ETHICS AND VULNERABLE ELDERS

ETHICS AND VULNERABLE ELDERS

The Quest for Individual Rights and a Just Society

Written and edited by

Pamela Teaster
Candace Heisler
Georgia Anetzberger

cognella®
SAN DIEGO

Bassim Hamadeh, CEO and Publisher
Seidy Cruz, Specialist Acquisitions Editor
Gem Rabanera, Project Editor
Abbey Hastings, Associate Production Editor
Emely Villavicencio, Senior Graphic Designer
Trey Soto, Licensing Specialist
Natalie Piccotti, Director of Marketing
Kassie Graves, Vice President of Editorial
Jamie Giganti, Director of Academic Publishing

Printed in the United States of America.

cognella | ACADEMIC PUBLISHING
3970 Sorrento Valley Blvd., Ste. 500, San Diego, CA 92121

Brief Contents

Contents

SECTION III.   Vulnerability: Care Arrangement   143

CHAPTER 15   Self-Neglect   225

*Carmel B. Dyer, MD, AGSF, FACP, John M. Halphen, JD, MD
and Jessica Lee, MS, MS*

CHAPTER 16   Older Adults in Correctional Settings   241

Anita N. Blowers, PhD

Foreword

Ethics and Aging: The Shadow of Vulnerability

Years ago, when I was doing interviews for my book about ethics and aging, I spoke with a cardiologist who said to me, "I can get patients to do whatever I want, depending on how I talk to them." I would not see his response as cynical, but rather as "owning" or recognizing the reality of power that he actually has as a physician. To imagine that all the cardiologist needed to do was tell the truth would be to ignore the facts of communication and of power. This reality of power is largely unacknowledged in contemporary bioethics. It seems to defeat our noblest ideals of autonomy and informed consent. Power lies in the shadow and so, too, is its correlate—vulnerability, which is the lack of power.

Our aspirations for bioethics are the heritage of the Enlightenment. A great pillar of the Enlightenment, the poet Goethe's last words were "more light." Here was the message of the Enlightenment—"more light," a promise of reason and, in our time, the ideal of autonomy. The greatest philosophers of modern times, Kant and Mill, have promoted this ideal of autonomy as the cornerstone of ethics. But the lived experience of advanced age is quite different. Advanced age—for every single reader of these words who lives long enough—will be an experience of dependency on others, on what Tennessee Williams memorably called "the kindness of strangers." For those of us who grasp that old age represents "our future selves," such a conclusion is profoundly unwelcome. We have spent our entire adult lives trying to be in control, to be free, to be independent. American culture is symbolized by the Statue of Liberty, and liberty remains our beacon at every age.

There is a story about the apocryphal Turkish folk hero Mulla Nasr Idin who was crawling around under a street lamp. A passerby asked what he was doing; he replied, "Looking for my key." The passerby asked where he'd lost it and Mulla answered, "over there in the dark." "Then why are you crawling under the street lamp?" asked the stranger. "There's so much light here," replied Mulla.

Ethics and Vulnerable Elders is a book that invites us to look deeper into the darkness, into the shadow of vulnerability that is the lived reality of old age. It engages the tools of the Enlightenment—applied ethics—and turns that light on groups and conditions of age that do not easily fit our preferred paradigm for right action: Just tell the truth and let people exercise their autonomy.

We know well enough that people who are poor, are ethnic minorities, or have compromised cognitive capacity, are all in a position in which they are vulnerable and easily oppressed or victimized. We insist upon rights for vulnerable people, and we even create institutional frameworks—such as Adult Protective Services—to enforce those rights. True, almost everywhere, Protective Services remains understaffed and underfunded. But if we think deeply about protecting the vulnerable, we may hope that the problem will be resolved if only we could provide vulnerable elders themselves with more money and power.

Is it really so? I once had occasion, during a fund-raising initiative at Hunter College, to meet Brooke Astor, the famous and wealthy benefactor of countless philanthropic endeavors in New York City. She was at the time nearly 100 years of age. Long after that we all came to learn that for years Astor had long been exploited by her son, Tony, later convicted of larceny and tampering with his mother's estate. The Astor case was a spectacular example of how even rich and powerful people, in conditions of advanced age and dependency, can be the target of elder abuse. It was also a reminder that not only strangers, but family members as well can be agents of abuse and exploitation.

This last point is important because it underscores the ways in which power and vulnerability intersect in ways that make it difficult for outsiders to intervene, even when we recognize that rights are being ignored. Ethical analysis often engages in debates about principles and procedures, ethics codes, and ethics committees. But in the end we are compelled to recognize what Isaiah Berlin enunciated in his seminal essay "Two Concepts of Liberty:" Namely, our highest ideals—e.g., autonomy and beneficence—can conflict. Applied ethics, as we see in the multiple cases described in this book, will struggle to cope with these dilemmas. This analytical exercise is important and indispensable, and the chapters in this book will give insights into the many different arenas where vulnerability puts rights at risk. But the exercise of analysis is not enough. Analysis can be an effort to look for our key under the street lamp instead of going into the darkness, into the shadow of vulnerability that looms in the last stage of life. *Ethics and Vulnerable Elders* draws us into that shadow even if we would prefer to look elsewhere.

We will make progress only by venturing into the shadow and asking ourselves at every juncture: Where do we have the power to protect the vulnerable? How do we exercise that power, and what do we know about the forces, often unseen, that constrain the power of elders themselves and those of us who try to intervene? Only by asking these difficult questions, as the authors do in this book, will we find the hope we need where we have too often been reluctant to turn the light on the shadow of vulnerability that will affect us all.

As an old man, at the end of his own life, Immanuel Kant was asked to name the basic questions of philosophy. There are only three, he replied: Who do we know? What should we do? And what may be hope? These are the same questions asked in the chapters of *Ethics and Vulnerable Elders*. The quest for individual rights demands nothing less than turning the light toward the shadow we know is there.

Harry R. Moody, PhD
Visiting Faculty, Creative Longevity
and Wisdom Program, Fielding Graduate University

Acknowledgments

We realize that no task of any importance is ever accomplished without the contributions of others. In this context, the authors are grateful for the work of Yuxin Zhao, Virginia Tech graduate research assistant, without whom the book's publication would have been significantly delayed. We also acknowledge the pioneering efforts of Tanya Fusco Johnson, whose *Handbook on Ethical Issues in Aging* inspired the publication of this textbook over 20 years earlier. We are most appreciative of the staff at Cognella, especially Jim Brace Thompson, Gem Rabanera, and Seidy Cruz, who assisted us with countless aspects of the book's production. Finally, we want to thank the authors of the book's forward and various chapters, who have added depth and wisdom to the textbook and have assisted us in meeting deadlines and chapter requirements.

Ultimately, however, it is often those less directly involved who not that truly enable task completion. This is true for our textbook as well. Therefore, the authors acknowledge and appreciate our family members and friends for their love, patience, and support as we labored toward completion of the book. Further, we recognize the importance of our students, whose thoughtful questions and insights as well as scholarly needs served to anchor the book's organization and core content throughout.

INTRODUCTION

Pamela B. Teaster, PhD
Virginia Tech

Georgia J. Anetzberger, PhD, ACSW
Case Western Reserve University

Candace J. Heisler, JD
National Trainer and Consultant

KEYWORDS

older adults
public administration
vulnerability
health care management
virtue ethics

ethics
elder abuse
elder and family law
multidisciplinary

Overview

The three of us, Teaster, Anetzberger, and Heisler, have been colleagues for over half a century. The topic that brought us together is elder abuse, which is the very same topic that brought us together to develop this textbook. In each of our specialties—public administration and gerontology, social work, and law, respectively—we recognized that the thread running through our disciplinary approaches to the topic of elder abuse is human vulnerability and an applied ethics approach. We propose that concept of vulnerability is very much like that of a prism, its different colors changing depending on how a light shines through it. As for applied ethics, we have long recognized that, while ethics is at the heart of prevention and intervention into the problem of elder abuse, research and theorizing have not positioned ethics as the primary facet through which to address the problem.

Consequently, when we were approached by Cognella to create an ethics book, we drew in our collective breaths, knowing that (a) a book of this nature is long overdue (one of this type has not been published in nearly 20 years), and (b) creating such a book would be a great challenge. The majority of books that attempt to address current ethical issues facing older adults have publication dates in the 1990s. A particular strength of our book is the unique approach of combining perspectives from social work, law, ethics, gerontology, and public policy. We determined that our unique contribution to such a book would rest on the intersection of ethics and vulnerability. We recognized that crafting such a textbook meant reaching out to a cadre of outstanding people who were not only highly knowledgeable in a respective content area but also able to take the content area and infuse it with applied ethics.

Thus, the purpose of this book is to produce a timely, dynamic, thought-provoking, and useful ethics textbook that employs a principled approach to ethics and that addresses current issues affecting vulnerable older adults. Our goal is to elucidate predominant current and future conundrums facing a vulnerable older adult population as well as to provide frameworks for their resolution. We envision that our book should be useful both as a primary and as a supplemental textbook in law schools and graduate schools with foci on gerontology; disability; social work; public health; elder, criminal, and family law; and health care management. Within this multidisciplinary edited volume are chapters that explore ethical issues affecting the unique and special population of older adults who are vulnerable.

The framework guiding each chapter is that the contributing author wrote on a specified topic but used a similar format. Drawing upon the most recent research, each chapter includes a summary; case study; discussion of applicable principles of ethics, including autonomy, beneficence, nonmaleficence, and justice; treatment of future dilemmas within the topical area; and 3–5 questions for further consideration. The 19 chapters of the book are organized into six sections. Chapter 1 sets the framework for the rest of the book and includes an important grounding in ethics by presenting key concepts and definitions to help the reader better consider information in the chapters that follow. Sections II–V are devoted to a particular set of vulnerabilities: Section II plumbs the vulnerabilities of compromised health (cognitive impairment, mental illness, and physical disability); Section III examines effective status (gender, ethnicity, sexual orientation, religion, and immigrants); and Section IV examines abuse, neglect, and exploitation (abuse, neglect, and exploitation; self-neglect; correctional settings; criminal victimization; and bullying).

What Is Ethics?

Ethics is a branch of philosophy that explores differences between what is a right action and what is a wrong one. Ethics explores morals, values, and virtues of human conduct, with an emphasis on the "ought" (Pozgar, 2012). Thus, ethics addresses how people and organizations ought to act or to proceed given a certain situation. It concerns universal concepts to help guide, regulate, prescribe, or understand both individual and group behavior (Teaster & Sokan, 2016). Ethics is derived from the Greek term *ethos*, meaning habit or custom. Most human beings strive to be ethical, and so understanding ethics has implications for how a person can live a well-informed life (Aristotle, 350 BCE). Though often standing in relation to the law, ethical principles do not carry the force of law (Darr, 2011). Many organizations promulgate codes of ethics or a set of rules that guide conduct of members of a profession.

Ethics as a Guide for Behavior and Action

Not every issue, question, or problem—heated or not—that arises among individuals is an ethical issue or dilemma, and it is important and instructive to understand the differences. Below is an explanation of what ethical issues are and what they are not.

Nonethical Problems, Disagreements, or Differences of Opinion

Sometimes, in fact, quite often, problems arise. They are nonethical if they are matters of personal preference and if they do not result in harm to another (Johnson, 1999). These problems concern differences in perspective or opinion. An example is an older adult's choice of ice cream—chocolate, vanilla, or strawberry. A problem of this nature is a matter of choice, preference, or availability, but it is not an ethical dilemma or an ethical issue.

Ethical Dilemmas

An ethical dilemma arises when a conflict occurs concerning ethical principles (e.g., autonomy, beneficence, nonmaleficence, and justice) discussed in detail below (Johnson, 1999). At issue could be which of these should prevail. Most often, the principle of autonomy stands in conflict with beneficence, nonmaleficence, and justice. In the 21st century, the principle of autonomy tends to prevail over the other principles unless there is a compelling and often life-threatening reason otherwise. A dilemma occurs between honoring the older adult's autonomy concerning withholding a medical procedure or acts of beneficence manifested by the duty to care and do all possible to save lives on the part of the health care professionals.

Ethical Issues

According to Callahan (1988), an ethical issue emanates from a conundrum over a single ethical principle rather than as a conflict between or among principles (Johnson, 1999). As so often concerns vulnerable and exploited older adults, should autonomy prevail so that a capacitated elder involved in a sweetheart financial scam be allowed to continue, even if nearly all the elder's (and the heirs') estate will be depleted and the elder will not have enough money left to live out his or her life?

Organization of Ethics

As a study, ethics has a number of branches, these being normative ethics, applied ethics, and metaethics. Derived from the discipline of philosophy, each informs an understanding of morality in a different way (Holstein & Mitzen, 2001; Holstein, Parks, & Waymack, 2011; Johnson, 1999; Moody, 1992; Veatch, 2016).

Normative Ethics

Normative ethics focuses on moral standards of human behavior—that which is good and right (Summers, 2009). Sometimes referred to as moral theory, this branch of ethics is involved in an examination of appropriate standards of human behavior, including what is considered appropriate moral behavior. Important to normative ethics is that the norms of behavior are general in nature (Veatch, 2016). An example of the application of appropriate norms of behavior would be giving a choice of apparel to a nursing home resident with mild cognitive impairment and asking his or her preference regarding what to wear for the day (Kane & Caplan, 1990).

Under the rubric of normative ethics is *action theory*, where the focus is not on the behavior or motives of the actor but rather on the action he or she is to undertake. The central question of action theory is what is the right action, and that question can be answered in a variety of ways (and they may conflict), using principles or theories discussed below. An example of an action is the dilemma between allowing a hoarding elder to stay in her home versus taking her out of her home to be in a safer environment. A second theory under normative ethics is *virtue theory* (Veatch, 2016). Rather than focus on the action, the emphasis of virtue theory is on the actor. If the actor is virtuous, then it would follow that the action that the actor would take is the right and moral action. For example, the virtuous geriatrician will provide the right kind of end-of-life care. A third issue addressed within normative ethics is that of *value theory*. In this strand, rather than a focus on the application of a principle, the focus is on what is valued (Annas, 2009; Veatch, 2016). For example, an honest and appropriate physician should speak with a patient about her treatment options in an end-of-life situation.

Metaethics

Rather than a focus on what is moral, metaethics examines the nature of morality itself. Metaethics plumbs basic ethical questions, including but not limited to the meaning of moral words, the genesis of moral values, the context and variance of morality, and the nature of what is a moral value (DeLapp, n.d.). According to Veatch (2016), metaethics deals with concerns of how we find answers to ethical questions and how to know that the answer we find is the right one. Importantly, metaethics examines how individuals and groups derive ethical meaning, which reflects how they determine their definitions of the good life and how it should be lived (Johnson, 1999). An example is how a population of elder interviewees might view self-neglect and ethical interventions.

Applied Ethics

Applied ethics has its grounding in the discipline of philosophy and is related to meta-ethics and normative ethics. Applied ethics arose in prominence due to the foment of the civil rights movement in the 1960s and the questioning of U.S. involvement in the Vietnam War (Johnson, 1999; Singer, 1986) as well as the questions that technology presented and that continue to this day. An increasingly global world as well as instantaneous communication via the Internet and smartphones have also increased the importance of applied ethics to varied problems, including those related to health and health care, safety, and vulnerability. Bioethics is a subset of applied ethics, which, in addition to addressing issues of those with moral standing, addresses those without it, including animals and artificial intelligence (Dittmer, n.d.). The application of applied ethics is the substance of this book. Often, the use of ethical principles is applied to a problem, which follows.

Principles

One way of addressing ethical problems is to make use of guiding principles, a major explanation of these being most notably articulated by Beauchamp and Childress (2012), a text first published in 1979 and now in its seventh edition. These four principles are particularly relevant to the health professions and so are salient for this textbook.

Autonomy

Autonomy is often regarded as primary among the four principles and concerns a person's right to make decisions, free from coercion, about his or her own life (Pence, 2015). Autonomy is highly prized and emphasized in the United States and other democracies, as it is associated with the right of an individual to make and execute plans concerning his or her person and destiny. Autonomy is notably associated with the harm principle articulated by John Stuart Mill (1859, p. 223),

> that the only purpose for which power can rightfully be exercised over any member of a civilized community, against his will, is to prevent harm to others. His own good, either physical or moral, is not a sufficient warrant. Over himself, over his own body and mind, the individual is sovereign.

Similarly, autonomy is often at stake in legal actions such as guardianship when, due to a court determination of incapacity, these rights of a vulnerable person are removed: the right to marry, the right to buy and sell property, and the right to contract (Teaster, Schmidt, Wood, Lawrence, & Mendiondo, 2010).

Beneficence

Beneficence is associated with being and doing good, as well as with kindness, generosity, and keeping others safe and is central to being moral (Beauchamp & Childress,

2012). Beneficence is grounded in being compassionate (Pence, 2015) for its own sake. In resolving an ethical dilemma, autonomy and beneficence may become competing principles. A classic example of the tension concerning autonomy and beneficence would be whether (or when) to limit or stop a cognitively impaired elder from driving an automobile.

Nonmaleficence

This principle literally means to do no harm or that clients or patients should not leave an encounter with a service provider worse than when they, entered it. According to Pence (2015, p. 17), "this crucial principle of medical ethics prohibits corruption, incompetence, and dangerous, nontherapeutic treatments." The principle of nonmaleficence guides research studies and protects subjects or participants from being harmed by an intervention or treatment. Pence (2015) remarks that nonmaleficence has an important concordance with autonomy—that individuals have a right to be left alone, particularly when they do not want help. An example of the application of the principle of nonmaleficence is when Adult Protective Services (APS) seeks to intervene in an elder self-neglect case. Should the individual have decisional capacity and be deemed competent, then state intervention in the guise of APS must not proceed.

Justice

The final of the four principles is justice, often associated with David Hume (2006) and John Rawls (2009). This principle reflects what is fair, equitable, and appropriate. Using this principle means treating people in a manner free from prejudice and distributing goods and resources equitably. Justice is used in research ethics to make sure that benefits and burdens are distributed equitably. An example of the application of justice to vulnerable older adults would be ensuring that lesbian, gay, bisexual, and transgender elders are recruited appropriately and justly as research participants as are heterosexual elders. Justice can also be distributive or criminal in nature, for example, when making a decision to prosecute a family member who has physically abused an older adult.

Predominant Ethical Theories

In addition to the four principles discussed above, there are a number of ethical theories that help guide ethical decision making. This section highlights the most applicable theoretical constructs for our text, on vulnerable older adults.

Virtue Ethics

Discussed briefly above under the section on normative ethics, virtue ethics is derived from Aristotle and Plato and emphasizes not that an action is moral or ethical but rather that the actor is moral and ethical. Medical professionals should make honest decisions about older adults' conditions because it is the right thing to do. Though it bears a relationship to the ethical theories below, what distinguishes it from the others is that the concept of virtue or virtuous character traits are at the heart of virtue ethics. Three concepts are associated with virtue ethics: arête, phronesis, and eudaimonia. In brief, arête is regarded as excellence or virtue, phronesis is defined as practical wisdom, and eudaimonia is equated with happiness or well-being and flourishing (Annas, 2009). Elders, by their life years, have a great deal of wisdom about the kind of medical treatment that they want.

Utilitarianism

Utilitarianism is associated with Jeremy Bentham and John Stuart Mill. Utilitarians hold that an action is ethical if it produces the greatest happiness for the most individuals. Hence, utilitarians are also regarded as consequentialists because, different from the character of the actor or actors making a decision or taking an action, or that the action necessarily would become universal law (as discussed below with Kantian ethics), the appropriate action or decision is one that maximizes the scope of happiness (Pence, 2015). When a law is enacted or amended, such as Medicare or Medicaid, lawmakers are generally acting in what they regard will product the greatest good for the most older people.

Kantian Ethics

Kantian ethics is attributed to German philosopher Immanuel Kant, who proposed a number of concepts related to ethical action. Kantian ethics are associated with deontological moral theory that suggests that the rightness or wrongness of an action is not dependent on its consequences but rather upon its adherence to a duty or responsibility to others. Kant proposed the Categorical Imperative, a formulation of which is that individuals' actions become a universal law. As such, Kantians are rule abiding and expect others to be so. In addition, Kant believed that individuals have inherent moral worth and that one of our responsibilities is to make decisions based on the inherent moral worth of persons. Related to older people with vulnerability such as those with dementia, Kantian ethics is instructive, as Kant would regard people with Alzheimer's disease as having moral worth, thus we are duty bound to respect them regardless of their cognitive capacity (Kantian Ethics, n.d.).

Theory of Justice

Although there are a number of ethical theories of justice, one of the most definitive and recent to emerge is that of John Rawls. Rawls recognized that human beings are motivated by self-interest and that they act based on a social contract established by the society in which they dwell. Rawls proposed that the right way to make a choice is through a thick *veil of ignorance*, one that obfuscates one's social standing, education, income, gender, location, and so forth. Because an actor cannot know his or her place in society, the actor will opt for equality "unless the difference favors the least well-off group" (Pence, 2015, p. 16), or Rawls's *difference principle*, which mandates that all citizens should have access to a baseline of resources (Veatch, 2016). As appropriate, older adult women as well as younger adult women should be included in drug trials because uptake at the cellular level also affects them.

Feminist Ethics

Feminist ethical theory or the ethics of care theory approaches the issue of vulnerable elders by examining the complex intersection of social and historical context, age, gender, race, ethnicity, socioeconomics, and sexual orientation in the lives of an increasingly diverse and often marginalized population of victims of elder abuse (Ploeg, Lohfield, & Walsh, 2013). For example, situating the social locations of old age and gender within the backdrop of inequality focuses scholarly attention on the significance of the relationship between abuse and social and economic power (Holstein et al., 2011). In many cultures, women tend to be economically and socially disadvantaged in comparison to men; consequently, gender itself may be a vulnerability. Without economic or social means, older women are very likely to remain in unsafe relationships (Koenig, Rinfrette, & Lutz, 2006). Also, in the United States, women were denied the right to vote until 1920.

Communicative Ethics

Communicative ethics, also called discourse ethics, is associated with German scholar Jurgen Habermas and more recently, Harry Moody. Communicative ethics bears some relationship to Rawls's theory of justice and with Kantian ethics. Central to communicative ethics is that a decision or action is universal when, in deliberation, each participant assumes the perspective of all others in order to determine if the decision should be adopted from their perspective. Habermas (1998) argues that Kant had a view of the individual as homogenous and so failed to recognize the roles of different individuals or cultures in shaping identities and, hence, rules by which to abide. Thus, Habermas maintained that a critical aspect of ethical decision making is that, through discourse and imagination all test the acceptability of a norm, not an individual alone. Moody (1992) extended Habermas' argument to older adults, both on micro- and macrosystem levels (Bronfenbrenner, 1986). In application, it is, in most cases, important to communicate honestly with an older adult about medical treatment decisions, including their burdens and their efficacy.

Challenges of Theories

No one theory or set of ethical theories has yet become universal or cross-cutting. Several reasons account for a lack of theoretical consensus. First, there is no consensus about which one or ones are most appropriate. Theories may not be used because decision makers are simply reacting to a problem rather than embedding a theory a priori. Second, theories may not work well for certain disciplines. For example, the disciplines of law and medicine operate on an understanding of the facts of a case. Third, multiple theories are rarely used together. Fourth, some models, frameworks, and theories also fail to pass the test of cultural embeddedness and do not translate across cultures (Roberto & Teaster, 2017).

Ethics, Older Adults, and Vulnerability

Ours is an aging society, and U.S. statistics are a testament to this demographic reality. According to the U.S. Census Bureau (2017), there were 47.8 million people age 65 and older on July 1, 2015, which accounted for 14.9% of the total population. The older adult population is projected to reach 98.2 million by 2060, or 1 in 4 U.S. residents, with adults aged 85 years and older comprising 19.7 million of that number. According to the Social Security Administration (2018), for men and women turning 65 in 2018, the average life expectancy for men is approximately 84.3 years and 86.6 years for women. Increasingly, older adults have better physical and mental health than ever before in history, and morbidity has been compressed to the last few years of life (Cutler, Ghosh, & Landrum, 2013).

Despite these gains, the incidence of disease and disability rises with age. The Medicare Current Beneficiary Survey indicates that 74% of Medicare beneficiaries residing in community settings are living with two or more chronic conditions (e.g., heart disease, hypertension, diabetes, arthritis, osteoporosis, pulmonary disease, stroke, Alzheimer's, Parkinson's, and cancers) (Joint Center for Housing Studies, 2014). About 1 in 4 adults age 50 and over has difficulty with hearing, vision, cognition, or mobility; for those age 85 and over this figure rises to more than 2 in 3. These limitations may affect older adults' capacity for self-care and living independently. The Department of Health and Human Services estimates that 70% of people who reach age 65 will need some type of long-term care in later life (Joint Center for Housing Studies, 2014).

Healthy older adults usually reside in their own homes. Adults living with chronic disease(s), dementia, or both tend to reside in their homes at the beginning of an illness but then may transition to other care settings where they can receive help in order to live safely and well. These settings may include living in the home of a family member or friend, continuing care retirement communities, group homes, assisted living facilities, nursing homes, and hospitals. According to the Pew Research Center (2016), in 1990, approximately one-fourth of women age 85 and older (27%) lived in nursing homes, whereas 13% did in 2014. Among men aged 85 and older, 17% lived in nursing homes in 1990 and 8% did so in 2014.

In addition to needing assistance with chronic physical health conditions, more than 16 million people in the United States are living with cognitive impairments (Family Caregiver Alliance, 2013), including but not limited to mild cognitive impairment, which affects 10% to 20% of people 65 and older, and age-related dementias, which affect 5 million people in that age group. Alzheimer's disease, the most serious and common impairment, accounts for between 60% and 80% of dementia cases and is the sixth leading cause of death in the United States (Kochanek, Murphy, Xu, & Tejada-Vera, 2016).

Physical difficulties, not mental health problems, including that of just growing old, can create a number of problems that become ethical issues and dilemmas for older adults and their families. Issues and dilemmas become even more confounding because, in addition to health problems and economic problems, they also create vulnerabilities among older adults, as discussed in the following section.

Vulnerability

For the purposes of this book, vulnerable refers to physical, mental, or social conditions that compromise a person's ability to carry out essential functions in daily living; safeguard him or her from abuse, neglect, or exploitation; or protect legal rights, thereby rendering the person at risk of harm or loss. The table of contents captures the broad origins of vulnerability: compromised health; effective status; care arrangement; and abuse, neglect, and exploitation. It also suggests potential effects.

The term *vulnerable* comes from early 17th century Latin *vulnerare*, meaning *to wound*. It is defined in the Merriam-Webster Dictionary (n.d.) as "susceptible to physical or emotional attack or harm," and if applied to a particular person "to be in need of special care, support, or protection because of age, disability, or risk of abuse or neglect." Although the term is employed in a variety of contexts, from informed consent in conducting research to safe sanctuary policies, vulnerability is most commonly used to describe the potential victims of elder abuse, including self-neglect, beginning with earliest recognition of the problem forward (e.g., Anetzberger, 1990; Bonnie & Wallace, 2003; Butler, 1975; Killick, Taylor, Begley, Anand, & O'Brien, 2015; Kosberg, 1983).

The understanding of vulnerability is neither as clear nor simple as suggested by its source or dictionary definition. Rather, the concept is vague, complex, and confusing (Peroni & Timmer, 2013). These perceptions may rest in part on the seemingly endless potential factors that underlie the origins and effects of vulnerability, which themselves can overlap. The literature on vulnerability suggests that it can arise from both conditions and circumstances. Conditions include disability or impairment (physical, mental, intellectual, or sensory), illness, frailty, or addiction (alcohol or drugs). Circumstances include history of mistreatment, loneliness, isolation, relocation (as with asylum seekers or those experiencing institutional displacement), power imbalances (due to differential status based on characteristics like income, gender, sexual orientation, gender identity, or ethnicity), or select settings (such as hospitals or inner-city crime-prevalent neighborhoods). Likewise, the identified potential effects of vulnerability are numerous and include perceived lack of control or helplessness; inability to care for or protect oneself or one's affairs; susceptibility to disease, harm, or suffering; loss of income or assets; violation of human rights; becoming a target of scams or quackery or a victim of crime or mistreatment; or death.

Kahana, Kahana, and Kinney (1990) offer a paradigm for late-life vulnerability that identifies the collapsed various origins as "stress" and effects as "outcomes." They also suggest that external resources (i.e., social, economic, and environmental) and internal resources (i.e., cognitive and personality) can serve as potential moderators. External resources may include sufficient income, family support, and access to formal services. Internal resources may include family history, lifestyle, and coping strategies. In this regard, it is generally thought that vulnerability only can be altered through the actions of others; the person identified as vulnerable cannot change the situation entirely on her or his own.

Although it appears that there is no universally accepted definition of vulnerability, there does seem to be more agreement around its variables. For example, vulnerability can be temporary or permanent, depending on the duration of its origins and impact of its effects. It may be objective or subjective, depending on the focus of interest, whether on measuring risk and identifying risk management interventions or understanding the experience of being vulnerable. Finally, vulnerability can be used to describe individuals, groups, or all persons. A more extreme stance is taken by Fineman (2008), who objects to anything but universal application, suggesting that vulnerability is an aspect of what it means to be human.

It may be, as Fineman suggests, that everyone is vulnerable, since we all have the capacity for experiencing suffering and loss. However, it is also true that some of us are more vulnerable than others (Stevens, 2013). As noted in the dictionary definition, age can be a particular determinant. In this regard, children are dependents by virtue of their immaturity and legal status, which render them at risk. Older adults, especially those in advanced old age, also experience increased vulnerability for reasons that include greater likelihood of impairment and disability, structural inequality, marginalization, and other problems (Atchley, 1990; Beaulieu, Crevier, D'Amours, & Diaz, 2015; Mysyuk, Westendorp, & Lindenberg, 2016). Accordingly, vulnerable elders may be classified as a subset of older adults. If so, they are a heterogeneous group, and old age alone cannot confer membership.

The identity of vulnerable elders as a group, or even for an individual, may be problematic. The label can come with negative connotations, potentially resulting in stigmatization or paternalism (Peroni & Timmer, 2013). Moreover, in a risk-adverse society like ours, it can serve to rob those so labeled of basic rights or experiences that give life meaning (Dunn, Clare, & Holland, 2008; MacLeod & Stadnyk, 2015). In addition, it can become a self-fulfilling prophecy, with subsequent personal curtailment of life adventures in deference to safety and security (Brown, 2010). Finally, labeling can lead to cautious practices in providing care or result in over regulation (Kane, 1990) or in how the law treats vulnerable individuals, as discussed below.

Role of Law

The roots of American law go back to the beginning of the country and earlier. The Founders wanted to create a government that was different from the perceived tyranny of the then English king and the many sovereigns who ruled with absolute power. Early American history is replete with examples of taxation without representation, class distinctions, and arbitrary rules and laws pressed on the American colonies by the distant English government. The Founders realized that law is the foundation of a free society. Indeed, "(t)here can be no free society without law administered through an independent judiciary. If one man can be allowed to determine for himself what is law, every man can. That means first chaos, then tyranny." (*United States v. United Mine Workers*, 1947). Their goal was to create a government of limited and divided power. The structure of American government that was created reflected these principles.

Laws are enacted to clarify the roles and power of government and the limits of power given to the three legal powers in the United States: the legislature, executive, and judiciary. In the *Federalist Papers* Hamilton wrote about the three branches, noting:

> Whoever attentively considers the different departments of power must perceive, that, in a government in which they are separated from each other, the judiciary, from the nature of its functions, will always be the least dangerous to the political rights of the Constitution; because it will be least in a capacity to annoy or injure them. The Executive not only dispenses the honors, but holds the sword of the community. The legislature not only commands the purse, but prescribes the rules by which the duties and rights of every citizen are to be regulated. The judiciary, on the contrary, has no influence over either the sword or the purse; no direction either of the strength or of the wealth of the society; and can take no active resolution whatever. It may truly be said to have neither FORCE nor WILL, but merely judgment; and must ultimately depend upon the aid of the executive arm even for the efficacy of its judgments. (1788, Number 78)

These distinctions were critical to the Founders' efforts to limit the power of the sovereign, the King of England, in accordance with the rule of law—that is, a principle under which persons, institutions, and entities are accountable to laws that are: (a) publicly promulgated, (b) equally enforced, (c) independently adjudicated, and (d) consistent with international human rights principles (U.S. Courts, n.d.).

Law can be described as a body of rules prescribed by a lawfully constituted authority which have binding legal force.[1] Violations are subject to sanctions or other legal consequences. Conversely, no one can be punished unless he or she has violated an existing law when she acted. As such, laws define what impermissible conduct is. Laws limit what a governmental body, corporation, or individual can do or under what circumstances each can seek redress from others. "The purpose of the law is to influence people's decisions—to channel the decisions in certain directions and away from other directions" (D'Amato, 2008, p. 8).

The U.S. Constitution is the paramount law of the country. In it, the Founders attempted to define the country's core values. Other core values, such as freedom of religion and speech and the right to free assembly, due process, and equal protection, were added in the Bill of Rights and subsequent amendments. The Founders created a system in which the legislative branch enacts laws; the executive branch sets policy, oversees the military, and enforces the laws; and the judicial branch interprets the law and determines the merit of legal actions. The federal courts "were designed to be the intermediate body between the people and their legislature" (Hamilton, 1788, Number 78) assuring that legislators, as the people's representatives, acted within their authority.

These branches of government were not designed to have equal power. Montesquieu (1748, p. 186) described the comparative power of the judiciary as "next to nothing." Hamilton (1788, Number 78) in the previously cited *Federalist Paper* wrote:

> It proves incontestably, that the judiciary is beyond comparison the weakest of the three departments of power; that it can never attack with success either of the other two; and that all possible care is requisite to enable it to defend itself against their attacks. It

---

1   See e.g., *United States Fidelity and Guaranty Co. v. Guenther* (1930).

equally proves, that though individual oppression may now and then proceed from the courts of justice, the general liberty of the people can never be endangered from that quarter; I mean so long as the judiciary remains truly distinct from both the legislature and the Executive. For I agree, that "there is no liberty, if the power of judging be not separated from the legislative and executive powers." And it proves, in the last place, that as liberty can have nothing to fear from the judiciary alone, but would have everything to fear from its union with either of the other departments; that as all the effects of such a union must ensue from a dependence of the former on the latter, notwithstanding a nominal and apparent separation; that as, from the natural feebleness of the judiciary, it is in continual jeopardy of being overpowered, awed, or influenced by its co-ordinate branches; and that as nothing can contribute so much to its firmness and independence as permanency in office, this quality may therefore be justly regarded as an indispensable ingredient in its constitution, and, in a great measure, as the citadel of the public justice and the public security.

The law is not necessarily based on majority rule. For example, grievances voiced by minority groups or by those who may hold minority opinions are entitled to be heard and to prevail in appropriate situations. When the majority infringes upon the rights of the minority, thus denying the minority right to legal equality, laws can be declared unconstitutional and repealed. American history is filled with examples of what was once viewed as lawful (though not ethical) conduct, including slavery, denial of the right to vote to women, African Americans, and Native Americans, and the forced removal of Native Americans from their traditional homes to distant and hostile locations, that have been overturned.

The examples mentioned above make the point that law is separate and distinct from ethics. While notions of what is lawful conduct may change over time, ethics tend to be more stable and fixed. Ethics are typically rooted in religious and philosophical principles; law may or may not be. Because laws may or may not be based in ethical behavior people can act lawfully while not acting ethically. For example, in a state without so-called Good Samaritan laws, a person can watch a person drown and not offer any assistance even when the onlooker could easily act. Because there is no duty to act, no matter how morally reprehensible, no legal sanction can be imposed. Justice Oliver Wendell Holmes in his article "The Path of Law" (1897, p. 459), wrote "If you want to know the law and nothing else, you must look at it as a bad man, who cares only for the material consequences which such knowledge enables him to predict. ... A [bad] man who cares nothing for an ethical rule which is believed and practiced by his neighbors is likely nevertheless to care a good deal to avoid being made to pay money, and will want to keep out of jail if he can." In contrast the "good man" finds reasons for his conduct both in the law and outside of it, "in the vaguer notions of conscience" (Holmes, 1897, p. 457). The example that follows highlights differences between ethical and lawful conduct.

Mr. H. has three adult children and has suffered several strokes, which have left him incontinent and completely dependent on his children for care. He lives with his sons and receives monthly social security and pension payments. His daughter was initially the full time caregiver but moved out months earlier and now visits her father on a weekly basis. When the daughter moved out, the two sons agreed that one brother would work, and the other would be primarily responsible for the father's care. Both used the father's funds to live and run the household.

The daughter noticed that since moving out, the house had become filthy. She discussed with her brother the need to take their father to the doctor. She visited each of the six weekends before police came to the house. She was last in her father's bedroom 5 weeks prior to the arrival of police, when she noticed the mattress had a hole in it, and there were feces-soiled clothes on the floor. She also stayed in the house overnight several weekends before police came.

Police were called when the father died. They observed that his body lay on a mattress rotted from constant wetness through to the metal springs. He had multiple large pressure ulcers over one-sixth of his body. The stench of urine and feces pervaded the entire house. An autopsy revealed that he had a yeast infection in his mouth and suffered from congestive heart failure, bronchial pneumonia, and hepatitis. Death was caused by septic shock due to the pressure ulcers which, in the opinion of the pathologist, were caused by malnutrition, dehydration, and neglect. Police arrested the two sons and the daughter for neglect of an elder and the sons for involuntary manslaughter. The court dismissed as to the daughter, finding that there was no duty to provide care for her father once she moved out and handed care off to her brothers. The fact that she visited and stayed overnight in the weeks and days prior to her father's death did not make her legally responsible. (*People v. Heitzman*, 1994)

The *Heitzman* case made its findings based on the law, and the finding is consistent with many other states that do not impose a duty on adult children to care for their aging parents or siblings. Those considering the case from an ethical perspective may arrive at a different conclusion, finding that the daughter's conduct failed to apply critical ethical principles of justice (fairness, nonmalfeasance—"do no harm"—and protection). She did not consider her father's preferences—a desire to live his final days in dignity and without pain and suffering.

CONCLUDING OBSERVATIONS

This chapter has provided readers with an explanation of its purpose and intention. We introduced readers to the concepts of applied ethics, ethical issues and dilemmas, ethical principles, and ethical theories. Following those definitions, we explained why we focus this textbook on older adults; and in particular, those who are vulnerable. To protect those who are old and vulnerable, we have the rule of law, the role of which concludes our introduction.

It is the hope of the authors that these concepts afford an important scaffolding for the topics that follow and that these chapters provide a solid grounding for the issues confronted by the chapter authors. We stress that none of the issues presented have tidy answers. However, they have considerations that can guide theory, research, and practice. Our hope is that they well prepare readers for present and future ethical dilemmas and issues. As we have structured the book, we hope that all readers join us in our ethical journey in pursuit of individual rights and a just society for all present and future vulnerable elders.

REFERENCES

Annas, J. (2009). Virtue ethics. In *The Oxford handbook of ethical theory*. Oxford: Oxford University Press.

Anetzberger, G. J. (1990). Abuse, neglect, and self-neglect: Issues of vulnerability. In Z. Harel, P. Erhlich, & R. Hubbard (Eds.), *The vulnerable aged: People, services, and policies* (pp. 140–148). New York, NY: Springer.

Aristotle. (350 BCE). *Nicomachean ethics (W. D. Ross, Trans.)*. Retrieved from http://classics.mit.edu/Aristotle/nicomachaen.html

Atchley, R. C. (1990). Defining the vulnerable older population. In Z. Harel, P. Erhlich, & R. Hubbard (Eds.), *The vulnerable aged: People, services, and policies* (pp. 18–31). New York, NY: Springer.

Baron de Montesquieu, C. S. (1748). *Spirit of laws* (Vol. I).

Beauchamp, T. L., & Childress, J. F. (2012). *Principles of biomedical ethics* (7th ed.). Oxford: Oxford University Press.

Beaulieu, M., Crevier, M., D'Amours, M., & Diaz, L. (2015). Financial exploitation of older women: A case analysis using the struggle for recognition theory. *Journal of Elder Abuse & Neglect, 27*, 489–499.

Bonnie, R. J., & Wallace, R. B. (Eds.). (2003). *Elder mistreatment: Abuse, neglect, and exploitation in an aging America*. Panel to Review Risk and Prevalence of Elder Abuse and Neglect, National Research Council, Washington, DC.

Bronfenbrenner, U. (1986). Ecology of the family as a context for human development: Research perspectives. *Developmental Psychology, 22*, 723–742.

Brown, K. (2010). *Vulnerable adults and community care*. Exeter, UK: Learning Matters.

Butler, R. N. (1975). *Why survive? Being old in America*. New York, NY: Harper & Row.

Callahan, J. C. (1988). *Ethical issues in professional life*. New York, NY: Oxford University Press.

Cutler, D. M., Ghosh, K., & Landrum, M. B. (2013). Evidence for significant compression of morbidity in the elderly US population. In *Discoveries in the Economics of Aging* (pp. 21–51). University of Chicago Press.

D'Amato, A. (2008). *A new (and better) interpretation of Holmes's prediction theory of law* (Working paper, Northwestern University, Chicago, IL). Retrieved from http://scholarlycommons.law.northwestern.edu/facultyworkingpapers/163

Darr, K. (2011). *Ethics in health services management* (5th ed.). Baltimore, MD: Health Professions Press.

DeLapp, K. M. (n.d.). Metaethics. In *Internet Encyclopedia of Philosophy*. Retrieved from http://www.iep.utm.edu/metaethi/

Dittmer, J. (n.d.). Applied ethics. In *Internet Encyclopedia of Philosophy*. Retrieved from http://www.iep.utm.edu/ap-ethic

Dunn, M. C., Clare, I. C. H., & Holland, A. J. (2008). To empower or to protect? Constructing the "vulnerable adult" in English law and public policy. *Legal Studies, 28*(2), 234–253.

Family Caregiver Alliance. (2013). Incidence and prevalence of the major causes of brain impairment. Retrieved from www.caregiver.org/caregiver/jsp/content_node.jsp?nodeid=438

Fineman, M. A. (2008). The vulnerable subject: Anchoring equality in the human condition. *Yale Journal of Law & Feminism, 20*(1), 1–23.

Habermas, J. (1998). The inclusion of the Other. In *Studies in Political Theory* (Parts VIII and IX of Chapter 1). Cambridge, MA: MIT Press.

Hamilton, A. (1788). *Federalist Papers* (Number 78).

Holmes, O. W. (1897). The path of law. *Harvard Law Review,* pp. 457, 459.

Holstein, M. B., & Mitzen, P. (Eds.). (2001). *Ethics in community-based elder care.* New York, NY: Springer.

Holstein, M. B., Parks, J. A., & Waymack, M. H. (2011). *Ethics, aging, and society: The critical turn.* New York, NY: Springer.

Hume, D. (2006). *An enquiry concerning the principles of morals* (Vol. 4). Oxford: Oxford University Press.

John Stuart Mill, The Collected Works of John Stuart Mill, Volume XVIII—Essays on Politics and Society Part I, ed. John M. Robson, Introduction by Alexander Brady (Toronto: University of Toronto Press, London: Routledge and Kegan Paul, 1977). Retrieved 6/12/2019 from the World Wide Web: https://oll.libertyfund.org/titles/233

Johnson, T. F. (Ed.). (1999). *Handbook on ethical issues in aging.* Westport, CT: Greenwood Press.

Joint Center for Housing Studies. (2014). *Housing America's older adults: Meeting the needs of an aging population.* Harvard University. Retrieved at https://www.aarp.org/content/dam/aarp/livable-communities/documents-2014/Harvard-Housing-Americas-Older-Adults-2014.pdf

Kahana, E., Kahana, B., & Kinney, J. (1990). Coping among vulnerable elders. In Z. Harel, P. Erhlich, & R. Hubbard (Eds.), *The vulnerable aged: People, services, and policies* (pp. 64–85). New York, NY: Springer.

Kane, R. A. (1990). Venerable and perhaps vulnerable: The nature and extent of vulnerability among the aged. In Z. Harel, P. Erhlich, & R. Hubbard (Eds.), *The vulnerable aged: People, services, and policies* (pp. 4–17). New York, NY: Springer.

Kane, R. A., & Caplan, A. L. (Eds.). (1990). *Everyday ethics: Resolving dilemmas in nursing home life.* New York, NY: Springer.

Kantian ethics. (n.d.). Retrieved from http://www.csus.edu/indiv/g/gaskilld/ethics/kantian%20ethics.htm

Killick, C., Taylor, B. J., Begley, E., Anand, J. C., & O'Brien, M. (2015). Older people's conceptualization of abuse: A systematic review. *Journal of Elder Abuse & Neglect, 27,* 100–120.

Kochanek, K. D., Murphy, S. L., Xu, J, & Tejada-Vera, B. (2016). Deaths: Final data for 2014. *National Vital Statistics Reports, 65*(4), 1–122.

Koenig, T. L., Rinfrette, E. S., & Lutz, W. A. (2006). Female caregivers' reflections on ethical decision-making: The intersection of domestic violence and elder care. *Clinical Social Work Journal, 34*(3), 361–372.

Kosberg, J. I. (1983). The special vulnerability of elderly parents. In *Abuse and maltreatment of the elderly* (pp. 263–275). Boston, MA: Wright-PSQ.

MacLeod, H., & Stadnyk, R. L. (2015). Risk: "I know it when I see it": How health and social practitioners defined and evaluated living at risk among community-dwelling older adults. *Health, Risk & Society, 17*(1), 46–63.

Mill, J. S. (1859). *On liberty.* London: Parker.

Moody, H. R. (1992). *Ethics in an aging society.* Baltimore, MD: Johns Hopkins University Press.

Mysyuk, Y., Westendorp, R. G. J., & Lindenberg, J. (2016). Older persons' definitions and explanations of elder abuse in the Netherlands. *Journal of Elder Abuse & Neglect, 28*, 95–133.

Pence, G. E. (2015). Medical ethics: Accounts of ground-breaking cases (7th ed.). New York, NY: McGraw-Hill Education.

People v. Heitzman, 9 C. 4th 189, 37 Cal. Rptr. 2d 236 (1994).

Peroni, L., & Timmer, A. (2013). Vulnerable groups: The promise of an emerging concept in European Human Rights Convention law. *International Journal of Constitutional Law, 11*(4), 1056–1085.

Pence, G. E. (2015). *Medical ethics: Accounts of ground-breaking cases.* New York, NY: McGraw-Hill Education.

Pew Research Center. (2016). Social and demographic trends. Retrieved from http://www.pewsocialtrends.org/2016/02/18/2-living-arrangements-of-older-americans-by-gender

Ploeg, J., Lohfeld, L., & Walsh, C. A. (2013). What is "elder abuse"? Voices from the margin: The views of underrepresented Canadian older adults. *Journal of Elder Abuse & Neglect, 25*(5), 396–424.

Pozgar, G. D. (2012). Healthcare ethics. In *Legal aspects of health care administration* (11th ed., pp. 367–398). Sudbury, MA: Jones and Bartlett Learning.

Rawls, J. (2009). *A theory of justice.* Cambridge, MA: Harvard University Press.

Roberto, K. A., & Teaster, P. B. (2017). Theorizing elder abuse. In *Elder abuse* (pp. 21–41). Cham, Switzerland: Springer International.

Singer, P. (Ed.). (1986). *Applied ethics.* Oxford: Oxford University Press.

Social Security Administration. (2018). Life expectancy. Retrieved on from https://search.ssa.gov/search?utf8=%E2%9C%93&affiliate=ssa&query=life+expectancy

Stevens, E. (2013). Safeguarding vulnerable adults: Exploring the challenges to best practice across multi-agency settings. *Journal of Adult Protection, 15*(2), 85–95.

Summers, J. (2009). Theory of healthcare ethics. In E. E. Morrison (Ed.), *Health care ethics: Critical issues for the 21st century* (pp. 3–40). Sudbury, MA: Jones and Bartlett.

Teaster, P. B., Schmidt, W. C., Wood, E. F., Lawrence, S. A., & Mendiondo, M. S. (2010). *Public guardianship: In the best interests of incapacitated people?* Santa Barbara, CA: ABC-CLIO.

Teaster, P. B., & Sokan, A. E. (2016). Ethical standards and practices in human services and health care for LGBT elders. In D. A. Harley & P. B. Teaster (Eds.), *Handbook of LGBT elders* (pp. 639–655). Cham, Switzerland: Springer International.

United States Fidelity and Guaranty Co. v. Guenther, 281 U.S. 34, 50 S.Ct. 165, 74 L.Ed. 683 (1930).

United States v. United Mine Workers, 330 U.S. 258 (1947).

US Census Bureau. (2017). Facts for features: Older Americans Month: May 2017. Retrieved from https://www.census.gov/newsroom/facts-for-features/2017/cb17-ff08.html

US Courts. (n.d.). Overview—rule of law. Retrieved from http://www.uscourts.gov/educational-resources/educational-activities/overview-rule-law

Veatch, R. M. (2016). *The basics of bioethics* (3rd ed.). New York, NY: Routledge.

Vulnerable. (n.d.). In *Merriam-Webster Online*. Retrieved from http://www.merriam-webster.com/dictionary/vulnerable

VULNERABILITY: COMPROMISED HEALTH

dvances in overall health care have enhanced the ability of older adults to live more healthfully and longer than ever before. Yet, even with such astounding advances—including the eradication of previously near-fatal diseases—incidences of disease and disability increase with age, with consequent limitations for those affected. Nearly three out of four Medicare beneficiaries living in the community do so with two or more chronic conditions, such as heart disease or arthritis. One in four adults age 50 and over has difficulty with hearing, vision, cognition, or mobility; and for those age 85 and over, this figure rises to more than 2 in 3. More than 1 in 10 older adults experience cognitive impairment, with Alzheimer's disease—the most serious and common of the age-related dementias—now the sixth leading cause of death in the United States. Finally, many older adults suffer from mental illness, particularly depression and anxiety. Limitations of compromised health such as these affect older adults' capacity for self-care and ability to live independently. In combination, they can be especially devastating.

In this section, chapters on cognitive impairment, mental illness, and physical disability show how these problems, taken individually or together, can significantly alter the life of an older person and the people around him or her. The chapters also reveal the centrality of both formal and informal caregivers for vulnerable elders, who daily confront the challenges of compromised health, challenges that often escalate with advanced age.

As you read these chapters, consider ethical concerns related to maintaining autonomy when an older adult has compromised cognitive capacity or mental health challenges. How does an older adult stay in the community and sustain relationships with others when she experiences debilitating chronic pain or has mobility limitations? What does society owe vulnerable older adults with compromised health—a critical issue with health care costs for this population requiring more and more of total health care expenditures in the United States? As will be revealed, these are just a few of the many ethical issues and dilemmas surrounding compromised health for older adults.

2

COGNITIVE IMPAIRMENT

Elizabeth J. Santos, MD, MPH
University of Rochester Medical Center

Corey Nichols-Hadeed, JD
University of Rochester Medical Center

KEYWORDS

cognitive impairment
executive dysfunction
crystallized intelligence
dementia

capacity
neurocognitive domains
fluid intelligence

CASE STUDY 2.1

Glenn Henderson brought his mother Mary for an evaluation at a memory disorders clinic. Mary is an 82-year-old woman whose husband Bill died about 6 months ago after a long illness. Mary was Bill's primary caregiver and had spent the last 2 years by his side administering all of his medications and bringing him to dialysis three times a week. Since Bill's death, Glenn and his siblings, Sarah and Jared, have noticed that Mary is not as sharp as she once was. Glenn is single, but he also has a very demanding job and runs his own company, so he cannot be there as often as he would like. Her daughter Sarah and Sarah's husband Luke are quite busy with their children and new grandchildren, but they live closest to Mary and usually help with household chores. Mary's other son Jared and his wife Kelly live several hours away, but Jared is in accounting and finance and had helped Bill and Mary with their financial planning.

All of Mary's children agree that something has changed, but they do not agree about what is wrong and what type of help she might need. Her daughter-in-law Kelly's mother died a few years ago with Alzheimer's dementia, and she was quite difficult to manage, responded to auditory hallucinations, wandered, was violent at times, and had to be placed in a skilled nursing facility. Given their experience with Kelly's mother, Jared and Kelly think that Mary is doing very well and that the other children are overreacting. Mary is calm and takes care of her hygiene. She is isolated and quiet since Bill's death, but Jared and Kelly do not think this is a problem. Her other children, Glenn and Sarah, are concerned because she asks them the same questions repeatedly and has forgotten the names of Sarah's children and grandchildren at times. They have also found pills on the floor and are worried that she is not taking her medication correctly. Mary does not think that she has any problems and says that though she misses Bill, she is happy enough living alone and staying in the house most of the time. Because she was unable to socialize throughout the past few years of Bill's illness, she has lost touch with many friends, some of whom have moved to retirement communities close to their children. Does Mary have cognitive impairment?

Cognitive Impairment

The concept of cognitive impairment is extremely complex and quantifying the amount of cognitive impairment a person has is an elusive goal. Scores on cognitive screening tools and a diagnosis of dementia cannot capture the range and myriad ways that one's mind works to get through the day, making both simple and sophisticated decisions. Many ways of describing neurocognitive domains exist, but the way described in the most recent *Diagnostic and Statistical Manual of Mental Disorders*, the diagnostic guide used by health care professionals throughout the world, includes six neurocognitive domains: Complex Attention, Executive Functioning, Learning and Memory, Language, Perceptual, and Social-Cognition.

Complex Attention includes sustained attention, divided attention, selective attention, and processing speed. **Executive Functioning** includes but is not limited to an even more complicated set of factors such as: planning, sequencing, responding to feedback, error correction, and mental flexibility. **Learning and Memory** is comprised of immediate, recent, and very long-term memory and implicit learning. **Language** involves both receptive and expressive forms such as naming, word finding, fluency, grammar, and syntax. The **Perceptual** domain consists of functions such as visual perception, which can be observed by problems with facial recognition, drawing, and inability to imitate gestures and pantomime use of known objects such as a hairbrush. **Social-Cognition** involves understanding and recognition of emotional states and the ability to consider other people's mental states. Inability to do this or a change in this domain is often recognized as a personality change.

Mental capacity is an essential concept to understand in relation to cognitive impairment and how this affects vulnerability (Moye & Marson, 2007). In general, if one has capacity, this means that one has the ability to make decisions. When we question a person's ability to make decisions, this is often due to our disagreement with the decision that person is making. Normally, for most high-level decisions, we presume that children lack capacity and adults have capacity. When evaluating someone for medical decision-making capacity, four elements are necessary to consider:

1. Does the patient express a preference/choice?

2. Is the patient able to attain a factual understanding of the relevant information provided?

3. Is the patient able to appreciate risks and benefits, and consequences of accepting or rejecting treatment?

4. Is the patient demonstrating rational thinking and logical decision making?

The last element, demonstrating rational thinking and logical decision making, can be quite difficult to assess and greatly affected by changes in any of the neurocognitive domains. However, a problem in one or more domains does not necessarily mean that someone lacks capacity to make decisions.

Capacity determinations can be complex due to the intersection of and distinctions between "competency and capacity" in the legal setting versus "capacity" in the medical/clinical setting (Santos & Nichols-Hadeed, 2017). Law and medicine have separate definitions of these terms, and they are often used interchangeably in error. The law uses the terms to declare a more permanent status of someone's cognitive abilities, and medicine uses the terms to gauge decision-making capacity in a specific situation. For example, under federal law governing pensions, bonuses, and veterans' relief, the Code of Federal Regulations defines mental incompetency as, "A mentally incompetent person is one who because of injury or disease lacks the mental capacity to contract or to manage his or her own affairs, including disbursement of funds without limitation" (38 C.F.R §3.353, 2018). A review of state law definitions of incompetency/incapacity demonstrated that each state provides its own state specific definition, varying in clarity and complexity (Demakis, 2013). The array of laws and legal definitions is further complicated by legal professionals' lack of knowledge regarding health conditions that develop with age (Soones, Ahalt, Garrigues, Faigman, & Williams, 2014). Physicians rely on the "psychiatric interview" standard to evaluate a patient's ability to make decisions at the time of the assessment (Brandl et al., 2007). When considering capacity, it is important to define what that term means in relation to the situation, and in doing so, to understand what systems are relevant—medicine, legal, or perhaps both.

Neurocognitive disorders include all types of dementias as well as more temporary states such as delirium, which can be caused by a multitude of medical illnesses, medications, substance use, and withdrawal from substances. A simplistic way to think of delirium is as an acute change in mental status that affects alertness and thinking. If you have ever seen anyone intoxicated by alcohol or drugs or under the influence of anesthesia after surgery, then you have seen examples of delirium. Most often, delirium is a temporary state that resolves quickly. However, if the cause of the delirium is not immediately recognized, multifactorial, ongoing and/or not easily treated, the delirium can be prolonged for months or even years. It is easy to imagine that during times of delirium, one may not have the capacity to make certain decisions, but may be able to make others. For example, an intoxicated person may make the poor decision to meet up with a former lover but may also have enough mental capacity to refuse to get into the car with an intoxicated driver.

A very simplistic and general definition of dementia is that of cognitive decline from a previous baseline in more than one neurocognitive domain that impacts daily function. Dementia usually is progressive depending on the etiology. There are numerous causes of dementia, which include Alzheimer's disease and Parkinson's disease, to name a few.

A frontotemporal dementia syndrome may initially manifest with personality and behavioral changes that draw attention before memory impairment is readily noted. Strokes occurring at any age may cause vascular dementia. Someone who already has a diagnosis of dementia is also at higher risk to develop delirium more quickly than someone without dementia who suffers from the same illness. For example, if two people have pneumonia, but one of them also carries a diagnosis of mild Alzheimer's dementia, the one with dementia is likely to appear more confused until the pneumonia is resolved and during that period of acute worsened confusion may not be able to make financial decisions. Once the pneumonia has resolved, both people may have the same capacity to make financial decisions. Therefore, a person's cognitive impairment may be permanent and progressive, but it may also be temporary and can change with different circumstances.

It is a common misconception that someone with a diagnosis of dementia or a major neurocognitive disorder does not have the ability to make decisions. It is also a common ageist misconception that older adults necessarily have cognitive impairment. In fact, though it is true that most people with cognitive impairment are older adults, cognitive impairment can be present in any age group. It is often more difficult for people to believe that a relatively young person has cognitive impairment; much time can go by before a younger person is acknowledged to have a problem, which can lead to increased opportunities for exploitation of a vulnerable younger adult as well.

There are cognitive processes that do change with age (Harada, Natelson Love, & Triebel, 2013) and one of the easiest ways to think about these changes is to consider the concepts of crystallized and fluid intelligence introduced by Raymond B. Cattell and Donald Hebb in the mid-20th century (Brown, 2016). Crystallized intelligence or abilities are skills and knowledge that we learn and practice over a lifetime. Examples of crystallized abilities include things like facts, general knowledge, math, and vocabulary. Fluid intelligence or abilities require flexibility to adapt to different situations and to use already learned crystallized knowledge to make logical decisions. It takes fluid intelligence to be able to understand new relationships and discern patterns. Abstract reasoning and problem solving are attributed to fluid intelligence. Crystallized and fluid abilities interact with each other as they work to help us make educated logical decisions related to the world around us; but as we age, fluid abilities are most often affected while crystallized abilities are more stable and may even improve with life experiences. Fluid cognitive domains that may diminish with age include executive function, processing speed, and psychomotor abilities.

Autonomy

Autonomy or self-determination is a core ethical principle often defined as respect for one's ability to make decisions (Beauchamp & Childress, 2012). In the context of cognitive impairment, this is an area fraught with conflict. Ideally, we would all like to be able to have our decisions respected and followed. When someone has cognitive impairment, as noted previously, one's decision-making capacity is often questioned. Though cognitive impairment may be present, the specific decision being made has to be considered in detail in order to determine the effect that cognitive impairment has on that decision. Decisions about driving and spending money are common areas of concern that test the premise of autonomy.

Returning to the case study at the beginning of the chapter, Glenn and Sarah are concerned about their mother's driving. Mary thinks their fears are unfounded. She doesn't go out much at all and when she does, she only drives short distances in the daytime when the weather is good. However, a few months ago, she went to a large grocery store where she usually shops and forgot where she parked. Mary called Sarah in a panic and Sarah had to come and help her find the car. After they found Mary's car, Sarah followed her home and watched helplessly as her mother drove over several curbs when she turned. Admittedly, Mary was quite shaken up over losing her car and was rather distracted when she drove home. Glenn believes that Mary should not be driving because she once got lost going to his office, but he had just recently moved, and it was in a new building.

Driving a car is an extremely complex task that involves many neurocognitive domains, and the decision to allow someone to continue driving is a frequently challenged test of autonomy. It is imperative to have good functioning in attention and perception. Many would assume that someone who was diagnosed with dementia would be unable to drive, but that is not necessarily true. Recall that a diagnosis of dementia is usually a progressive decline in more than one neurocognitive domain, but it does not mean that all of them are affected. One could have severe problems with speech and personality changes, perhaps due to a stroke, but have no problems with visual and motor skills or attention needed to drive. In comparison, a younger adult may not have any neurocognitive deficits that are as easily notable as problems with speech, but more subtle problems with attention and learning that impair driving. In the latter case, cognitive impairment is present but may go unnoticed. The most reliable way to evaluate ability to drive is to complete a formal driving evaluation.

CASE STUDY 2.2

Mary drove Bill to dialysis for over two years prior to his death. After his death, she continued to drive but only drove short distances to nearby stores. Mary became very upset that Glenn and Sarah were questioning her ability to drive. After explaining how complex a task driving a car is, they all agreed that Mary should have a formal driving evaluation that could be more objective. In the meantime, Mary also agreed that she would not drive if she was emotionally distraught but would spend at least 30 minutes calming down before she tried to drive anywhere.

For many years, Jared has managed Mary and Bill's finances, but they never arranged for him to officially be appointed as power of attorney. Jared set up all of their bills to be paid automatically through their bank accounts when his father became ill. Unfortunately, when there is a new bill that is not on automatic payment, Mary has to write a check. This past winter, one of the pipes froze and burst in her basement. Luckily after Bill's death, Mary had moved many of their memorabilia and pictures upstairs from the basement so that she could look at them and reorganize, so nothing valuable was destroyed by the water damage. She called Glenn, who was out of town on a business trip. He immediately called the plumber, but their usual plumber was unavailable, so Glenn was forced to call an emergency plumber he found in the phone book. The emergency plumber fixed the pipe, but charged Mary over $2000, which Glenn thought was excessive. Mary told Glenn that the plumber offered to fix several other plumbing issues while he was there and that raised the price. Her explanation is very plausible, but Glenn is concerned that Mary is unable to manage her money and is vulnerable to scam artists and contractors.

Another frequently challenged test of autonomy is financial capacity, the right to control how one's money is spent. There is growing evidence that even mild executive dysfunction can affect financial decision-making capacity and can contribute to vulnerability resulting in financial exploitation (Marson et al., 2000). Recall that executive function involves planning, sequencing, responding to feedback, error correction, and mental flexibility. When one makes financial decisions like paying bills, manipulating bank accounts, and investing money, one needs to understand why the money is being moved, where the money is coming from, and where the money is going. If one cannot comprehend any one of these issues and lacks the mental flexibility to understand any changes in the sequence of events revolving around the movement of money, then it is possible for one to be unable to manage one's money. It is not uncommon that someone who is unable to manage her money retains the capacity to choose a power of attorney, as that comprises a different set of criteria and is a much more straightforward decision in comparison to ongoing changing circumstances that are associated with financial management. Of course, one who does have executive dysfunction may be at higher risk for manipulation and may be influenced to choose a power of attorney that is less than ideal. It is best to make those types of decisions long before one has cognitive impairment, if at all possible.

CASE STUDY 2.3

Mary was never comfortable managing the finances and left all of those decisions to Bill and Jared. Mary trusts her children and would allow any of them to act as her power of attorney, and she has agreed to discuss this with all of them. Since Jared lives a few hours away and Glenn is often traveling for business, Mary thought that her daughter Sarah would be most likely able to help her manage any bills that come up suddenly. She does want Jared to continue to manage all of her ongoing steady finances.

Beneficence

The ethical principal of beneficence is grounded in doing well for others, in other words, providing a benefit to others in some way (Beauchamp, 2013). There is some ethical debate over how far the obligation of beneficence reaches in terms of what extent of benefit is morally obligated. This is especially true of medicine, where degrees and levels of care from prevention to maintenance cover a range of professional obligations.

CASE STUDY 2.4

Though Mary's children are not in agreement about her level of cognitive impairment, they want to consider any medication clinical trials she could participate in. Jared saw a *60 Minutes* television show about Alzheimer's dementia and thinks that everyone should participate in clinical trials to further medical knowledge. Sarah is worried that Mary might not actually be given medication, but that she would be placed in the placebo arm of the trial. Glenn is ambivalent about participation in research. One of Glenn's friends is currently enrolled in a clinical trial for a lung cancer treatment, and he has watched him become very ill with treatment. Of course, it is not clear whether or not his friend is in the control arm or the treatment arm of the study, but his friend is constantly nauseous and can no longer go to their biweekly dinners.

One example of an ethical dilemma concerning vulnerable adults with cognitive impairment is the process of developing effective medical treatment. We try to discover preventive measures and curative treatments for every disease and in doing so, we need to test the treatments on the individuals suffering from the disease. In the case of medications for dementia, this can be very difficult to do. All research subjects must participate voluntarily and with informed consent. We know that not all people who carry diagnoses of dementia lack capacity to give informed consent. However, a subject with dementia who may initially consent to participate in the trial may lose the ability to give informed consent during the trial. To create treatments for dementia, we need to use subjects with dementia. In order to benefit others, including their families, many patients with dementia want to participate in clinical trials. How can we safeguard the vulnerable adult with cognitive impairment during a medication clinical trial?

CASE STUDY 2.5

Mary does not think she has cognitive impairment and therefore does not believe that she would qualify for a clinical trial. There is ongoing research on preventative measures prior to development of dementia, and she thinks she might want to participate in that type of research study. However, she is hesitant to allow any blood draws, and she has anxiety that worsens when she is in an MRI machine, so she will not allow head imaging either. Although Jared is encouraging and Sarah wants her to consider a trial, Mary is reluctant. Participation in the studies must be voluntary and, in this case, Mary is not willing.

Mary's children are concerned that Mary is not taking all of her medications regularly, including her diabetes medications. For the past several years, she has devoted her time to caring for Bill and as a result has neglected her own health. Her blood pressure and blood glucose have both increased since Bill's death. She is no longer restricting her diet now that she doesn't have to cook diabetic-friendly meals for Bill, but she should be cooking them for herself. Glenn accompanied her to her primary care physician's appointment and was warned that her kidney functions were worsening. When Glenn took her home after the appointment, he found out that since her husband died, she has been ordering prepared meals and upon inspection, her cupboards are full of unhealthy snacks. There is also some concern that Mary may not be able to cook as well as she once did. She prepared her traditional candied yams and potatoes au gratin as side dishes for Thanksgiving last year and mistakenly switched the sugar and salt in each dish. The physician advised that she should not try to multitask, but rather follow only one recipe at a time to improve her focus.

The previous example described wanting to benefit others, but let us consider treatment that directly benefits someone with cognitive impairment. Hemodialysis is a method used to cleanse toxins from blood when kidneys are damaged, and it is very often required due to renal failure caused by diabetes. When renal failure causes toxins to build up in the bloodstream, many sequelae can follow, including delirium and finally death. In addition to experiencing a more acute confusional state like delirium, adults with progressive cognitive impairment or dementia may also require hemodialysis. Hemodialysis usually takes several hours and requires the patient to sit calmly connected to a machine while the patient's blood is removed, cleansed, and returned. This can be a very trying process for anyone. For a patient who also has cognitive impairment, acutely or chronically, it can be a confusing process (Davidson & Holley, 2008; Feely, Albright, Thorsteinsdottir, Moss, & Swetz, 2014). Additionally, it is not uncommon for agitation to be associated with cognitive impairment, which makes sitting calmly for several hours to endure hemodialysis very difficult. Capacity to make the choice to endure hours of hemodialysis three times a week requires at least a basic understanding of the steps involved and risks and benefits of enduring this treatment that may last for many years. If a patient with worsening and progressive cognitive impairment becomes agitated and refuses to cooperate with the procedure, how should we proceed? Can we proceed? If the only way to safely conduct the hemodialysis is to sedate the patient every time, should we do this?

CASE STUDY 2.6

Mary is at risk for diabetic nephropathy. If she does not control her blood glucose, her kidney function will continue to deteriorate, and then she may need hemodialysis, like her husband did. Mary is very aware of how taxing hemodialysis can be. She drove Bill to dialysis three times a week and waited with him for many hours every day. She also saw him endure the pain and repeated surgeries to create arteriovenous fistulas. She was present at the dialysis center when other patients became frustrated and aggressive, even pulling out their tubing, and she was scared. Mary is not sure she would want to go through dialysis like Bill did and promises to follow a stricter diet again.

Nonmalfeasance

For physicians, the ethical principle of nonmalfeasance has long been conceived as the principle "first, do no harm" (Beauchamp & Childress, 2012). We must avoid treatments that might cause harm to the patient, but many treatments do have side effects that must be endured to be effective. In the example above, patients undergoing hemodialysis suffer through hours of treatment in order to remove dangerous toxins from their blood.

Let us consider another common dilemma facing patients diagnosed with dementia and their families, namely whether or not to start anticholinergic medication such as Donepezil (Gauthier, Leuzy, Racine, & Rosa-Neto, 2013). All medications have some risk of side effects, and Donepezil is no exception. Donepezil is a first-line treatment for Alzheimer's dementia in the effort to slow down the progression of the illness, but it is far from a cure. Many patients suffer from disturbing side effects, such as diarrhea and vivid dreams or nightmares. Too often patients do not already have advance directives but defer to the substituted judgment of their families. If it is clear that the patient does not have sufficient capacity to make the decision whether or not to start medication, the decision may rest with a designated health care proxy, guardian, or otherwise trusted family member. However, even if the patient lacks full capacity to make an informed decision, he or she may be the one experiencing the side effect and may refuse to take the medication that the family or guardian wants him or her to take. Is it worth going against the patient's stated refusal to take this medication if he or she is being harmed by medication side effects?

CASE STUDY 2.7

During the cognitive screening testing, Mary scored 21/30 on the Montreal Cognitive Assessment (MoCA), indicating some cognitive impairment with a "normal" score being >26/30. She admits that with Bill gone, she is also more depressed and anxious to be home alone. Her children think she's always been a rather anxious person, but she never was treated for anxiety. Anxiety can adversely influence her score on cognitive testing, causing her to be less attentive to the questions. Mary further has experienced a lot of heartburn and Gastroesophageal Reflux Disease, which is likely due to anxiety. Her children want her to take any medications that will help her cognition now, but Mary is ambivalent about taking more medications. When she hears that a possible side effect of any of the anticholinergic medications may be gastrointestinal upset, she becomes more adamant that she doesn't want to take them. Since her anxiety seems also to be influencing her cognition negatively, her children want her to take anti-anxiety medication as well. After seeing the results of her cognitive screening, her children believe that she cannot make any decisions and want to be able to decide what medications she takes. Her physician discusses issues related to decision-making capacity described above and though they are not convinced that she cannot make the decision to refuse medication, they let Mary voice her concerns. Mary was swayed by her children's concern and agreed to a trial of Donepezil.

Another common occurrence is the difficult choice to pay for medication that is not covered by insurance or is very expensive even with insurance. Memantine is the only FDA-approved medication for moderate to severe dementia of the Alzheimer's type, but for many patients, even with insurance it can be prohibitively expensive. There may be tension between family members who want to "do everything" for their loved one, but limited incomes and the cost of caring for loved ones may already be quite a financial load. A patient with dementia may already feel guilty, hopeless, and like a burden to his or her family, and she may not want to spend the money for medication that is not curative, preferring to leave more of his or her estate to her family. In this case, the patient with dementia may be refusing to start medication because of the perceived financial burden to his or her family rather than any physical harm.

CASE STUDY 2.8

Unfortunately, after only a few days, Mary developed such extreme diarrhea that she was taken to the emergency room, and the Donepezil was discontinued. Her family called the physician in a panic because they wanted her to continue some type of cognitive-sparing medication. The physician talked with them about trying the Rivastigmine patch with the hope that it would be less likely to cause diarrhea, and they agreed to try it. When they went to the pharmacy to pick up the prescription, it was over $400, and the pharmacist said that Mary's insurance would not cover it. They did not pick up the prescription but again called the physician's office to find out if they could speak with the insurance company. Because Mary was not officially diagnosed with Alzheimer's dementia, the insurance company refused to pay for the patch, which was not on their formulary. The insurance company did have Rivastigmine tablets on the formulary, though they are at the highest tier. Of course, given her experience in the emergency room, Mary is even more reluctant than ever to start any medication.

Justice

The principle of justice is most often linked with equality and fairness (Beauchamp & Childress, 2012; Feinsod & Wagner, 2008). In the realm of health care, the concept of distributive justice deals with concerns about who decides and who gets which treatments. Justice is affected by many factors such as age, residence, social status, ethnicity, disability, and insurance, to name a few. Stigmatized groups may be devalued and face more injustice (Yang & Kels, 2017).

For adults with cognitive impairment, it may be even more difficult to discern when something is fair or not. A score on a cognitive screening tool such as a Montreal Cognitive Assessment (MoCA) can tell us about certain cognitive domains that might be impaired, but this score cannot directly translate into a description of functional ability. For example, two people may both score 21 out of 30 on the MoCA, where greater than or equal to 26 is usually "normal," but this does not tell us anything about their ability to drive a car, an extremely complex task. Inattention, distraction, anxiety, hearing loss, and depression all can contribute to someone's poor performance on the MoCA. To have the most objective measure of driving ability, a formal driving evaluation is required rather than relying on scores from cognitive screening. Would it be fair to automatically stop anyone from driving who scores less than 26 on the MoCA?

It is easy to see how the presence of cognitive impairment creates vulnerability and can cause ethical concerns, and in the context of medical care this is especially true. As explored in this chapter, the ethical principles of autonomy, beneficence, nonmalfeasance, and justice require careful, ongoing consideration, especially when the subject of concern has cognitive impairment. Given the complexity of the interface between medical care, ethics, and cognitive impairment, it is not surprising that, more often than not all, of these principles need to be considered and may be in conflict with one another. Arriving at an ethical decision may cause conflict. It is also important to recognize that cognitive impairment and capacity are not static and can change over time, which will necessarily influence decisions and how autonomy is evaluated.

DISCUSSION QUESTIONS

1. Whose concerns matter most? The adult with cognitive impairment or the guardian?

2. How does one's cognitive ability influence our understanding of equality and fairness?

3. Does someone's ability or lack thereof to participate in community, productivity, generativity, and family add to or subtract from one's worth? How do you decide someone's worth to society?

4. Think of a scenario in your own life where two ethical principles are competing. How do you prioritize? How would someone's cognitive function affect that decision?

5. Consider a longitudinal research study involving a new treatment with follow-up over several years. How can you minimize harm to the study subjects whose ability to give informed consent many change over time?

REFERENCES

Beauchamp, T. (2013). The principle of beneficence in applied ethics In *The Stanford Encyclopedia of Philosophy*. Retrieved from https://plato.stanford.edu/archives/win2016/entries/principle-beneficence

Beauchamp, T., & Childress, J. (2012). *Principles of biomedical ethics* (7th ed.). New York, NY: Oxford University Press.

Brandl, B., Dryer, C. B., Heisler, C. J., Otto, J. M., Stiegel, L. A., & Thomas, R. W. (2007). *Elder abuse detection and intervention: A collaborative approach.* New York, NY: Springer.

Brown, R. E. (2016). Hebb and Cattell: The genesis of the theory of fluid and crystallized intelligence. *Frontiers in Human Neuroscience, 10*, 606. doi:10.3389/fnhum.2016.00606

Davidson, S. N., & Holley, J. L. (2008). Ethical issues in the care of vulnerable chronic kidney disease patients: The elderly, cognitive impaired, and those from different cultural backgrounds. *Advances in Chronic Kidney Disease, 15*(2), 177–185.

Demakis, G. J. (2013). State statutory definitions of incompetency/incapacity: Issues for psychologists. *Psychology, Public Policy, and Law, 19*, 331–342.

Determinations of incompetency and competency, 38 C.F.R. §3.353 (2018).

Feely, M. A., Albright, R. C., Thorsteinsdottir, B., Moss, A .H., & Swetz, K. M. (2014). Ethical challenges with hemodialysis patients who lack decision-making capacity: Behavioral issues, surrogate decision-makers, and end-of-life situations. *Kidney International, 86*, 475–480.

Feinsod, F. M., & Wagner, C. (2008). The ethical principle of justice: The purveyor of equality. *Annals of Long-Term Care, 1*(1).

Gauthier, S., Leuzy, A., Racine, E., & Rosa-Neto, P. (2013). Diagnosis and management of Alzheimer's disease: Past, present and future ethical issues. *Progress in Neurobiology, 110*, 102–113.

Harada, C. N., Natelson Love, M. C., & Triebel, K. L. (2013). Normal cognitive aging. *Clinical Geriatric Medicine, 29*(4), 737–752.

Marson, D. C., Sawrie, S. M., Snyder, S., McInturff, B., Stalvey, T., Boothe, A., ... & Harrell L. E. (2000). Assessing financial capacity in patients with Alzheimer disease: A conceptual model and prototype instrument. *Archives of Neurology, 57*(6), 877–884. doi:10.1001/archneur.57.6.877

Moye, J., & Marson, D. C. (2007). Assessment of decision-making capacity in older adults: An emerging area of practice and research. *Journals of Gerontology: Series B, 62*(1), 3–11.

Santos, E. J., & Nichols-Hadeed, C. (2017). Medical decision-making capacity and ethical considerations. In X. Dong (Ed.), *Elder abuse: Research, practice and policy* (pp. 229–246). Champ, Switzerland: Springer International.

Soones, T., Ahalt, C., Garrigues, S., Faigman, D., & Williams, B. A. (2014) "My older clients fall through every crack in the system": Geriatrics knowledge among legal professionals. *Journal of the American Geriatric Society, 62*(4), 734–739. doi:10.1111/jgs.12751

Yang, T. Y., & Kels C. G. (2017). Ethical considerations in electronic monitoring of the cognitively impaired. *Journal of American Board of Family Medicine, 30*, 258–263.

3

MENTAL HEALTH AND ELDER ABUSE

Donna Cohen, PhD

Professor, Department of Child & Family Studies
College of Behavioral & Community Sciences
University of South Florida

KEYWORDS

mental health	behavioral health
elder abuse	case studies
interventions	emotional trauma
homicides	ethics

Overview

Elder abuse and mental health disorders/symptoms are both geriatric challenges, and they are independently related to premature morbidity and mortality if not detected and managed with appropriate interventions by trained professionals. Unfortunately, little systematic research has focused on the association of elder abuse and mental health, specifically mental illness as a risk factor and/or consequence of elder abuse. Because the relatively small number of studies uses the terms mental health/illness, psychiatric disorders, or psychological distress to refer to the emotional trauma associated with elder abuse, these labels will be used interchangeably. This chapter reviews the limited research about the relationship of elder abuse and the mental health of older persons as well as the mental health of family members who perpetrate abuse, presents two case studies, describes ethical challenges of interventions with vulnerable older persons, and identifies future research priorities and their implications for practice and policies that integrate the fields of elder abuse and mental health. Mental health care and elder abuse intervention networks are not often available and accessible in many communities in the United States, and they do not have adequate numbers of trained geriatric manpower to respond appropriately.

Introduction

Both mental health conditions and elder abuse can contribute to vulnerability in older persons, and each may interact with other factors that harm or increase susceptibility to harm in later life. These include but are not limited to age-related comorbid conditions and frailty, sensory impairments, functional losses and disabilities, disadvantaged socio-economic status, inadequate relational networks and supports, stress associated with late-life losses, lack of available and accessible health care or home- and community-based care, unsafe housing and degraded neighborhoods, and exposure to unsafe conditions and disasters (Mechanic & Tanner, 2007). Likewise, poor mental health and elder abuse can each be consequences for vulnerable older adults who are either being mistreated or in danger of mistreatment, and who are unable to protect themselves (Teaster, 2002).

Mental health problems affect a significant proportion of older adults and are the single greatest cause of health disability (Cohen & Eisdorfer, 2011). A total of 5.2 million older Americans have Alzheimer's disease and related dementias, and that number is estimated to triple to 14 million to 16 million in 2050. Between 5.6 and 8 million older people (14% to 20%) have a diagnosable behavioral health condition—mood disorders, anxiety disorders, substance abuse disorders, and personality disorders—and that number is expected to double by 2030. Within this population, about 3% to 5% are estimated to have a serious mental disorder (schizophrenia, bipolar disorder, or chronic depression). Beyond diagnosed disorders, 1 in 5 older people misuse alcohol and/or drugs, and about 10% to 20% of community-residing older persons have depressive symptoms.

Psychiatric symptoms and disorders impair older adults' ability to live safe, secure, and healthy lives. Unfortunately, mental health problems frequently go unrecognized and untreated, which affects a person's ability to care for herself or himself; access health and community care; maintain relationships with family and friends; and recognize danger that increases the risk for deteriorating physical and mental health, poor quality of life, and unnecessary disability (Cohen & Eisdorfer, 2011).

Elder abuse can lead to any number of serious consequences for victims, including physical injuries and deteriorating physical and behavioral health, resulting in increased medical costs, premature nursing home placement, and untimely heightened mortality rates (Dong, Chen, Chang, & Simon, 2013; Lachs, Williams, O'Brien, & Pillemer, 2002; Schofield, Powers, & Loxton, 2013; Yunis, Hairi, & Yuen, 2017). The prevalence of elder abuse marks it as an emergent public health and public mental health epidemic (Teaster & Hall, 2018).

All older persons can be abused, but the presence of mental health conditions increases the risk of being victimized (Anetzberger, 2012; Jones, 2015). The sequential relationship between mental health and elder abuse is unknown given the paucity of longitudinal studies (Cooper, Blanchard, Selwood, Walker, & Livingston, 2010; Dong et al., 2013; Lachs, Williams, O'Brien, Hurst, & Horwitz, 1997). However, a large body of cross-sectional studies has identified that both victim factors and perpetrator factors are associated with an increased risk of abuse (Dong et al., 2013). Victims and perpetrators are heterogeneous groups with great variability in their contributing characteristics. Understanding the interactive features within both groups that increase victimization of older adults is a priority research area.

Research about the ecological relationships of the many victim–perpetrator variables affecting the increased risk of abusive behaviors is limited (Roberto, 2017). Victim factors associated with elder abuse include advancing age, income, presence of a behavioral health condition(s), cognitive impairment, and the victim–perpetrator relationship (Labrum, 2017; Pillemer, Burnes, Riffin, & Lachs, 2016). Perpetrator factors include age, male gender, employment/financial problems, drug and/or alcohol use, psychiatric diagnosis, history of psychiatric hospitalization, receiving mental health treatment, and arrest history (Labrum, 2017; Pillemer et al., 2016). Interaction factors include financial and personal care assistance to relatives with mental illness, living together, sustained personal contact, perpetrators who take actions to set limits on the behaviors of victims with mental illness, and informal management of finances by older perpetrators for relatives with poor behavioral health (Labrum, 2017).

Mental Health Consequences Associated With Elder Abuse

Both community- and clinic-based studies have demonstrated that poor mental health and adverse psychosocial circumstances of older persons, especially depression, anxiety, post-traumatic stress disorder, and loneliness, are associated with an increased risk of being abused (Acierno et al., 2010; Dong, Beck, & Simon, 2010; Dong et al., 2011; Dong et al, 2013; Lachs et al., 1997; Natan, Lowenstein, & Eisikovits, 2010), and the prevalence of these conditions is higher than seen in nonvictims (Winterstein & Eisikovits, 2005). Persons who experience repeated abuse show higher levels of psychiatric distress (Fisher & Regan, 2006; Luo & Waite, 2011). Demographic characteristics of persons with mental health conditions that increase abuse risk include advanced age, low educational attainment, and female gender. However, these studies vary in sample size, selection criteria, and the definition of abuse.

The few published population prospective studies show that elder abuse is more devastating on mental health than physical health, and victims experience lengthy recovery times with a diminished quality of life (Comiijs, Pot, Smit, Bouter, & Jonker, 1998; Dong et al., 2011; Labrum, 2017). However, the multiple interactive variables that contribute to the negative mental health consequences of abuse over time are not understood.

The level of psychological distress and severity of symptoms and conditions differs depending on the type and frequency of abuse (Begle et al., 2011; Coker et al., 2002). Older persons who experience any form of elder abuse report greater distress than those who are not abused (Luo & Waite, 2011). Older women who are subjected to repeated episodes of abuse or multiple types of abuse have higher levels of depression or anxiety (Fisher & Regan, 2006). Verbal abuse rather than physical abuse of both genders is the strongest predictor of psychological distress (Pico-Alfonso et al., 2006).

CASE STUDY 3.1

Abuse of an Older Woman With Multiple Mental Health Problems

This case study describes a series of events that began when an older woman who was misusing alcohol was physically abused by a hired home caregiver. After the woman's two daughters discovered the abuse, they became more involved in their mother's hands-on care. The incidents that occurred thereafter led to the discovery of the mother's other health problems, inadequate clinical decisions, and a temporary rift in the daughters' relationship.

NL had been in a functional alcoholic marriage for 50 years, and after her husband died, leaving her a widow at age 72, her daily alcohol consumption increased steadily. NL began to neglect herself and her home and withdrew from family and friends. Her daughters, BL and ML, were concerned about her poor hygiene, confusion, social withdrawal, and multiple falls. They had tried unsuccessfully for years to intervene with their parents' alcohol misuse, and now that NL was alone, she told them she was an adult who could do what she wanted.

NL agreed to hire a live-in housekeeper, but four women quit the position over a 6-month period because NL was so difficult. She yelled at them constantly for not doing things the way she wanted and refusing to buy her wine. NL also accused them of stealing her money and clothes, eating her food, and having male friends over at night. The fifth housekeeper lasted 2 months, and BL and ML hoped that her world had stabilized. However, when BL visited one afternoon, she found her mother tied to the bedposts, gagged, and zipped into a sleeping bag. BL called the police who arrested the housekeeper when she returned. The police report described several bruises and cigarette burns on NL's body.

BL and ML then hired 24/7 care from an agency, which NL grudgingly accepted. Again, NL was not an easy client. Her memory problems worsened, and she complained of not sleeping at night, bugs in her bed, difficulty breathing, seeing people and hearing voices in her head and choking on poison gas being pumped into her home. BL visited her mother frequently since she lived close by and pleaded with her to see a doctor. NL refused, and discussions always escalated into angry confrontations. NL accused both BL and the agency caregivers of stealing her money and plotting together to kill her by chopping her into pieces with a chain saw in the shed. ML did not believe what her sister said her about their mother, and when she visited, NL would often be unpleasant but did not show the same bizarre behavior.

When NL was hospitalized for a broken hip after a fall, additional tests showed that she had cancer. After recovering from surgery, she began radiation therapy, and BL moved her mother into her home. NL was often agitated and combative. NL denied she had cancer, and although she complained about pain, she often refused to take her medications and accused BL of hiding them so she would die.

One day, when BL took her mother to a health care team meeting at the cancer center, a team member informed her that he believed she was psychologically abusing her mother by threatening to kill her. BL was told that state law required them to report this to Adult Protective Services, and they were taking NL into protective custody.

BL was shocked by the alleged abuse and tried reaching her sister, who did not return her phone calls for a week.

When ML finally called, she told BL that their mother had called many times crying because BL was hurting her, and she wanted help to escape. BL contacted an elder law attorney, and both met with an advocacy representative and the chair of the ethics committee at the cancer center. BL was troubled that the doctors and other team members did not understand that her mother had severe memory problems and a history of paranoia. She had never threatened or abused her mother.

The ethics committee review concluded that NL's clinical team had not met an acceptable standard of care. They had not only violated her patient rights since she was not competent to consent but also had not properly investigated accusations of abuse. NL was not given a mental status screening examination or referred for a psychiatric consultation, standard institutional protocol to assess elder abuse. The intake form BL had completed noted that NL had a history of cognitive problems and paranoia but had refused to see a doctor. Staff chart notes at the cancer center indicated that NL was often confused and paranoid.

NL was finally given psychiatric and neurological evaluations at the cancer center and was diagnosed with Wernicke-Korsakoff Syndrome. Psychological testing indicated that she did not have the capacity to understand and consent to her treatments. The consent forms were signed by the social worker without a witness, and there was no evidence that anyone had tested her understanding of the procedures to diagnose and treat her cancer.

The ethics committee recommended that the chief of geriatric oncology meet with NL and her daughters to discuss guardianship. A court date was set, but NL's health deteriorated rapidly, and she was transferred to hospice care. BL and ML repaired their relationship with psychotherapy, and they were able to care for their mother, who died several months later.

This case raises several common problems and ethical dilemmas for families. A history of challenging parental health behaviors and difficult parent–adult child interactions can interfere with decision making, particularly when parents have been unwilling to seek medical help. In this situation, the daughters first believed that NL's persistent drinking was the behavior of an autonomous adult to make that decision, even though it was not a good decision. As NL deteriorated, BL and ML did not know where to find help from aging services, community agencies, as well as physicians and social workers at local hospitals. They believed that NL was competent to live this way, even with the behavioral problems and intolerance of caregivers. Talking with a physician about NL's behaviors might have led to earlier intervention. However, family members are not to be blamed entirely since resources are often not available, accessible, or publicized.

This case also illustrates violations of the principles of beneficence, nonmaleficence, and respect for a person's rights and dignity as well as lack of adherence to professional standards of informed consent and proper evaluation in clinical settings. Health care centers should have and follow standard elder abuse protocols. Clinicians should routinely ask questions about elder abuse and neglect, even when older patients are cognitively impaired, since some patients may still have the capacity to report being hurt or threatened. However, as in this narrative, patients with more severe dementia and/or paranoid ideation may falsely accuse caregivers of physical, sexual, and psychological threats and assaults. It is important to conduct a mental status examination and, if needed, to refer the patient for appropriate psychiatric evaluation.

When older persons are severely demented, it is critical to find a knowledgeable informant other than the suspected perpetrator. However, this can be challenging for several reasons. Other informants may not be available, or in this case, relatives may falsely accuse the caregiver or other family members of abuse. It requires sensitivity to interview several persons and also maximize the privacy and confidentiality of everyone being interviewed.

Elder Abuse by Relatives With Mental Illness

It is well-known that a sizeable group of individuals, most often family members, with a history of or current mental problems perpetrates elder abuse (Anetzberger, 2012; Labrum, 2017). Estimates are that 16% to 38% of all perpetrators have a history of mental illness (Labrum & Solomon, 2015), but prevalence varies depending on data sources: victim reports, history of mental illness, psychiatric hospitalizations, and cases reported to aging services. Results of the National Elder Mistreatment Study (Acierno et al., 2010) indicate rates from 19% to 28%.

The most common interpretation, which has not been empirically tested, is that these family members are highly dependent on their victims, many of whom are older parents (Labrum & Solomon, 2015). When circumstances or changes in victim and/or perpetrator functioning disrupt the dependency balance, perpetrators may feel threatened by perceptions of lost stability, increasing the risk of abusive behavior. However, any number of victim and/or perpetrator characteristics may mediate the beliefs and behaviors of abusive perpetrators. Only one study to date has gone beyond describing the phenomenon to examining the extent to which perpetrator and victim characteristics and their interactions are associated with physical, psychological, and financial abuse. Labrum (2017) did a secondary analysis of survey data completed by community adults in the United States age 55 years and older, where 243 respondents reported having a relative with psychiatric disorder(s). Respondents answered two areas of questioning: whether and how often they experienced physical, financial, or psychological abuse by their relative with a psychiatric disorder over the past 6 months; and the occurrence, level, and frequency of caregiving they provided to their relative with a psychiatric disorder over the past 6 months.

Rates of physical, financial, and psychological abuse of respondents were 15%, 19%, and 41% respectively, and 8% reported multiple types of abuse or repeated occurrences of specific acts. The co-occurrence of all types of abuse was statistically significant: 47% of respondents who were physically abused also experienced financial abuse and 81% experienced psychological abuse; of respondents who experienced financial abuse, 36% experienced physical abuse and 83% experienced psychological abuse; and of respondents who were abused psychologically, 29% experienced physical abuse and 39% experienced financial abuse.

Physical abuse was significantly less likely when relatives with a psychiatric disorder were receiving treatment and was significantly more likely when respondents lived with their relative and when respondents engaged in high levels of limit-setting behaviors with their relative. Financial abuse was significantly less likely when relatives with psychiatric disorders were receiving treatment. However, financial abuse was significantly more likely when relatives were reported to have used illegal drugs. Psychological abuse was significantly less likely when relatives with psychiatric disorders were reported to take their medications and when respondents were the parent of their relative. Psychological abuse was significantly more likely when respondents lived with their relative, provided high levels of financial assistance, and used frequent limit-setting behaviors with their relative.

The rates of 15%, 19%, and 41% for physical, financial, and psychological abuse are markedly higher than the estimates of 1.6%, 5.2%, and 4.6% reported in the National Elder Mistreatment study (Acierno et al., 2010). Thus, abuse of older persons by relatives with psychiatric disorders is more common than previously recognized. Research is critical not only because of the estimated sizeable prevalence of different forms of abuse but also the significant co-occurrence of different forms of abuse that seriously compound the negative impact on victims.

Elder Abuse by Relatives With Serious Mental Illness

Labrum and Solomon (2015) proposed that most perpetrators with mental illness have a serious mental illness (SMI)—major depression, bipolar depression, or schizophrenia, but data are lacking. They described the first socioecological model to guide research to examine whether perpetrators of abuse, especially physical abuse, are persons with SMI, many of whom are care recipients and not caregivers. The conceptual model identifies the interactions of variables in five layered domains: victim factors (demographics, physical and mental health, social isolation); perpetrator factors (demographics, clinical characteristics, violence and/or criminal history, and psychosocial factors); relationship factors (dependency, living arrangement and frequency of contact, relationship quality, psychological and physical aggression); community factors (low income, social disadvantages, access to mental health treatment); and societal factors (ageism, attitudes towards violence, beliefs about persons with disabilities). No research to date has examined risk factors for elder abuse by persons with SMI. The major underlying assumption of this conceptual model is that the association of SMI with violent behavior causes elder abuse, but this has not been demonstrated in the abuse literature to date.

CASE STUDY 3.2

Elder Abuse Where Both Victim and Perpetrator Have Mental Health Problems

This case study examines the lethal consequences when a family caregiver with major depression and a personality disorder attacks her mother who has dementia and an anxiety disorder. DG, the fourth of five children, was born to FE in 1954. DG was an energetic woman with many talents in the performing arts. She was an outstanding student and graduated high school in the early 1970s. DG married after graduation, but the marriage ended shortly thereafter. She moved to Nashville in the mid-1970s to pursue a new life and career as a country western singer. DG was successful singing in commercials and music videos, and during this time she met her second husband, AG. They lived in Nashville until the early 1990s when they moved to Las Vegas, and both found rewarding jobs in the entertainment industry.

In 1999, DG began lengthy visits to Virginia to help her oldest sister care for their father who was bedridden from multiple strokes. DG was a devoted caregiver over a 2-year period, and she cared for his many needs on a daily basis at the nursing home. The ongoing stress led to DG being hospitalized for severe depression. After her father died in 2001, DG stayed in Virginia to care full time for her mother who had severe dementia, anxiety, and behavioral disturbances. She and her sister tried tirelessly to find home care for their mother, but home care was scarce, and they did not have the financial resources to obtain outside help. Although two brothers lived next door, both refused to be involved. After DG's sister was unable to help because of her own health issues, DG quickly became exhausted trying to meet her mother's unrelenting demands. She was hospitalized again for severe depression and prescribed Paxil. After being released, DG went to a community mental health center for follow-up and returned to her role as the primary caregiver. However, the situation rapidly declined for both mother and daughter for several reasons. The community mental health center closed, leaving DG without monitoring and management of her depression. Her mother's dementia progressed with increasing personal care needs, paranoia, and aggressive behavioral disturbances. As the sole caregiver she was a captive of her role without respite or assistance.

NL began stealing and hiding prescription medications, including DG's Paxil. DG claimed to have gone through withdrawal from lack of the antidepressant, and on May 2, 2002, she found a Paxil pill in her purse and took it. She then put her mother to bed and allegedly had two drinks. At one point in the evening, DG found her mother sitting on the toilet. DG said she was unclear about what happened next, which she attributed to her withdrawal from Paxil. DG thought her mother was yelling, and when DG tried to help her off the toilet, they began an angry and violent physical exchange. Neighbors called law enforcement who found NL dead on the bathroom floor with large amounts of blood, multiple bruises, and shoeprints on her upper torso. The crime scene investigation revealed that the shoe prints matched the bottoms of DG's tennis shoes. The coroner's report cited the cause of death as multiple blunt force trauma, the worst of which resulted in a crushed chest and multiple broken ribs.

At trial, DG's defense attorney argued that DG had a long history as a devoted caregiver to both her father and mother prior to this incident. DG was the sole caregiver and without psychiatric treatment, she suffered from increasingly severe depression and involuntary intoxication because of the drug withdrawal, all reasons DG should not be convicted of her mother's murder. A geriatric psychologist testified to DG's lengthy hands-on history of devotion to both parents, the intense stress of caregiving without help, her mental health issues—including the impact the closing of the mental health center had on the escalating severity of her depression—and the high risk for lethal violence. A pharmacology expert testified to the issue of Paxil intoxication. However, the judge ruled that DG's defense proved the conditions necessary for first-degree murder since she was not taking the medication properly.

In April 2004, DG was sentenced to 30 years in prison for murder, with 14 to be served and then 16 years on supervised probation. The judge acknowledged mitigating circumstances in his ruling, including her caregiving history, sole responsibility for her mother's care, a documented history of trying to find home care, and the impact of the closing of the mental health center. The judge also took into account the testifying psychologist's research in several areas: the high prevalence of severe interpersonal violence when family members care for relatives with dementia at home, especially when caregivers are depressed and live alone with the patient (Paveza et al., 1992); and the prevalence and role of mental illness in family caregivers who kill relatives (Cohen, Krajewski, & Toyinbo, 2017). He appreciated the high risk for lethal behavior but commented that most research focused on older spouses who killed and not adult children.

This tragedy highlights the potential for lethal consequences in vitally exhausted, depressed caregivers and also illustrates how social, political, and economic factors that are beyond a caregiver's control contribute to a full-court press on their well-being and ability to care. It also underscores the unfortunate circumstances of many family members who are trying their best to care. Good care requires people willing to care, able to care, and having the resources to care, as well as a community to help them care (Cohen & Eisdorfer, 2011). Sadly, DG was willing to care but encountered brick walls to continue to care and have the resources to do so.

Family Caregiver Homicides: The Ultimate Abuse

Homicides of dependent older people by family caregivers violate ethical, moral, and legal values and have long-term effects on families and the communities where they occur. Although family caregiver homicides (FCHs) have attracted media attention, sustained public debate and an investment in research have not occurred. Karch and Nunn (2010) conducted one of the few studies using data from states enrolled from 2003 to 2007 in the National Violent Death Reporting System, and they identified three FCH subtypes: 31% were intentional homicides of the victim only, 25% were homicide by neglect, and 44% were homicide-suicides. Victims were women (63%), widowed (42%), non-Hispanic (97%), White (88%), killed at home (92%) with a firearm (35%) or by intentional neglect (25%) by a husband (31%) or son (22%). A total of 48% were 80 years and older, 42% were 50–79 years old, and 9% were 18–49 years old.

The national prevalence of FCHs in the United States is unknown because there is no national surveillance system. However, prevalence will be low given data from the Bureau of Justice Statistics. In 2011, there were 13,200 homicide deaths among persons aged 18 years and older in the United States, and of those, 2,410 victims were 50–64 years old and 510 were 65 years and older (Cooper & Smith, 2011). How many of these victims were killed by family caregivers is not known. However, FCHs will not be frequent events, given the low number of older homicide victims, most of whom are killed by non-family, but this does not negate the value of research. FCHs are an extraordinary form of family violence, and it is important to identify what combination of factors leads family members to kill to develop strategies for prevention.

A recent 36-year retrospective national newspaper surveillance study estimated that the U.S. prevalence of FCHs increased from 0.8 to 1.1 per million. This is statistically correct from 1980 to 2015, with the highest state prevalence rates in the western and northeastern census regions (Cohen et al., 2017). Characteristic of victims and perpetrators were consistent over time. About 90% of perpetrators were men and 90% of victims were women. The most common perpetrator–victim relationships were spouses/intimate partners (80%) followed by adult children killing parents (19%). Most victims (78%) were killed with a firearm. The most common victim health conditions, in descending order, included dementias, cancer, and cardiovascular diseases, accounting for 56% to 75% of all reported conditions. The suicide attempt/completion rate steadily increased from 5 in 10 to 9 in 10, and the legal consequences for those who did not suicide were variable. The most common sentence was manslaughter or second-degree murder (20%). Priority research areas include determining national and state prevalence rates, clarifying the many interacting FCH antecedents, understanding why men are perpetrators, decreasing the vulnerability of women, identifying factors contributing to state variation in prevalence, understanding why perpetrators homicide-suicide, and evaluating factors that influence legal decisions about perpetrators who do not suicide.

Homicide-suicides involving older couples are the result of a confluence of factors that overwhelm devoted family caregivers, most often husbands, with no history of violence or criminal behavior (Cohen & Eisdorfer, 2011). Perpetrators' decision making becomes impaired by depression and other mental health problems; physical exhaustion; frustration with the lack of trained geriatric health professionals and available, affordable home-based services; and isolation from family and friends. The pressures of these multiple interacting stressors fuel hopelessness and helplessness about the circumstances that compromise rational thinking, leading to lethal violence. Research is lacking about factors that mediate FCH by adult child perpetrators. Although grown children may have close relationships with older parents, the nature of the intimacy is unlike that of older spouses. Beliefs about responsibility for the welfare of parents and other factors may interact to increase the risk of FCH. These may include family conflict, disruptions in work and family life, and the strain of long distance caregiving. Adult child perpetrators are equally likely to be either male or female.

Killings with attributions of mercy raise many complex and emotional issues (Cohen & Grabert, 2001). These include but are not limited to the value and sacredness of human life; the rights of any person to determine that the life of a loved one is no longer worth living and to kill them; the burdens on family members caring for catastrophically ill relatives; the responsibilities of health care professionals as well as family members and other persons in the community to detect, intervene, and prevent these tragedies; as well as legal guidelines to deal with these circumstances.

There is no distinction in U.S. criminal law between caregiver homicides with compassionate or merciful motivations and killing for any other reason. A compassionate killing by a devoted family caregiver is a deliberate homicide. As seen in the case study, the law provides for identification of mitigating as well as aggravating circumstances in judicial decisions. A review of the outcomes of criminal proceedings from case studies shows there is significant variability in the way law enforcement, prosecutors, and judges deal with family caregivers who kill (Cohen & Grabert, 2001; Cohen, Krajewski, & Toyinbo, 2017; Lavi, 2009). Sometimes charges are not made or are dropped. Sentences range from time served with probation and mental health care to incarceration from one year to life.

The emerging data about the nature of FCHs provide a framework for legal applications in criminal proceedings. Killing another human being is not a socially acceptable action, and compassionate homicides should not be institutionalized. However, there are many mitigating factors to be considered in this narrow band of spousal killings, and there should be a range of options in the courts. These circumstances could be argued as an affirmative defense, based upon the impaired mental state of the perpetrator struggling to care for himself and a spouse in the context of many inadequacies in the health and community-based care systems. It is not logical that these complex, lethal situations, which reflect significant shortcomings in our society's ability to deal with the needs of an aging society, be decided in a court of law without consideration of the full context of the killing.

Need for Ethical Standards of Practice

Elder abuse poses difficult and complex ethical considerations that many health care professions, including the mental health professions, have not sufficiently addressed in training curricula and research standards, continuing education, clinical practice, and professional policies (IOM, 2014; Qualls, Segal, Norman, Niederehe, & Gallagher-Thompson, 2002; Scheider, 2012). The many health care disciplines vary in the attention given to ethical considerations in their professional codes of conduct. For example, social work (Donovan & Regehr, 2010), nursing (Chang & Daly, 2011; Ludwick & Silva, 2003; Neno & Neno, 2005), and occupational therapy (Crepeau, Cohn, & Schell, 2003) have been attentive to elder abuse ethical and legal issues in surprising contrast to psychology, a field with clearly defined clinical and research focus in geropsychology (APA, 2010; Lysack, Lichtenberg, & Schneider, 2011). Health care professionals and government representatives working with older people, such as adult protective services professionals and law enforcement, must function within the ethical codes of their respective professional and institutional organizations as well as local, state, and federal laws. Frequently, the former are too general, ambiguous, or even contradictory, and professionals must rely on legal statutes and court decisions. It is unfortunate that professional and institutional codes suffer from a lack of clarity in defining elder abuse. Although state and federal laws as well as the research literature provide general descriptions of elder abuse, there is no consensus among researchers and policy makers about specific definitions of elder abuse and its subtypes (Anetzberger, 2012; Beaulieu & Leclerc, 2006). Definitions of elder abuse and criteria applied to define victims and perpetrators vary across states (Zeranski & Halgin, 2011), which makes it difficult to interpret what constitutes elder abuse as well as appropriate ethical and legal responses (Anetzberger, 2005).

CONCLUDING OBSERVATIONS

Although there is clear evidence that individuals with histories or current diagnoses of mental health problems perpetrate elder abuse, the few available studies have only described the occurrence of the relationship (Labrum & Solomon, 2015). There is a dearth of information about the interaction of the many possible victim, perpetrator, psychosocial, and ecological factors that contribute to an increased risk for abuse of victims by perpetrators with different types of psychiatric disorders and symptoms. Despite the scant number of prospective and retrospective longitudinal studies, the available knowledge base about the association of mental illness and elder abuse clearly underscores the significance of developing interventions. The three most commonly available interventions for victims include advocacy services, support groups, and family care conferences, but empirical evaluations of effectiveness are lacking. Collaborations between professionals in mental health and elder abuse are important priorities to develop a strong base of data for evidence-based strategies to detect, intervene, and prevent elder abuse (Jackson & Hafemeister, 2013). There would be a Nobel Prize for discoveries to identify and clarify the timeline of inter-acting antecedents, risk factors, and precipitating circumstances that lead to harm to vulnerable older adults.

Substantive strategies are needed to improve ways to analyze and resolve ethical considerations and dilemmas in the development of specific protocols for evaluating and responding to elder abuse when mental health issues are prominent in victims and/or perpetrators. The following areas need to be addressed to improve elder abuse practices when mental health problems are present:

- Creation of clear, uniform definitions and guidelines to improve surveil-lance of abuse and provide decision trees to help professionals intervene and/or prevent abuse, given the lack of evidence-based data that are inher-ent in current practices;

- Development of specific ways to disseminate information about defini-tions and guidelines to the many disciplines involved in elder abuse and mental health;

- Establishment of a research agenda to identify and clarify the many dynamic factors that interact in cases of suspected and detected elder abuse;

- Development of guidelines and algorithms to translate research findings into practice and policies;

- Implementation of platforms and mechanisms to open discussions about the many concerns, values, and beliefs during training, supervision, and continuing education of different health and elder abuse professionals;

- Focus on strategies to facilitate communication and collaborations among health care professionals and other service providers that identifies ways to balance the principles of beneficence and nonmaleficence with concerns for privacy and confidentiality;

- Improvement of curricula for education at all levels of training to cover laws, ethical codes, definitions, and value conflicts in managing elder abuse;

- Improvement of continuing education curricula about practical and ethical issues in management of elder abuse; and

- Implementation of strategies across professions and institutions to continually improve the clinical and ethical management of elder abuse.

DISCUSSION QUESTIONS

1. What are the elder abuse laws in your state, and how do they compare in comprehensiveness and clarity with regard to definitions of subtypes of elder abuse, criteria for victims and perpetrators, ethics, and responses to elder abuse in other states in the United States? Choose one state in a different region.

2. What mental health and elder abuse professional networks and resources exist in your local community and your state?

3. What should be the core components of an elder abuse protocol in medical settings when mental health problems are an issue with suspected and validated elder abuse victims and/or perpetrators? Identify the relevance of the ethical issues of the rights of persons to autonomy, truthfulness, and confidentiality. How can the principles of beneficence and nonmaleficence be preserved?

4. What should be the ethical components of education and training curricula in your profession or chosen profession for detecting, evaluating, and responding to elder abuse when victims and/or perpetrators have mental health problems?

5. A major legal case that brought significant attention to FCHs in the United States was Gilbert v. State of Florida 487 So.2d 1185 (1986). Roswell Gilbert was convicted of first-degree murder for killing his wife who had Alzheimer's disease. Read the following journal article: Hanks, R. S. (1995). The limits of care: A case study of legal and ethical issues in filial responsibility. *Marriage & Family Review, 21*(3–4), 239–257. Legal perspectives on the prosecution and defense of caregivers who kill are argued within criminal laws. However, the ethical perspectives on caring in the context of family relationships, where the caring interactions show people who cherish and value each other, is complex. Central to the ethics of caregiving is a focus on family relationships and shared decision making rather than individuals and individual decision making. What are your thoughts about the morality of caregivers taking the life of dependent, vulnerable relatives?

REFERENCES

Acierno, R., Hernandez, M. A., Amstadter, A. B., Resnick, H. S., Steve, K., Muzzy, W., & Kilpatrick, D. G. (2010). Prevalence and correlates of emotional, physical, sexual, and financial abuse and neglect in the United States: The National Elder Mistreatment Study. *American Journal of Public Health, 100*(2), 292–297.

American Psychology Association. (n.d.). Elder Abuse & Neglect in Search of Solutions. Retrieved from https://www.apa.org/pi/aging/resources/guides/elder-abuse.

Anetzberger, G. (2005). The reality of elder abuse. *Clinical Gerontologist, 28*(1–2), 1–25.

Anetzberger, G. (2012). *The clinical management of elder abuse.* New York, NY: Routledge.

Beaulieu, M., & Leclerc, N. (2006). Ethical and psychosocial issues raised by the practice in cases of mistreatment of older adults. *Journal of Gerontological Social Work, 46*(3–4), 161–186.

Begle, A. M., Strachan, M., Cisler, J. M., Amstadter, A. B., Hernandez, M., & Arcierno, R. (2011). Elder mistreatment and emotional symptoms among older adults in a largely rural population: The South Carolina elder mistreatment study. *Journal of Interpersonal Violence, 26,* 2321–2332.

Chang, E., & Daly, J. (2012). Transitions in Nursing—E-Book: Preparing for Professional Practice. Elsevier Health Sciences.

Cohen, D., & Eisdorfer, C. (2011). *An integrated textbook of geriatric mental health.* Baltimore, MD: Johns Hopkins University Press.

Cohen, D., & Grabert, B. (2001). The elusive concept of mercy killing. *Journal of Mental Health and Aging, 7*(2), 203–206.

Cohen, D., Krajewski, A. T., Toyinbo, P. (2017). *A newspaper surveillance study of the estimated prevalence and characteristics of family caregiver homicides involving older victims in the United States, 1980–2015* (Final Report to the Borchard Foundation Center on Law and Aging, Burbank, CA).

Coker, A. L., Davis, K. E., Arias, I., Desai, I., Sanderson, M., Brandt, H. M., & Smith, P. H. (2002). *American Journal of Prevention Medicine, 23,* 260–268.

Comijs, H. C., Pot, A. M., Smit, J. H., Bouter, L. M., & Jonker, C. (1998). Elder abuse in the community: Prevalence and consequences. *Journal of the American Geriatrics Society, 46,* 885–888.

Cooper, C., Blanchard, M., Selwood, A., Walker, Z., & Livingston., G. (2010). Family carers' distress and abusive behavior: Longitudinal study. *British Journal of Psychiatry, 196,* 480–485.

Cooper, A., & Smith, E. L. (2011). Homicide trends in the United States, 1980–2008 (NCJ 236018). *Washington, DC: US Department of Justice. Office of Justice Programs. Bureau of Justice Statistics.*

Crepeau, E. B., Cohn, E. S., & Schell, B. A. B. (Eds.). (2003). *Willard & Spackman's occupational therapy.* Philadelphia: Lippincott.

Dong, X., Beck, T., & Simon, M. A. (2010). The association of gender, depression, and elder mistreatment in a community-dwelling Chinese population: The modifying effect of social support. *Archives of Gerontology & Geriatrics, 50,* 202–208.

Dong, X., Chen, R., Chang, E. S., & Simon, M. (2013). Elder abuse and psychological well-being: A systematic review and implications for research and policy—a mini review. *Gerontology, 59,* 132–142.

Dong, X., Simon, M. A., Beck, T. T., Farran, C., McCann, J. J., Mendez-de Leon, C. F., ... & Evans, D. A. (2011). Elder abuse and mortality: The role of psychological and social wellbeing. *Gerontology, 57,* 549–558.

Donovan, K., & Regehr, C. (2010). Elder abuse: Clinical, ethical, and legal considerations in social work practice. *Clinical Social Work Journal, 38*(2), 174–182.

Fisher, B. S. & Regan, S. L. (2006). The extent and frequency of abuse in the lives of older women and their relationship with health outcomes. *Gerontologist, 46*, 200–209.

Institute of Medicine. (2014). *Dying in America: Improving quality and honoring individual preferences near the end of life.* Washington, DC: The National Academies. Retriced from http://www.nationalacademies.org/hmd/~/media/Files/Report%20Files/2014/EOL/Report%20Brief.pdf

Jackson, S., & Hafemeister, T. L. (2013). Understanding elder abuse: New directions for developing theories of elder abuse occurring in domestic settings. *Research in Brief, National Institute of Justice.*

Jones, J. T. (2015). *Abuse of elders with mental illness: Generally an international and specifically a United States perspective* (Research Paper No. 2015–20, University of Louisville Law School, Louisville, KY).

Karch, D., & Nunn, K. C. (2010). Characteristics of elderly and other vulnerable adult victims of homicide by a caregiver: National Violent Death Reporting System—17 U.S. states, 2003–2007. *Journal of Interpersonal Violence, 26*(1), 137–157.

Labrum, T. (2017). Factors related to abuse of older persons by relatives with psychiatric disorders. *Archives of Gerontology and Geriatrics, 68*, 126–134.

Labrum, T., & Solomon, P. L. (2015). Physical elder abuse perpetrated by relatives with serious mental illness: A preliminary conceptual social-ecological model. *Aggression and Violent Behavior, 25*, 293–303.

Lachs, M. S., Williams, C., O'Brien, S., Hurst, L., & Horwitz, R. (1997). Risk factors for reported elder abuse and neglect: A nine-year observational cohort study. *Gerontologist, 37*, 469–474.

Lachs, M. S., Williams, C. S., O'Brien, S., & Pillemer, K. A. (2002). Adult protective service use and nursing home placement. *The Gerontologist, 42*(6), 734–739.

Lavi, S. J. (2009). *The modern art of dying: A history of euthanasia in the United States.* Princeton, NJ: Princeton University Press.

Ludwick, R., & Silva, M. (2003). Ethics: Errors, the Nursing Shortage and Ethics: Survey Results. *Online Journal of Issues in Nursing, 8*(2).

Luo, Y., & Waite, L. J. (2011). Mistreatment and psychological well-being among older adults: Exploring the role of psychosocial resources and deficits. *Journal of Gerontology B: Psychological Sciences and Social Sciences, 66*, 217–229.

Lysack, C., Lichtenberg, P., & Schneider, B. (2011). Effect of a DVD intervention on therapists' mental health practices with older adults. *American Journal of Occupational Therapy, 65*(3), 297–305

Mechanic, D., & Tanner, J. (2007). Vulnerable people, groups, and populations: Societal view. *Health Affairs, 26*(5), 1220–1230.

Natan, M. B., Lowenstein, A., & Eisikovits, Z. (2010). Psychosocial factors affecting elders' maltreatment in long-term care facilities. *International Nursing Review, 57*, 202–208.

Neno, R., & Neno, M. (2005). Identifying abuse in older people. *Nursing Standard, 20*(3).

Paveza, G., Cohen, D., Eisdorfer, C., Freels, S., Selmal, T, Ashford, J. W., ... & Luchins, D. (1992). Severe family violence an Alzheimer's disease: Prevalence and risk factors. *Gerontologist, 32*(4), 493–497.

Pico-Alfonso, M. A., Garcia-Linares, M. I., Celda-Navarro, N., Blasco-Ros, C., Echeburua, E., & Martinez, M. (2006). The impact of physical, psychological, and sexual intimate male partner violence on women's mental health: Depressive symptoms, posttraumatic stress disorder, state anxiety, and suicide. *Journal of Women's Health, 15,* 599–611.

Pillemer, K., Burnes, D., Riffin, C., & Lachs, M. S. (2016). Elder abuse: Global situation, risk factors, and prevention strategies. *Gerontologist, 56*(S2), S194–S205.

Qualls, S. H., Segal., D. L., Norman, S., Niederehe, G., & Gallagher-Thompson, D. (2002). Psychologists in practice with older adults: Current patterns, sources of training, and need for continuing education. *Professional Psychology: Research and Practice, 33,* 435–442.

Roberto, K. A. (2017). Perpetrators of late life polyvictimization. *Journal of Elder Abuse & Neglect, 29*(5), 313–326.

Scheider, E. M. (2012). Elder abuse: Ethical and related considerations for professionals in psychology. *Ethics and Behavior, 22*(1), 75–87.

Schofield, M. J., Powers, J. R., & Loxton, D. (2013). Mortality and disability outcomes of self-reported elder abuse: A 12-year prospective investigation. *Journal of the American Geriatrics Society, 61,* 679–683.

Teaster, P. B. (2002). *A response to the abuse of vulnerable adults: The 2000 Survey of State Adult Protective Services.* Newark, DE: National Center for Elder Abuse.

Teaster, P. B., & Hall, J. E. (Eds.). (2018). *Elder abuse and public health.* New York, NY: Springer.

Winterstein, G. M., & Eisikovits, Z. (2005). The experience of loneliness of battered old women. *Journal of Women's Aging, 17,* 3–19.

Yunis, R. M., Hairi, N. N., & Yuen, C. W. (2017). Consequences of elder abuse and neglect: A systematic review of observational studies. *Trauma, Violence, & Abuse,* 1–17.

Zeranski, L., & Halgin, R. P. (2011). Ethical issues in elder abuse reporting: A professional psychologist's guide. *Professional Psychology: Research and Practice, 42*(4), 294.

4

PHYSICAL DISABILITY

Brigid Prayson, BA
The Ohio State University College of Medicine

Elizabeth O'Toole, MD
MetroHealth Medical Center, Case Western Reserve School of Medicine

Bette Bonder, PhD, OTR, FAOTA
Cleveland State University

KEYWORDS

physical disabilities
older and vulnerable people
medical, social, and environmental

activity limitation
quality of life

Overview

This chapter discusses physical disabilities in older adults with an emphasis on ethical considerations. This chapter serves as an overview of the topic but is not intended to be all encompassing.

The Americans With Disabilities Act defines a disability as a "physical or mental impairment that substantially limits one or more major life activity" (ADA National Network, 2019). Physical disabilities present in a myriad of ways and can be variably defined depending on the context. For example, physical disability could be a label used by an individual to self-describe functional limitations, or it can be a formal medical or legal distinction based on specific evidence or criteria.

This chapter begins with brief presentations of two case reports, which will be referenced throughout the chapter to help illustrate certain concepts. They are followed by a general overview of physical disability, including commonly employed categorization and classification schemes, information on prevalence of physical disabilities and manifestations, as well as special considerations in the older (and vulnerable) population. The chapter then turns to a discussion of key ethical principles to consider when addressing physical disability in the lives of older and vulnerable people.

Common considerations and a framework for an approach to working with older adults living with physical disabilities will also be presented. It is important to remember that older adults are, by definition, survivors who have lived through adversity. The problems they face—medical, social, and environmental—are often complex. The strategies and strengths upon which these individuals have depended over time are important resources. Finally, the chapter concludes with some discussion questions to spur application of the information presented.

Case Studies

CASE STUDY 4.1

MH

MH is a 74 year old woman with a medical history of chronic obstructive pulmonary disease (COPD) and diabetes. She is fiercely independent, although she has begun to struggle in completing daily tasks like housekeeping and grocery shopping. She gets winded very easily, has poor stamina, and has pain in her feet. In addition, her vision has significantly deteriorated over the last few years.

CASE STUDY 4.2

AZ

AZ is an 83 year old man who had a stroke that has left him wheelchair dependent. He reports that he "feels bad," asking his children for help and stressing that he does not want to be a "burden." He has stopped going to the community activities he once loved to attend, as he would need assistance with transportation. AZ has recently had episodes of chest pain but does not think it is an emergency and does not want to bother anyone with having to take time off from work to take him to see a doctor or go for testing.

Background Information

Definitions of Terms in Disability

The dialogue and vocabulary surrounding disabilities has changed in the last few decades. Perhaps most notably, the newer classification schemes for disability take into account the context or environment in which the disability manifests. The World Health Organization (WHO) released a new classification system called the International Classification of Functioning, Disability and Health (ICF) in 2001. This approach to conceptualizing and categorizing disability proposes that disability is a universal experience; that is, every person will experience some degree of disability at some point. The term that applies to a range of presentations and encompasses a spectrum of severities. Indeed, disabilities may variably affect different abilities to perform or participate in certain activities such as mobility (e.g. ambulation, altering or holding body posture, or manipulating objects); self-care; forming and maintaining relationships; engaging in major life domains such as school, work, and finances; and participating in social settings and community (CDC, 2017).

A document outlining terminology was published by the WHO in 2002 in order to have more informative and comprehensive labels for an individual's circumstances. It was recognized that medical diagnosis provides little detail on the humanistic aspects of an illness, including severity or impact on ability to perform tasks. The WHO stratification of disability combines aspects of the medical model of disability, as an attribute of the person stemming from a disease, injury, or health condition requiring medical treatment to "correct," with the social model of disability, in which disability is understood to be endogenous to society rather than the individual and is therefore deserving of a societal or political treatment since the problem is related to the environment rather than of the individual (ICF, 2002).

Dimensions to Disability

The WHO describes three dimensions of disability: body function and structure impairments, activity limitation, and participation restriction. The major elements classifying disability facilitate the identification of potential interventions and prevention strategies where applicable. *Impairment* refers to the actual anatomical and physiological function at a structural level, for example, the nerve damage MH (in the first case study) has sustained secondary to her diabetes, or in the second case study, the decreased motor function and depression resulting from the lack of blood flow to portions of AZ's brain following his stroke. Importantly, impairment is not synonymous with disability. *Impairment* refers to the medical impairment, while *disability* is the inability to perform a given activity as a result of the interface or combination of the medical impairment and the context or environment (Cocchiarella, 2018).

Activity limitation refers to the limitations an impairment places on one's ability to perform certain actions. For example, MH's COPD makes it hard for her to breathe and thus hard for her to exercise, and AZ's stroke has limited activities like walking.

Participation restrictions refer to limitations in one's ability to engage in social or functional activities such as obtaining health care, pursuing recreational activities, working, etc. Participation restrictions for MH might include difficulty going on hikes with her friends while AZ's participation restrictions might include the inability to go golfing or fishing (CDC, 2017). Environmental factors are also important in classifying disability, as these affect the way impairment, activity limitation, and participation restrictions occur or are experienced (ICF, 2002).

Disability Categories

The American Community Survey (ACS), a national survey performed by the U.S. Census Bureau, outlined six major disability categories (ACS, 2008). These include difficulties due to physical, mental, or emotional problems that result in impairments in (a) hearing, (b) vision, (c) cognition, (d) ambulation (e.g., walking, ascending/descending stairs), (e) self-care (e.g. bathing, dressing), and (f) independent living (e.g., difficulty doing errands). In reality, many people present with disabilities that cross multiple domains. For example, someone with severe arthritis might have trouble walking, going up stairs, dressing, and consequently doing errands (Erickson, Lee, & von Schrader, 2017).

As an example of the frequency of disability in the older population, according to Cornell University's DisabilityStatistics.org report based on data from the American Community Survey, the prevalence of ambulatory disability among Americans over the age of 65 was approximately 22.5% (90% MOE of ± 0.16, n = 574,734) in 2016 (Erickson et al., 2017). Ambulatory disabilities can inhibit the ability of an otherwise functional individual to partake in many aspects of life.

In addition to coping with a physical disability, many older adults face the added effects of also having a cognitive or psychological disability. Other chapters in this book discuss other forms of disability, but it is important to recognize that physical, cognitive, and psychological disabilities may coexist. Indeed, diseases such as Alzheimer's disease are quite common and occur in older people both with and without physical disabilities. While the Alzheimer's Association (2018) reports that 1 in 10 persons over the age of 65 has Alzheimer's dementia, the percentage of those with Alzheimer's disease increases with age and is reportedly 38% in those 85 years and older. Problem solving, adapting to challenging situations, and navigating daily life activities may be complicated for those with a physical disability who are also contending with a psychological or cognitive disability. Having a combination of disabilities makes it more likely that an individual will require assistance and support with activities of daily living. It also might mean the individual requires additional help or support with decision making or may be unable to make decisions regarding personal health and care. For example, in the second case study, AZ has had a stroke, lives relatively independently, and has avoided seeking medical attention for chest pain. If he also had a diagnosis of depression or dementia, define the nature of his situation and about appropriate response by caregivers might well need to change. There would be concern about whether his decision-making capacity has been affected by his psychological or mental decline and if such developments play a role in his decision not to seek help in the face of a potentially life-threatening health situation. It might also raise questions about his ability to continue living independently.

Individual's Experience of Disability

An individual's experience with disability may vary based on the course of the condition causing it. Physical disabilities can be progressive, as in the case of osteoarthritis and multiple sclerosis, or they can be stable as is true of a traumatic brain injury or spinal cord injury. Disabilities may also be transient and remitting or permanent and chronic. The needs of and supports required by individuals with stable disabilities and those with progressive disabilities may differ. The perception of well-being and adaptation may also differ based on the individual and context. Disabilities may be present at birth or develop at any age over the course of one's life. Thus, elderly patients may have lived with long-term chronic physical disabilities, such as cerebral palsy or congenital blindness, or they may be continuously adapting to later age onset conditions such as progressive neuromuscular decline or heart disease.

A broad range of diseases contributes to the development of physical disability in older people. Among the most common medical conditions leading to physical disability are hypertension, osteoarthritis, cancer, lung dysfunction, diabetes, and stroke. These pathologies are strikingly common, with hypertension affecting over half of those over 65 years of age and osteoarthritis afflicting nearly 50% (Manini, 2011). Additionally, physical disability may result from general muscle weakness or the burden of being tethered to medical equipment as in the case of oxygen dependence.

Older adults with physical disability may find themselves in a vulnerable position due to the limitations of the disability itself, dependence on those providing care or services, and the interaction between the disability and the environment. The fatigue and breathlessness that MH experiences may present particular problems when she has to walk a distance from the bus stop to get to the grocery store, but not be limiting if she wants to see a movie. AZ is likely to have difficulty using public transportation even if his community has a service for people with physical limitations, while MH may find this kind of service a great help.

When working with people experiencing physical disability, it is important to remember that the disability represents only one aspect of the person. Other facets of capacity and personhood remain essential considerations. The complexity of interaction between individuals, physical disabilities, and the environment may raise ethical issues.

Applicable Ethical Principles and Approaches

Ethical dilemmas arise for people with disabilities and their caregivers for many reasons, including when accessing needed services. For example, AZ is no longer able to independently get to the doctor's office and has to call on a family member for help. He may feel he must sacrifice some autonomy when involving others in arranging health care encounters and may believe that he must balance his needs for frequent appointments with the family's needs to carry on with their own lives. These activity limitations and potential participation restrictions implicate ethical principles of autonomy and justice.

Autonomy

Autonomy is a major ethical principle to be considered and explicitly addressed in the context of an older adult who has a physical disability. The physical disability may itself limit independence and increase reliance on others for assistance with daily tasks, resulting in loss of autonomous decision making and conflicts in implementation of decisions. Recalling MH, the woman with COPD and diabetes, her loss of stamina and foot pain may mean she can no longer walk to the nearby grocery or bank as she once did. She now must rely on others, including community social services, to get her where she needs to go or to do the errands for her. She can no longer take care of these tasks when she chooses but must now fit her needs into the schedule of others and the contours of program requirements.

Physical limitations associated with a physical disability can affect decision making ability or opportunities. Those with sensory limitations, such as vision or hearing loss, may require large-text written instructions, sound amplification, or similar modifications to be able to fully participate in decision making and to obtain necessary information or resources for making informed decisions. While these seem like straightforward accommodations, they are not always available and the need for them is not always recognized. Even when such accommodations are recognized, there may be associated costs that make them difficult to implement, putting the individual in the situation of having to rely on other people. Family members, such as adult children, are often involved in the older person's major life decisions, including significant medical decisions. Having a parent with a sensory disability, like deafness or vision problems, might result in adult children taking a more dominant role in decision making for ease of pragmatic progress and discourse. For example, it is conceivable that MH could be seen in the emergency department for a serious medical issue and decisions might be made between her son and providers; in the hectic and time-pressured setting of an emergency department, it may be easier to get information from her son, have a discussion with him, and have him sign necessary documents.

When interacting with an older adult who has a physical disability, it is important to actively support independence and preserve the individual's opportunity to participate in activities and decision making. As with all individuals, it is essential to assess the individual's decision-making capacity if it is in question. Direct communication with the individual is critical, but efforts to assure this are not always made. Sometimes care providers presume that a family member or an aide accompanying someone with a physical disability serves as that person's voice. They may assume that a person with a physical disability also has cognitive limitations or impaired functional status for decision making. Such assumptions and associated behaviors by others involved with an older individual with disability may severely undermine the autonomy of the individual and violate principles of autonomy, social justice, and beneficence. They negatively impact opportunities for the individual to exercise self-determination and can lead to unjust decisions and potential harm. Ethical decision making requires adherence to these principles, even when less convenient or requiring extra effort to engage with the older adult. For example, although it may take extra time to listen to someone with Parkinson's disease formulate his or her thoughts, that person is likely to be mentally capable of making choices and may be very frustrated, insulted, or offended if others deny autonomy to him or her by seeking a more expeditious decision from someone else. Further, such practices could actually decrease the effectiveness of medical and rehabilitation strategies and even contribute to the person developing depression (Miller, Noble, Jones, & Burn, 2006).

Though limitations on autonomy can be imposed by others, some older people may subscribe to the so-called "elderly mystique," which contends that the potential for growth, development, and continuing engagement in old age virtually disappear when a person has a disability. Older adults espousing this belief may self-limit their autonomy and independence (Cohen, 1988). Further, pervasive ageism and gerophobia (a relative fear of older adults), combined with a notion of biological inferiority and dependence can result in negative effects from well-intentioned but paternalistic practices by care providers, both formal and informal. If older people are regarded as inferior to younger, more able counterparts, they are considered to be unable to attain their own goals and fulfill their own needs; so they, as well as those around them, recalibrate their expectations and goals to lower standards (Cohen, 1988).

Autonomy is an important factor in successful aging with disability. Molton and Yorkston (2017) conducted a study using nine focus groups comprised of adult individuals who were 45 years or older and diagnosed with one of the following: spinal cord injury, multiple sclerosis, muscular dystrophy, or post-polio syndrome, to explore successful aging among the increasing aging population of individuals with disabilities. Autonomy and choice in decision making, psychological resilience, psychological adaptability, social participation and engagement, accessible and adequate medical care, and accessible supports and aids to meet needs were identified as important for successful aging for those with a long-standing disability. Study findings also indicate that those aging with a long-term, early-onset disability may have had a different life course as compared to those who have aged into a disability. Further, autonomy can extend beyond decision-making ability to include such activities as instructing and guiding caregivers and being engaged in interests and pursuits. In short, the study showed that for an older person with a physical disability, choosing what one wants to do is more important than doing what one has to do.

Context or setting may also foster loss of autonomy. This can be a particular issue in long-term care facilities or hospitals, which are frequently a part of the life experience of an older individual with a disability. In these kinds of settings, the older person with a disability is vulnerable. Dependence on others, including paid caregivers, creates a power dynamic that may result in feelings of loss of independence and actual loss of control and autonomy. The surveillance characteristic of such controlled environments may have a similar effect. Responses by staff (nurses, physical therapists, occupational therapists, etc.), especially those that allow the older person choice (e.g., where to sit at meals, whether to go to the craft room or to an exercise class, when to be bathed or dressed), have been seen to improve a resident's short- and long-term perception of autonomy. Indeed, the mere action of intentionally focusing on the wishes of the older person with disabilities for activities may improve the person's sense of autonomy (Anderson, Runge, Hoff, & Puggard, 2009).

Balancing Beneficence and Nonmaleficence

The balance between beneficence and nonmaleficence is a common ethical issue that arises when working with an older person with physical disability. Care providers, while intending to help a person and avoid harming him or her, may force a decision, intervention, treatment, or lifestyle change on a person who does not actually want it. Thus, despite being well-intentioned, their efforts to help the person—their beneficence—may not be consistent with nonmaleficence if the individual is stripped of the right to make personal choices. Making explicit efforts to ensure decisions and actions are made to meet the desire, priorities, and choices of the individual rather than those of the family or a medical professional is important. What might seem like the appropriate choice from the perspective of a physician, a social worker, or a family member may be quite different from that of the individual.

One example of this is the common scenario of differing perceptions of the relative priorities of safety versus freedom or independence. Supporting safety can be harmful when it conflicts with the individual's priority of independence, regardless of risk. The individual may not want to take what others see as the safe approach or, alternately, may decline a recommended medical procedure because there is a relatively greater risk to his or her mental, social, or psychological well-being. Balancing the patient's autonomy with the provider's responsibility to act with beneficence and nonmaleficence can lead to challenging situations when making treatment decisions. In this situation, it might be useful to consider whether the decision would be pressed upon a younger adult or an older adult who does not have a disability to clarify the basis for the decision.

Of course, cultural considerations must be taken into account when assessing ethics and weighing social values and personal preferences. As mentioned in Chapter 6, individual autonomy may be more or less valued and defined in different ways by different cultural groups (c.f. Fung, 2013). Dynamics and perceptions of older adults may vary across cultures. In some societies, older people are venerated and their decisions are innately respected; while in other cultures, it is expected that adult children will look after their aged parents and be the decision makers for them. Still other cultures may have collectivist decision making with the whole family weighing in on decisions. The concept of cultural competence is not new and has long been considered a standard of quality health care. It has been explored in many contexts, including in the context of end-of-life decision making (Koenig, 1997) as well as in providing culturally appropriate geriatric health care. The individual's interpretation of a disability may be related to elements of her culture. For example, how family members interact or feel obligations to one another, or the meaning of suffering and the individual's response may be culturally based. Because there are cultural differences even in the overarching ethical principles viewed as crucial in differing cultures, it can be helpful to gather information about the client's and family's beliefs, perhaps using narrative ethics (Lo, 2010). The narrative ethics approach may allow exploration and better understanding of the individual's beliefs and life experience, the impact of disability on the person, and expectations for care and outcomes.

Social Justice

Another ethical principle to consider when dealing with older people with disabilities is justice and perhaps more specifically social justice. Equity in care can be challenging to attain for elderly people with physical disabilities. Parameters on options are set by outside parties, such as insurance companies, nursing homes, or hospital administrators, as well as the government, which are involved in allocating funding and directing resources. Older people and those with physical disabilities often require a disproportionate amount of resources to aid with special needs and additional supports they require to perform the same activities as their younger or more able-bodied counterparts. The needs or desires of older people with disabilities may not always be deemed worthy of receiving resources. Decisions are made about such issues as how many resources should be spent on rehabilitation for a patient like AZ if he sustains another stroke, given competing demands for social funding and when there are limited resources for people across the age spectrum. Additionally, decisions about health care costs, who will pay for them, and what resources are available are often left to third parties and society at large. What then, is the societal responsibility to ensure that the older person with a physical disability is offered and able to attain equal quality service? How are the needs of such individuals weighed in the context of limited resources? And how can the temptation to use resources because they are available be balanced against the wishes of an older person who may not want aggressive intervention?

Fair and equitable relations between an individual and society are required for social justice. This encompasses addressing barriers to optimal health care and health maintenance practices, including preventive medicine and environmental modifications to facilitate function as well as assuring that there are educational materials, access to transportation, and appropriate medical equipment that can be used with those who have physical disabilities. Such actions achieve social justice while making it more likely that health screenings and other services routinely available to the general population are equally available to those with physical disabilities. Of course, decisions about receiving services remain the choice of the individual recalling that some older adults may not want services, even when care providers insist on them because Medicare or some other funder covers them.

Occupation has been highlighted as a critical component of quality of life and meaning in life among those with advanced age. Occupation, in this context, is more than one's vocation. Occupation refers to meaningful function in life. As one ages and develops a disability or one's functional ability declines with a progressive disability, an individual may be forced to alter or even relinquish one's occupation. It is natural with aging to have changes in occupations. For example, one's role as a parent shifts and morphs as children mature and function independently, one may retire after working, or one might have to give up certain hobbies due to physical changes. Recalling the case study of AZ, prior to his stroke he was an avid golfer who organized and led the men's group golf outings at his club. Since his stroke, he has been unable to get out onto the golf course and has given up his role organizing the outings.

Continuing to have meaningful activities and function in life are important to the health and wellness of people, regardless of medical condition. It is important for older adults with disabilities to remain engaged in activities and roles that are self-affirming and confirm self-efficacy and significance. Occupational justice ensures that those with disabilities have equal opportunity for participation in meaningful occupation (Wilcock & Townsend, 2000). Consequently, it is important that those providing care for older adults with physical disabilities consider the meaningful roles and activities of the individual and help facilitate and support their engagement in such activities (Bonder, 2018).

Technology can be a powerful tool to support justice for those with physical disabilities. This may take many forms, such as hearing aids and glasses for those with sensory disabilities; motorized or manual wheelchairs and canes for those with mobility issues; lightweight oxygen tanks and distribution devices for those with respiratory or circulatory issues; electronic communication devices, including telehealth options that decrease the need for travel; and personal automated medication distribution systems to support ability to reliably take medications; and so on. In addition to appliances and mechanical instruments to aid those with physical disabilities, Internet technology provides access to websites with educational materials, blogs facilitating advice and sharing of collective knowledge, and applications for mobile devices such as those offering lists of local restaurants that are accessible to persons using wheelchairs, walkers, or canes. Modern technology will continue to play a pivotal role in the quality of life of those with physical disabilities, regardless of age, providing opportunities for connectedness to those who might be vulnerable to physical isolation. At the same time, the many benefits of technology for those with physical disabilities must be balanced with risks such as misinformation, vulnerability to scams or being taken advantage of, and access to personal data that can be misused for criminal purposes such as identity theft, financial abuse, fraud, or theft.

Application to the Older Vulnerable Adult With Physical Disability

Unfortunately, older adults with physical disabilities are frequently victims of all forms of elder abuse. Those working with older adults living with physical disabilities must remain aware of the potential for abuse. Estimates for prevalence of elder abuse based on self-report indicate that approximately 10% of elders have experienced some form of reported elder abuse (Lachs & Pillemer, 2015). This reported figure is undoubtedly an underestimate of the true prevalence, as some affected individuals may have been unwilling to report and survey methods excluded data from those not capable of giving informed consent to participating, such as those with cognitive impairments or dementia. According to the WHO, 1 in 6 people aged 60 years and older has been subjected to elder abuse in the past year. This problem is likely to get worse with the growing aging population. Indeed, physical health issues and functional impairment were found to be reliable risk factors for elder mistreatment (Lachs & Pillemer, 2015). Those with a physical disability who are dependent on others for critical support, such as food preparation or assistance with activities of daily living, may be unable to fully exercise their autonomy because of caregiver influence or fear of negative responses from care providers. The opinion of an individual with a disability may not be solicited or welcomed by the caregiver, and the individual's thoughts or requests may be frustrating to the caregiver, thus limiting the individual's opportunity for self-determination. Caregivers may find their role inconvenient, unpleasant, or burdensome. Older adults who are dependent may be vulnerable to mistreatment from others who may not be fully respectful of them or aware of their own ethical obligations to adhere to principles of autonomy, beneficence, and justice (among others). Some caregivers may neglect those they are supposed to be helping, or become hostile, violent, or abusive while delivering care. Caregivers may face pressures when trying to balance maintaining their own lives with caring for an older person in need of support. Caregiving may be further complicated when a *care recipient* becomes abusive toward the caregiver as may happen when the care recipient is affected by dementia.

Ethical delivery of care can be affected by the power dynamic in the relationship between a caregiver and an older adult. Balancing care provision and needed support to avoid stifling the recipient's autonomy can be difficult. Conflicts of interest may occur between the needs of the dependent adult and those of the caregiver. There may be an increased risk for mistreatment when individuals are isolated in their own homes and unable to direct and supervise a caregiver or are receiving care in a nursing home. An elderly individual with physical disabilities may not be able to summon help or function independently enough to risk addressing mistreatment or be able to access or follow through with outside support.

Verbal abuse of older people is particularly prevalent and is associated with poorer quality of life. One study attempted to further elucidate the relationship between verbal mistreatment and quality of life and found that verbal abuse was related to social functioning, role limitation, and declining mental health (Fulmer, Rodgers, & Pelger, 2014). Based on analysis of nine studies evaluating data from six countries, rates of elder abuse are even higher in institutional settings, such as nursing homes, with a disturbing 2 out of 3 staff members (64.2% of those surveyed) admitting having committed abuse in the last year (WHO, 2018).

Caring for an Older Adult With a Physical Disability

Based on the information discussed above about older persons with disabilities, the challenges of adhering to ethical principles in care contexts, and the risks for abuse and exploitation, we propose a set of guidelines to frame an approach to care and decision making with older adults experiencing physical disability:

1. Respect the individual's autonomy and right to self-determination by specifically identifying the individual's relevant values and health care goals. Avoid assumptions or presumptions about what the individual's preferences, goals, or values may be or if the person's preferences and values may conflict with the values or goals of others involved with the individual.

2. Identify the individual's strengths and explore what the barriers to achieving these preferences, values, and goals could be.

3. Determine who and what resources are available to support the individual's values, achieve the desired goals, and address barriers.

4. Consider what ethical principles are involved to guide decision making.

CASE STUDY 4.3

Applying the Guidelines

Let's see how this framework might be used in the case of MH. MH is a 74-year-old woman with a medical history of chronic and progressive COPD and diabetes. Although she puts a very high value on her independence, she is now having difficulty with tasks like housekeeping and grocery shopping because of her shortness of breath and poor stamina. Walking and other activities are limited by worsening pain in her feet.

Applying Guideline Point 1

1. An approach to MH should include meeting with her to discuss her goals and priorities for her care.

2. She states that her goals are to remain living in her home, to be as comfortable as possible, and to have the best quality of life she can for the rest of her life.

3. What are her perceptions of her physiologic condition/impairments, her related activity limitations, and resultant participation restrictions? We need to understand her perceptions of the impact of health conditions on her life experience. Are there discrepancies between her assessments and those of others? Are these discrepancies factual or do they represent a difference of opinion or difference of priorities?

4 She may recognize the decline in her functioning and value her independence so highly that she is willing to tolerate some safety risk rather than move into a more supportive environment. However, her family may feel she is unsafe and want her to move to a nursing facility where her physical needs could be met.

5 After further exploration with MH, we find that she has always enjoyed being with others and is lonely living alone. She cannot be as active outside the home because of her limited tolerance for movement (requiring a wheelchair and oxygen) and difficulty getting out of the house. She no longer participates in lunches, playing cards, or seeing movies with her friends. Previously, opportunities to participate have been important factors in optimizing her quality of life. Applying the WHO dimensions to disability, MH has significant body function impairments, activity limitations, and participation restrictions.

Applying Guideline Point 2

1. MH may have several barriers to overcome in attempting to achieve her goals.

2. MH has identified goals that reflect her values. Unfortunately, her goal of living at home (maximizing autonomy) conflicts with her goal to optimize her quality of life (addressing her participation restrictions). In addition, while MH's preferences should be the paramount concern, the worries of her family who support her also have to be addressed in some way. If MH perceives a proposed accommodation as a diminishment of her autonomy or sense of self, this would create another barrier.

3. Cost, ability to pay, and availability could be barriers to providing a variety of potential supports, including home assistance (adequate assistance with meals, house cleaning, personal care and companionship), facilitated social opportunities such as appropriate transportation to community activities (senior centers or adult day care, for example), or moving to a more supportive environment. How acceptable would these arrangements be to her?

Applying Guideline Point 3

Identify resources that might be available (personal, interpersonal, financial, technological, community, societal) to overcome barriers. Are resources accessible to her and is she willing to use them?

Applying Guideline Point 4

Supporting the individual's autonomy/self-determination requires ongoing assessment of the individual's capacity for health care decision making. It also requires facilitation of the individual's role as primary decision maker whenever possible. As MH has a progressive, serious condition, she should be given the opportunity to express her wishes for current and future care. Care providers should be mindful of and take opportunities when patients are able to obtain the best available evidence of patient values and perspectives. After a determination of her capacity to make health care decisions, a discussion with MH about her goals for future medical care, the likely course of her lung disease and diabetes, and her wishes for future health care including possible resuscitation in the event of a cardiopulmonary arrest would be prudent. Determining whom she would trust to make her health care decisions if she became unable would also be very important. The results of these discussions should be documented and advance directives utilized appropriately. These discussions and decisions should be revisited regularly, especially if there is a change in condition or support.

In assessing the viability of options and resources, care must be taken to balance the rights of others in the situation, so that the principles of autonomy, beneficence, nonmaleficence, and justice are considered from the perspectives of family members and others as well. For example, if MH insisted on smoking in bed with her oxygen on respecting her autonomy would not justify putting others at risk.

CONCLUDING OBSERVATIONS

Opportunities for optimal quality of life for older adults with physical disability are improved if those working with them (a) recognize the dimensions of the disability (body function and structure impairments, activity limitation, and participation restriction) and the impact these have on the individual; (b) determine and address the individual's goals, strengths and need for support; (c) avoid assumptions; and (d) attend to and facilitate adherence to ethical principles, including autonomy, beneficence, nonmaleficence, and justice.

Effective strategies for best preserving the rights of older people with physical disabilities, implementing protections to prevent mistreatment, and utilizing appropriate mechanisms to help enhance quality of life require a thoughtful and individualized approach.

DISCUSSION QUESTIONS

Consider MH. Her family is concerned that she is no longer safe living by herself because of her limited ability to respond to an emergency and her risk for falls.

1. How would you think about a recommendation of a move from living independently to an assisted living facility and who should be involved in making a plan for MH?

2. Would your recommendation change if she were 90 years old? Why or why not?

3. What role does the family play in making decisions for her care? Does your response change if demands would be placed on the family to implement the intervention decisions?

Consider AZ. He has discontinued his community activities and avoids medical care. He says this is because he does not want to burden others and would need help to maintain his activities.

1. Why might he make that decision?

2. What other concerns would you have about the impact of his decreased activity and participation on his health and quality of life?

VG is a 70-year-old woman with a history of cerebral palsy. She uses a walker for short distances around her apartment and a motorized wheelchair outside her apartment. She has weakness of her left hand but has use of her right. Her cognition is intact, but she has a hearing deficit. She very much wants to attend her granddaughter's wedding 200 miles away. Her children think the trip will be too much for her.

1. What specific barriers would she face and what would be necessary for her to achieve her goal?

2. How can health care professionals weigh VG's wishes against those of the family? Are there strategies that might help them reach a workable compromise?

REFERENCES

American Community Survey. (2008). Disability Statistics. Retrieved from http://www.disabilitystatistics.org/sources-DS.cfm

ADA National Network. (2019). What is the definition of disability under the ADA? Retrieved from https://adata.org/faq/what-definition-disability-under-ada

Anderson, M., Runge, U., Hoff, M., & Puggard, L. (2009). Perceived autonomy and activity choices among physically disabled older people in nursing home settings: A randomized trial. *Journal of Aging and Health, 21*(8), 1133–1158. doi:10.1177/0898264309348197

Alzheimer's Association. (2018). Facts and figures. Retrieved from https://www.alz.org/alzheimers-dementia/facts-figures

Bonder, B. (2018). Meaningful occupation in later life. In B. R. Bonder & V. D. Bello-Haas (Eds.), *Functional performance in older adults* (4th ed., pp. 61–73). Philadelphia, PA: Davis.

Centers for Disease Control and Prevention. (2017). Disability and health. Retrieved from https://www.cdc.gov/ncbddd/disabilityandhealth/disability.html

Cocchiarella, L. (2018). Disability assessment and determination in the United States. UptoDate. Retrieved from https://www.uptodate.com/contents/disability-assessment-and-determination-in-the-united-states

Cohen, E. S. (1988). The elderly mystique: Constraints on the autonomy of the elderly with disabilities. *Gerontologist, 28*(1), 24–31.

Erickson, W., Lee, C., & von Schrader, S. (2017). *Disability statistics from the American Community Survey (ACS)*. Ithaca, NY: Cornell University Yang-Tan Institute.

Fulmer, T., Rodgers, R. F., & Pelger, A. (2014). Verbal mistreatment in the elderly. *Journal of Elder Abuse & Neglect, 26*(4), 351–364. doi:10.1080/08946566.2013.801817

Fung, H. H. (2013). Aging in culture. *Gerontologist, 53*, 369–377. doi:10.1093/geront/gnfo24

ICF. (2002). *Towards a common language for functioning, disability and health*. Geneva: World Health Organization. Retrieved from http://www.who.int/classifications/icf/icfbeginnersguide.pdf

Koenig, B. A. (1997). Cultural diversity in decisionmaking about care at the end of life. In M. J. Field & C. K. Cassel (Eds.), *Approaching death: Improving care at the end of life*. Retrieved from https://www.ncbi.nlm.nih.gov/books/NBK233599

Lachs, M., & Pillemer, K. (2015). Elder abuse. *New England Journal of Medicine, 373*, 1947–1956. doi:10.1056/NEJMra1404688

Lo, M. M. (2010). Cultural brokerage: Creating linkages between voices of lifeworld and medicine in cross-cultural clinical settings. *Health, 14*, 484–504.

Manini, T. (2011). Development of physical disability in older adults. *Current Aging Science, 4*(3), 184–191.

Miller, N., Noble, E., Jones, D., & Burn, D. (2006). Life with communication changes in Parkinson's disease, *Age and Ageing, 5*(3), 235–239. Retrieved from https://doi.org/10.1093/ageing/afj053

Molton, I. R., & Yorkston, K. M. (2017). Growing older with a physical disability: A special application of the successful aging paradigm. *Journals of Gerontology: Series B, 72*(2), 290–299. Retrieved from https://doi.org/10.1093/geronb/gbw122

Wilcock, A. A., & Townsend, E. (2000). Occupational terminology interactive dialogue. *Journal of Occupational Science, 7*, 84–86.

World Health Organization. (2018, June 8). Elder abuse. Retrieved from http://www.who.int/news-room/fact-sheets/detail/elder-abuse

VULNERABILITY: EFFECTIVE STATUS

I n Section II, the effects of status, including gender, race and ethnicity, sexual orientation, religion, and immigrant status on an older person's vulnerability are examined. These aspects often overlap and intersect with one another, and so must be considered through the multifaceted prism of compromised health; care arrangement; and abuse, neglect, and exploitation.

This section will demonstrate that older adults of color; immigrants; and gay, lesbian, bisexual, and transgender older persons may be hesitant or unwilling to accept treatment, pursue legal remedies, and/or accept governmental services. Often, their choices are derived from personal or historical experiences of oppression, discrimination, marginalization, and invisibility. The chapter on race and ethnicity, shows readers how cultural values guide the making of important decisions, often in ways that seem contrary to Western principles of autonomy. Understanding these perspectives will assist professionals in working with clients and patients from diverse backgrounds while avoiding causing distress, offense, or harm.

As pointed out in several chapters, status can be an obstacle to effective care or other intervention, or a powerful and beneficial aspect of effective victim- or patient-centered care. For example, the authors of the chapter on religion describe how proselytizing or projecting personal religious views on patients can undermine a physician's ability to maintain a patient-focused perspective. Alternatively, when the physician provides the patient with an opportunity to freely discuss his or her spiritual history, the doctor encourages personal and informed decisionmaking.

As you explore this section, think about how professionals ethically can best serve clients and patients from unfamiliar ethnic, racial, and religious traditions in ways that protect an older adult's autonomy. Consider how a nursing facility can assure that gay and lesbian residents are treated fairly in admission and visitation policies (justice). Consider further how a social worker in a hospital can obtain information about a patient's religious beliefs in a way that assists the patient in making informed medical decisions (nonmaleficence) and allows the hospital to deliver patient-centered care (beneficence).

These chapters provide powerful examples to challenge thinking about diverse older adults whose long lives often have been filled with injustice and discrimination because of their gender, sexual orientation, race, ethnicity, religion, and/or immigrant status.

5

CONSIDERING GENDER AND ETHICS: A CONTEXTUAL APPROACH TO WORKING WITH OLDER PERSONS

Sharon Bowland, PhD
University of North Texas

Beth Halaas, EdD, MSW
Eastern Washington University

KEYWORDS

gender	older persons
life course	practice
framework	ethics
social work	

Overview

There is ample documentation about how gender role stereotypes, social norms, and social policies privilege men over women and negatively influence health and well-being for marginalized groups such as transgender persons and women of color. These inequalities are embedded in the fabric of our society and are often unquestioned and hidden until we dig deeper into our assumptions and biases. Practitioners frequently use an ethical lens that does not consider the influence of gender on life course decision making; nevertheless, research has documented the association of gender with certain vulnerabilities in older women such as financial difficulties, chronic health conditions, and violence and abuse (Crimmins, Kim & Hagedorn, 2008; Murtagh & Hubert, 2004; Shumaker & Hill, 1991; Wilke & Vinton, 2005). Men also experience gender-related vulnerabilities based on life course experiences such as serving in combat. However, given space limitations, we will confine our exploration of gender and ethical decision making to the experiences of women, including women of color, with some consideration of the experience of transgender persons.

This chapter will analyze the gender context of ethical decision making and practice. We recognize that older women are influenced by intersectionality (the conjunction of their multiple identities including gender, gender identity, age, race/ethnicity, religion, socioeconomic status, and sexual orientation), which can amplify experiences of oppression and vulnerability. We will challenge practitioners to become more effective by expanding their ethical decision making frameworks to include gender-related considerations.

Definitions of Gender

We do not make essentialist claims (that men and women are fundamentally different from one another); nevertheless, we think it is important to consider the lived experience of gender in a society where binary definitions (male or female) largely define the experience of older women and transgender adults. Thus, we take a social constructionist view of gender development; namely, that the meaning of gender has been fashioned collectively, and that as gendered persons we are given messages about what capacities to develop and what capacities to ignore. We recognize the powerful influence of gender messages and expectations on development over the life course. We also tend to accept gender role expectations without thinking critically about whether these promote an unjust society (Sherwin, 2007). This injustice begins with personal pressure to fill stereotypical roles. There are many implicit expectations to enact gender roles that in later life may translate into inequality and vulnerability.

Life Course Perspective

Historical and Economic Factors

Messages about who we are as gendered persons are grounded in history. When we are born matters. Thus, we recommend viewing the experiences of older women and transgender persons through the lens of a life course perspective. To do this we must probe social, historical, and economic forces that shape individual lives (Elder, Johnson, & Crosnoe, 2003) and cultural identities (race, ethnicity, sexual orientation, and/or gender identity) (Walker, 2004). Before World War II, women's work occurred primarily in the household. During the war, however, more women worked outside the home. At the end of the war women returned to working in the home, and the ideal of the suburban housewife was celebrated (National Organization for Women, n.d.). In the 1960s, the number of women in the workforce increased due to the availability of birth control and pressure from the growing feminist movement (Toossi & Morisi, 2017). The percentage of women in the workforce steadily increased from the 1960s to 1999, when it reached a high of 60%. In 2015, it was at 56.7% (Toossi & Morisi, 2017). The U.S. Census found that in 2015, women made 80% of what males did (Proctor, Semega, & Kollar, 2016). This pay gap persists even though more women than men attend college and are joining professions that were previously dominated by men (Lopez & Gonzalez-Barrera,

2014). These statistics point to ongoing economic inequality for women, both nation-ally and internationally, that accumulates over the life course. The cumulative results are lower amounts of personal savings, pensions, social security benefits, and health insurance coverage. Additionally, women have higher vulnerability due to race/ethnicity and poverty after divorce or widowhood. Decisions such as becoming a caregiver for a sick parent rather than continuing one's career until retirement age likely have strong implications for economic resources in older adulthood.

Cohort

The date of our birth has an important influence on gender messages that women and transgender persons receive about gender roles and norms. Examples include Baby Boomers (those born after World War II) and the Silent Generation (those born during the Great Depression). Transgender older persons who are Baby Boomers have faced major discrimination based on their gender identity, while our current cohort of young adults are growing up at a time more accepting of variability in gender identity and expression. Millennials, those born around the turn of the 21st century, often discard binary understandings of gender (male and female) and advocate for increased recog-nition and rights for transgender persons. While our notions of gender are changing dramatically, older persons frequently experience a great deal of discrimination over the life course as they challenge gender roles and identities. These effects are compounded when persons had multiple experiences of oppression and discrimination.

Women's Development

Historically, our understanding of human development has largely been focused on what is normative for male development (Surrey, 1985). Dr. Jean Baker Miller and her colleagues (JBMTI, n.d.) reexamined women's development in light of gender socialization that favors autonomy over a self that is developed through relationships (Miller, 1986a; Miller & Stiver, 1986). Relational-Cultural Theory (RCT) began as a response to psychoanalytic theories that held separation/autonomy as a goal for both men and women's psychological and social development (Jordan, Kaplan, Miller, Stiver, & Surrey, 1991). The relational/cultural model also drew on the work of moral development theorist Carol Gilligan (1982), who in her observations of girls and boys suggested that girls appeared to be more greatly influ-enced in their decision making by an ethic of care rather than an ethic of justice. Women have frequently operated in relationships of mutual dependency. In contrast to previous theories, the above scholars held that the goal of psychological development is actually learning how to connect with others rather than learning how to make autonomous decisions. The RCT suggests that holding onto oneself in the midst of one's relationships and embracing positive messages from one's own culture is what furthers development.

Trauma and Vulnerability

Calasanti (2010) asserted the importance of examining the intersection between gender and age to assess the impact of social inequality. Older women experience elevated levels of vulnerability as they age. Some factors for consideration are the cumulative effects of violence and abuse, chronic health conditions, and financial insecurity due to caregiving or divorce. Power inequalities that occur among women, women of color, and transgender persons over the life course continue into older adulthood, aided by ongoing racial discrimination, cultural conceptions of gender roles, and policies that privilege some over others in the workplace. Research examining gender as a factor in health tends to support the existence of these disparities. Women live longer than men; they also have more chronic conditions (Murtagh & Hubert, 2004). Our health care system, however, focuses more energy and resources on those with terminal illness rather than on those with chronic conditions such as arthritis or osteoporosis. This focus leads to health disparities for women. Without correction, the impact of chronic conditions will continue to be large, manifesting as slow decline, disability, and diminished quality of life (Murtagh & Hubert, 2004). A similar decline has been demonstrated in Latin American women over the age of 60 (Alvarado, Zunzunegui, Béland, & Bamvita, 2008). Through examination of cross-national data in five Latin American countries, investigators found that women were more likely to be in frail physical health than men, and to have more chronic conditions (Alvarado et al., 2008).

A key study in understanding the life course impact of childhood experiences on health in later life is the Adverse Childhood Events Study (Fellitti et al., 1998). There is some evidence that women experience higher rates of childhood sexual abuse (CSA) and witness more domestic violence (Afifi et al., 2008; Cavanaugh, Petras, & Martins, 2015), while men are more likely to report physical abuse in childhood (Afifi et al., 2008). Rates of reported CSA differed between men and women who participated in the study (25% for women and 16% for men). Related to domestic violence, women are 7 to 14 times more likely than men to endure a profound injury in a relationship with their intimate partner (Tjaden & Thoennes, 2000), and two to three times more likely to identify fear of being injured in an intimate relationship (Morse, 1995). Kessler, Sonnega, Bromet, Hughes, and Nelson (1995) found that women were more likely than men to experience sexual assault and molestation that led to post-traumatic stress disorder. In a rare study on intimate partner violence for those aged 45 and older, women reported the same rates of violence as those who were younger (Wilke & Vinton, 2005). The women over age 45 were more likely to have health and mental health concerns and chose to stay in their intimate relationship with an abusive partner. Multiple studies indicate that women are more likely than men to experience anxiety and depressive disorders (Afifi et al., 2008; Cavanaugh et al., 2015) and to experience hopelessness (Haatainen et al., 2004).

Transgender Persons and Vulnerability

The National Transgender Discrimination Survey (NTDS) (Grant et al., 2011) reported data from over 6,000 transgender and gender nonconforming persons between the ages of 18 and 89. Thirteen percent of participants were 55 years of age and older. All persons in the survey, especially persons of color and those with low incomes, experienced high levels of discrimination in education, housing, and health care. Furthermore, they reported discrimination in accessing health care (28%), including being refused services (19%) and in finding a culturally responsive physician. Latino/a participants reported the highest rates of discrimination in health care settings such as the ER and mental health clinics among all other ethnic categories, while African American transgender participants were computed to be at highest risk for physical assault in health care settings (Grant et al., 2011).

The U.S. Transgender Survey (Grant et al., 2011) found that transgender respondents had three times the unemployment rate as the general U.S. population (James et al., 2016). The NTDS reported that 41% of the survey respondents had made at least one suicide attempt. Among transgender adults in the NTDS (Grant et al., 2011), 26% reported being physically assaulted and 10% reported being sexually assaulted due to prejudice based on gender expression or transgender identity. There are indicators from other research that sexual violence rates are much higher when looking at the data from a life course perspective (Kenagy, 2005; Kenagy & Bostwick, 2005). In another study, transgender persons over age 50 were found to be at higher risk than their lesbian, gay, and bisexual contemporaries for experiencing threats, as well as verbal and physical abuse (Fredricksen-Goldsen et al., 2011). Transgender persons continue to face issues of inequality, despite progress made in LGBTQ rights over the past decade (Auldridge, et. al., 2012; Knochel, et. al., 2002).

Ethical Considerations

Beauchamp and Childress (1979) developed general guiding principles that were intended to inform decision making for health and well-being. Robinson (2011), a critic of traditional ethical frameworks, suggested that the focus in ethics is often on values such as independence, self-determination, and rights, while deemphasizing the value of interdependency, relationships, and positive connection. Other feminists who critique models of ethical decision making (Held, 2006; Sherwin, 2007) see these models as promoting inequality because they are blind to gender and ignore the lived experiences of women. Guiding principles may be too abstract and idealized to be connected to the contexts in which ethical decisions are required (Edwards & Mauthner, 2002; Held, 2006; Sherwin, 1989; Sherwin, 2007). An example is an older woman who stays in her unsafe housing community to be with her friends. Disruption of relationships is often not considered in health care decision making. Feminist ethicists question the notion that it is possible to act autonomously and without constraint. More recently Beauchamp (2007) acknowledged the importance of developing rules to apply to specific situations and saw the necessity of addressing the larger social and social justice contexts in which decisions are based. The social justice issue in the example above is the lack of protection for a vulnerable older person living in a high-crime community. Providers and practitioners should consider the contexts in which decisions are made.

Held's (1995) analysis of ethics and decision making suggests that ending oppression of women necessitates using multiple perspectives to address ethical concerns, and not just a one-size-fits-all model. Another consideration for ethical decision making is the importance of recognizing that there are power differentials in relationships. Thus, it will be important for providers to acknowledge power imbalances in reciprocal relationships with patients by discussing these differences and empowering older persons, who often defer to providers, to direct their own health care (Sherwin, 1989). Gilligan's writings and the work of Baker Miller and colleagues give credence to healthy development being rooted in relationships and decision making being rooted in an ethic of care

(Held, 2006). Women often have different motivations from men for decision making in a multitude of contexts in their lives. These contexts are related to preserving the quality of their lives and the lives of those with whom they have relationships.

As we have seen in the analysis above, our decision making is influenced by historical events and cultural norms. Ethical decisions are not only about autonomous decision making but also include the web of relationships and one's cultural heritage (Held, 2006). Focusing on gender-based inequities as they relate to the care and provision of services for older persons is paramount for ethical practice. Furthermore, consideration of a life course perspective provides practitioners with a lens through which to consider social justice and intersectionality. We will now introduce a practice framework that can assist practitioners in assessing older persons with increased gender sensitivity.

Practice Framework

An ethics of care framework (Sherwin, 2007), in contrast to Beauchamp and Childress's (1979) principles, would consider the importance of interdependent relationships in making health care decisions. Seen from the context of how one functions, Grewal et al. (2006) identified attributes such as *attachment, role, enjoyment, security,* and *control* as more contextual measures of the quality of life. Indeed, conceptual perspectives that focus on quality of life, instead of those that privilege autonomy and beneficence, are inherently better suited to account for the complex circumstances of gender. For example, an older woman with grave medical concerns and financial strains might avoid a doctor visit if her main concern is to maintain a home for her dependent daughter and granddaughter who are living with her. She may abandon self-care for the "good" of the family, denying her decline and fearing her medical needs might swamp the family by using up the limited income on which they all depend. As RCT (Jordan et al., 1991) suggests, her primary concerns may be preserving relationships as opposed to following principles and moralities (Edwards & Mauthner, 2002). Thus, the well-being of the family would be taken into consideration in care planning for the patient (McAuley, Teaster, & Safewright, 1999).

Developing a gender-sensitive practice framework, applicable for a variety of helping professions, is an important step toward implementing ethically sound interventions for older persons. Use of a comprehensive practice framework which does not solely revolve around one's medical condition is especially pertinent for work with women in challenging social or environmental situations. The Practice Framework for Older Persons (PFOP) presented here relies heavily on the use of certain capabilities tied to gender inequity conceptualized by Robeyns (2003) and rooted in Amartya Sen's (1993) conception of capability as related to quality of life. In addition, the framework incorporates a life course perspective not often found in practice milieus. The applicability of Sen's capability approach has been utilized in many areas, including human development (Fukuda-Parr, 2003), health (Mitchell, Roberts, Barton, & Coast, 2017), gender inequality (Robeyns, 2003), communication for development and social change (Jacobson, 2016), and economic evaluations of health and social care (Coast et al., 2008). Use of a capability perspective acknowledges the distinction between *means* and *opportunities* (Sen, 2005) and allows for a critical analysis of how, for example, gender impacts one's capitalization of resources. The PFOP is a practice framework that includes 11 task areas, which considers past and current realities for an older person. By considering a life course context of means and opportunities, a more complete picture can be drawn about a person's unique wants, needs, and desires. Although originally developed with gender in mind, the PFOP is particularly beneficial for women and transgender persons given ethical demands for practice paradigms that consider gender fluidity and personal agency. The PFOP also takes into account the relational context of decision making for women.

Application of Practice Framework for Older Persons

The PFOP is relevant for many older persons. Practitioners can use the PFOP questions as they explore key task areas such as safety, shelter, finances, and health during the assessment process. In order to take into account a life course perspective, a past considerations column is included in the framework. Past considerations questions enable practitioners evaluating older persons to identify the cumulative advantage and disadvantage of experiences that occur along the way in a person's life.

Additionally, there are specific questions included in the right-hand column that could elicit gender-based concerns. If someone is experiencing domestic violence, for instance, has this been a pattern across the life course, or is it an isolated incident occurring in the present? How we answer this and other life experiences has implications for intervention and ethical decision making. As with a chronic illness, persons may need different kinds of interventions if they have, for instance, experienced a pattern of domestic abuse over a long period of time or if they report gender discrimination in the workplace. Safety is the primary consideration for abuse, but others may include how to mobilize a family system that has enabled the abuse to continue. The gendered impact of life course events continues, for instance, when an older woman experiences domestic abuse and her grown male children identify with their father and perpetuate emotional abuse in their relationship with their mother. It will be important to look at the pattern of abuse across her life course to determine where current supportive relationships exist to empower and protect her. Domestic violence may also impact access to pension income for an older woman, especially if she does not have a consistent work history.

It is crucial for human services organizations to not only serve older persons, but also to offer care and resources that are both person-centereed and applicable regardless of demographic background, and culture. While the PFOP was developed with gender inclusivity in mind, it can be modified to emphasize a variety of intersectionality elements. The "past" and "current" considerations of each task area (second and third column) can be adapted to reflect a specific population or subgroup. Using the PFOP for planning and quality improvement purposes will hopefully broaden organizational perspectives about how different aspects of service delivery are inclusive and tailored to meet the needs of an older person. For example, program processes such as intake, assessment, service planning, and discharge planning can be evaluated to determine if each of the task areas of the PFOP are covered. In addition, the task areas can be used as a guide for training practitioners working with older persons.

CASE STUDY 5.1

Ms. Rose M. is a 61-year-old African American woman who has been referred to a social worker at a low-income health clinic to discuss why she hasn't been following through on her previously agreed plan to exercise. Her biggest complaint is hip pain. She takes medications for blood pressure, congestive heart failure, diabetes, arthritis, and gout. She also reports bladder incontinence. In addition to her physical problems, Ms. M. reports she has a history of domestic violence, depression, and substance abuse. Ms. M. is divorced and has been sober for 2 1/2 years. Ms. M. lives alone in mixed-age public housing. She reports that it is difficult to stay clean and sober when living around younger people who are using drugs every day. She also states there are ongoing safety concerns (sexual harassment, strangers creeping into the building each night) in this setting. She is not old enough for Medicare and does not qualify for disability. Her unemployment from a job in fast food service has run out. She has a history of discrimination in the workplace. She fears she will be unable to get another job due to age discrimination and because she is Black. Ms. M. has children who live close by but with whom she has minimal contact. She has begun to reestablish a relationship with her children; there has been a long estrangement due to her substance abuse. She acknowledges that she has regrets about her parenting. She says she is living her life "one day at a time." She wants a better relationship with her family and a job with an income.

CONCLUDING OBSERVATIONS

An ongoing challenge for the helping professions is to adopt practices and policies that do not reinforce gender stereotypes and inequalities (Calasanti, 2010). As providers of services from a multitude of fields, we need to ask what practices or policies in our own unique settings contribute to existing patterns of oppression (Sherwin, 2007). Relations of family, friendship, and group identity have largely been missing from ethical frameworks; indeed, our constructs about health are often more attuned to the financial marketplace. Furthermore, idealized frameworks do not particularly apply to decision making for end-of-life care, mental illness, loneliness, and disconnection. People are often treated as moral agents that are expected to make autonomous decisions and practice guidelines do not deliberate about gender differences, discrimination, life course, or age. The PFOP is intended to be applicable for numerous practice domains (for example, social work, nursing, and public health) and for a variety of practice levels (such as case planning, program development, community approaches, and professional development). The consideration of one's means and opportunities, cohort, history, and life course further enhances our ability to understand a person's unique desires and needs and sets the stage for ethical and social justice–oriented practice.

TABLE 5.1 Practice Framework for Older Persons (PFOP)

Task Areas	Past Considerations	Current Considerations	Gender-Specific Questions
Health	Did person have access to appropriate mental health resources, if needed, in their past?	What is person's current mental status?	*Does person have debilitating medical conditions that are not appropriately responded to by the medical system?*
	Did person enjoy a healthy physical past?	Is person physically healthy?	*How does person's desire to protect relationships shape their decisions on seeking health care?*
	What is the person's history with mobility?	Is person mobile?	
Safety	What is person's history with bodily integrity and safety?	Does person enjoy a life without violence or harm to physical self?	*Has person experienced domestic violence?*
		Is person's bodily integrity currently being maintained?	
		Is person safe?	
		Does person feel safe?	
Domestic Work & Nonmarket Care	Was person able to raise children and/or take care of others?	Does person maintain relationships with those in their prior care?	*Does person still provide care for others? What are the circumstances of this caregiving? Do others depend on person emotionally and financially?*
Shelter	Did person benefit from regular shelter throughout their life?	Does person currently have shelter?	*How does person's desire to protect relationships shape their decisions on moving to safer housing?*
	Has person's living environment been consistently safe?	Does person currently live in a safe and pleasing environment?	
Financial	Was person able to work in the labor market or undertake projects?	Does person have sufficient monetary and health care benefits and resources?	*Will finances be affected if person needs to separate from one or more family members?*
Relationships	What has been the history of person's social relations?	What is present status of social relations?	*Are person's relationships built on certain gender expectations or norms?*

Task Areas	Past Considerations	Current Considerations	Gender-Specific Questions
Spirituality	Did person have freedom to follow or not follow religious principles?	Does person currently have the freedom to follow or not follow religious principles?	*How is religion a source of support or a source of spiritual distress?*
Respect & Dignity	Has person historically felt politically empowered?	Does person currently feel politically empowered?	*Does person feel listened to and feelings taken into consideration by significant people in their life?*
	Has person been respected by family and friends in their past?	What is person's current situation in regard to positive social opportunities?	*Does person experience gender bias in ways family and others respond to their requests and needs (being dismissed, judged)?*
	Does person have a history of being respected by their community?	Does person currently feel respected in their community?	*Does person have a history of discrimination based on expected gender identity and roles?*
Leisure Activities	Has person historically had access to leisure activities?	Is person able to engage in leisure activities?	*Does person feel comfortable participating in activities which are traditionally associated with another gender?*
Agency/Time Autonomy	Does person have a history of and comfort level with making decisions about how they spend their time?	Is person able to exercise autonomy in allocating one's time?	*If person is not able to exercise agency with one's time, is it based on gender restrictions?*
Education & Knowledge	What is person's educational background?	Is person able to use and produce knowledge?	*Has person's access and expectations relating to education been based on gender?*

Note: Based on ideas from Ingrid Robeyns, "Sen's Capability Approach and Gender Inequality: Selecting Relevant Capabilities," *Feminist Economics*, vol. 9, no. 2-3, pp. 71-72. Taylor & Francis Group, 2003.

DISCUSSION QUESTIONS

1. Apply the PFOP to the above case study. What information about Rose is still needed?

2. How will you include the experience of racial discrimination in your assessment and intervention with Ms. M.?

3. Given how our individual privilege (class, race, gender) impacts our worldview, which questions in the PFOP framework will be most challenging for you to relate to?

4. Assume Ms. M. identifies as being transgender. Which task areas in the PFOP might you explore further?

5. In what ways could technology be used to help Ms. Rose with any of her concerns?

6. Considering your agency and professional focus, which of the PFOP task areas are most often overlooked when assessing an individual's situation?

REFERENCES

Afifi, T. O., Enns, M. W., Cox, B. J., Asmundson, G. J., Stein, M. B., & Sareen, J. (2008). Population attributable fractions of psychiatric disorders and suicide ideation and attempts associated with adverse childhood experiences. *American Journal of Public Health, 98*(5), 946–952. Retrieved from https://doi.org/10.2105/AJPH.2007.120253

Alvarado, B. E., Zunzunegui, M.-V., Béland, F., & Bamvita, J.-M. (2008). Life course social and health conditions linked to frailty in Latin American older men and women. *Journals of Gerontology: Series A, 63*(12), 1399–1406. Retrieved from https://doi.org/10.1093/gerona/63.12.1399

Auldridge, A., Tamar-Mattis, A., Kennedy, S., Ames, E., & Tobin, H. P. (2012). *Improving the lives of transgender older adults: Recommendations for policy and practice*. Services and Advocacy for GLBT Elders, and the National Center for Transgender Equality. Retrieved from https://transequality.org/issues/resources/improving-lives-transgender-older-adults-full-report

Beauchamp, T. L. (2007). The four principles approach to health care ethics. In R. E. Ashcroft, A. Dawson, H. Draper, & J. R. McMillan (Eds.), *Principles of health care ethics* (2nd ed., pp. 3–10). West Sussex, UK: Wiley.

Beauchamp, T. L., & Childress, J. (1979). *Principles of biomedical ethics*. New York, NY: Oxford University Press.

Calasanti, T. (2010). Gender relations and applied research on aging. *Gerontologist, 50*(6), 720–734. Retrieved from https://doi.org/10.1093/geront/gnq085

Cavanaugh, C. E., Petras, H., & Martins, S. S. (2015). Gender-specific profiles of adverse childhood experiences, past year mental and substance use disorders, and their associations among a national sample of adults in the United States. *Social Psychiatry and Psychiatric Epidemiology, 50*(8), 1257–1266. Retrieved from https://doi.org/10.1007/s00127-015-1024-3

Coast, J., Flynn, T., Natarajan, L., Sproston, K., Lewis, J., Louviere, J., & Peters, T. (2008). Valuing the ICECAP capability index for older people. *Social Science & Medicine, 67,* 874–882. Retrieved from https://doi.org/10.1016/j.socscimed.2008.05.015

Crimmins, E. M., Kim, J. K., & Hagedorn, A. (2008). Life with and without disease: Women experience more of both, *Journal of Women & Aging, 14*(1–2), 47–59. Retrieved from https://doi.org/10.1300/J074v14n01_04

Edwards, R., & Mauthner, M. (2002). Ethics and feminist research: Theory and practice. In M. Mauthner, M. Birch, J. Jessop, & T. Miller (Eds.), *Ethics in qualitative research* (pp. 14–28). Thousand Oaks, CA: Sage.

Elder, G. H., Johnson, M. K., & Crosnoe, R. (2003). The emergence and development of life course theory. In J. T. Mortimer & M. J. Shanahan (Eds.), *Handbook of the life course* (pp. 3–19). Boston, MA: Springer.

Felitti, V. J., Anda, R. F., Nordenberg, D., Williamson, D. F., Spitz, A. M., Edwards, V., & Marks, J. S. (1998). Relationship of childhood abuse and household dysfunction to many of the leading causes of death in adults: The Adverse Childhood Experiences (ACE) Study. *American Journal of Preventive Medicine, 14*(4), 245–258. Retrieved from https://doi.org/10.1016/S0749-3797(98)00017-8

Fredriksen-Goldsen, K. I., Kim, H.-J., Emlet, C. A., Muraco, A., Erosheva, E. A., Hoy-Ellis, C. P., ... & Petry, H. (2011). *The aging and health report: Disparities and resilience among lesbian, gay, bisexual, and transgender older adults.* Seattle, WA: Institute for Multigenerational Health. Retrieved from http://www.age-pride.org/wordpress/wp-content/uploads/2011/05/Full-Report-FINAL-11-16-11.pdf

Fukuda-Parr, S. (2003). The human development paradigm: Operationalizing Sen's ideas on capabilities. *Feminist Economics, 9,* 301–317. Retrieved from https://doi.org/10.1080/1354570022000077980

Gilligan, C. (1982). *In a different voice: Psychological theory and women's development.* Cambridge, MA: Harvard University Press. Retrieved from https://doi.org/10.1111/j.1471-6402.1985.tb00902.x

Grant, J. M., Mottet, L. A., Tanis, J., Harrison, J., Herman, J. L., & Keisling, M. (2011). *Injustice at every turn: A report of the national transgender discrimination survey.* National Center for Transgender Equality and National Gay and Lesbian Task Force. Retrieved from http://www.thetaskforce.org/static_html/downloads/reports/reports/ntds_full.pdf

Grewal, I., Lewis, J., Flynn, T., Brown, J., Bond, J., & Coast, J. (2006). Developing attributes for a generic quality of life measure for older people: preferences or capabilities? *Social Science & Medicine, 62,* 1891–1901. Retrieved from https://doi.org/10.1016/j.socscimed.2005.08.023

Haatainen, K., Tanskanen, A., Kylmää, J., Honkalampi, K., Koivumaa-Honkanen, H., Hintikka, J., & Viinamaki, H. (2004). Factors associated with hopelessness: A population study. *International Journal of Social Psychiatry, 50*(2), 142–152. Retrieved from https://doi.org/10.1177/0020764004040961

Held, V. (2006). *The ethics of care: Personal, political, and global.* New York, NY: Oxford University Press.

Jacobson, T. (2016). Amartya Sen's capability approach and communication for development and social change. *Journal of Communication, 66*, 789–810. Retrieved from https://doi.org/10.1111/jcom.12252

James, S., Herman, J., Rankin, S., Keisling, M., Mottet, L., & Anafi, M. A. (2016). *The report of the 2015 US transgender survey.*

Jean Baker Miller Training Institute. (n.d.). Relational-Cultural Theory. Retrieved from https://www.wcwonline.org/JBMTI-Site/relational-cultural-theory

Jordan, J., Kaplan, A., Miller, J. B., Stiver, I., & Surrey, J. (1991). *Women's growth in connection: Writings from the Stone Center.* Cambridge, MA: Harvard University Press.

Held, V. (1995). *Justice and care: Essential readings in feminist ethics.* Routledge.

Kenagy, G. P. (2005). The health and social service needs of transgender people in Philadelphia. *International Journal of Transgenderism, 8*(2–3), 49–56. Retrieved from https://doi.org/10.1300/J485v08n02_05

Kenagy, G. P., & Bostwick, W. (2005). The health and social needs of transgender people in Chicago. *International Journal of Transgenderism, 8*(2–3), 57–66. Retrieved from https://doi.org/10.1300/J485v08n02_06

Kessler, R. C., Sonnega, A., Bromet, E., Hughes, M., & Nelson, C. B. (1995). Posttraumatic stress disorder in the National Comorbidity Survey. *Archives of General Psychiatry, 52*, 1049–1060. Retrieved from https://doi.org/10.1001/archpsyc.1995.03950240066012

Knochel, K. A., Croghan, C. F., Moone, R. J., & Quan, J. K. (2010). Ready to serve? The aging network and LGB and T older adults. Retrieved from https://www.n4a.org/files/ReadyToServe1.pdf

Lopez, M. H., & Gonzalez-Barrera, A. (2014). Women's college enrollment gains leave men behind. *Pew Research Center.* Retrieved from https://www.pewresearch.org/fact-tank/2014/03/06/womens-college-enrollment-gains-leave-men-behind

McAuley, W. J., Teaster, P. B., & Safewright, M. P. (1999). Incorporating feminist ethics into case management programs. *Journal of Applied Gerontology, 18*(1), 3–24. Retrieved from https://doi.org/10.1177/073346489901800101

Miller, J. B. (1986a). *Toward a new psychology of women* (2nd ed.). Boston, MA: Beacon Press.

Miller, J. B. (1986b). *What do we mean by relationships?* (Working paper, Jean Baker Miller Institute at Wellesley Centers for Women, Wellesley, MA).

Miller, J. B., & Stiver, I. (1997). *The healing connection: How women form relationships in therapy and in life.* Boston, MA: Beacon Press.

Mitchell, M., Roberts, T., Barton, P., & Coast, J. (2017). Applications of the capability approach in the health field: A literature review. *Social Indicators Research, 133*, 345–371. Retrieved from https://doi.org/10.1007/s11205-016-1356-8

Morse, B. J. (1995). Beyond the Conflict Tactics Scale: Assessing gender differences in partner violence. *Violence and Victims, 10*, 251–272.

Murtagh, K. N., & Hubert, H. B. (2004). Gender differences in physical disability among an elderly cohort. *American Journal of Public Health, 94*(8), 1406–1411.

National Organization for Women. (n.d.). Founding. Retrieved from https://now.org/about/history/founding-2/

Proctor, B. D., Semega, J. L., & Kollar, M. A. (2016). Income and poverty in the United States: 2015 (Report Number P60-256, US Census Bureau, Washington, DC). Retrieved from https://www.census.gov/library/publications/2016/demo/p60-256.html

Robinson, R. (2011). *The ethics of care: A feminist approach to human security.* Philadelphia, PA: Temple University Press.

Robeyns, I. (2003). Sen's capability approach and gender inequality: Selecting relevant capabilities. *Feminist Economics, 9,* 61–92. Retrieved from https://doi.org/10.1080/1354570022000078024

Sen, A. (1993). Capability and well-being. In M. Nussbaum & A. Sen (Eds.), *The quality of life* (pp. 30–66). New York, NY: Oxford University Press.

Sen, A. (2005). Human rights and capabilities. *Journal of Human Development, 6*(2), 151–166. Retrieved from https://doi.org/10.1080/14649880500120491

Sherwin, S. (1989). Feminist and medical ethics: Two different approaches to contextual ethics. *Hypatia, 4*(2), 57–72. Retrieved from https://doi.org/10.1111/j.1527-2001.1989.tb00573.x

Sherwin, S. (2007). Feminist approaches to health care ethics. In R. E. Ashcroft, A. Dawson, H. Draper, & J. R. McMillan (Eds.), *Principles of health care ethics* (pp. 79–85). West Sussex, UK: Wiley.

Shumaker, S. A., & Hill, D. R. (1991). Gender differences in social support and physical health. *Health Psychology, 10*(2), 102–111. Retrieved from https://doi.org/10.1037/0278-6133.10.2.102

Surrey, J. (1985). *Self-in-relation: A theory of women's development.* Retrieved from http://www.wcwonline.org/pdf/previews/preview_13sc.pdf

Tjaden, P., & Thoennes, N. (2000). *Full report of the prevalence, incidence and consequences of violence against women: Findings from the National Violence Against Women Survey.* Washington, DC: National Institute of Justice.

Toossi, M., & Morisi, T. L. (2017). *Women in the workforce before, during, and after the Great Recession.* Spotlight on Statistics, U.S. Bureau of Labor Statistics. Retrieved from https://www.bls.gov/spotlight/2017/women-in-the-workforce-before-during-and-after-the-great-recession/pdf/women-in-the-workforce-before-during-and-after-the-great-recession.pdf

Walker, M. (2004). Relational-cultural theory: A framework for development across the life span. In D. Comstock (Ed), *Diversity and development: Critical contexts that shape our lives and relationships* (pp. 25–46). Belmont, CA: Brooks-Cole.

Wilke, D. J., & Vinton, L. (2005). The nature and impact of domestic violence across age cohorts. *Affilia, 20,* 316–328. Retrieved from https://doi.org/10.1177/0886109905277751

6

VULNERABILITY, EFFECTIVE STATUS, AND ETHNICITY

Donna Benton, PhD

Kylie Meyer, MSc

Jeanine Yonashiro-Cho, PhD

Elizabeth Avent, MSG

Ayesha Dixon, MSG, MPA

Janeth Marroletti Velazquez

KEYWORDS

patient-centered decision making	autonomy
biomedical principles of beneficence	nonmaleficence
justice	race and ethnicity
intersectionality	older adult

Overview

Why would an African American older adult be suspicious of participation in research? When can training on cultural competency hinder provision of services to a Chinese American family? How can adherence to patient-centered decision making decrease autonomy when addressing housing decisions for a Hispanic older adult? In this chapter, we will discuss biomedical principles of beneficence, nonmaleficence, justice, and autonomy as they relate to race and ethnicity. In doing so, we seek to equip students with the knowledge they need to begin answering these difficult questions and others like them during encounters with multicultural patient and client populations.

When thinking about working with others from diverse races and ethnicities, it is helpful to use a theory to help understand observed situations and guide approaches for intervention and resolution. Theory can be paired with guiding principles—beneficence, nonmaleficence, justice, and autonomy—to make sure that interactions with clients and patients are respectful and uphold dignity. For example, when encountering a client or patient who expresses beliefs or opinions that are difficult to understand, application of theory can help identify the information necessary to provide quality care to a person, while principles guide actions that are based on information presented.

It is critical to understand the theories of intersectionality and cumulative inequality to when faced with an ethical dilemma while working with older adults. **Intersectionality** is a concept referring to the complex ways in which people's experiences over the life course and in old age emerge from the interconnectedness of their social identities (race, gender, socioeconomic class) within systems of inequalities (Calasanti & Giles, 2018). Intersectionality posits that the effects of characteristics such as race, ethnicity, age, gender, sexual orientation, geographic location, and socioeconomic status overlap with each other. The inequalities stemming from these characteristics in society are not mutually exclusive or additive, but reinforcing (Brown, 2011). **Cumulative inequality** theory, like intersectional approaches (Calasanti & King, 2015), acknowledges that inequalities experienced in one life domain "spill over" into others, to perpetuate accumulation of advantage or disadvantage over the life course (Ferraro & Shippee, 2009; Ferraro, Shippee, & Schafer, 2009). The roots of inequality may begin before an individual is born and contribute to his or her unique experiences of inequality into later life.

In this chapter, we focus on how ethnicity and perceived race can influence encounters with providers in health and social service settings that often occur at older ages. **Race** is a social construct based on "phenotypic genetic expression rather than as a biological construct" (Ford & Kelly, 2005). Moreover, Beutler, Brown, Crothers, Booker, and Seabrook (1996) remind researchers that while race has limited biological validity, it still functions as a social-psychological and social-political construct. As such, it serves as a proxy to help explain variations in factors such as health care, housing, and education between racial groups. **Ethnicity,** in contrast, refers to cultural factors such as nationality, language, ancestry, and religion to name a few examples. Ethnicity is an entirely social-political construct that not which is fluid and may change over time (Ford & Kelly, 2005). This chapter does not explicitly discuss other characteristics that shape a person's life course in order to minimize redundancy with several other chapters in this textbook. It is important, however, to apply the theories of intersectionality and cumulative inequality to more fully understand the case studies presented. Each case study describes encounters that complicate the application of principles of beneficence, nonmaleficence, justice, and autonomy when working with populations from various racial/ethnic groups, and potentially increased vulnerability if handled insensitively. This chapter focuses on African American, Latino/Hispanic, and some Asian populations because they represent the largest ethnic and racial groups in the United States and are more likely to be represented in research and population profiles.

Changing Demographics

Data taken from the last census shows that the older population in 2015 was more than 46 million, but it is projected to be more than 98 million by 2060 (Mather, Jacobsen, & Pollard, 2015). We are seeing a more racially and ethnically diverse older adult population as the lifespans of these groups increase. The older African American (non-Hispanic) population is expected to grow from 9% in 2014 to 12% in 2060. The older Asian population (which includes Hawaiian and Pacific Island population) made up 4% of the older population in 2014 but will jump to 9% by 2060. This increase will also by accompanied by an increase in longevity. Hispanic older adults will be the largest population in the future, with this ethnic group making up 22% of older adults in 2060 as compared to 8% in 2014. The term Hispanic or Latino refers to persons of Mexican, Cuban, Puerto Rican, South or Central American, or other Spanish culture or origin regardless of race. Overall, from 2015 to 2060 it is projected that the number of African American older adults will triple, the number of Hispanic older adults will more than quintuple, Asian American older adults will more than double, and the number of White older adults will less than double. Other key demographic factors for the diverse aging population include variations in socioeconomic status, education, living arrangements, health status, and marital status, to name a few examples. All of these demographics intersect to make an older adult more or less vulnerable to the challenges associated with advancing age. (U.S. Census, 2016a). Note that there is a paucity of data on projected aging trends for Native Americans and Alaska Natives. In 2015, only .5% and .1% of persons over the age 65 were Native Americans and Alaska Natives respectively. (U.S. Census, 2016a). Because of the limited data, we will only focus our discussion on the other four racial/ethnic groups.

Problems of Aggregation of Ethnic Groups

Aside from numbers, the racial/ethnic elders of the future will be diverse in terms of their individual cohort experience related to their unique cultural experiences. As successive generations age, it will be critical that clinicians understand that complex factors influence how decisions are made when providing services and supports to ethnically diverse older adults. Let's look at case example.

CASE STUDY 6.1

Mr. Harold Lee, a 79-year-old naturalized Chinese American man was brought to the hospital after experiencing a stroke. He was accompanied by his wife Sylvia Kubota-Lee, an 82-year-old American-born Japanese woman. Mrs. Kubota-Lee held the health care power of attorney for her husband. While clinicians assessed her husband, Mrs. Kubota-Lee was led to registration to complete hospital registration and insurance paperwork. After half an hour, she was approached by a case worker who handed her a stack of papers in Chinese. As the worker paused to wait for her response, Mrs. Kubota-Lee explained that she only spoke and read English and would not be needing Medicaid or SSI. The worker quickly apologized and explained that the hospital staff had flagged her case as part of a special cultural service program. He helped her complete the paperwork in English before taking her to see her husband.

Shortly thereafter, Mr. and Mrs. Lee were joined by their middle-aged children, two adult sons and a daughter. Once they were present, Mrs. Lee noticed that hospital staff would often direct their questions or comments to her children, especially her eldest son. Frustrated, she found herself having to interrupt the conversation to ask questions or ask her son to raise specific issues or make relevant medical decisions. When she complained to the charge nurse, the nurse apologized and explained that the staff had engaged in cultural competency training and had been avoiding talking about negative topics with her out of respect for her culture.

   Justice is the fair and equitable treatment of individuals. The case study highlights justice-related issues because the aggregation of ethnic subpopulations into broader racial category of Asian negated differences that were important for assisting this family. For this family, income and language were not actual barriers for service utilization. However, this does not mean that they did not need to be provided services that met their cultural needs. For the Lees, use of public funds or a translator may not have been required; however, equity recognizes that not everyone starts from the same place. Therefore, a service provider should still assess the family needs for factors such as food preferences, knowledge of resources, immigration status, and cultural background, just to name a few factors. Providing an individualized assessment will help mitigate factors that result from **cumulative inequality**. Cumulative inequality contributes to individual-level heterogeneity in socioeconomic status, life experiences, language use, emigrant history, and immigration status (Hoeffel, Rastogi, Ouk Kim, & Shahid, 2012) of older adults and must be acknowledged in order to provide quality services to an individual in a group. Information and profiles of Asian and Hispanic populations have been routinely aggregated in research studies over the past few decades. Aggregation of cultural groups is not unique to the Asian population; it also commonly occurs with the Latino/Hispanic population. For example, the U.S. census separates Hispanics into racial categories (non-Hispanic Black or non-Hispanic White), which sometimes is confusing to people who identify more with culture based on nation of origin and not the concept of race. Because of historical issues of racial policies in the United States, the cultural diversity among and between Asian and Hispanic/Latino populations is often ignored, and instead, these populations are listed as single racial groups. For other populations such as Native Americans or Pacific Islanders, aggregation serves to make them invisible by being labeled as "other." Therefore, it is not surprising that staff in this example incorrectly guessed the racial and ethnic background of the wife while trying to apply their limited knowledge of Asian cultural groups. The staff generalized information that they learned about Asian culture (talking to the male in the room, limited English proficiency) without first considering individual cultural variations because of learning about stereotypical profiles based on aggregated research data.

Stereotyping and Microaggressions

Culturally stereotyping individuals by their ethnic background or other characteristics can lead to personal insult, harm to the patient–provider relationship, compromised care, and future avoidance of service utilization (Kagawa-Singer & Blackhall, 2001).

Stereotyping occurs when the cultural norms and characteristics of one ethnic or cultural group are broadened to the larger group and applied to individuals for which they are culturally inappropriate or even offensive (Nadal, Vigilia Escobar, Prado, David, & Haynes, 2012; Sue, Bucceri, Lin, Nadal, & Torino, 2007).

In the case of Mrs. Kubota-Lee, the staff's broad application of cultural knowledge learned in class, without regard to her actual needs and care preferences, resulted in the perpetuation of **microaggressions** and misunderstandings. This in turn led to personal offense, decreased personal agency, and diminished quality of care for both Mrs. Kubota-Lee and her husband. **Macroaggressions** are verbal and nonverbal insults, whether intentional or unintentional, that communicate hostile, derogatory, or negative messages to persons based solely upon their marginalized group. These so-called hidden messages can invalidate the group identity or demean them, relegating them to an inferior status. Assumptions of Mrs. Kubota-Lee's need for language assistance without prior indication of need may be perceived as insulting, especially to a natural-born U.S. citizen. Moreover, incorrectly assessing an individual's ethnic identity may also evoke offense and anger from the misrepresented party. Similarly, the tendancy of hospital staff to interact with the couple's adult children appears to have arisen in response to cultural preferences and norms practiced by some Asian ethnic groups and individuals (Hicks & Lam, 1999; Kagawa-Singer & Blackhall, 2001; Wuensch et al., 2013; Yonashiro-Cho, Cote, & Enguidanos, 2016), though they are in direct conflict with the patient's care preferences and advance care planning, potentially constituting an ethical and legal infringement.

Cultural Competency and Assessment

Many cultural competency programs and practices appear positive and in many ways can be exemplary in their efforts to improve culturally competent care. However, practitioners should understand that the application of these programs and approaches to specific encounters with older adults from various ethnic and cultural groups must still be approached on a case-by-case basis. **Cultural imperialism** is the process and practice of promoting one culture over another. Often this occurs during colonization, whereby one nation overpowers another—typically one that is economically disadvantaged and/or militarily weaker. The dominant country then forces its cultural beliefs and practices onto the conquered nation. Culture can be imposed in a variety of ways, such as through creating new laws and policies concerning what specific types of education, religion, art, and language are to be used. Let's look at the case of housing zoning laws. In many cities, neighborhoods don't allow for building so-called granny flats in single-family zoned neighborhoods. The zoning is consistent with the dominant cultural value of autonomy and independency across age groups. But for groups that value family over autonomy, such as Asian/Pacific Islander and Latino older adults, these laws can make it difficult for social services to implement culturally appropriate, ethical service goals within the dominant culture's housing policies (Pynoos, Feldman, & Ahrens, 2004).

Cultural History

Individuals' willingness to participate in programs and services may be influenced by the intersection of personal and cultural histories, particularly if zoning law experiences include episodes of injustice and discrimination. For example, an 88-year-old Japanese American who was an adolescent and lived through the Japanese internment may resist placement in formal institutions (e.g., nursing facilities), despite need for such care. The internment was from 1942 to 1946 and involved the unlawful detainment of persons of Japanese ancestry without cause after the bombing of Pearl Harbor, which resulted in the loss of their freedom, homes, and businesses as well as their armed domestic imprisonment in destitute government-run encampments. For African Americans, history of discrimination in access to quality long-term care contributes to differences in utilization patterns between them and White Americans. Negative social experiences for aging ethnic immigrants, such as experiences of injustices inflicted in their country of origin or ancestry, may result in a distrust of the government, formal authority figures, or dissimilar individuals into older adulthood. Resulting trauma and mistrust can span generations, with consequences on myriad encounters with service professionals not attuned to historical cohort differences. In reviewing literature on why ethnic groups are less likely to participate in research, Moreno-John et al. (2004, p. 99S) concluded that "African Americans, Latinos, and American Indians have all experienced a loss of cultural and traditional lifestyles, and issues of mistrust of mainstream society continue for many ethnic minorities, irrespective of their immigration status." This conclusion was found again among a racially and ethnically diverse group of family caregivers. In the study by Scharlach et al. (2006), Native American and African American participants indicated that historical adversity impacted them both negatively and positively. For example, they pointed out that there were service barriers in the community when they needed help. On the other hand, they said this also made them more committed to providing help in the community, brought families closer, and made caregiving a blessing.

While experiences may seem equivalent, a review by Ayalon and Gum (2010) of perceived major lifetime discrimination (events that impact socioeconomic status) and everyday discrimination (assaults to one's character) concluded that even though both Black and Hispanic older adults represent ethnic minority groups, perceived exposure to discrimination in Hispanics is more consistent with the experiences of Whites than those of Blacks. Hispanics in their study reported fewer incidents of everyday discrimination than Blacks but still higher than Whites. As this study suggests, it is important that generalizations are not made about similarities or differences between ethnic and racial groups. As Dale Berra stated when asked about how he compared to his father Yogi Berra: "You can't compare me to my father. Our similarities are different."

Cohort Differences Within Ethnic Groups

For many ethnic minorities, low rates of participation in scientific research are related to mistrust in addition to socioeconomic limitations, language and literacy issues (Moreno-John, et al 2004).

CASE STUDY 6.2

Mr. Jones is a 75-year-old African American man who lives in rural Mississippi. While attending a senior center, a young man doing his internship asked Mr. Jones if he would participate in a research program to help improve services to older adults at risk for dementia. The program would help Mr. Jones decide and sign an advance directive for health care and also power of attorney for financial decisions should they be needed. The intern explained that research suggests that Blacks have a higher risk for developing Alzheimer's disease compared to Whites. Mr. Jones said he would have to talk to his family and pray about this before making a decision. Mr. Jones's wife said this was a bad idea because she recalled being a young adult in the 1970s and hearing about African American men in Tuskegee, Alabama, deliberately infected with syphilis by doctors. She feared that the researcher might be trying to give her husband Alzheimer's disease. His daughter Vanessa disagreed, saying that helping others had always been important to her father and having help with advance directives would help the family know what to do if Mr. Jones became seriously ill in the future. Mr. Jones, while respecting his spouse's belief, felt that maybe he should give the program a try as long as it did not involve taking medication. Their youngest daughter, 44-year-old Vanessa, was an MSW with an emphasis in aging. She had not lived in Mississippi in over 25 years (since going away to college to study) and lives in San Francisco. She said that they should participate in programs like the one her father has been offered because it means Blacks will receive better care for memory problems in the future. In addition, she said she wants to know how to make decisions for her parents when she becomes their caregiver in the future.

As this case underscores, it is important to recognize and anticipate differences among members of the same racial and/or ethnic group. Among this family of African Americans, each member has experiences that modify their willingness to participate in research. The daughter's attitude is shaped by differences in education and cohort. Mrs. and Mr. Jones's understanding of and historical closeness to the Tuskegee research are shaping their decision. Also, the daughter's interest in research is related to her lack of historical experience with negative aspects of research. For the daughter, informed consent is more the norm, which may increase her willingness to participate in research. Another cohort difference is the daughter's desire to have in writing what type of health and financial decisions her parents would like in the future.

Ethical Issues Related to Beneficence and Nonmaleficence

When patients cannot make decisions for themselves and have no record of how they would like their care handled, health care professionals must respect the desires of a patient's family. Respecting the family's wishes can sometimes be at odds with what professionals perceive to be in the best interest of patients. Roughly 40% of Americans will become incapable of making their own health care decisions near the end of life

(Koss & Baker, 2017), but just half of older adults have completed an advance directive or living will (Pew Research Center, 2009). There are significant disparities between non-Hispanic White Americans and non-Hispanic African Americans in advance care planning. Across settings, African Americans are less likely than White Americans to have an advance directive. One study found that only 30% of African Americans in nursing homes had an advance directive compared to 70% of White Americans; among those receiving home health, only 13% of African Americans had advance directives compared to roughly over 30% of White Americans (Lloyd, 2011).

Acknowledging and respecting differences can support the best interests of families and patients who have complex relationships and attitudes towards health care and other social institutions. Lack of awareness or knowledge about advance care planning was found as a barrier to completing advance directives not only among African Americans, but also among other minority racial groups (Hong, Yi, Johnson, & Adamek, 2017). Although these aspects must be considered when caring for and interacting with African American older adults and their families, we must also remember that issues of beneficence will occur with many racial and ethnic groups. Moreover, cohort differences exist within ethnic groups, like Mr. Jones and his daughter. This is exemplified by research showing increasing rates of advance directive completion among African American families over time (Portanova, Ailshire, Perez, Rahman, & Enguidanos, 2017). Zsembik (1996) points out that the complex interplay of social norms of the ethnic group, economic constraints, acculturation, and age may account for differences within Hispanic families. Therefore, when a service provider is faced with ethical decisions related to minimizing harm, it is important to remember to look at cohort differences within the group.

Culture and Elder Abuse

What should a social worker do if the family of an African, Chinese, or Hispanic immigrant insists that their father with middle-stage Alzheimer's disease and very limited income has the right to buy gifts for the family, rather than spend money on Western medications? Moreover, the family also believes that the father's memory and behavior challenges are a normal part of aging. According to the family, the older adult prefers complementary and alternative medicines, such as prayer, herbs, or vitamins because they are perceived to be healthier than Western medicines. In this case, the belief system of the family, income, age, and culture combine to raise an ethical dilemma related to autonomy and beneficence. A service provider may think that family members are taking advantage of their father's diminished capacity to use his income (fiduciary abuse) and want to make a report to adult protective services. However, another service provider may assess the situation and feel that education about dementia and ongoing case management is a better solution. In both cases, the vulnerability of the older adult is not just related to age but also to long-held cultural traditions related to elder respect, acceptance and beliefs about aging, and income. In a study of older Canadians by Clarke and Bennett (2013), use of self-care in chronically ill older adults reflected a means of maintaining control and a sense of self. There is little in the literature related to persons from minority cultures that suggests that the desire to maintain a sense of self while coping with a chronic illness does not apply to non-White ethnic older adults. Thus, for Asian, Black, and Hispanic families, maintaining the autonomy of their older family member—even when it may be viewed as problematic by social and health care professionals—is a priority. Awareness of a potential ethical issue of autonomy versus safety has to be considered to part of cultural competency for social service provider. This is not to imply that elder abuse should be ignored, but interventions should be tailored to improve care within a culturally appropriate model.

Faith and Health

Religious beliefs are another very important reason that African Americans sometimes refuse to complete advance directives. Religion is a major source of guidance for many African Americans faced with challenging decisions about end-of-life care. Only 40% of African Americans believe there are circumstances in which a person should have the right to die compared to 75% of White Americans (Pew Research Center, 2009). In Bullock's (2006) study, African Americans recounted stories of people coming out of comas and recovering after being given a grim prognosis as a basis of their beliefs. They also recounted putting their faith in God and not the doctors, because they believe that God is in control. This also ties into African Americans' distrust of health care providers, as they believe doctors are often incorrect about prognoses.

In addition, African Americans' beliefs about what constitutes a "good death" often does not align with what health care providers define as such. Bullock (2006) found that some African Americans believe a good death can be achieved when all life-sustaining measures are used. Among African Americans with an advance directive, 23.8% opted for prolonged care; while just 3.3% of White Americans and 13.3% of Hispanics did so (Portanova et al., 2017). Opting out of life-sustaining treatments is not necessarily at odds with palliative medical care that emphasizes patient comfort, but it can make hospice care less desirable for African American families, who may be uncomfortable with hospice care, associating withholding of treatment with negligent or subpar care (Johnson, Kuchibhatla, & Tulsky, 2008).

Although health care providers should expect to see variation among patient populations and their families in their attitudes towards life-prolonging care and advance directives, there are ways to consistently apply the principals of beneficence and nonmaleficence across cases. Understanding and respect for different attitudes and beliefs—even when these might not align with professionals' perspectives and opinions—can build trust and lead to better care.

Family Caregiving and Autonomy

The term *Hispanic* or *Latino* refers to persons of "Mexican, Cuban, Puerto Rican, South or Central American or other Spanish culture or origin regardless of race" (US Census,

2016). The Hispanic older adult population in the United States is rapidly growing and now accounts for 17% of adults 65 years and older (US Census, 2016). This is projected to grow in future years. Hispanics currently account for 70% of the population living in the following four states: California, Texas, Florida, and New York (Administration of Community Living, 2015).

Autonomy of the individual is a principle inherent in Western culture and institutions, and it asserts that individuals have the right to make choices for themselves. However, autonomy as it is applied in the United States and other Western countries can conflict with more family-centered values shared by many Hispanic families (Del Río, 2010; Elliott, 2001). Among Hispanic families, it is often important for the family to participate in decisions that are left to individuals in non-Hispanic families. By understanding the importance of family in the Hispanic older adult population and including them in decisions, the autonomy of the individual is not jeopardized but enhanced.

For example, consider the case of Maria Rosa, who is an 85-year-old Hispanic woman who speaks only Spanish and lives with dementia and diabetes. Maria Rosa's family is worried that she can no longer live on her own, so they hold a meeting and decide that their mother would stay with her daughter Yessenia. Taking care of aging family members is often highly valued amongst Hispanic families. It is one aspect of *familismo*, or emphasis on family loyalty and cohesion. Familismo is one reason Hispanic families are more likely than other populations to reject the use of formal services such as home care or social support services (Angel, Rote, Brown, Angel & Markides, 2014; Scharlach et al., 2006). Eighty-four percent of Hispanic caregivers reported that they believed that caregiving was an expectation within their upbringing, and 70% reported it would bring shame on their family not to accept their caregiving role (Cucciare, Gray, Azar, Jimenez, & Gallagher-Thompson, 2010). Sending an aging parent to a skilled nursing facility is considered especially egregious (Scharlach et al., 2006). A social worker approached the family about placing Maria Rosa in a nursing home rather than with Yessina, explaining that Maria Rosa's care needs were complex. Yessenia explained that to do so was shameful and that a nursing home is not an option for her family. However, a study by Herrera, Angel, Venegas, and Angel (2012) reminds us that while cultural factors may account for higher rates of caregiving in the community, there is also a lack of culturally appropriate long-term care facilities; economic constraints and lower access also may contribute to usage. These factors combine to underscore the ethical issues around equal access to long-term care options for older adults and their family caregivers.

In lieu of formal services, in many Hispanic families, the daughter takes on the caregiving role. While many daughters derive a sense of satisfaction from taking care of an aging parent, in cases where there is perceived pressure or lack of choice, caregiving can be burdensome (Mendez-Luck & Anthony, 2015). In the case above, although Yessina agreed with her family to bring her mother to live with her, part of her reason for doing so could be to abide by social norms and expectations. It is clear this decision created considerable difficulty; she expressed struggling to balance care for her mom with existing responsibilities to her children and employment. Fulfilling a perceived duty to the family can, in this way, align with individual choice while also requiring considerable sacrifice for the individual.

There are other reasons that Hispanic families choose not to use formal services, in addition to a preference that the family provide care. Formal services are expensive, and Hispanic families often have fewer means than non-Hispanic families (Semega, Fontenot, & Koller, 2015). Hispanic caregivers specifically spend an average of 44% of their total annual income on out-of-pocket costs related to caregiving—more than African Americans, Asian Americans, and White Americans (Rainville, Skufca, & Mehegan, 2016). In the case study presented, it is not entirely clear whether Yessenia is hesitant about formal services because she is uncomfortable with using them or because of the high costs. Lack of awareness can also contribute to low rates of formal service use among Hispanic families (Scharlach et al., 2006). Indeed, Yessenia demonstrates considerable interest in some types of services when she learns about them, and is grateful that the social worker shared these with her. All of these reasons could contribute to decisions on whether to use supports and services.

The focus of family-level decision making is also notable throughout this case. Another aspect of familismo is reference to the family when making decisions. Hispanic families often express preference to make important decisions as a unit rather than unilaterally. Family decisions are also a value for other ethnic groups. This preference stems from different understandings of the self. In Western cultures, the self is perceived as an independent and autonomous entity, even though there are many points during the life course when one must rely on others (Del Río, 2010). In contrast, amongst Hispanic families—like many other non-Western cultures—the self is recognized in reference to others (Aranda & Knight, 1997). Thus it is important that decisions that affect the family be made together. Autonomous decision making, rather than being empowering, can be burdensome and isolating since presumably others will be affected by any major decisions (Elliott, 2002).

Cases like that of Maria Rosa and her family demonstrate that including family members in health care and social services decisions does not necessarily undermine autonomy when the patient desires this and consents. Nor should providers assume that autonomy is being circumvented when family members defer to others or refuse to make decisions alone even when they could rightfully do so. Importantly, understandings and application of autonomy will vary both within and between cultures (Elliott, 2002). Practitioners should be aware of the possible nuances of this ethical principle when providing services to racially and ethnically diverse client populations and should defer to patients and their families, as appropriate, on how decisions affecting care should be made.

CONCLUDING OBSERVATIONS

Although most providers strive to adhere to principals of beneficence, nonmaleficence, justice, and autonomy when assisting their clients and patients, failure to understand and appreciate the role of race/ethnicity can violate these principals and cause harm to individuals and families. Person-centered and ethical service provision necessitates equal treatment to prevent undue vulnerability, but how services are provided may vary due to factors related to race and ethnicity. Still, variation in services should be considered with the client or patient and family as appropriate.

Of note, ethical service provision is not achieved by abiding to a strict set of rules. Rather, it calls for dynamic approaches and flexible understandings. Applying theoretical lenses of intersectionality and cumulative inequality can help providers navigate these situations by identifying the right questions to better achieve understanding. For example, why would an African American older adult refuse advance care planning that could help his wishes be known when he cannot make health care decisions?

From there, principled application of knowledge can help guide decisions on next steps. Because he has reason to distrust medical institutions and providers, and believes these documents will be misused, additional actions should be taken to increase trust, including clarifying what these documents can do, explaining how they are used by providers, and discussing ways to ensure they will not be misused.

Culturally skilled practice calls for, first, the assessment of individual patient and caregiver needs and preferences, and second, the provision of culturally concordant care and services to meet identified needs. For example, a good approach that can work with many ethnic older adults is, rather than assume language services are needed, have staff wear badges that indicate their ability to speak another language. Engaging in culturally skilled practice provides patients with a safe place to exercise their personal agency to choose to receive culturally tailored services and interventions to the extent that these approaches are desired.

We must also be aware that not all changes provide equality. For example, Artiga and Foutz (2016) report that, despite coverage gains under the Affordable Care Act, nonelderly Hispanics, Blacks, and Native Americans and Alaska Natives remain significantly more likely than Whites to be uninsured. Overall, people of color account for more than half (55%) of the total 32.3 million nonelderly uninsured. There are a number of differences in the characteristics of the uninsured by race and ethnicity that affect their eligibility for coverage. Understanding these vulnerabilities may help inform outreach and enrollment efforts. Moreover, this inequality will continue across the lifespan and begin to expand by normal changes with age.

Importantly, racial/ethnic minority status does not necessarily contribute to increases in vulnerability. Although the cases described above illustrate how these characteristics can expose racial/ethnic minority populations to uncomfortable, offensive, and even harmful situations, racial/ethnic minority status can also be protective. For example, in the case study about Mrs. Rosa, Yessenia could draw on her family as a resource to help make decisions about how best to assist her mother, potentially reducing the stress of this decision. African American and Hispanic families generally view caregiving as a positive and fulfilling life event. The wrong approach, such as treating caregiving as a burden, could alienate a family needing intervention. In the same way racial/ethnic minority status is not a confirmed liability, though in some circumstances these populations experience increased risk of harm in U.S. society. The increased vulnerability that occurs because of the intersection of history, race, culture, and age might be mitigated by coping skills learned and applied across a lifetime.

Providers can attenuate vulnerability related to racial/ethnic status through an evidence-based approach to providing care and careful application of the principles described. Where a robust evidence base does not exist due to the systemic omission of racial/ethnic differences in existing research, principled service delivery is particularly important. As the United States becomes a more multicultural society, providing culturally competent services to diverse ethnic and racial groups will not be optional.

It will, as it should, be ethically mandatory. This chapter provides tools to help meet these demands.

DISCUSSION QUESTIONS

1. In what ways have historical factors have shaped social services usage by ethnic minorities?

2. How does the ethical principle of autonomy serve as a barrier when providing housing options for African American or Hispanic older adults?

3. What are the specific identities or traits that intersect to make older Japanese Americans vulnerable to inequalities? How might these differ for an immigrant Hispanic older adult?

4. Explain how cumulative inequality can change over cohorts through developmental and cultural process.

5. How have caregiving roles affected minority families?

6. What measures might be taken to improve end-of-life planning for future generations?

REFERENCES

Administration of Community Living. (2015). A statistical profile of older Hispanic Americans. Retrieved from https://www.acl.gov/sites/default/files/Aging%20and%20 Disability%20in%20America/Statistical-Profile-Older-African-Ameri.pdf

Angel, J. L., Rote, S. M., Brown, D. C., Angel, R. J., & Markides, K. S. (2014). Nativity status and sources of care assistance among elderly Mexican-origin adults. *Journal of Cross-Cultural Gerontology, 29*(3), 243–258.

Aranda, M. P., & Knight, B. G. (1997). The influence of ethnicity and culture on the caregiver stress and coping process: A sociocultural review and analysis. *Gerontologist, 37*(3), 342–354.

Artiga, S., & Foutz, J. (2016). Key facts on health and health care by race and ethnicity. Retrieved from https://www.kff.org/disparities-policy/report/ key-facts-on-health-and-health-care-by-race-and-ethnicity

Ayalon, L., & Gum, A. (2011). The relationships between major lifetime discrimination, everyday discrimination, and mental health in three racial and ethnic groups of older adults. *Aging & Mental Health, 15*(5), 587–594.

Beutler, L. E., Brown, M. T., Crothers, L., Booker, K., & Seabrook, M. K. (1996). The dilemma of factitious demographic distinctions in psychological research. *Journal of Consulting and Clinical Psychology, 64*(5), 892–902. Retrieved from http://dx.doi.org. libproxy1.usc.edu/10.1037/0022-006X.64.5.892

Brown, G. K. (2011). Understanding horizontal inequalities: The role of civil society. In *Overcoming the Persistence of Inequality and Poverty* (pp. 203–230). Palgrave Macmillan, London.

Bullock, K. (2006). Promoting advance directives among African Americans: A faith-based model. *Journal of Palliative Medicine, 9*(1), 183–195. Retrieved from https://doi.org/10.1089/jpm.2006.9.183

Calasanti, T., & Giles, S. (2018, April 25). The challenge of intersectionality [Web log post]. Retrieved from http://www.asaging.org/blog/challenge-intersectionality

Calasanti, T., & King, N. (2015). Intersectionality and age. In J. Twigg & W. Martin (Eds), *Routledge handbook of cultural gerontology* (pp. 193–200). Oxfordshire, UK: Routledge.

Clarke, L. H., & Bennett, E. V. (2013). Constructing the moral body: Self-care among older adults with multiple chronic conditions. *Health, 17*(3), 211–228.

Cucciare, M. A., Gray, H., Azar, A., Jimenez, D., & Gallagher-Thompson, D. (2010). Exploring the relationship between physical health, depressive symptoms, and depression diagnoses in Hispanic dementia caregivers. *Aging Mental Health, 14*(3), 274–282.

Del Río, N. (2010). The influence of Latino ethnocultural factors on decision making at the end of life: Withholding and withdrawing artificial nutrition and hydration. *Journal of Social Work in End-of-Life & Palliative Care, 6*(3–4), 125–149.

Elliott, A. C. (2001). Health care ethics: Cultural relativity of autonomy. *Journal of Transcultural Nursing, 12*(4), 326–330.

Ferraro, K. F., & Shippee, T. P. (2009). Aging and cumulative inequality: How does inequality get under the skin? *Gerontologist, 49*(3), 333–343. Retrieved from https://doi.org/10.1093/geront/gnp034

Ford, M. E., & Kelly, P. A. (2005). Conceptualizing and categorizing race and ethnicity in health services research. *Health services research, 40*(5p2), 1658–1675. Retrieved from https://doi.org/10.1111/j.1475-6773.2005.00449.x

Ferraro, K. F., Shippee, T. P., & Schafer, M. H. (2009). Cumulative Inequality Theory for research on aging and the life course. In V. L. Bengston, D. Gans, N. M. Pulney, & M. Silverstein (Eds.), *Handbook of theories of aging* (pp. 413–433). New York, NY: Springer.

Herrera, A. P., Angel, J. L., Venegas, C. D., & Angel, R. J. (2012). Estimating the demand for long-term care among aging Mexican Americans: Cultural preferences versus economic realities. In J. Angel, F. Torres-Gil, & K. Markides (Eds.), *Aging, health, and longevity in the Mexican-origin population* (259–276). Boston, MA: Springer.

Hicks, M. H. R., & Lam, M. S. C. (1999). Decision-making within the social course of dementia: Accounts by Chinese-American caregivers. *Culture, Medicine and Psychiatry, 23*(4), 415–452.

Hoeffel, E., Rastogi, S., Ouk Kim, M., & Shahid, H. (2012). *The Asian population: 2010* (Report for the US Census Bureau). Retrieved from https://www.census.gov/prod/cen2010/briefs/c2010br-11.pdf

Hong, M., Yi, E.-H., Johnson, K. J., & Adamek, M. E. (2017). Facilitators and barriers for advance care planning among ethnic and racial minorities in the U.S.: A systematic review of the current literature. *Journal of Immigrant and Minority Health*. Retrieved from https://doi.org/10.1007/s10903-017-0670-9

Johnson, K. S., Kuchibhatla, M., & Tulsky, J. A. (2008). What explains racial differences in the use of advance directives and attitudes toward hospice care? *Journal of the American Geriatrics Society, 56*(10), 1953–1958.

Kagawa-Singer, M., & Blackhall, L. J. (2001). Negotiating cross-cultural issues at the end of life: "You got to go where he lives." *Journal of the American Medical Association, 286*(23), 2993–3002.

Koss, C. S., & Baker, T. A. (2017). A question of trust: Does mistrust or perceived discrimination account for race disparities in advance directive completion? *Innovation in Aging, 1*(1), igx017. Retrieved from https://doi.org/10.1093/geroni/igx017

Lloyd, J. (2011, January 7). Study: Blacks less likely to have living wills, DNR orders. *USA Today*, p. 3A.

Mather, M., Jacobsen, L. A., & Pollard, K. M. (2015). Aging in the United States. *Population Bulletin, 70*(2).

Mendez-Luck, C. A., & Anthony, K. P. (2015). Marianismo and caregiving role beliefs among US-born and immigrant Mexican women. *Journals of Gerontology Series B: Psychological Sciences and Social Sciences, 71*(5), 926–935.

Moreno-John, G., Gachie, A., Fleming, C., Nápoles-Springer, A., Mutran, E., Manson, S., & Pérez-Stable, E. (2004). Ethnic minority older adults participating in clinical research. *Journal of Aging and Health, 16*(5_suppl), 93S–123S.

Nadal, K. L., Vigilia Escobar, K. M., Prado, G. T., David, E. J. R., & Haynes, K. (2012). Racial microaggressions and the Filipino American experience: Recommendations for counseling and development. *Journal of Multicultural Counseling and Development, 40*(3), 156–173.

Pew Research Center. (2009). *End-of-life decisions: How Americans cope.* Washington, DC: Author. Retrieved from http://www.pewsocialtrends.org/2009/08/20/end-of-life-decisions-how-americans-cope

Portanova, J., Ailshire, J., Perez, C., Rahman, A., & Enguidanos, S. (2017). Ethnic differences in advance directive completion and care preferences: What has changed in a decade? *Journal of the American Geriatrics Society, 65*(6), 1352–1357.

Pynoos, F., Feldman, P. H., & Ahrens, J. (Eds.). (2004). *Linking housing and services for older adults: Obstacles, options, and opportunities.* New York, NY: Haworth Press.

Rainville, C., Skufca, L., & Mehegan, L. (2016). *Family caregiving and out-of-pocket costs: 2016 report* (Report, American Association of Retired Persons). Retrieved from http://www.aarp.org/content/dam/aarp/research/surveys_statistics/ltc/2016/family-caregiving-cost-survey-res-ltc.pdf

Scharlach, A. E., Kellam, R., Ong, N., Baskin, A., Goldstein, C., & Fox, P. J. (2006). Cultural attitudes and caregiver service use: Lessons from focus groups with racially and ethnically diverse family caregivers. *Journal of Gerontological Social Work, 47*(1–2), 133–156.

Semega, J. L., Fontenot, K. R., & Kollar, M. A. (2017). *Income and poverty in the United States: 2016* (Current Population Report, US Census Bureau). Retrieved from https://www.census.gov/content/dam/Census/library/publications/2017/demo/P60-259.pdf

Sue, D. W., Bucceri, J., Lin, A. I., Nadal, K. L., & Torino, G. C. (2007). Racial microaggressions and the Asian American experience. *Cultural Diversity and Ethnic Minority Psychology, 13*(1), 72–81.

US Census Bureau. (2016). *Population division, annual estimates of the resident population by sex, age, race, and Hispanic origin for the United States and States: April 1, 2010 to July 1, 2015.* Retrieved from https://www.giaging.org/documents/A_Profile_of_Older_Americans__2016.pdf

Wuensch, A., Tang, L., Goelz, T., Zhang, Y., Stubenrauch, S., Song, L., ... & Fritzsche, K. (2013). Breaking bad news in China—the dilemma of patients' autonomy and traditional norms. A first communication skills training for Chinese oncologists and caretakers. *Psycho- Oncology, 22*(5), 1192–1195.

Yonashiro-Cho, J., Cote, S., & Enguidanos, S. (2016). Knowledge about and perceptions of advance care planning and communication of Chinese-American older adults. *Journal of the American Geriatrics Society, 64*(9), 1884–1889. Retrieved from http://doi.org/10.1111/jgs.14261

Zsembik, B. A. (1996). Preference for co-residence among older Latinos. *Journal of Aging Studies, 10,* 69–81.

SEXUAL ORIENTATION

Jeffrey Mostade, PhD
Kent State University

Varun Umesh Shetty, MD
University of Pittsburg Medical Center

KEYWORDS

lesbian	transgender
bisexual	marginalized
vulnerable	immigrant
older adult	intersectionality
gay	

Overview

In professional interactions with older adults, the richness of life often becomes a vital factor in understanding both the person and their predicament. Whether an attorney, counselor, nurse, physician, social worker, parole officer, psychologist, gerontologist, or public health researcher, the intersections of race/ethnicity, culture, cohort, class, sex, gender, ability, and sexual orientation with aging are unavoidable when understanding and working with clients. Vulnerable adults are just that, and the population of lesbian, gay, and bisexual older adults is especially vulnerable to misapprehension, misunderstandings, and misinterpretations, with both internal and external barriers to accessing services.

This chapter includes a review of the terminology and background information on lesbian, gay, and bisexual older (age 65 and older) adults as well as a discussion of the concept of vulnerability and ethical applications to this population. Two case studies are employed to illuminate the conceptual understandings in the chapter.

Background Information and Terminology

A National Resource Center on LGBT Aging (Grant, 2010) study reported that there were approximately 1.5 million older (aged 65 and older) lesbian, gay, bisexual, and transgender (LGBT) adults in the United States. This number is expected to grow to approximately 3.5 million to 7.2 million individuals by 2030, as Baby Boomers age into this profile (Teaster, White, & Kim, 2016). This population is expected to face the typical challenges of aging, including medical health considerations, mobility, psychological health, and maintenance of social systems of support (Stoukides, Holzer, Ritzau, & Burbank, 2006), concurrent with the effects of racism, homophobia, transphobia, and the effects of a possible lifetime of living and coping with stigma, marginalization, discrimination, and invisibility (Burbank & Burkholder, 2006).

Cohort effects are varied and important for this population, as the understanding of what it means to be LGBT has shifted enormously during the lives of the oldest old (85 and older, born 1933 and earlier) to the most recent cohort of the youngest old (65 years, born 1953 and earlier), in 2018. Diversity and extremely different cohort experiences render this a community lacking in communal experiences. The hidden nature of the population increases the difficulty of identification, as well as the provision of resources to support the vulnerable older LGBT adult. Text box 7.1 provides definitions of terms to be used throughout this chapter.

BOX 7.1

Sexual Orientation and Gender

Gay refers to any person who has sexual, affectional, and/or romantic orientation toward other persons of the same sex. In general, this has come to refer to gay men, but it can reference gay men or lesbian women.

Lesbian refers to a woman who has sexual, affectional, and/or romantic orientation only toward other women.

Bisexual refers to a person who is oriented toward people of both sexes and may have sexual, affectional, or romantic attractions. This does not necessarily mean that they must be equally attracted to people of both sexes or that they must be involved with people of both sexes concurrently.

A transgender person is understood to be someone who may be born biologically as one sex but may "identify emotionally, physiologically and psychologically with another sex or gender expression" (Robinson-Wood & Weber, 2016, p. 69). Transgender people may be gay, lesbian, bisexual, heterosexual, or asexual. A person whose personal experience of their gender identity is congruent with their understood biological sex is considered to be cisgender (Robinson-Wood & Weber, 2017). The umbrella term *transgender* can range from transsexual people who have had gender reassignment surgery, to people who

---

choose to use hormone therapy to address secondary sex characteristics but elect not to have gender reassignment surgery, to those people refusing to identify with either gender and those refusing gender categorization. This community traditionally includes cross-dressing people and intersex people. Although transgender people can be of any sexual orientation, they have historically been included under the LGBT umbrella.

Homophobia references general societal negative attitudes toward lesbians and gay men, as well as internalized homophobia, a "set of negative attitudes and affects towards homosexuality in other persons and towards homosexual features in oneself" (Burbank & Burkholder, 2006, p. 178).

There is no agreed-upon criterion for the definition of a gay, lesbian, or bisexual person. Primarily, people must self-identify as gay, lesbian, or bisexual to be construed as such. The question can focus on identity or behavior (Knauer, 2011). Consequently, although we know very little about LGBT people in general, we know even less about the experience of LGBT older adults in the aggregate. The limitations caused by definitions and sampling ensure that we know even less about older LGBT people of color, older lesbians, and LGBT people of different ability, by income, religion, or any other criteria of interest when assessing, predicting, and providing culturally appropriate services to vulnerable older LGBT adults.

The complexity in measuring the actual population of vulnerable older LGBT adults and their specific health considerations has as much to do with definition as with outreach to this population (Knauer, 2011). This attitude toward society occurs in part because this population grew up in a time when a same-sex sexual orientation was considered medically diagnosable, criminal, and socially deviant (Burbank & Burkholder, 2006; Choi & Meyer, 2016; Knauer, 2011). Existing demographic information for this community show differences from the larger societal profile in the rates of education, income, the number of committed relationships, the proportion who live alone, and the number without children. This group seems to be more highly educated, more likely to live alone, less likely to be partnered or formerly married and less likely to have children (Burbank & Burkholder, 2006). The MetLife study on LGBT Aging (Metlife Mature Market Institute & Lesbian and Gay Aging Issues Network of the American Society on Aging, 2010) shows that bisexual people have a very different experience than gay men, lesbian women, or transgender people. They have significantly fewer friends, are far less likely to self-identify as LGBT, and are consequently more guarded with others.

A person is not considered vulnerable simply because of their sexual orientation or gender identity. Although there is some vulnerability implied by a public LGBT identity due to stigma, discrimination, and prejudice, researchers in British Columbia have identified external and internal risk factors in the identification of vulnerable older adults. Internal risk factors include increasing age, female gender, mental illness, cognitive impairment, and problems with activities of daily living. External factors include a lack of a social network, care provider dependence, living alone, lack of community resources, inadequate housing, unsanitary living conditions, high-crime neighborhood, adverse life events, and poverty (Culo, 2011).

Health Considerations and Vulnerable Aging

Older adults are already a highly diverse group of persons in regard to age, culture, socioeconomic states, sex, gender, physical ability, mental health, health status, living environments, and social arrangements. The interactions among a person's identities and experiences are "separate, joined, reciprocal, internal and contextual" (Hawley & Mostade, 1999, p. 318). An older person with somewhat limited mobility suddenly becomes a vulnerable older adult if their oxygen machine ceases to function or transportation becomes unavailable.

Identifying populations of vulnerable older LGBT adults creates an opportunity to offer resources that can interrupt or delay the transition from functional independence to a situational or chronic vulnerability (Stoukides et al., 2006). Specific vulnerability will vary depending on the individual, the population, the experience, and the resources available, highlighting the need for careful assessment.

LGBT Aging and Health Considerations

The LGBT community is not monolithic. Its members' experiences vary by gender and sex as much as they do by class and ethnicity. In addition to health considerations and barriers to service, both internal and external, the gay community has some theorized strengths in response to assuming a stigmatized aging identity, first characterized as "crisis competence" by Kimmel (1978). It was reported in the MetLife study of Baby Boomers (2006) that older LGBT people felt they had developed greater resilience and better support networks as a result of being out as LGBT people and members of that community. Kimmel's (1978) research from 40 years ago helped positively change the stereotype of lonely, depressed, older gay men. He was one of the first researchers to call for addressing stigmatization and the provision of targeted services for older gay men. A study of this population by D'Augelli, Grossman, Hershberger, and O'Connell (2001) found that the majority of participants had good self-esteem and adjustment. Lower rates of internalized homophobia seem to be associated with higher rates of self-esteem, self-disclosure of one's LGBT status, and less loneliness (D'Augelli et al., 2001).

Internalized homophobia has pronounced effects on the health and social status of older LGBT people and has been associated with substance abuse, suicidal ideation, and depression (Amadio & Chung, 2004; Burbank & Burkholder, 2006). Older lesbian, gay, and bisexual people exhibit increased prevalence of mental health problems, disability, physical limitations, and disease compared to heterosexual people (Choi & Meyer, 2016). Furthermore, lesbian, gay, and bisexual seniors are more vulnerable because they have a higher risk of social isolation than older adults who do not identify as such (Cahill, South, & Spade, 2000).

Gay Men

Although Kimmel's earlier mentioned research showed theorized crisis competence, more recent research shows social and health risks. Older gay men have a higher risk of poor physical health and also of living alone; at the same time, both older gay men and older bisexual men show lower rates of obesity than heterosexual men (Fredriksen-Golden, Kim, Barkan, Muraco, & Hoy-Ellis, 2013). The Centers for Disease Control and Prevention (CDC) reports that gay, bisexual, and other men who are attracted to men show higher rates of HIV and other sexually transmitted diseases, higher rates of tobacco and substance use, and increased prevalence of depression (CDC, 2017).

Lesbian Women

Lesbians are at risk because they are female, and many have experienced adverse life events. Older lesbians show increased health-related issues compared with heterosexual woman primarily due to health factors and high-risk behaviors, as they seem to have similar rates of chronic illness. Lesbians and bisexual women show a higher risk for cardiovascular disease and obesity (Fredriksen-Golden et al., 2013). Older lesbians have been found to have higher rates of obesity and tobacco and alcohol use (Burbank & Burkholder, 2006). Other risk factors include never having had children and a decrease in the use of health screening examinations compared to heterosexual women. Older lesbian women showed higher rates of heavy drinking than did bisexual women (Fredriksen-Golden et al., 2013). A higher percentage of older lesbians seems to be partnered than the corresponding percentage of older married woman (Herdt, Beeler, & Rawls, 1997), again from a smaller, geographically limited study. Health information for older women is also conflated because presumably the data for bisexual women have been combined with that of heterosexual women and then compared to older lesbian women (Burbank & Burkholder, 2006).

Bisexual People

Older bisexual men have been associated with a higher risk of poor physical health and a higher likelihood of living alone than heterosexual men. Bisexual men also report higher rates of diabetes and lower incidence of testing for HIV than older gay men (Fredriksen-Golden et al., 2013). In studies, older bisexual women showed lower rates of excessive drinking than did older lesbian women; both older bisexual and lesbian women showed lower rates of sexually transmitted infections (Fredriksen-Golden et al., 2013). In addition, bisexual women are at higher risk of cardiovascular disease and obesity than heterosexual women (Fredriksen-Golden et al., 2013).

LGBT older adults as a group have higher rates of disability, poorer mental health, and higher consumption of both tobacco and alcohol (Fredriksen-Golden et al., 2013; Teaster et al., 2016). A lifetime of workplace discrimination and the disenfranchisement of their families of choice often causes economic vulnerability (Grant, Koskovich, Frazer, & Bjerk, 2010). Psychological reactions to a lifetime of discrimination, stigmatization, and fear vary (Cahill et al., 2000), depending on individual resilience and resources. Social isolation, associated in older adults with increased risk of mortality (Steptoe, Shankar, Demakakos, & Wardle, 2013), has been discussed in the literature as a concern for the LGBT community since 2000 (Cahill et al., 2000; Grant et al., 2010).

Social isolation does not necessarily mean living alone but rather refers to the lack of regular meaningful interaction with others. Such interaction can be provided in the community, in group activity, with friends, and with family. Isolated adults are more likely to be older, unmarried, and possess lower socioeconomic status and education levels (Steptoe et al., 2013). Compared to 90% of LGBT research respondents who reported having no children, only 20% of non-LGBT older adults had no children (Cahill et al., 2000). This potential social isolation caused by a historically lower incidence of part- nered households (Herdt et al., 1997) and the previously mentioned lack of children as social opportunities is exacerbated by the reluctance of members of the community to engage with a social system (e.g., hospital, social worker, LGBT center) that was previously seen as a potential source of oppression. Heterosexual households develop support communities that may or may not be broad but are usually multigenerational. LGBT older adults have depended on friends and families of choice (Brennan-Ing, Seidel, Larson, & Karpiak, 2013) for support, but their network is often only a single generation deep; that is, many older adult caregivers are friends as well as older adults themselves.

Many of the greatest health concerns lie in barriers to health care and aging ser- vices, which include discrimination, problems with accessing services, and the lack of support for older LGBT people and their partners and other informal caregivers (Fredericksen-Goldsen et al., 2011). There is also a clear lack of community resources that target the LGBT community (Auldridge & Espinoza, 2013), particularly those who struggle with medical comorbidities and other risk categories. LGBT people of color experience the greatest number of institutional barriers and have the poorest health outcomes which, in general, follows a life of intersecting multiple identities and the associated discrimination (Auldridge & Espinoza, 2013). The classic example is the older Black lesbian, who potentially has experienced ageism, racism, sexism, and homophobia, often even within these various communities of identity.

Racial/Ethnic and Cultural Considerations

Race is now understood as a social construct rather than a biological one (Marks, 2008). Due to the lack of biological markers, race is of even lesser utility when considered in terms of a racial understanding of a vulnerable older adult. The experiences of these individuals of the same race can be highly disparate and distinct. From a utility per- spective, race is too broad a concept to inform planning.

At the same time, skin color and other morphological attributes are and have been an unavoidable part of racist history, oppression, discrimination, and the lived experience of many older adults in the United States. Perceived race and perceived sexual orienta- tion have formed the basis for many instances of discrimination in the experience of many older LGBT adults.

Older gay men, lesbian women, and bisexual people have vastly different experi- ences when other personal identities and their associated experiences are considered. "LGBT people of color experience more psychological distress, financial instability, limited access to culturally competent care and housing inequality than" their European American counterparts (Robinson-Wood & Weber, 2016, p. 66). It is beyond the scope of this chapter to delineate each possible identity, culture, cohort, ability difference, religion, or national origin, but this brief survey of some of the distinctive effects of marginalization on older LGBT people is important to understand them, determine how to provide ethical services, and to demonstrate the importance of an intersectional approach to assessments.

The paucity of research that has been done with LGBT older adults suggests they share many of the same concerns that other older adults share: income stability, healthy choices in living, and maintaining social and community engagement (Anetzberger, Ishler, Mostade, & Blair, 2004). However, even these conclusions are of little utility as there has been little concerted effort toward research that is inclusive and reflective of the actual communities represented in the LGBT spectrum or in the U.S. census (Kimmel, Rose, & Did, 2006).

Whether African American, Hispanic, Asian American/Pacific Islander, Native American/Alaska Native, LGBT older adults of color face racial, economic, and gender disparities and will constitute 40% of the elder community in the United States by 2050 (Auldridge & Espinoza, 2013). Millions of older LGBT people face a lack of culturally competent care and the associated discriminations that come from within and without their communities of color.

Cohort

Along with their experiences of discrimination and prejudice by sex and race/culture, the historical time during which a client lived and reached adolescence becomes of almost paramount importance to understanding them. Their lived experience varies depending on the decade during which an individual came of age, especially in the 1940s, 1950s, 1960s, or 1970s. Men and women were still dishonorably discharged because of their sexual orientation from the U.S. armed forces during this time (U.S. Naval Institute, 2018). The psychosocial issues for successive cohorts shifts with the attitudes and experiences common at the time.

The cohort, however, does not provide a monolithic experience for LGBT people living in these periods. Different age cohorts had different experiences depending upon race/ethnicity and culture, including both their experience of the prevailing racial attitudes coupled with their experience of homophobia, as well as their experiences of within-group prejudice against an LGBT identity within their ethnic/racial community, along with the special racism within the gay community toward people of color.

Living Environments

The older LGBT population likely includes many living in nursing homes, assisted living facilities, congregate living facilities, and other environments facilitating health care later in life. This group also includes older LGBT people living in prison and jail environments. What could they possibly have in common? Although completely different, these environments can cause LGBT older adults to once again question their transparency and whether they choose to be out with their fellow residents or staff.

LGBT older adults may face discrimination from personal caregivers, health care staff, agencies, community workers, neighbors, or family members as well as institutionalized homophobia and transphobia in the form of policies, nonrecognition of important relationships, and lack of access to culturally affirming health and supportive care (White & Gendron, 2016). In prisons, it may be important for older prisoners to deny their sexual orientation for reasons of personal safety. Although some individuals may develop some personal resilience, friendship networks, and stigma management following a lifetime of discrimination and fear of discrimination (White & Gendron, 2016), individuals in residential settings face correspondingly less control over their environments and may choose to retreat into the closet, the traditional form of safety from the broader community. In all cases, the solutions should include increased and careful research, staff education, and inclusive policies.

Global Health Considerations and Immigrant LGBT Elders

The older LGBT population outside of the United States, especially in low–middle income countries (LMIC), is an extremely heterogeneous cohort. It includes individuals from different cultures and socioeconomic strata, with differing personal sexual identities, languages, perceptions, economic, and even legal statuses. Data on the older LGBT population are scarce or even lacking in some national surveys for LGBT populations in these countries (India HIV/AIDS Alliance, 2012). Textbox 7.2 provides definitional information about different cultural groups within the LGBTQ population.

BOX 7.2

Ethnicity and Culture

African American or *Black* can encompass—and fail to capture—such diverse ethnic or cultural experiences as Afro-American, Afro-Caribbean, or West Indies heritage, or living as a Black immigrant from an African nation or another continent (Harley, 2016).

Native American and Alaska Native peoples represent over 500 language and cultural groups, so their experience as LGBT people will be unique to their cohort and location (Harley & Alston, 2016).

Asian American and Pacific Islander (AAPI) people come from such diverse ethnic and cultural locations as South Asia, including India, Afghanistan, Pakistan, Sri Lanka, and Bangladesh; the Far East; and Southeast Asia (Japan, China, Vietnam, and more than 20 other ethnicities, countries of origin, and language groups). They also include Pacific Islanders, whose historic origin lies in Guam, Hawaii, and other Pacific Islands (Reeves & Bennett, 2003). Fifty-nine percent of the current U.S. AAPI population was born in another country (Pew Research, 2017).

European American as a group represents distinct ethnic, language, and cultural origins and norms from approximately 50 countries (Otis, 2016)—e.g., Great Britain, Ireland, Germany, Italy, Poland, France, Cyprus, Greece, Montenegro, and Latvia.

Latino/a American or *Hispanic* refers to a diverse group of people with ethnic or cultural heritage from 23 different countries including Equatorial Guinea on the continent of Africa. The umbrella term *Latino/a* can include recent immigrants as well as families whose ancestors lived in North America before the founding of the United States (Aguilera-Titus & Deck, 2018).

At present, 72 countries in the world have laws that criminalize homosexuality, of which eight countries have laws that punish homosexuality by death (Carroll & Mendos, 2017). Several countries that have regressive LGBT laws also score poorly on the HelpAge Global AgeWatch Index, a comparative data set examining quality of life in older adults (Scobie et al., 2015). In addition to chronic diseases such as cardiovascular disease and diabetes, LGBT seniors are at an increased risk of being HIV positive (CDC, 2017). HIV may deepen social isolation due to stigma, cause economic insecurity, and worsen health outcomes in the elderly (Tyagi, 2016). Some countries have laws that actively prevent outreach to LGBT populations (Beyrer, 2014). Criminalizing homosexuality makes an already vulnerable population even more vulnerable by hindering HIV prevention and treatment efforts. Complicating matters further is the regressive attitude of health care practitioners toward older LGBT individuals and individuals with HIV (Ama, Shaibu, & Burnette, 2016). This worsens the already existing problem of poor access to health care for the elderly in LMIC countries. Older LGBT individuals in war-torn countries or those escaping persecution may have additional mental health problems such as depression, anxiety, and post-traumatic stress disorder (PTSD). LGBT seniors are also at risk of violence from the community as well as local law enforcement (Gridley & Kothary, 2016).

Older LGBT immigrants in the United States may experience such compounded vulnerability due to their age, sexual orientation, and immigrant status (Sokan & Davis, 2016). Within this group, the legal status of immigrants (refugee, legal immigrant, or undocumented immigrant) has a significant influence on the individual's socioeconomic status and access to health care. LGBT refugees may be doubly marginalized as they may be escaping discriminatory laws in their own country, be ostracized by their family and friends, and find themselves socially isolated (Gridley & Kothary, 2016).

Ethical Service With Vulnerable Older LGBT Adults

Each vulnerable older LGBT adult potentially presents an ethical conundrum to the professional providing services, solutions, policy, or research. An ethical approach to service that is reflective and grounded in action can be transprofessional (Schon, 1983). It is of little utility to attempt a generalized approach to vulnerable LGBT adults without taking into account the external experiences of individual adults or the effects of discrimination, stigma, and lack of access to education and health care as well as the internal psychology of the client, including internalized homophobia, sexism, racism, classism, ableism, and the degree of trust and or alienation toward organizations or society. There are barriers to service with older vulnerable LGBT adults that are both organizational and psychological (Anetzberger et al., 2004), but overcoming these barriers falls within the ethical responsibility of the organizations and professionals providing service delivery and outreach (Teaster & Sokan, 2016).

The editors of this book refer primarily to the application of the principles of biomedical ethics as defined by Beauchamp and Childress (2001). Autonomy, the right for an individual to make his or her own choices; beneficence, the principle of acting with the best interest of the other in mind; nonmaleficence, the principle of "above all, do no harm," as stated in the Hippocratic oath; and justice, the concept that emphasizes fairness and equality among individuals. The profession of counseling considers a fifth grounding concept to be that of fidelity, or the ability to address the ethical imperative through loyalty, the honoring of commitment, and the correct application of the principles of one's profession (Kitchener, 1984).

Ethical service to vulnerable older LGBT adults requires flexibility and curiosity while honoring the five ethical principles. We have an ethical obligation to minimize or eliminate the external barriers to service such as provider ageism or homophobia, lack of identification and outreach, and cultural naiveté. We also have an ethical obligation as individuals and as organizations to anticipate and ameliorate the internal barriers to service that exist on the part of the client: internalized homophobia, distrust of organizations and societal intrusion, and a lack of multigenerational linkage to the greater LGBT society.

There is a historical reluctance on the part of great portions of the LGBT community to self-identify or engage with community organizations. The knowledge and awareness lies with us as professionals; assuming the responsibility for effectively bridging these external and internal barriers to service with the elder LGBT community can allow us to more effectively identify and serve the most vulnerable in these communities. We can begin to apply these ethical principles through discussion applied to the following case studies. Use the case studies to frame your own service, whatever your profession. Applying the knowledge you have acquired with basic ethical principles, write down a plan for service for these two case studies.

CASE STUDY 7.1

Depression and Self-Neglect

Olivia Alvarez is a 77-year-old Puerto Rican immigrant woman who was recently referred to you by her niece, a 57-year-old married woman with whom Olivia has recently come to live. The niece is worried that her never-married aunt may have problems beyond the arthritis and COPD that brought her to live with them in the first place: "We moved her to the suburbs with us after her roommate died and she wasn't able to keep up her house alone. The kids are all gone, we have the room, but she stays in her room, crying more days than not, not eating. We are worried about her."

On meeting Olivia, you find a quiet, reserved woman who makes eye contact hesitantly while she is speaking. She reports that she moved to the United States when she was 20 years old, working in a factory until she retired at age 65. Olivia owned her own home, which she shared with her best friend Mary, a White woman. Olivia looks away when she speaks of Mary and seems wistful. She details a history of high-functioning, blue-collar unmarried women with stable incomes, friends, and a home. A cigarette smoker for most of her life, she describes her increasing struggles with COPD and arthritis pain. Olivia attempts to keep the discussion focused on her health issues rather than her sadness.

What are some of the external influences on Olivia's decisions in her life? She was a Puerto Rican immigrant who arrived 57 years ago; she speaks excellent English as a second language with the barest trace of an accent; she is 77, well into older age status, with chronic health conditions, mobility issues, and suspected major depression due to the loss of a close friend. What would change about this situation if Olivia had been in a romantic or affectional relationship with Mary? If Olivia had lost her life partner, would we look at her differently?

Olivia's case also poses ethical challenges. Olivia's right to privacy versus greater clinician understanding, which might allow more effective help, raises the issue of autonomy. Additionally, issues of beneficence include: How can we validate Olivia's feelings without violating her privacy? Is it possible that Olivia is a lesbian? Does she even understand her friendship with Mary in that way? An important issue of nonmaleficence also arises: If Olivia has kept this a secret from her family, what information is necessary to work with her without being overbearing? Olivia's case can help illustrate the discussions in this chapter. Reflect on your emotional responses and how your understanding may require an increasingly ethical and affirming response to this client.

Olivia may not want anyone else to recognize the significance of her roommate relationship—she may not have understood it in any way as a lesbian relationship, and/or she may be worried about homophobia and discrimination from her family of origin who are now her caregivers. Consider her culture: She is a Puerto Rican who emigrated to the United States in 1940 when beliefs and feelings about gay or lesbian relationships—let alone identities—may have been stigmatized or unthinkable. Olivia may recognize homophobia in her family, or she may perceive this based on her own internalized homophobia that comes as a result of the interaction of cohort, historical effects, and culture.

This intentional decision to allow Olivia her privacy with hopes for increased trust recognizes her autonomy. It is also beneficent because it is in the best interest of the client, and nonmaleficent as this decision in itself causes no immediate harm. Justice is present because it strives to both recognize the history, self-determination, and privacy of the individual while seeking to make a space for the client to self-identify if she chooses. Olivia faces ageism, racism, sexism, and the social erasure represented by social and internalized homophobia. As stated above, these effects, both internal and external, of intersectional experiences are not additive but exponential. We need to be subtle, careful, and thoughtful in approaching vulnerable LGBT older adults such as Olivia Alvarez or Howard Sprague, who is described below.

CASE STUDY 7.2

Mental Health and Relationship Issues

Howard Sprague, a 67-year-old recently retired European American university professor, has been referred for a consultation by his partner of 17 years (husband for 3 years), Krit Songkhla, a 77-year-old Thai immigrant and owner of a small boutique. Krit reports that Howard "hasn't been himself" in the past year, sharing that Howard has become enraged over inconsequential matters and had lost his way twice on the way to usual destinations. Krit reports trying to discuss these issues with Howard, but

Howard has been quite defensive, attributing his behavior to the stress of retiring. Krit reports that Howard has always managed their joint assets and that he acts quite paternally regarding that responsibility. Howard accompanied Krit to the session today and states that he knew it was time for a consult when he "foolishly" invested most of their joint retirement savings following a tip from a friend, losing most of it. They are coming to you for advice. Howard is increasingly vulnerable as he is showing signs of possible mild cognitive impairment; additionally, he is suddenly far less stable financially than they had planned as a couple.

Reflecting on the ethical issues in this case includes examining the autonomy of Howard and Krit to make their financial decisions in the way that they always have. Is the recent loss an aberration of the market or incompetent decision making? Beneficence and justice involve assessing this case in light of the careful considerations of intersectionality. This is an intercultural marriage between a European American man and a Thai man. It is not quite an intergenerational marriage, but age-wise they are a decade apart. Taking into account the cohort of the time at which each was raised, Howard was born in 1951 and entered adolescence in 1964 in Brooklyn, New York; while Krit was born in 1941 in what was then the Kingdom of Thailand, experienced war with Japan during his childhood, and entered adolescence in Bangkok in 1954. He emigrated when he was 30 years old, in 1971. Is Howard's impulsiveness and sudden anger indicative of a mental health concern? An issue of nonmaleficence can include how to examine their financial relationship while respecting their autonomy in making these decisions, including poor ones. Whichever professional service you are providing to this couple, it may be the case that Howard will need a referral for assessment of his cognition and mood. Once Howard's assessment is complete, the couple will need to adjust to their new financial circumstances.

Many current aging LGBT adults are concerned about their futures. They worry that they won't have access to LGBT-competent aging services, they worry about discrimination in assisted living and long-term care, and they worry about having to go back into the closet to stay safe (Sackett, 2018). In many ways, the future of service to vulnerable LGBT older adults belongs to you. Previous generations of professionals seemed to have little recognition of this complex population, let alone an opportunity to develop reflective practice. It's important to develop knowledge and awareness while attempting to develop these skills. You have a small amount of knowledge; an ethical response to service challenges you to query your own awareness of your feelings about service with older LGBT adults and how they may facilitate or impede your own ethical, effective service with this population. How will this information affect your own practice?

DISCUSSION QUESTIONS

1. How will an understanding of the history of a client's culture and ethnicity have an impact on your assessment of an LGBT vulnerable adult?

2. Name at least four ethical principles used for decision making when working with older adults. Give an illustrative example.

3. Older LGBT adults may hold prejudiced beliefs about organizations because of previous experiences of homophobia, forming a psychological, internal barrier to receiving services. Talk about how to form an ethical organizational response.

4. How might racial/ethnic identity affect an older LGBT client's vulnerability?

5. "Can't I just ignore this client's sexual orientation?" Talk about this ethically.

6. How would accurate identification and counting of this underserved population affect ethical services for vulnerable LGBT older adults?

REFERENCES

Aguilera-Titus, A., & Deck, A. F. (2018). Hispanic/Latino presence in the USA and the church. Retrieved from http://www.usccb.org/issues-and-action/cultural-diversity/resources/upload/presence-hispanic-latino.pdf

Ama, N. O., Shaibu, S., & Burnette, J. (2016). Healthcare providers' (HCPs) attitude towards older adults with HIV and AIDS in Botswana. *Journal of AIDS and HIV Research, 8*(10), 136–149. doi:10.5897/JAHR2016.0389

Amadio, D. M., & Chung, Y. B. (2004). Internalized homophobia and substance abuse among lesbian, gay and bisexual persons. *Journal of Gay & Lesbian Social Services, 17*(1), 83–101.

Anetzberger, G. J., Ishler, K. J., Mostade, J., & Blair, M. (2004). A community dialogue series focused on the issues and concerns of older gays and lesbians. *Journal of Gay & Lesbian Social Services, 17*(1), 23–45.

Auldridge, J., & Espinoza, R. (2013). *Health equity and LGBT elders of color: Recommendations for policy & practice.* New York: Services & Advocacy for GLBT Elders (SAGE). Retrieved from https://sageusa.org/resources/publications.cfm?ID=203

Beauchamp, T. L., & Childress, J. (1979). *Principles of biomedical ethics.* New York, NY: Oxford University Press.

Beyrer, C. (2014). Pushback: The current wave of anti-homosexuality laws and impacts on health. *PLoS Medicine, 11*(6). doi:10.1371/journal.pmed.1001658

Brennan-Ing, M., Seidel, L., Larson, B., & Karpiak, S. E. (2013). Social care networks and older LGBT adults: Challenges for the future. *Journal of Homosexuality, 61*(1), 21–52. doi:10.1080/00918369.2013.835235

Burbank, P., & Burkholder, G. (2006). Health issues of lesbian, gay, bisexual and transgender older adults. In P. Burbank (Ed.) *Vulnerable older adults: Health care needs and interventions* (pp. 149–165). New York, NY: Springer.

Cahill, S., South, K., & Spade, J. (2000). *Outing age: Public policy issues affecting gay, lesbian, bisexual, and transgender elders.* New York, NY: Policy Institute of the National Gay and Lesbian Task Force.

Carroll, A., & Mendos, L. R. (2017). *State-sponsored homophobia 2017: A world survey of sexual orientation laws: Criminalization, protection and recognition.* Geneva: International Lesbian, Gay, Bisexual, Trans and Intersex Association (ILGA). Retrieved from http://ilga.org/downloads/2017/ILGA_State_Sponsored_Homophobia_2017_WEB.pdf

Centers for Disease Control and Prevention. (2017). *HIV among people aged 50 and over.* Atlanta, GA: US Department of Health and Human Services. Retrieved from https://www.cdc.gov/hiv/group/age/olderamericans/index.html

Choi, S. K., & Meyer, I. H. (2016). *LGBT aging: A review of research findings, needs, and policy implications.* Los Angeles, CA: Williams Institute.

Culo, S. (2011). Risk assessment and intervention for vulnerable older adults. *British Columbia Medical Journal, 53*(8), 421–425. Retrieved from www.bcmj.org/articles/risk-assessment-and-intervention-vulnerable-older-adults

D'Augelli, A. R., Grossman, A. H., Hershberger, S. L., & O'Connell, T. S. (2001). Aspects of mental health among older lesbian, gay, and bisexual adults. *Aging and Mental Health, 5*(2), 149–158.

Fredriksen-Golden, K. I., Kim, H. J., Barkan, S. E., Muraco, A., & Hoy-Ellis, C. P. (2013). Health disparities among lesbian, gay, and bisexual older adults: Results from a population-based study. *American Journal of Public Health, 103,* 1802–1809. doi:10.2105/ajph.2012.301110

Grant, J. M. (2010). *Outing age 2010: Public policy issues affecting lesbian, bi, gay and transgendered elders.* New York City: National Gay & Lesbian Task Force Policy Institute. Retrieved from www.thetaskforce.org/static_html/downloads/reports/reports/outingage_final.pdf

Grant, J. M., Koskovich, G., Frazer, M. S., & Bjerk, S. (2010). *Outing age 2010: Public policy issues affecting gay, lesbian, bisexual and transgender elders.* Washington, DC: National Gay and Lesbian Task Force.

Gridley, S. J., & Kothary, V. (2016). Immigrant and international LGBT health. In J. M. Ehrenfeld & K. L. Ekstrand (Eds.), *Lesbian, gay, bisexual, and transgender healthcare: A clinical guide to preventive, primary and specialist care* (pp. 391–403). New York, NY: Springer International. Retrieved from https://link.springer.com/chapter/10.1007/978-3-319-19752-4_22

Harley, D. A. (2016). African-American and Black LGBT elders. In D. A. Harley & P. B. Teaster (Eds.), *Handbook of LGBT elders: An interdisciplinary approach to principles, practices and policies* (pp. 105–134). New York, NY: Springer.

Harley, D. A., & Alston, R. J. (2016). American Indian, Alaska native and Canadian aboriginal two-spirit/LGBT elderly. In D. A. Harley & P. B. Teaster (Eds.), *Handbook of LGBT elders: An interdisciplinary approach to principles, practices and policies* (pp. 135–158). New York, NY: Springer.

Hawley, L., & Mostade, S. J. (1999). Transcending the culture of prejudice to a culture of pride as a counselor. In J. McFadden (Ed.), *Transcultural counseling: Bilateral and international perspectives* (2nd ed., pp. 317–339). Alexandria, VA: American Counseling Association.

Herdt, G., Beeler, J., & Rawls, T. W. (1997). Life course diversity among older lesbians and gay men: A study in Chicago. *Journal of Gay, Lesbian and Bisexual Identity, 2,* 231–247.

India HIV/Aids Alliance. (2012). Pehchan baseline survey. Retrieved from https://indiahivaidsalliance.wordpress.com/category/pehchan

Kimmel, D. C. (1978). Adult development and aging: A gay perspective. *Journal of Social Issues, 34,* 43–71. doi:10.1111/j.1540-4560.1978.tb02618.x

Kimmel, D., Rose, T., & Did, S. (2006). *Lesbian, gay, bisexual and transgender aging: Research and clinical perspectives.* New York, NY: Columbia University Press.

Knauer, N. J. (2011). *Gay and lesbian elders: History, law and politics in the United States.* Burlington, VT: Ashgate.

Kitchener, K. S. (1984). Intuition, critical evaluation and ethical principles: The foundation for ethical decisions in counseling psychology. Counseling Psychologist, 12(3), 43–55.

Marks, J. (2008). Race: Past, present and future. In B. Koenig, S. S.-J. Lee, & S. S. Richardson (Eds.), *Revisiting race in a genomic age* (pp. 21–38). New Brunswick, NJ: Rutgers University Press.

MetLife Mature Market Institute, American Society on Aging and Zogby International (2006) Out and Aging: The MetLife Study of Lesbian & Gay Baby Boomers, retrieved from https://www.lgbtagingcenter.org/resources/resource.cfm?r=31

Metlife Mature Market Institute & Lesbian and Gay Aging Issues Network of the American Society on Aging. (2010). Out and aging: The MetLife study of lesbian and gay baby boomers. *Journal of GLBT Family Studies, 6*(1), 40–57.

Otis, M. D. (2016). European LGBT elders. In D. A. Harley & P. B. Teaster (Eds.), *Handbook of LGBT elders: An interdisciplinary approach to principles, practices and policies* (pp. 177–198). New York, NY: Springer.

Pew Research Center. (2017). Five key findings about LGBT Americans. Retrieved from http://www.pewresearch.org/fact-tank/2017/06/13/5-key-findings-about-lgbt-americans

Reeves, T., & Bennett, C. (2003). *The Asian and Pacific Islander population in the United States: March 2002.* Washington, DC: US Census Bureau.

Robinson-Wood, T., & Weber, A. (2016). Deconstructing multiple oppressions among LGBT older adults. In A. D. Harley & P. B. Teaster (Eds.), *Handbook of LGBT elders: An interdisciplinary approach to principles, practices, and policies* (pp. 65–81). New York, NY: Springer.

Sackett, V. (2018, March 27). LGBT adults fear discrimination in long term care. *AARP: Family & Friends.* Retrieved from http://www.aarp.org/home-family/friends-family/info-2018/lgbt-long-term-care-fd.html

Schon, D. (1983). *The reflective practitioner: How professionals think in action.* Burlington, VT: Basic Books.

Scobie, J., Amos, S., Beales, S., Dobbing, S. G., Knox-Vydmanov, C., Mihnovits, A., & Mikkonen-Jeanneret, E. (2015). *Global AgeWatch Index 2015: Insight report summary and methodology.* London: HelpAge International. Retrieved from http://www.helpage.org/global-agewatch/reports/global-agewatch-index-2015-insight-report-summary-and-methodology

Sokan, A. E., & Davis, T. (2016). Immigrant LGBT elders. In D. A. Harley and P. B. Teaster (Eds.), *Handbook of LGBT elders: An interdisciplinary approach to principles, practices and policies* (pp. 261–284). New York, NY: Springer.

Stoukides, J., Holzer, C., Ritzau, J., & Burbank, P. (2006). Health issues of frail older adults. In P. Burbank (Ed.), *Vulnerable older adults: Health care needs and interventions* (pp. 3–19). New York, NY: Springer.

Steptoe, A., Shankar, A., Demakakos, P., & Wardle, J. (2013). Social isolation, loneliness, and all-cause mortality in older men and women. *Proceedings of the National Academy of Sciences of the United States of America, 110*(15), 5797–5801. Retrieved from http://doi.org/10.1073/pnas.1219686110

Teaster, P. B., & Sokan, A. E. (2016). Ethical standards and practices in human services and health care for LGBT elders. In D. A. Harley and P. B. Teaster (Eds.), *Handbook of LGBT elders: An interdisciplinary approach to principles, practices and policies* (pp. 639–656). New York, NY: Springer.

Teaster, P. B., White, J. T., & Kim, S. (2016). Family relationships of older LGBT adults. In D. A. Harley & P. B. Teaster (Eds.), *Handbook of LGBT elders: An interdisciplinary approach to principles, practices and policies* (pp. 43–64). New York, NY: Springer.

Tyagi, P. (2016). *HIV in India: Why are older people the forgotten story?* London: HelpAge International. Retrieved from http://www.helpage.org/blogs/prakash-tyagi-869/hiv-in-india-why-are-older-people-the-forgotten-story-1024

US Naval Institute. (2018). Key dates in US policy on gay men and women in military service. Retrieved from https://www.usni.org/news-and-features/dont-ask-dont-tell/timeline

White, J. T., & Gendron, T. L. (2016). LGBT elders in nursing homes, long-term care facilities and residential communities. In D. A. Harley & P. B. Teaster (Eds.), *Handbook of LGBT elders: An interdisciplinary approach to principles, practices and policies* (pp. 417–437). New York, NY: Springer.

Resources

LGBT Aging Center: https://lgbtagingcenter.org/resources/resources.cfm?a=3

8

RELIGION

Abebaw Mengistu Yohannes, PhD
Department of Physical Therapy, Azusa Pacific University, Azusa, California

Harold G. Koenig, MD
Duke University Medical Center, Durham, North Carolina
King Abdulaziz University, Jeddah, Saudi Arabia
School of Public Health, Ningxia Medical University, Yinchuan, China

KEYWORDS

religion	depression
elderly	anxiety
religiosity	ethical
chronic condition	quality of life
social support	spirituality

Overview

Despite great medical advances in treating chronic conditions, a significant proportion of older people are living with incurable pain and distress, terminal disease, and increased physical disability that impairs quality of life. Given these challenges, older people often seek meaning in life or desire for a transcendent connection. Spirituality is an important element of person-centered care. There is sufficient evidence to suggest that religious or spiritual involvement is related to better mental, social, behavioral, and physical health. Thus, evaluating spiritual distress (suffering) may help in tailoring appropriate interventions according to the patient's wishes and needs. Furthermore, religion/spirituality may be an underappreciated resource that health care professionals could employ to enhance holistic patient-centered and integrated care of chronically ill, seriously ill, and terminally ill older patients. This chapter advocates for the inclusion of religion as part of the assessment and treatment of vulnerable older adults, specifically incorporating ethical issues as part of routine clinical practice. It also highlights barriers, practical assessment approaches, and specific strategies for providing spiritual care to those in later life.

Background

In 2010, persons over age 65 years numbered 524 million worldwide. That number is projected to triple to over 1.5 billion by 2050 (National Institute on Aging, 2011). At the same time, there will be a three- to four-fold increase, respectively, in persons aged 75 and older and 85 and older living with chronic conditions. (Mather, 2016; Wolff, Starfield, & Anderson, 2002). We should celebrate longevity while recognizing and preparing for the potential consequences of chronic diseases, with an increasing disease burden to individuals and society involving escalating health care costs and an expanding of both formal and informal care needs. Traversing a long-life course means encountering a myriad of important life events, including the loss of close friends and family members, a dwindling social network, suffering from incurable diseases such as dementia, and succumbing to terminal diseases such as cancer. Elderly people are increasingly vulnerable to these important life events and may experience social isolation, disorientation, desperation, fear, and often dependency on family and others, sometimes accompanied by loss of hope (Zimmer et al., 2016).

Despite great medical advances in treating chronic conditions, a significant proportion of older people are living with incurable pain and distress, terminal disease, and increased physical disability that impairs quality of life. Older people often seek meaning in life or desire for a transcendent connection. Expressions of religiosity and spirituality and higher involvement in religious and spiritual activities are common at this time, significantly more so than among younger people. For example, a recent World Values Survey examined religiosity in the 13 most highly populated countries, representing 60% of the global population. The percentage of individuals older than 60 who self-rated as religious ranged from 16.6% in China to 100% in Pakistan (Inglehart et al., 2014). Religious people derive significant benefits from their religious activities, which help build social ties and support networks, as well as increase disease-prevention and health-promotion behaviors; for example, reducing the prevalence of cigarette smoking and alcohol use disorders (Agrawal, Grant, Haber, & Madden, 2017; Idler, Blevins, Kiser, & Hogue, 2017; Meyers, Brown, Grant, & Hasin, 2017).

Evidence suggests older people who are religious and engage in a public religious activity at least weekly, despite battling chronic diseases, exhibit higher levels of life satisfaction and better psychological well-being and coping mechanisms compared to nonreligious elders as shown in Table 8.1. Patients report that when their doctors involve them in spiritual discussions, they feel that they are receiving more holistic care and feel empowered that their religious beliefs have been addressed as part of medical management; they also feel stronger doctor–patient relationships (Ellis, Vinson, & Ewigman, 1999; Hebert, Jenckes, Ford, O'Connor, & Cooper, 2001; MacLean et al., 2003; Meyers et al., 2017; Puchalski & Ferrell, 2010;).

This is where religion often separates those who cope from those who despair or experience deep remorse, frustration, or anger in the midst of adverse life events. This chapter explores the role of religion and spirituality in the life of older people with chronic diseases, and examines the impact of religion on physical, psychological, and emotional hardships in the context of their social networks. It then examines how to incorporate religion and spirituality during a patient encounter with a case example,

TABLE 8.1   The Potential Benefits of Religiosity and Spirituality

- Lower levels of depression
- Lower levels of anxiety
- Higher rates of resilient reintegration following traumatic life events
- Positive relationships with friends and relatives
- Better life satisfaction or happiness
- Reduced all causes of mortality
- Better lifestyle (e.g., not smoking or indulging with alcohol)
- Better coping mechanism with adverse life events
- Experiencing peace and comfort from God

including ethical issues and best practices to address the spiritual needs of chronically ill older adults, especially those toward the end of life.

Defining Religiosity and Spirituality

Determining the difference between religiosity and spirituality is difficult for any single culture or society. These concepts have similar common characteristics that involve personal information and the search for ultimate truth (Koenig, 2012). A religious person often defines himself or herself as being spiritual, so that spirituality often encompasses religiosity (Koenig, 2012). However, religion around the world generally includes specific foundational principles that are organized around distinct systems of beliefs, practices, and rituals within a community of believers.

Spiritual care is one of the domains in palliative care that includes attending to the spiritual, religious and existential issues in patient care (World Health Organization [WHO], n.d.). In 2009, a consensus experts conference report defined spirituality as an "'aspect of humanity that refers to the way individuals seek and express meaning and purpose and the way they experience their connectedness to the moment, to self, to others, to nature and/or to the significant or sacred" (Puchalski, et al, 2009, page 887). On the other hand, religiosity is described as a means by which individuals express their spirituality by the adoption of values, beliefs, and ritual practices that offer answers to major questions about life and death (Lai et al., 2016; Puchalski, 2012; Puchalski et al., 2009). Pargament (1997) defines religion as a process, a search for significance in ways related to the sacred. The sacred encompasses the concepts of God and the divine transcendent, but it is not limited to notions of higher powers. These attributes or qualities become sanctified by their associations with or representation of holiness or transition from hopelessness to wholeness (Haug, Dabnbolt, Kvigne, & DeMarinis, 2016; Milsten, 2008). It is much easier to quantify religiosity than spirituality. Religiosity can be measured in objective ways, using frequency of activity such as a ritualistic practice and/or the attendance at places of worship. In contrast, spirituality is more difficult to precisely measure as it is based on indirect personal experiential terms such as the search for meaning, truth, peace, personal fulfilment, and connectedness with others, as well as feeling a personal relationship to a higher power (Zinnbauer et al., 1997). Existential well-being is a related but separate concept not necessarily connected with a higher power. It is a term which we define along the lines provided by MacDonald

(2000): Existential well-being "pertains to spirituality as expressed through a sense of meaning and purpose for existence and a perception of self as being competent and able to cope with the difficulties of life and limitations of human existence." (MacDonald, 2000, page 187)

Religion and Population-Based Studies

Studies have shown an association between higher levels of public religious attendance and lower risk of depressive symptoms (Koenig et al., 1998; Yohannes, Koenix, Baldwin, & Connolly, 2008) and mortality among U.S. adults (Musick, House, & Williams, 2004; Li, Stampfer, Williams, & VanderWeele, 2016). A recent 10-year longitudinal health retirement survey study (Idler et al., 2017) of individuals age 50 or older found that religious attendance lowered mortality risk by 40% compared to nonattendance. Furthermore, another longitudinal survey (Li et al., 2016) over 16 years of follow-up showed that in women (n = 74,534), frequently attending religious services lowered the risks of all-cause mortality by 33%, cardiovascular mortality by 27%, and cancer mortality by 21% compared to women who never attended religious services. In contrast, specific religious affiliation was not associated with risk of mortality.

Terminal Disease and Religion

Living with incurable chronic disease is challenging. Such disease dramatically affects every dimension of physical, emotional, psychological, social, and spiritual life (Selman, Young, Vermandere, Stirling, & Leget, 2014). Spirituality is an important aspect of person-centered medical care, particularly for patients with cancer as they try to cope with their illness from diagnosis through treatment (Puchalski, 2010). A diagnosis of cancer often heralds a shortened lifespan and therefore may spark deeper existential issues that could trigger profound suffering and distress. In a qualitative study (n = 15), Pascal and Endacott (2010) explored ethical and existential challenges and experiences of older adults following a diagnosis of cancer. Participants described existential challenges that included experiencing anxiety and uncertainty about both recurrent and metastatic disease. Furthermore, uncertainty served as a wake-up call and precipitated ethical challenges (Pascal & Endacott, 2010). Such challenges involved finding meaning in surviving and questioning morals, values, and relationships. This type of ethical crisis strikes to the core of human beliefs, violating basic assumptions about our sense of control and ability to predict the future (Brenan, 2006; Leung & Esplen, 2010). In essence, this kind of crisis is emotionally draining and psychologically devastating, often involving social isolation along with ambiguity, loss of freedom, and fear of death (Brenan, 2006). Hence, health care professionals need to be ready to respond when the patient raises these types of concerns either in a clinic or in a hospital setting and provide appropriate support and emotional space. It may also involve referral to a member of the clergy for a meaningful spiritual conversation. Failure to respond to these types of concerns and lack of engagement by providers may be considered an ethical violation (Benzen & Berg, 2005).

The WHO defines palliative care as an approach that improves the quality of life of patients and their families facing problems associated with life-threatening illness, through the prevention and relief of suffering by means of early identification, assessment, and treatment of pain; this type of care integrates the physical, psychosocial, and spiritual aspects of patient care (WHO, n.d.).

Studies have shown that early referral to palliative care and intervention may improve quality of life and reduce symptom intensity and depressive symptoms, and increase personal satisfaction with care in patients with advanced cancer (Greer et al., 2018; Haun et al., 2017; McDonald et al., 2017; Vantbutsele et al., 2018). However, a review of the literature suggests that the effects on mortality and major depression are uncertain (Haun et al., 2017). In contrast, a recent randomized controlled study that investigated the benefits of palliative care in patients with advanced cancer and higher levels of depression who received intervention had a lower mortality risk (Hazard ratio = 0.963, confidence interval [0.933, 0.993], p = .018) even when controlling for demographics, cancer site, and illness-related variables (Prescott et al., 2017).

Scope of Spiritual Beliefs in the United States

The importance of spirituality to patients and health care professionals (physicians and nurses) is accepted by both popular opinion polls and clinical practice guidelines. In 2017, a Gallup survey found that approximately 80% of U.S. adults believe in God or a universal spirit and that 75% consider religion important in their life (Newport, 2017). Over 90% of medically ill hospitalized patients believe spiritual health is as important as physical health, while 77% expressed positive attitudes toward physicians who addressed spiritual issues (King and Bushwick, 1994), and over 40% used faith to cope with their illness (King & Bushwick, 1994). Failure to respond to these types of concerns and lack of engagement may mean the provider is failing to address the ethical principle of nonmaleficence (do no harm). These attitudes are particularly paramount for older people who are hospitalized with terminal illness and approaching death, some of whom may wish to discuss their faith and even have their physician pray with them (Koenig, 1998). It is important to balance patient desires (self-determination) with the physician's beliefs/religion, which may come into play when the physician does not share the patient's religious affiliation or religious views. Religion and spirituality may or may not be sources of comfort, support, and healing for older adults with life-threatening illness (Hebert et al., 2001), and it is the health professional's job to determine the patient's preferences. The Joint Commission now encourages a spiritual assessment upon hospital admission and requires it for certain patients, like those receiving palliative care or those admitted for substance abuse problems (Joint Commission, 2010). Despite this guidance, spiritual assessment and spiritual care provisions for older people with serious or life-threatening illnesses remain underutilized.

Barriers to Spiritual Care

There are several patient, physician, and administrative barriers that prevent patient-centered spiritual care as shown in Table 8.2. Potential patient barriers include lack of knowledge about the opportunity to receive spiritual care and fear that their physician may be uninterested or unable to address their spiritual needs. In contrast, physicians often report lack of time to do so, difficulty in identifying patients who desire a discussion of spiritual issues, and the misunderstanding that addressing spiritual concerns is not part of the physician's role (Ellis, 1999). In addition, overburdened health care professionals who are primarily responsible for medical care tasks often leave staff to address other needs of patients including spiritual care (Koenig, 2014). System failures may include inadequate spiritual care training for physicians and staff and lack of recognition of spiritual issues in vulnerable patients, as well as employers' perspectives that emphasize productivity instead of holistic patient care (Koenig, 2014; Post, Puchalski, & Larsen, 2000). In contrast, potential facilitators to spiritual assessment and provision may include a good relationship with the physician, shared life priorities, and physician personality (e.g., calm, down to earth, compassionate, assuring, and caring), physician knowledge about spiritual health, qualities of openness and approachability, and use of a screening tool to assess spirituality (Ellis & Campbell, 2004).

TABLE 8.2   Barriers to Spiritual Assessment and Provision

Patient-level barriers

- Lack of motivation
- Vulnerability
- Not believing in spiritual care
- Cognitive impairment
- Distrust of doctors
- Fear that doctors are uninterested in spirituality (of the patient or the physician himself or herself)
- Fear of disclosing deeper issues in their life
- Comorbidities (e.g., severe of depression or dementia)

Health care professionals' (physicians, nurses, etc.) barriers

- Time constraints
- Inadequate training in spiritual care
- Low regard for patient spiritual care
- Overburdened by the workload
- Not knowing professional boundaries
- Uncertainty in identifying patients with spiritual needs
- Concerns about projecting beliefs onto patients
- Not utilizing spiritual screening instruments
- Negative attitudes of peers toward spiritual care

Organizational-level barriers

- Lack of adequately trained clergy
- Emphasis on physician productivity rather than patient-centered care
- Lack of space and environment for spiritual concerns
- Limited access to support professional development in spiritual care
- Lack of equipoise between effort and reward

Ethical Issues

Spiritual care is part of a holistic approach to patient-focused care. There is increasing interest in and recognition that both in research and clinical practice, clinicians must address a patient's medical condition in terms of autonomy, beneficence, maleficence, and justice (Torry, 2017).

Autonomy

In critically ill older patients, there is concern regarding autonomy when providing spiritual care to those patients admitted to intensive care units with advanced stages of cancer. It is both ethical and important to discuss religious beliefs and/or practices, whether or not the patient initiates such a discussion. In this scenario, the health care practitioner needs to make no assumptions; rather, the practitioner should receive information from the patient by conducting a spiritual history and responding accordingly. In one survey (Ellis, 1994), over 50% of the physicians were concerned about projecting their own beliefs onto patients. Given this concern, physicians should carefully and respectfully maintain a patient-centered perspective—not projecting their own beliefs onto patients but instead initiating a spiritual history and allowing the patient to guide this discussion. In contrast, proselytizing patients by forcing their own beliefs on vulnerable patients is highly ethically questionable. Furthermore, the physician should not imply that religious involvement is necessary to stay healthy or that those who become sick don't have enough faith; such implications add to a patient's suffering. As older people become physically ill, they are most likely to be vulnerable and reliant on religion as it provides "coping resources include powerful cognitions (strongly held beliefs) that give meaning to difficult life circumstances and provide a sense of purpose" (Koenig, 2012, p.7)

Furthermore, respect for the autonomy of the patient requires that health care professionals assist the patient to make his or her own informed choices. For example, if by fasting a patient might compromise his or her recovery and adversely affect his or her health, then the provider has a duty to provide sufficient information to the patient that will enable him or her to decide whether to continue fasting as part of a religious practice. The provider should be nonjudgmental when the patient's values conflict with his or her own beliefs and discuss the issue with compassion and empathy.

Beneficence and Nonmaleficence Issues

It is important to recognize ethical concerns about the positive correlation between spirituality and various indices of health. As mentioned earlier, critics challenge such findings based on methodological issues and question whether religious activity will promote health or that sickness will result from a lack of faith. (Koenig, Larson, & Larson, 2001). Nevertheless, several well-conducted cross-sectional and longitudinal studies have demonstrated small to moderate benefits from religious involvement in improving longevity, reducing pain and anxiety, enhancing quality of life, and promoting health behaviors (Koenig, 2012).

For example, a patient who identifies as a Jehovah's Witness may need a blood transfusion to undergo heart surgery, but the patient's religious beliefs do not allow for such medical treatment. In such a scenario, the negative consequences (i.e., including adverse events such as death) must be clearly explained in the presence of witnesses and the patient's decision must be documented in the medical notes. If the patient has the capacity to do so, he or she ultimately has the right to make their own medical decisions. The physician's role is to provide appropriate and complete information about the procedure and be respectful of the patient's decisions, listen, gather information, and accept the patient's choice.

Ethical principles of beneficence and nonmaleficence carry over into soliciting participation in research. As with other kinds of research, spiritual care research should include an explanation of the potential risks (nonmaleficence), benefits, the nature of the research (including that participation is entirely voluntary), and assure that the study subject/patient has adequate time to consult with family and friends (and his or her physician, in some cases) prior to engaging in the study. It is imperative that the study subject/patient gives written informed signed consent prior to entering into the study.

Justice

The provider should allocate a similar amount of time to discussing the benefits and risks of either addressing spiritual issues in the context of the medical encounter or referring the patient to pastoral care for the addressing of patients' spiritual needs. This should be done whether the physician initiates such discussions or whether the patient brings up the subject. It is unethical to exclude individuals from spiritual care because of their color, gender, ethnicity, religion, or sexual orientation (Ellis & Campbell, 2004). The purpose of the spiritual assessment is to identify spiritual beliefs, needs, practices, and resources that may positively impact the patient's health (Saguil & Phelps, 2012). For health care professionals, incorporating patient spirituality brings the potential benefits of improving communication, increasing resiliency, and providing comfort to severely ill patients in the midst of their distressing situations.

There are many older adults who believe in God or a higher power, as well as many who are atheist or agnostic (does not think it is possible to determine if there is a god), who reside in long-term care settings (e.g., nursing homes or assisted living facilities). Therefore, health care providers in these facilities need to be trained to take a spiritual history so that they can identify the spiritual needs of patients and develop a plan for someone to address them. Health care professionals and staff should also encourage residents to continue to build relationships within their communities of faith (Richards, 2005). Furthermore, when care providers address spiritual needs in these long-term facilities, the residents may develop a sense of hope and peace (Leeuwen, Tiesinga, Jochemasen, & Post, 2007). In order to support patient spirituality in these settings, (a) the institutions need to incorporate spirituality into their mission and vision statements; (b) assessing and addressing need to be part of the services they provide; and (c) spiritual resources must be made available to residents, including spiritual activities and reading materials (Meyers, 2006). Finally, staff need to be trained to take a spiritual history in order to foster a culture of spiritual support in their workplace, so that they can create a more positive and enriching environment for residents to live in (Meyers, 2006).

Unmet Spiritual Needs

In a recent U.S. study (Gonclaves, Lucchetti, Menezes, & Vallada, 2015) that compared the informants' reports about the end-of-life care for patients age 65 years and older in a two-time frame point (2000 and 2011–2013), spiritual care remains unaddressed, for 72.4% and 58.3% of individuals, respectively. In a separate study conducted in Switzerland (Teno, Freedman, Kasper, Gozalo, & Mor, 2015), a cross-sectional analysis revealed that the factors that contribute to poor quality of life in elderly hospitalized patients 65 years and older undergoing post-acute rehabilitation were increased comorbidities, elevated depressive symptoms, and unmet spiritual needs. This underscores the relevance of spirituality/religiosity as an essential component of quality of life in medically ill elderly patients. Initiating and addressing unmet spiritual needs for elderly patients with advanced incurable diseases has the potential to improve patients' health-related quality of life and in alleviating existential distress (such as grappling with the nature of existence and of knowledge we will die) (Bornet, Truchard, Rochat, Pasquier, & Monod, 2017; Leung & Esplen, 2010). Practical approaches to improving unmet spiritual needs in older hospitalized patients involve the use of simple questionnaires such as the Spiritual Distress Assessment Tool (Monod, Martin, Spencer, Rochat, & Bula, 2012). It has five items, and scores on a 4-point scale range, from 0 (no evidence of unmet spiritual needs) to 3 (evidence of severe spiritual need) with a maximum score of 15 points. Spiritual distress is defined as a score > 5. It is a valid and reliable tool. However, its efficacy in an intervention is unknown. Findings do suggest that the single question *Are you at peace?* on a visual analog scale that ranges from 0 to 10 provided the level of peacefulness in patients with serious illnesses (Steinhauser et al., 2006) and strongly correlates with emotional and spiritual well-being of older people with physical illness. In addition, the HOPE (H- sources of hope, strength, comfort, meaning, peace, love, and connections; O- the role of organized religion for the patient; P- personal spirituality and practices; E- effects of on medical care and end of life decisions) (Anadarajah & Hight, 2001) can be used for detailed spiritual assessment. These questions provide a formal tool to assess a patient's spirituality and facilitate discussion with the patient in a clinical practice setting. Thus, addressing spiritual issues may help health care professionals to tap into a potential resource of healing and/or coping (Saguil & Phelps, 2012).

Ethical Practice Steps for Integrating Spiritual Assessment Into Patient Care

The pastoral care field concerns the assessment and addressing of spiritual needs among medically ill patients. Although there is still a lack of consensus over the core of what constitutes a spiritual need and how best to measure that, most health care professionals in the field advocate assessing the following: (a) taking a spiritual history; (b) listening actively to identify patient fears and hopes; (c) practicing compassionate care; (d) being attentive to all dimensions of patient and family needs; (e) incorporate spiritual practices as part of the care plan; and (f) involving chaplains as members of the interdisciplinary health care team (Koenig, 2002; Koenig, 2013; Koenig, 2018; Puchalski, 2001; Saguil & Phelps, 2012).

The following points may guide as a step-by-step approach to integrate spiritual assessment into the care of the patient.

1. Spiritual history: It is worth explaining why a spiritual assessment is important and the positive impact this assessment may have on patient health and identifying the help the patient may need as part of his or her care plan. Incorporating a spiritual history during an initial new patient evaluation is important, e.g., prior to hospital admission. When probing the patient, the following questions may help to facilitate discussions of spiritual needs: "Do you have a religious or spiritual support system to help you in times of need? Do you have any religious beliefs that might influence your medical decisions? Do you have any other spiritual concerns that would like someone to address?" (Koenig, 2002). In addition, it creates an opportunity for conversation about values and beliefs and uncovers coping and support mechanisms patients may have such as family and church. This helps the health care professional to recognize when cases need to be referred to chaplains or counselors for unmet spiritual needs to be addressed. The spiritual history should be patient centered, and proselytizing and ridiculing patients' beliefs are unacceptable (Koenig, 2002; Puchalski, 2001).

2. Listening actively to a patient's fears and hopes: It is paramount to listen actively in order to find out whether a patient derives comfort from his or her religious and spiritual beliefs. This encompasses spending time with the patient and letting him or her talk—not providing advice or trying to find solutions (Saguil & Phelps, 2012). It is critical that when discussing spiritual issues such as fears and hopes with the patient, the health care professional should listen actively and support where appropriate, without guiding or leading the patient to make a decision (Koenig, 2002; Puchalski, 2001). The health care professional (e.g. physician or nurse) should be sensitive and affirmative when the patient raises spiritual issues so that he or she feels honored, respected, and valued in a clinical setting. Puchalski (2001) states compassionate care requires the health care professional to walk with people in the midst of their pain and spiritual struggle, to be partners with patients rather than experts dictating information to them.

3. Being attentive to all dimensions of patient and family need: Psychosocial issues including physical, psychological, and emotional issues need to be addressed as part of a holistic care plan in order to deal with spiritual concerns for the patient and family. In addition, it is advisable to create a safe place and environment that allows the patient to initiate discussion of spiritual issues (Koenig, 2002; Puchalski, 2001). Furthermore, when identifying spiritual issues from the patient, it is advisable to make an effort to incorporate them as a part of patient care plan. This involves referring the patient to chaplains or pastoral counselors for in-depth spiritual support and treatment.

4. Accommodate: In acute hospital or other inpatient settings, accommodate the environment to meet the patient's spiritual needs, such as ensuring that

someone provides a prayer rug for a Muslim patient or a priest provides Holy Communion to a Catholic patient (Koenig, 2002; Saguil & Phelps, 2012).

5. Avoid value imposition: Being clear about respect for the patient's values and experience will help to avoid the problems of coercion or proselytizing (Koenig, 2002; Puchalski, 2001; Saguil & Phelps, 2012).

As the health care professional, be aware of the power imbalance. This is especially important when dealing with critically ill patients about spiritual issues. It is important to show empathy, compassion, and understanding for the patient's values and beliefs in order to build trust and create a conducive environment for effective communication (Koenig, 2002; Puchalski, 2001; Saguil & Phelps, 2012).

There are clear boundaries that physicians or allied health care professionals should be aware of and respect; for example, do not propose religion to nonreligious patients or force a spiritual history if the patient is not religious, unless the patient raised it during consultation. It is important not to pray with a patient prior taking a spiritual history unless prompted by the patient. Finally, the activity should be patient centered and patient directed (Koenig, 2013). For a more detailed description of best practices with regard to integrating spirituality into the care of older patients, the reader is referred elsewhere (Koenig, 2013).

There are some important ethical issues that require in-depth exploration beyond the scope of this chapter. For example, there may be situations where physicians will not order certain treatments based on their own religious beliefs. A physician with strong beliefs regarding the preservation of life might be asked to prescribe life-ending drugs in a state that permits this, or he or she might not want to give a do-not-resuscitate order. In such circumstances, the physician or staff may need to refer a patient to another provider who will do what the patient wishes (after psychiatric and palliative care evaluations to rule out treatable causes for the patient's disease). Basically, the principle is that all actions should be patient centered; if health professionals feel that their religious beliefs conflict with what the patient wants done, then they need to provide alternative ways to meet the patient's needs. Indeed, religion/spirituality may play an important role in addressing these important decisions (e.g., legal and social issues), and this needs to be thoroughly discussed with the patient's family and clergy.

Suggestions for Research

Given the potential for religious and spiritual interventions to enhance mental, social, behavioral, and physical health among older persons, it is important to gain a better understanding of the connection between spirituality, religiosity, and health in older adults from every ethnic, cultural, and religious background. Thus, future research should focus on examining longitudinal associations, the mechanisms by which religiosity and spirituality impact on health outcomes, and the conducting of clinical trials to test the efficacy of spiritually integrated interventions. For more information in this regard, see Koenig (2018).

CONCLUDING OBSERVATIONS

Many older adults have religious beliefs and practices that they use to cope with illness and make sense of the existential struggles that often accompany aging. These beliefs often influence the medical decisions that patients make; and for the many reasons described in this chapter, health professionals should assess and address the spiritual needs of older adults whom they encounter in health care settings. Religion/spirituality may be an underappreciated resource that health care professionals could tap into that will enhance the care of chronically ill, seriously ill, and terminally ill older patients. The vast majority of research suggests that religious or spiritual involvement is related with better mental, social, behavioral, and physical health. Nevertheless, further research is needed to examine the benefits and risks for religious/spiritual interventions, as these may prove to enhance the health care and quality of life of older adults.

CASE STUDY 8.1

A 70-year-old man who lives alone in an apartment, presented to an outpatient medical clinic with chronic obstructive pulmonary disease (COPD) and complaints of gradually worsening exertional dyspnea and chest discomfort. For 4 weeks, he had not been able to do light household work. The patient's medical history indicated that he had a pulmonary embolism in 2016 and treatment for lung cancer in 2017, and he had a history of depression and anxiety symptoms as of 2015. His current medications included diazepam, albuterol, simvastatin, calcium/vitamin D, amitriptyline, and Tiotropium.

The patient reported that he often felt restless and anxious because of dyspnea on exertion and experienced feelings of tiredness. The medications he was taking, however, did not help to relieve his dyspnea, depression, or anxiety. He reported to the physician that his life had ended since the beginning of his COPD 15 years ago. He said he felt sad and hopeless, had lost 10 pounds in the past 8 weeks, had little appetite, and felt quite fragile. A recent chest X-ray and biopsy showed a benign tumor in his right lung.

When the physician took a spiritual history, the man said that he attended church services only twice a year on Christmas and Easter. He reported that he felt God was punishing him for his bad behavior in the past, and he felt guilty about it. He says that he occasionally prays for relief, but there has been no change in his condition. He indicated that he is tired of living and wishes that God would take him home. During the clinic visit, he expressed his frustration and despair to the doctor and asked him what he should do. What would be the next step to address this patient's physical and spiritual problems?

Reviewing the Case

The spiritual history revealed that the patient was struggling with a number of spiritual and emotional concerns. Possible recommendations could include treatment of his depression and referral to a chaplain to address his spiritual concerns. If the doctor felt that the patient's COPD was terminal, then referral to the palliative care team (which hopefully would include a chaplain) would also be appropriate in an attempt to provide holistic care. The chaplain would conduct a spiritual assessment of his or her own and then address the patient's frustration and resentment that he may have toward God. The chaplain is likely to do a lot of listening, and may—if the patient desires—include prayer and even referral to a local church of the patient's denomination in order to broaden his social network and increase his social support over the long term.

CASE STUDY 8.2

A 65-year-old Muslim patient has type 2 diabetes and is insulin dependent. This is the month of Ramadan. She comes to the clinic for a routine check-up for her diabetes. Is it appropriate for the physician, who knows that the patient is Muslim, to ask about her fasting?

Reviewing the Case

It is important for the physician to have a conversation with the patient about her fasting by asking how the role of religion plays out in her life and whether she is fasting for Ramadan. If religion is important to her and she is fasting (or planning to fast), then the physician should show respect for her religious beliefs in an atmosphere of kindness and compassion, but should nevertheless explain the potential health consequences on her diabetes of fasting. The patient might or might not be aware that fasting during Ramadan is not obligatory if doing so would adversely affect her health. If the patient does not know or is not sure, the physician might suggest that she consult with the imam of the mosque that she attends. Alternatively (or in addition), the physician may adjust her insulin dose so that this lowers her risk of hypoglycemic episodes during her times of fasting. The important points here are that the clinician would take a spiritual history, show respect for the patient's religious beliefs, and work with the patient within the context of her faith to optimize her physical health.

DISCUSSION QUESTIONS

1. Why do you think religion/spirituality is important for older people with terminal disease?

2. Is there evidence that addressing spiritual issues is as important as treating physical health?

3. How confident are you in taking a spiritual history when evaluating a patient with advanced lung cancer?

4. What are the strengths and weaknesses of available literature in terms of spiritual care provision for critically ill elderly patients?

5. How would you incorporate (integrate) spiritual care as part of routine clinical practice in your chosen field in the future?

6. What did you learn after reading and reflecting on this chapter about religion and physical health?

7. As a group, discuss a care plan for addressing unmet spiritual needs for older people from different faith groups (e.g., for patients with Muslim or Christian faith).

REFERENCES

Agrawal, A., Grant, J. D., Haber, J. R., Madden, P. A.F., Heath, A.C., Bucholz, K. K., Sartor, C.E. Differences between White and Black young women in the relationship between religious service attendance and alcohol involvement. American Journal of Addiction 2017; 26(5); 437–435.

Anadarajah, G., & Hight, E. (2001). Spirituality and medical practice: Using the HOPE questions as a practical tool for spiritual assessment. *American Family Physician, 63*(1), 81–89.

Benzen, E., & Berg, A. (2005). The level of and relation between hope, hopelessness and fatigue in patients and family members in palliative care. *Palliative Medicine, 19*, 234–240.

Bornet, M.-A., Truchard, E. R., Rochat, E., Pasquier, J., & Monod, S. (2017). Factors associated with quality of life in elderly hospitalized patients undergoing post-acute rehabilitation: A cross-sectional analytical study in Switzerland. *BMJ Open, 7,* e018600.

Brenan, J. (2006). A conflation of existential and spiritual beliefs. *Psycho-Oncology, 15,* 933–934.

Ellis, M. R., & Campbell, J. D. (2004). Patients' views about discussing spiritual issues with primary care physicians. *Southern Medical Journal, 97*(12), 1158–1165.

Ellis, S. (1999). The patient-centred care model: holistic/multiprofessional/reflective. *British Journal of Nursing, 8*(5), 296–301.

Ellis, M. R., Vinson, D. C., & Ewigman, B. (1999). Addressing spiritual concerns of patients: Family physicians' attitudes and practices. *Journal of Family Practice, 48*(2), 105–109.

Gonclaves, J. P. B., Lucchetti, G., Menezes, P. R., & Vallada, H. (2015). Religious and spiritual interventions in mental health care: A systematic review and meta-analysis of randomized controlled trials. *Psychological Medicine, 45*, 2937–2949.

Greer, J. A., Jacobs, J. M., El-Jawahri, A., Nipp, R. D., Gallagher, E. R., Pirl, W. F., ... & Temel, J. S. (2018). Role of patient coping strategies in understanding the effects of early palliative care on quality of life and mood. *Journal of Clinical Oncology, 36*(1), 53–60.

Haug, K. S., Dabnbolt, L., Kvigne, K., & DeMarinis, V. (2016). Older people with incurable cancer: Existential meaning-making from a life-span perspective. *Palliative and Supportive Care, 14*(1), 20–32.

Haun, M. W., Estel, S., Rücker, G., Friederich, H. C., Villalobos, M., Thomas, M., & Hartmann, M. (2017). Early palliative care for adults with advanced cancer. *Cochrane Database of Systematic Reviews, 6,* CD011129.

Hebert, R. S., Jenckes, M. W., Ford, D. E., O'Connor, D. R., & Cooper, L. A. (2001). Patient perspectives on spirituality and the patient-physician relationship. *Journal of General Internal Medicine, 16,* 685–692.

Idler, E., Blevins, J., Kiser, M., & Hogue, C. (2017). Religion, a social determinant of mortality? A 10-year follow-up of the Health and Retirement Study. *PLoS One, 20*(12), e0189134.

Inglehart, R., Haerpfer, C., Moreno, A., Welzel, C., Kizilova, K., Diez-Madrano, J., ... & Puranen, B. (Eds.). (2014). *Wave 6 2010–2014 Official Aggregate v.20150418.* Madrid: World Values Survey Association. Retrieved from http://www.worldvaluessurvey.org/WVSDocumentationWV6.jsp

Joint Commission. (2010). Advancing effective communication, cultural competence, and patient- and family-centered care: Roadmap for hospitals. Oakbrook Terrace, IL. Author. Retrieved from https://www.jointcommission.org/assets/1/6/ARoadmap-forHospitalsfinalversion727.pdf

King, D. E., & Bushwick, B. (1994). Beliefs and attitudes of hospital inpatients about faith healing and prayer. *Journal of Family Practice, 39*(4), 349–352.

Koenig, H. G. (1998). Religious attitudes and practices of hospitalized medically ill older adults. *International Journal of Geriatric Psychiatry, 13*(4), 213–224.

Koenig, H. G. (2002). An 83-year old woman with chronic illness and strong beliefs. *Journal of the American Medical Association, 288*(4), 487–493.

Koenig, H. G. (2012). Religion, spirituality, and health: The research and clinical implications. *Internationally Scholarly Research Network Psychiatry, 278730.*

Koenig, H. G. (2013). *Spirituality in patient care (3rd ed.).* Philadelphia, PA: Templeton Press.

Koenig., H., G. (2014). The Spiritual Care Team: Enabling the Practice of Whole Person of Medicine. Religions, 5:1161–1174

Koenig, H. G. (2018). *Religion and mental health: Research and clinical applications.* New York, NY: Academic Press.

Koenig, H. G., Larson, D. B., & Larson, S. S. (2001). Religion and coping with serious medical illness. *Annals of Pharmacotherapy, 35*(3), 352–359.

Lai, C., Luciani, M., Galli, M., Morelli, E., Del Prete, F., Ginobbi, P., ... & Lobardo, L. (2016). Spirituality and awareness of diagnoses in terminally ill patients with cancer. *American Journal of Hospices and Palliative Medicine, 34*(6), 505–509.

Leeuwen, R. V., Tiesinga, L. J., Jochemasen, H., & Post, D. (2007). Aspects of spirituality concerning illness. *Journal Compilation, 21,* 482–489.

Leung, D., & Esplen, M. J. (2010). Alleviating existential distress of cancer patients: Can relational ethics guide clinicians? *European Journal of Cancer Care, 19,* 30–38.

Li, S., Stampfer, M. J., Williams, D. R., & VanderWeele, T. J. (2016). Association of religious service attendance with mortality among women. *JAMA Internal Medicine, 176*(6), 777–785.

MacDonald, D. A. (2000). Spirituality: Description, measurement, and relation to the five factor model of personality. *Journal of Personality, 68,* 153–197.

MacLean, C. D., Susi, B., Phifer, N., Schultz, L., Bynum, D., Franco, M., ... & Cykert, S. (2003). Patient preference for physical discussion and practice of spirituality. *Journal of General Internal Medicine, 18*(1), 38–43.

Mather, M. (2016). Fact sheet: Aging in the United States. Population Reference Bureau. Retrieved from http://www.prb.org/Publications/Media-Guides/2016/aging-united-states-fact-sheet.aspx

McDonald, J., Swami, N., Hannon, B., Lo, C., Pope, A., Oza, A., ... & Zimmermann C. (2017). Impact of early palliative care on caregivers of patients with advanced cancer: Cluster randomized trial. *Annals of Oncology, 28*(1), 163–168.

Meyers, J. L., Brown, Q., Grant, B. F., & Hasin, D. (2017). Religiosity, race/ethnicity, and alcohol use behaviors in the United States. *Psychological Medicine, 47*(1), 103–114.

Meyers, S. (2006). Role of the social worker in old versus new culture in nursing homes. *Social Work, 51*(3), 273–277.

Milsten, J. M. (2008). Introducing spirituality in medical care: Transition from hopelessness to wholeness. *Journal of the American Medical Association, 299*(20), 2440–2441.

Monod, S., Martin, E., Spencer, B., Rochat, E., &v Bula, C. (2012). Validation of the spiritual distress assessment tool in older hospitalized patients. *BMC Geriatrics, 12*, 13.

Musick, M. A., House, J. S., & Williams, D. R. (2004). Attendance at religious services and mortality in a national sample. *Journal of Health and Social Behavior, 45*(2), 273–285.

National Consensus Project for Quality of Palliative Care. (2013). *Clinical practice guidelines for quality of palliative care* (3rd ed.). Retrieved from http://www.national-coalitionhpc.org/ncp-guidelines-2013

National Institute on Aging. (2011). *Global health and aging* (Report, National Institutes of Health). Retrieved from http://www.who.int/ageing/publications/global_health.pdf

Newport, F. (2017). Update on Americans and religion. Gallup. Retrieved from http://news.gallup.com/poll/224642/2017-update-americans-religion.aspx

Pargament, K. I. (1997). *The psychology of religion and coping: Theory, research, practice.* New York, NY: Guilford Press.

Pascal, J., & Endacott, R. (2010). Ethical and existential challenges associated with a cancer diagnosis. *Journal of Medical Ethics, 36*(5), 279–283.

Post, S. G., Puchalski, C. M., & Larsen, D. B. (2000). Physicians and patient spirituality: Professional boundaries, competency and ethics. *Annals of Internal Medicine, 132*(7), 578–583.

Prescott, A. T., Hull, J. G., Dionne-Odom, J. N., Tosteson, T. D., Lyons, K. D., Li, Z., ... & Bakitas, M. A. (2017). The role of a palliative care intervention in moderating the relationship between depression and survival among individuals with advanced cancer. *Health Psychology, 36*(12), 1140–1146.

Puchalski, C. M. (2001). The role of spirituality in health care. *Baylor University Medical Center Proceedings, 14*, 352–357

Puchalski, C., Ferrell, B., Virani, R., Otis-Green, S., Baird, P., Bull, J, Chochinov, H., Handzo, G., Nelson-Becker, H., Prince-Paul, M., Pugliese, K., Sulmasy, D. (2009) Improving the quality of spiritual care as a dimension of palliative care: the report of the Consensus Conference. Journal of Palliative Medicine, 12(10):885–904.

Puchalski, C. M. (2010). Religion, medicine and spirituality: What we know, what we do not know and what we do. *Asian Pacific Journal of Cancer Prevention, 10* (Supplement 3), 45–49.

Puchalski, C. M. (2012). Spirituality in the cancer trajectory. *Annals of Oncology, 23*(Supplement 3), iii49–iii55.

Puchalski, C., & Ferrell, B. (2010). *Making health care whole.* West Conshohocken, PA: Templeton Press.

Puchalski, C., Ferrell, B., Virani, R., Otis-Green, S., Baird, P., Bull, J., ... & Pugliese, K. (2009). Improving the quality of spiritual care as a dimension of palliative care: The report of the consensus conference. *Journal of Palliative Medicine, 12*, 885–904.

Richards, M. (2005). Spirituality and social work in long-term care. *Journal of Gerontological Social Work, 45*(1–2), 173–183.

Saguil, A., & Phelps, K. (2012). The spiritual assessment. *American Family Physician, 86*(6), 546–550.

Selman, L., Young, T., Vermandere, M., Stirling, I., & Leget, C. (2014). Research priorities in spiritual care: An international survey of palliative care researchers and clinicians. *Journal of Pain and Symptom Management, 48*(4), 518–531.

Steinhauser, K. E., Volis, C. L., Clipp, E. C., Bosworth, H. B., Christakis, N. A., & Tulsky, J. A. (2006). "Are you at peace?": One item to probe spiritual concerns at the end of life. *Archives of Internal Medicine, 166*(1), 101–105.

Teno, J. M., Freedman, V. A., Kasper, J. D., Gozalo, P., & Mor, V. (2015). Is care for the dying improving in the United States? *Journal of Palliative Medicine, 18*(8), 662–666.

Torry, M. (2017). Ethical religion in primary care. *London Journal of Primary Care, 9*(4), 49–53.

Vanbutsele, G., Pardon, K., Van Belle, S., Surmont, V., De Laat, M., Colman, R., ... & Deliens, L. (2018). Effect of early and systematic integration of palliative care in patients with advanced cancer: A randomized controlled trial. *Lancet Oncology, 19*(3), 394–404. doi:10.1016/S1470-2045(18)30060-3.

Wolff, J. L., Starfield, B., & Anderson, G. (2002). Prevalence, expenditures, and complications of multiple chronic conditions in the elderly. *Archives of Internal Medicine, 162*, 2269–2276.

World Health Organization. (n.d.). WHO definition of palliative care. Retrieved from http://www.who.int/cancer/palliative/definition/en

Yohannes, A. M., Koenig, H. G., Baldwin, R. C., & Connolly, M. J. (2008). Health behavior, depression and religiosity in older patients admitted to intermediate care. *International Journal of Geriatric Psychiatry, 23*, 735–740.

Zimmer, Z., Jagger, C., Chiu, C.-T., Ofstedal, M. B., Rojo, F., & Saito, Y. (2016). Spirituality, religiosity, aging and health in global perspective: A review. *SSM- Population Health, 2*, 373–381.

Zinnbauer, B. J., Paragament, K. I., Cole, B., Rye, M. S., Butter, E. M., & Belavich, T. G. (1997). Religion and spirituality: Unfuzzying the fuzzy. *Journal for the Scientific Study of Religion, 36*, 549–564.

9

OLDER IMMIGRANTS

Tenzin Wangmo, PhD
Institute for Biomedical Ethics
University of Basel, Switzerland

KEYWORDS

older immigrants
culture
policy
barriers

layers of vulnerability
health and social care
legal regulations

Overview

Older immigrants constitute almost one-fifth of the older adult population of the United States. Their proportion will double by 2060. Increasing migration and consequent aging in the host nation as well as migration at old age underscore the importance of understanding immigrants' aging experiences, their health and social concerns, and finding appropriate ways to address them. Older immigrants face unique obstacles when compared with native-born older adults. These include challenges associated with language, culture, and legal regulations. These barriers hamper access to health and social care systems affecting older migrants' overall well-being. This chapter uses the layers of vulnerability approach to analyze these barriers and to assess ways to minimize them. The chapter will begin with the ethical principle of vulnerability followed by a brief overview of regulatory, health, social, and familial contexts that shape the lives of older immigrants. It will then underpin different factors that make an older immigrant more prone to harm using the layers of vulnerability approach. Finally, the chapter will elucidate some mechanisms to overcome or mitigate these different layers of vulnerability through individual, familial, and policy initiatives to ensure older immigrants are cared for and enabled to live an old age with dignity.

The author wishes to thank colleagues, Christopher Poppe, Dr. Priya Satalkar, Dr. Eloise Gennet, and Dr. Eva de Clercq, for their suggestions for this chapter.

Introduction

International migration now occurs more often than in the past. The United Nations (2018) concluded that in 2017, 258 million people migrated from one country to another. The United States is one of the top receiving nations for international migrants among high-income countries. According to the latest data from the U.S. Census Bureau (2017), there were 43.8 million foreign-born persons in 2016, constituting 13.6% of the total population. From the current population of immigrants, 7.5 million (17.1%) were 65 years or older in 2016. This group is anticipated to increase to 26.4 million (38.1%) in 2060. In the same period, the proportion of native-born older adults in the United States is projected to increase from 17.1% to 26.2% (U.S. Census Bureau, 2017), underlining that the proportion of older immigrants will grow at a faster rate than that of native-born older adults. Such growth means that policy makers and service providers must be prepared to address the challenges of the increasingly heterogeneous older adult population of the United States in such a manner that their rights as individuals are respected and that no additional harm is placed upon them. In this chapter, the ethical principle of vulnerability (Kemp & Rendtorff, 2007), and in particular, the layers of vulnerability approach is used to analyze factors that compromise the well-being of older immigrants. Vulnerability is one of the central principles of European bioethics along with autonomy, integrity, and dignity (Kemp & Rendtorff, 2007). The four principles of medical ethics (i.e., autonomy, beneficence, nonmaleficence, and justice) (Beauchamp & Childress, 2001) will be used to reinforce the vulnerability approach wherever needed.

Vulnerability

Kemp and Rendtorff (2007) conceptualize vulnerability as follows: "(a) It expresses the finitude and fragility of life which, in those capable of autonomy, grounds the possibility and necessity for all morality. (b) Vulnerability is the object of a moral principle requiring care for the vulnerable" (p. 10). This principle necessitates not only protection of an individual's autonomy, integrity, and dignity but also necessitates obligations that those who are vulnerable are protected.

Hence, unlike the field of research ethics, where vulnerability is traditionally associated with so-called vulnerable populations and defined as an increased risk of harm or decreased capacity to protect oneself from harm (Coleman, 2009; Council for International Organizations of Medical Sciences [CIOMS], 2016; Oviedo Convention on Biomedical Research, 2005; World Medical Association, 2017), in European bioethics and law vulnerability is considered to be a universal human condition. In research situations, the groups that are categorized within the vulnerable label include minors, pregnant women, prisoners, and persons with mental illness, but also those who lack education and/or language competency, belong to minority racial and ethnic groups, are immigrants, and are poor (CIOMS, 2016). The labeling approach has been criticized because it designates an entire population (e.g., minors, pregnant women, immigrants, persons living in low-income countries) as being vulnerable. In doing so, it ignores within-group variations and is in some ways a form of paternalism. The labeling approach is too broad and static. In response, more nuanced ways of understanding vulnerability have been put forth (Coleman, 2009; Kipnis, 2001; Rogers, Mackenzie, & Dodds, 2012). In the case of older immigrants, the labeling approach to vulnerability terms all older immigrants as vulnerable and thus in need of protection. Older immigrants are not all prone to the same risks. Great heterogeneity exists within this group as well and different protections are necessary to address their specific vulnerabilities.

Layers of Vulnerability

The layers of vulnerability approach (Luna, 2009) will frame the discussion of vulnerabilities that older immigrants face in their host nation. This approach underlines that there are different factors that make an individual vulnerable, that a removal of a vulnerability-causing factor will reduce the overall vulnerability, and that when situations change, vulnerability may evolve. Thus, vulnerability is not a fixed label but a dynamic one that evolves based on the situation in which the person finds himself or herself. Each factor (i.e., layer) individually acts as a cause of additional vulnerability and no factor is built upon the other (i.e., there is no hierarchy).

Different factors make older immigrants vulnerable to varying extents. These include sociodemographic factors, such as gender, education, income, time spent in the host nation, personal resources, and social network. Further factors that make them vulnerable include political and social conditions that place them at higher risk such as discrimination in accessing employment, health care, and social benefits; as well as legal restrictions making them ineligible for means-tested or old-age benefits (discussed in the next few sections). Nevertheless, these vulnerabilities do not affect all older immigrants equally. Some immigrants may never face any such *additional vulnerability* and may be as vulnerable as a native-born older person. For example, an older immigrant from Europe who came to the United States in his early 20s and was educated in the United States, speaks the language fluently, has had a good professional career, and at old age is as economically self-sufficient as any of his native-born peers, is as vulnerable as a native-born peer would be. Older immigrants to the United States who are not of European origin are discussed further. Our discussion here only entails the *additional vulnerabilities* and not those that an older adult may face due to his or her advanced age and related deteriorating health and mental conditions, ageism, or living in nursing homes.

Older Immigrants in the United States

Federal Regulations Affecting Older Immigrants

Older immigrants living in the United States come from many different countries. Most immigrants are from Latin America, followed by Asia and Europe (Radford, 2019). Many have entered the United States as highly skilled persons during their prime ages and have aged in place, while others have moved to the country as parents of highly skilled immigrants who became U.S. citizens (O'Neil & Tienda, 2014). Others have fled their home countries at younger ages or even at old ages with few resources to help them integrate into the host nation.

The Immigration and Nationality Act of 1965 was instrumental in changing the demographic makeup of the United States because it removed the nationality quota that had limited the number of non-Europeans immigrating to the United States (O'Neil & Tienda, 2014). Furthermore, this act included parents of U.S. citizens within the definition of family members who were eligible for immigration. There was no cap in how many visas could be issued to family members of U.S. citizens. Carr and Tienda (2013) concluded that in the last few decades new citizens continue to sponsor more family members including greater numbers of family members 50 years and older. Thus, the proportions of older adults entering the United States through family reunification has increased steadily (Wilmoth, 2012). This development has also meant that increasing numbers of older immigrants have been eligible for means-tested federal benefit programs designed to help those who are economically disadvantaged—Supplementary Social Income (SSI) and Medicaid. These two programs support persons with disabilities and low incomes, including older immigrants, to help them meet their basic financial and health needs.

To curb the number of persons eligible for means-tested federal benefits, two restrictions were introduced: the 1996 Personal Responsibility and Work Opportunity Reconciliation Act and 1996 Illegal Immigration Reform and Responsibility Act. These two regulations excluded newly arrived older immigrants from accessing means-tested federal benefits. That is, for a period of 5 years, newly arrived older immigrants are dependent on their sponsoring family members for both economic and health needs. This dependence raises a question as to whether these two regulations mitigate or reinforce the vulnerability of older immigrants.

In addition, those arriving at old age are not eligible for Social Security and Medicare, two resources that provide economic and health security to adults 65 years and older. These two old-age benefits require that the recipient have worked in the United States for 40 quarters (Borjas, 2011). Thus, to qualify, immigrants who have migrated at an older age are incentivized to work even after they reach the age of 65 in order to fulfill the 40 quarters of work requirements.

Access to Financial and Health Care Support: An Issue of Justice and Autonomy?

Evident from the above discussion is that age at immigration is an important layer of vulnerability for older immigrants' well-being. Those immigrants who came to the United States at younger ages and who have worked in the country will have higher incomes at old age and are eligible for Social Security and Medicare, similar to native-born older adults. In contrast, those who migrated at older ages will have lower incomes in light of their inability to work or not having fulfilled necessary work requirements to qualify for old-age benefits. Not surprisingly, late-life immigrants have higher poverty rates than those who migrated at earlier stages of their lives (Wilmoth, 2012). Late life immigrants are more dependent on SSI and Medicaid (O'Neil & Tienda, 2014). Nguyen (2012) stated that the financial insecurity faced by older immigrants (newly immigrated and lacking legal status) is worsened by regulations that exclude them from means-tested social benefits, revealing—as noted above—ethical concerns. In a study with 15 low-income older Korean immigrants, Yoo and Zippay (2012) found that for these older persons, it was not family members but neighbors, churches, and senior centers that were the primary sources of support. Furthermore, these older Koreans identified SSI as a source of financial security that allowed them to live independently and reduced their dependence on their family members. Finally, Torres, Munoz, and Becerril (2016) concluded that Latino elders lack financial security even though they may have worked for decades in the United States. This was because they were employed in low-paying jobs and/or lacked legal status, constituting additional layers of vulnerability.

As described in the prior discussion, Medicaid and Medicare are two health care benefits available to older adults in the United States. Older immigrants who are newly or recently arrived and those lacking legal status are less likely to have health insurance than U.S.-born older adults. Living without health insurance is likely to affect their health and health-seeking behaviors (Stewart & London, 2015).

Language competency also greatly affects older immigrants' access to health care in the host nation and adds a different layer of vulnerability. Thus, those with limited language proficiency face higher health burdens than those with less or no problems communicating in the host language (Chow, 2010; Kim et al., 2011). Poorer linguistic competence limits older immigrants' ability to use health care services: they face more barriers and have greater psychological distress than those with less or no linguistic problems. Similarly, Nguyen (2012) concluded that length of stay in the United States, availability of insurance, and language competency affected older immigrants' access to health care. These layers of vulnerability require mitigation to address justice- and autonomy-related issues in access to care.

Intergenerational Relations: Beneficence and Nonmaleficence

Since the enactment of Social Security, caring for older people has primarily become a state obligation rather than a family concern. The availability of social safety nets has significantly impacted intergenerational relationships (Bengtson & Oyama, 2007; Bengtson & Roberts, 1991). That is, the cultural norm of our society toward filial piety[1] has weakened in the past few decades (Fingerman, Pillemer, Silverstein, & Suitor, 2012; Gans & Silverman, 2006). Several studies have focused on the continuation of filial piety despite migration of the child from rural areas to cities and from less developed countries to developed ones (Nesteruk & Marks, 2009; Şenyürekli & Detzner, 2008). Migration is changing intergenerational relationships.

A systematic review of older Chinese immigrants reported that although there are higher filial expectations from their children among older Chinese immigrants than older Whites (Lin, Bryant, Boldero, & Dow, 2015), those expectations from children of older Chinese immigrants are changing. Specifically, while some older Chinese immigrants were dependent on their children, many live independently, making critical the

---

[1]   Filial piety is a based in Confucian principles and describes the child's duties and obligations to parents which include as examples, financial and physical care and support, respect, and obedience. (Dong & Xu, 2016).

availability of public housing and other supports. Another example of such changing expectations is the choice made by some older immigrants to live close to their children rather than living with their children (Diwan, Lee, & Sen, 2011). Ajrouch (2005) arrived at similar findings among older Arab immigrants who stated that they appreciated the support provided by their children but preferred to be independent and not a burden. Treas (2008–2009) cautioned against commonly held beliefs that immigrant families are traditional, immigrant elders have high authority within their families, and that immigrant life guarantees happiness and security.

Related to the issue of filial piety is loneliness that older immigrants face in their new country. Treas and Mazumdar (2002) reported that limited mobility and language deficiencies of older immigrants result in isolation. Feelings of loneliness and isolation in their host nation are also a result of expectations of support from children, particularly male children (Alvi & Zaidi, 2017). Furthermore, older immigrants feel lonelier than native-born older adults (de Jong Gierveld, Van der Pas, & Keating, 2015) due to linguistic and cultural differences. However, their isolation is worsened by (a) heavy domestic responsibilities in their children's households, (b) their children's tendency to overprotect their parents and shield them from the practical aspects of life in the new country, and (c) the sacrifices that they make to put the needs of their children and grandchildren before themselves (Treas & Mazumdar, 2002). These situations raise ethical issues of beneficence and nonmaleficence on the part of the children. For instance, isolation and loneliness are situations that could result in harm to the older immigrant and may remain hidden if the older person does not vocalize those experiences to his or her children, or if the children to not respond to these situations.

CASE STUDY 9.1

Case Studies[2, 3]

Mrs. Li is a 69-year-old Chinese immigrant living in New York City. She came to the United States as a young undergraduate student in the 1970s. She worked her entire life as a health care professional and is now retired. She lives with her husband.

---

2   Four case studies reveal different factors that make older immigrants *more* prone to harm when compared to a native-born older adult. Embedded within each case could be particularly charged ethical dilemmas where, for example, autonomy might be at risk or where they have to make critical medical decisions like treatment refusal or palliative care. These situations however are not highlighted in the case studies and thus the scope of these case studies is limited. However, these ethically charged medical situations will constitute further layers of vulnerability and will need other resources or solutions, which is beyond the scope of this chapter. In line with the focus of this chapter, the emphasis here is on broader situations and conditions that impose additional vulnerability on older immigrants, rather than on very specific medical situations.

3   The fictional case studies presented use only female immigrants to avoid a vulnerability discussion surrounding gender (e.g., inherent vulnerability described by Rogers et al., 2012) and gender-related migration patterns (e.g., men migrating before their spouses) which are significant but also beyond the scope of this chapter.

Mrs. Sharma is 80 years old. She is originally from India and came to the United States 15 years ago as part of family reunion when her son became a U.S. citizen. She speaks limited English and has no working experience in the United States. During her first decade, she lived with her son and helped with household activities. She now lives alone.

Mrs. Ngo is a 75-year-old widow and lives in Dallas with her daughter, a U.S. citizen. She came from Vietnam a year ago. She speaks no English. She does the housework and is often alone at home. Her contact with other Vietnamese people is also very limited.

Mrs. Garcia is 70 years old, speaks fluent English, and is from Mexico. She has lived in the United States for many decades and worked mostly in low-paying odd jobs. She possesses no legal residency; however, both of her children were born in the United States. She lives with one of them.

Applying Layers of Vulnerability Approach to the Case Studies

Table 9.1 shows factors that make these older immigrants vulnerable to varying degrees. The additional vulnerabilities that they face are due to their life course and history of migration. For instance, late-life immigrants (i.e., those who migrated at old age and are unable to work) and older immigrants with no legal status face different challenges than those who immigrated legally at a younger age or at an age that still enabled them to work in the United States. Also, those older immigrants (regardless of legal status) who have lived for many years in the host nation but chose or did not feel the need to integrate (i.e., those living in self-sufficient ethnic neighborhoods) would face similar challenges associated with language competence like newly arrived older immigrants who lack language competency. Furthermore, their old age also means that they will not be able to gain employment and even though they are of legal retirement age, they

TABLE 9.1   Factors that Make Older Immigrants Vulnerable

Vulnerable due to ...	Mrs. Li	Mrs. Sharma	Mrs. Ngo	Mrs. Garcia
Language	No	Yes	Yes	No
Income (e.g., does not qualify for Social Security)	No	Yes	Yes	Yes
Dependency (on family members to access health, social, and community services)	No	Yes	Yes	No
Isolation/Loneliness	No	Yes	Yes	No
Legal status (i.e., does not qualify for means-tested benefits)	No	No	Yes	Yes
Citizen status	No	No	Yes	Yes
Discrimination	Yes	Yes	Yes	Yes

are not entitled to old-age benefits and perhaps even means-tested since they may not fulfill eligibility requirements (Borjas, 2011; Population Research Bureau, 2013).

The case studies display four different immigration histories: (a) legal migration as a young adult and aging in place in the United States; (b) legal migration at old age more than a decade ago; (c) legal migration at old age only recently; and (d) illegal migration decades ago. Their migration histories and sociodemographic characteristics affect them in different ways, although they have the same underlying denominators: gender, being an older person, and health characteristics (health was not specified in the case studies). In the case of Mrs. Li, an immigrant who was educated and had worked her entire life in the United States, she can function in her host country well in light of her socioeconomic status, and her vulnerability as an older immigrant is minimal. This is because, as someone who worked in the United States until retirement, she qualifies for Medicare and Social Security and possibly has additional savings that secure her old age. Her language competency and work experience in health care are strong indicators that she will not face additional barriers to accessing health care. Because she and her husband are childless, they may face vulnerability related to lack of social support and when they become unable to drive and increasingly physically limited, they will need greater formal support and possibly institutionalization in a nursing home. However, native-born childless older adults may also face such a situation. The additional risk of harm that Mrs. Li might face is discrimination due to her ethnic origin in different facets of her life, despite her linguistic and cultural integration.

Unlike Mrs. Li, Mrs. Sharma is limited by her ability to speak English (although she speaks some English) and has mostly lived with her son's family since she came to the United States. Her social interactions beyond the family have been minimal, resulting in possible feelings of loneliness and isolation. She does not receive Social Security because she lacks the required 40 quarters of work credits in the country. Her residency in the United States over the last 15 years makes her eligible for SSI and Medicaid, which now allows her to live on her own and exercise her autonomy in personal daily life situations. However, the factors that make her vulnerable—that is, limited language competency, income insecurity, loneliness/isolation, and dependence on her family—constrict her ability to exercise her choices. More specifically, her lack of English language skills will translate into several barriers for her in accessing health, social, and community services, as well as small interactions with non-Indians in daily situations. Furthermore, she is dependent on her child (and possibly grandchildren) to facilitate her access to these services (e.g., doctor's visits) as well as to understand what happens in those situations. For instance, when accessing medical treatment, she may not fully understand the medical information, why a specific treatment is provided, and what alternatives are available. Therefore, in such specific situations, her ability to provide informed consent is limited.

Ms. Ngo is a recent immigrant and speaks no English. As a result, her vulnerabilities are in some situations greater than that of the other two older immigrants already described. Ms. Ngo is completely dependent on her daughter for economic security since she does not qualify for any old-age benefits or means-tested benefits. Furthermore, her lack of English-speaking linguistic skills and cultural understanding deepens her dependence on her daughter, thereby clearly restricting her choices and abilities to act independently and making her a ward of her daughter. In Vietnam, she was able to manage all her health and social needs, in addition to meeting her basic personal daily needs. Now, in the United States, her status has changed from that of an independent parent to that of a dependent parent.

Finally, Mrs. Garcia's case study may well represent the experiences of many older immigrants who came from Latin America decades ago and remained undocumented, and hence under the radar of the government. As an immigrant who has lived in the country for decades, she fortunately does not face challenges associated with linguistic and cultural competence. She is able to communicate with friends and others and manage her life in the United States. Unlike the other older women, she may never qualify for either old-age or means-tested benefits in light of her illegal status in the United States (even though she may have paid taxes as part of her employment using a fake Social Security number). Her situation underscores justice concerns and thereby social responsibility of the host nation. She will face economic insecurity as she grows older, health insecurity with deteriorating health needs, and very important concerns related to access to health care. Furthermore, she may face an additional challenge of deportation should she be identified by federal authorities. Fear of deportation may result in avoiding accessing health care even when direly needed.

Toward Justice: Addressing Vulnerabilities Affecting Older Immigrants

Many factors make older immigrants susceptible to additional layers of vulnerability in their host nations. The additional risks that they face necessitate actions from different stakeholders to protect their dignity and integrity, make them capable of exercising their autonomy, and ensuring justice. Most often discussed in the literature are vulnerabilities linked to language deficiency and economic insecurity (Borjas, 2011; Derose, Escarce, & Lurie, 2007; Kim et al., 2011; Nam, 2012;). Lacking or limited language competency means that they face greater difficulties accessing basic health and social care services, as well as in their daily lives. For instance, Mrs. Sharma and Mrs. Ngo would require communication support in order to fully understand information when seeking any sort of formal and informal care in the United States. Hence, they are dependent on their children or other family members to make health care appointments, visit hospitals, and arrange for other formal care-related encounters. Additionally, their children or other family member must accompany them to all such visits, affecting when older immigrants can access health care. Two concerns are underscored: older immigrants' limited ability to act autonomously and their families' willingness and ability to act in the best interest of the older immigrant. Mrs. Ngo's situation is worsened by her ineligibility for social benefit programs. Although the situation for Mrs. Ngo is transitional, it is permanent for Mrs. Garcia due to legal regulations.

Table 9.2 presents ways to overcome the vulnerabilities delineated in Table 9.1. The three stakeholders—the older person, his or her family, and the host nation—can each work toward enhancing the capabilities of the older immigrants to help reduce and remove these sources of vulnerabilities. In the next few paragraphs, some of these mechanisms pointed out in Table 9.2 will be differentiated at the micro level of the individual, the meso level of the family, and the macro level of the state.

TABLE 9.2 Addressing Vulnerabilities that Challenge Older Immigrants

Layers of Vulnerability	How can it be addressed?
Language	• Strong motivation and willingness on the part of older immigrants to learn the host language[1] • Availability of opportunities to learn the local language in an age-sensitive manner and at low cost (or free of cost)[3] • Dispersing of information in languages that older immigrants can understand[3] • Access to translators at health and social institutions that care for older immigrants[3] • Ensuring that translators are culturally adept to properly and adequately work as mediators[3]
Income	• Older immigrants and their families need to assess and understand the value of employment to qualify for old-age benefits, and make practical plans[1,2] • Opportunities to engage in work must be made available (if the older person chooses to work even after retirement) and support to make the older person capable of doing so (e.g., skills training, language training)[3] • Measures to support older immigrants should their sponsoring family members become unable to provide the necessary care[3] • For those who are eligible, access to social welfare should be made possible with least possible legal and bureaucratic hurdles and with no fear of discrimination or stigmatization[3]
Dependency of family	• When deciding to migrate at old age, obtain information about the situation that they will face in the host nation[1] • Family members should encourage their older parents to learn the local language and familiarize themselves with the culture[2] • Providing older parents with opportunities (within their cultural community as well as those available from the community in general) and support that enable them to seek health care and social services on their own[2] • Making exceptions for SSI and Medicaid in light of individual family situations to mitigate possible elder abuse and violations of human rights[3]
Isolation/ Loneliness	• Speaking about feelings of loneliness and isolation with their children and finding solutions as a family[1] • Family members should allow older parents to manage basic activities on their own, e.g. shopping, understanding public transportation[2] • Family members need to understand that older parents are susceptible to loneliness, even if parents do not speak about it openly[2] • Putting into place services and events that would make participation in senior centers more attractive for older immigrants[3] • Social and community services could team with religious institutions to engage older immigrants into activities taking place in the community[3]
Legal status and citizenship	• Older immigrants must know that lack of citizenship may exclude them from specific social insurance plans. Thus, they would also need to plan and put efforts into ensuring that they gain citizenship[1] • Informing older immigrants about their rights to naturalization[3] • Having support in place for older immigrants who do not have writing skills, computer knowledge, and income to apply for citizenship even when they fulfill citizenship requirements[3] • Developing a legal pathway for older undocumented immigrants to gain residency status[3]
Discrimination	• Policy-level initiatives to reduce discrimination[3] • Public awareness of rights of minorities and need for cultural sensitivity and inclusion[3]

Note: [1]Measures from the part of the older immigrant (micro); [2]Support from the family members (meso); [3]Policy level solutions from the host nation (macro).

Micro Level: The Older Immigrant

With respect to linguistic proficiency, older immigrants must be motivated to learn the language of their host country. Doing so would be immensely beneficial for all facets of life, from taking public transportation to communicating illness symptoms with a physician. Furthermore, attending language classes will also allow older immigrants to meet peers and possibly reduce loneliness, as attaining some level of language proficiency would enable them to communicate in daily life situations. For those older immigrants who migrate in their 50s and later, it is critical that they understand the long-term benefits of gaining employment to become eligible for Social Security and Medicare. Older immigrants should seek knowledge from friends and family members who have immigrated previously about life in the host nation to prepare themselves for their new lives. For instance, it might help to know how the host nation works, and about changes in familial relationships that can occur due to the new context. Such prior knowledge and emotional preparedness may reduce feelings of intergenerational dissonance.

Meso Level: The Family

Within the family, dissonance between ideals of filial piety and actual support from children in the host nation can lead to negative feelings and experiences (Ajrouch, 2005; Lin et al., 2015). Feelings of loneliness and disappointment that older immigrants may experience and their inability to express them to their family members due to dependence on the sponsoring child is a vulnerability that may be solvable with clear communication within the family. As noted in Table 9.2, family members can address loneliness and isolation faced by older immigrants by actively engaging them in activities and services that could make the older person more capable and less dependent or isolated. That is, first, family members could encourage older persons to learn the new language and help them overcome shyness associated with learning at an old age. Second, the sponsoring children could encourage their older family members able to work to gain employment, even though such communication would require a cultural paradigm shift. An older parent may view such encouragement as a breach of filial piety and lack of deference. Further, this might also mean older immigrants have to work in jobs that would be below their qualification levels. Such changes might be particularly difficult in cultures where a woman may have never worked in the home country. Therefore, it might be valuable at the family level when the sponsoring child (and other children) and the older parent(s) have a clear plan of action on how the older parent(s) could be supported in the United States in the long term in light of the latter's eligibility or ineligibility to social benefit programs and the former's economic situation.

Macro level: The State

Stated earlier, language proficiency on the part of the older person is critical in accessing health care services. The availability of free or affordable language classes for older immigrants would be a positive incentive on the part of the host nation. Additionally, language and cultural competence of health care providers are also necessary to ensure good doctor–patient relationships and trust in the health care system (Sandhu et al., 2013). Availability of health information in the language that the older immigrant can understand, or taking the time to ensure understanding of the information received by the older immigrant will help reduce vulnerability associated with access to health care. It may also be useful to ensure that certain hospitals or general practitioners specialize in serving older immigrant populations (Kowoll et al., 2018). Fear of discrimination and actual experience of discrimination when accessing health care is a vulnerability that older immigrants face (Derose et al., 2007; Lauderdale, Wen, Jacobs, & Kandula, 2006; Viruell-Fuentes, Miranda, & Abdulrahim, 2012). Thus, the state could support resources to ensure that professionals working in health care and particularly in so-called migrant-friendly hospitals receive training on language, cultural sensitivity, and discrimination so that their patients feel respected, listened to, and taken seriously.

Furthermore, state support in the form of SSI and Medicaid may help ensure the independence of the older immigrants from their family members and enable them to live an independent life like many other older persons in the United States (Nyugen, 2012; Yoo & Zippay, 2012).

While significant legal restrictions concerning eligibility for programs exist, and are a reality with which older immigrants must live, blind adherence to regulations that do not consider changing family situations (e.g., loss of job of the sponsoring child, elder abuse within the family) is hardly conducive to realities that some older immigrants and their families may face. Thus, exceptions in SSI and Medicaid regulations that promote human dignity and protect the more vulnerable older immigrants from violence and exploitation will remove risks associated with being completely dependent on financially limited or abusive family members. Undocumented older immigrants are in a much more precarious situation because they fail to fulfill all requirements necessary to become eligible for access to social benefit plans (both old-age and means-tested social and health benefits). Fear of deportation may mean that they will not access any services even when in dire need. Solutions at the macro level are needed to protect these older immigrants who fall completely under the radar of all social benefit plans enacted to provide a dignified old age.

CONCLUDING OBSERVATIONS

Immigration to a new country brings with it challenges that needs mitigation in order to provide justice and a just society. Older immigrants who legally migrated decades earlier, who were either educated or gained education in the United States and were employed most likely will never face many challenges that undocumented older immigrants or older immigrants who came to the United States at older ages confront. The latter groups could not earn work credits due to their legal status or old age, lack educational and language skills, and remain isolated from critical cultural and regulatory knowledge. Thus, they face more challenges in all facets of their lives than a native-born or an integrated older immigrant. The additional vulnerabilities that these newly relocated or undocumented older immigrants encounter are complex. Personal, familial, and policy resources can help reduce and remove them.

The chapter used the layers of vulnerability approach to analyze additional challenges that older immigrants face and which limit autonomy in many ways. Responding to the layers of vulnerability of older immigrants is thus a concern of justice on the part of the host nation. In ensuring justice, the host nation works toward enhancing the capabilities of its new residents and citizens. On the part of family members, it is their responsibility to work in the best interest of their older parents, while the older person himself or herself chooses to use the available opportunities to sharpen his or her capabilities and become more able to function in the society consistent with his or her needs.

The layers of vulnerability elucidated in this chapter are not exhaustive. The chapter focused on broader contexts and conditions that place older immigrants at higher risk of harm. It did not discuss specific health care encounters or particular ethically charged decision-making situations (e.g., palliative care, refusal of treatment, or institutionalization in a nursing home). These ethically charged situations constitute further layers of vulnerability, requiring other solutions to overcome them, some of which are addressed in other chapters of this book.

Professionals (e.g., health care staff, social workers, and government employees) who work with older immigrants must assess specific vulnerabilities that place the particular person at higher risk of harm in light of his or her current overall situation. Doing so would enable the service provider to determine how existing resources could address a particular vulnerability and examine other measures to solve other vulnerabilities in the future.

DISCUSSION QUESTIONS

1. Beyond the vulnerability principle, when seeking health care, what other ethical principles are necessary to consider in the case of (a) an older immigrant with limited linguistic competence; (b) an older immigrant showing signs of dementia; (c) decisions concerning institutionalizing an older immigrant with dementia; and (d) an older immigrant who appears isolated and is showing signs of malnutrition.

2. Are federal policies ethically justified even when they might pose harm to older immigrants?

3. What are the responsibilities of the host nation toward its new members?

4. Because vulnerabilities are different from one older immigrant to another, how would you seek to understand these differences in practice?

5. Which vulnerabilities would you address first and why?

REFERENCES

Ajrouch, K. J. (2005). Arab-American immigrant elders' views about social support. *Aging and Society, 25,* 655–673.

Alvi, S., & Zaidi, A. U. (2017). Invisible voices: An intersectional exploration of quality of life for elderly south Asian immigrant women in a Canadian sample. *Journal of Cross Cultural Gerontology, 32,* 147–170.

Beauchamp, T. L., & Childress, J. F. (2001). *Principles of biomedical ethics.* New York, NY: Oxford University Press.

Bengtson, V., & Oyama, P. (2007). *Intergenerational solidarity: Strengthening economic and social ties* (Background paper, United Nations, New York, NY).

Bengtson, V.L., & Roberts, R.E. (1991). Intergenerational solidarity in aging families: An example of formal theory construction. *Journal of Marriage and the Family, 53*(4), 856–870.

Borjas, G. J. (2011). Social Security eligibility and the labor supply of older immigrants. *Industrial and Labor Relations Review, 64,* 485–501.

Carr, S., & Tienda, M. (2013). Family sponsorship and late-age immigration in aging America: Revised and expanded estimates of chained migration. *Population Research Policy Review, 32,* 825–849.

Chow, H. P. H. (2010). Growing old in Canada: Physical and psychological well-being among elderly Chinese immigrants. *Ethnicity & Health, 15,* 61–72.

Coleman, C. H. (2009). Vulnerability as a regulatory category in human subject research. *Journal of Law Medicine and Ethics, 37,* 12–18.

Council for International Organizations of Medical Sciences. (2016). *International ethical guidelines for health-related research involving humans.* Geneva: Author. Retrieved from https://cioms.ch/wp-content/uploads/2017/01/WEB-CIOMS-EthicalGuidelines.pdf

de Jong Gierveld, J., van der Pas, S., & Keating, N. (2015). Loneliness of older immigrant groups in Canada: Effects of ethnic-cultural background. *Journal of Cross-Cultural Gerontology, 30,* 251–268.

Derose, K. P., Escarce, J. J., & Lurie, N. (2007). Immigrants and health care: Sources of vulnerability. *Health Affairs, 26,* 1258–1268.

Dong, Xinqi & Xu, Ying. (2016). Filial Piety among Global Chinese Adult Children: A Systematic Review. *Research & Reviews: Journal of Social Sciences, 2* (1), 46–55. Diwan, S., Lee, S. E., & Sen, S. (2011). Expectations of filial obligation and their impact on preferences for future living arrangements of middle-aged and older Asian Indian immigrants. *Journal of Cross-Cultural Gerontology, 26,* 55–69.

Fingerman, K., Pillemer, K., Silverstein, M., & Suitor, J. (2012). The Baby Boomers' intergenerational relationships. *Gerontologist, 52,* 199–209.

Gans, D., & Silverstein, M. (2006). Norms of filial responsibility for ageing parents across time and generations. *Journal of Marriage and Family, 68,* 961–976.

Kemp, P., & Rendtorff, J. D. (2007). The Barcelona Declaration: Towards an integrated approach to basic ethical principles. *Synthesis Philosophica, 46,* 239–251.

Kim, G., Worley, C. B., Allen, R. S., Vinson, L., Crowther, M. R., Parmelee, P., & Chiriboga, D. A. (2011). Vulnerability of older Latino and Asian immigrants with limited English proficiency. *Journal of American Geriatrics, 59,* 1246–1252.

Kipnis, K. (2001). Vulnerability in Research Subjects: A Bioethical Taxonomy. *Online Ethics Center for Engineering and Research. National Academy of Engineering of the National Academes* http://www.onlineethics.org/cms/8087.aspx

Kowoll, M. E., Meyer-Kühling, I., Degen, C., Gladis, S., Zeier, P., & Schröder, J. (2018). Elderly migrants in outpatient and inpatient care services in Baden-Württemberg/Germany. *Psychiatry Research, 260,* 130–137.

Lauderdale, D. S., Wen, M., Jacobs, E. A., & Kandula, N. R. (2006). Immigrant perceptions of discrimination in health care: The California Health Interview Survey 2003. *Medical Care, 44,* 914–920.

Lin, X., Bryant, C., Boldero, J., & Dow, B. (2015). Older Chinese immigrants' relationships with their children: A literature review from a solidarity-conflict perspective. *Gerontologist, 55,* 990–1005.

Luna, F. (2009). Elucidating the concept of vulnerability: Layers not labels. *International Journal of Feminist Approaches to Bioethics, 2,* 121–139.

Nam, Y. (2012). Welfare reform and older immigrant adults' Medicaid and health insurance coverage: Changes caused by chilling effects of welfare reform, protective citizenship, or distinct effects of labor market conditions by citizenship. *Journal of Aging and Health, 24,* 616–640.

Nesteruk, O., & Marks, L. (2009). Grandparents across the ocean: Eastern European immigrants' struggle to maintain intergenerational relationships. *Journal of Comparative Family Studies,* 77–95.

Nguyen, D. (2012). The effects of sociocultural factors on older Asian Americans' access to care. *Journal of Gerontological Social Work, 55,* 55–71.

O'Neil, K., & Tienda, M. (2014). Age at immigration and the incomes of older immigrants, 1994–2010. *Journals of Gerontology, Series B: Psychological Sciences and Social Sciences, 70,* 291–302.

Oviedo Convention on Biomedical Research. (2005). Additional protocol to the Convention on Human Rights and Biomedicine, concerning biomedical research. Retrieved from https://rm.coe.int/168008371a

Pew Research Center. (2018). Origins and destinations of the world's migrants, 1990–2017. Retrieved from http://www.pewglobal.org/2018/02/28/global-migrant-stocks/?country=US&date=2017

Population Reference Bureau. (2013). Elderly immigrants in the United States. *Today's Research on Aging, 29,* 1–9.

Radford, J. (2019). Key findings about U.S. immigrants. Pew Research Center. Retrieved from https://www.pewresearch.org/fact-tank/2019/06/03/key-findings-about-u-s-immigrants/

Rogers, W., MacKenzie, C., & Dodds, S. (2012). Why bioethics needs a concept of vulnerability. *International Journal of Feminist Approaches to Bioethics, 5,* 11–38.

Sandhu, S., Bjerre, N. V., Dauvrin, M., Dias, S., Gaddini, A., Greacen, T. ... & Priebe, S. (2013). Experiences with treating immigrants: A qualitative study in mental health services across 16 European countries. *Social Psychiatry Psychiatric Epidemiology, 48,* 105–116.

Şenyürekli, A. R., & Detzner, D. F. (2008). Intergenerational relationships in a transnational context: The case of Turkish families. *Family Relations, 57,* 457–467.

Stewart, K. A., & London, A. S. (2015). Falling through the cracks: Lack of health insurance among elderly foreign-and native-born Blacks. *Journal of Immigrant and Minority Health, 17,* 1391–1400.

Torres, A., Munoz, J. A., & Becerril, R. (2016). Elderly undocumented Latinos and their retirement strategies. *Sociology Faculty Publications, 1.* Retrieved from https://scholarworks.lib.csusb.edu/cgi/viewcontent.cgi?referer=https://www.google.com/&httpsredir=1&article=1000&context=sociology-publications

Treas, J. (2008–2009). Four Myths About Older Adults in America's Immigrant Families. *Generations, 32,* (4), 40–45.

Treas, J., & Mazumdar, S. (2002). Older people in America's immigrant families: Dilemmas of dependence, integration, and isolation. *Journal of Aging Studies, 16,* 243–258.

United Nations. (2018). *International migration report—highlights.* New York, NY: Author. Retrieved from http://www.un.org/en/development/desa/population/migration/publications/migrationreport/docs/MigrationReport2017_Highlights.pdf

US Census Bureau. (2017). 2017 national population projections tables. Retrieved from https://www.census.gov/data/tables/2017/demo/popproj/2017-summary-tables.html

Viruell-Fuentes, E. A., Miranda, P. Y., & Abdulrahim, S. (2012). More than culture: Structural racism, intersectionality theory, and immigrant health. *Social Science & Medicine, 75,* 2099–2106.

Wilmoth, J. M. (2012). A demographic profile of older immigrants in the United States. *Public Policy and Aging Report, 22,* 8–11.

World Medical Association. (2017). WMA Declaration of Helsinki—ethical principles for medical research involving human subjects. Retrieved from https://www.wma.net/policies-post/wma-declaration-of-helsinki-ethical-principles-for-medical-research-involving-human-subjects

Yoo, J. A., & Zippay, A. (2012). Social networks among lower income Korean elderly immigrants in the U.S. *Journal of Aging Studies, 26,* 368–376.

VULNERABILITY: CARE ARRANGEMENT

C hapter 1 suggested that vulnerability can arise from circumstances, or alternatively from conditions. The chapters comprising this section on care arrangement explore select circumstances which can render older adults vulnerable to harm or loss. This is accomplished by examining the implications of formal service delivery and the effects of care setting. The receipt of formal services can occur in the older adult's own dwelling or a nearby agency, as you will discover in the chapter on home and community-based services, or it can happen in another dwelling, as examined in the chapter on residential long-term care. The remaining two loci for formal services considered in this section, health care and end-of-life care, enable delivery either at home or elsewhere, such as in a hospital or nursing facility.

Readers may wonder how formal service receipt potentially can cause an older adult harm or loss. As our chapter authors reveal, it may happen as a result of power imbalances between caregiver and care recipient, illustrated by differences in knowledge and capacity. It also may occur when the situation of the older adult is characterized by resource scarcity; for example, if something other than present care is locally nonexistent or has restrictive eligibility. Similarly, setting can foster harm or loss—at home if the dwelling lacks accessibility or is unsafe, or elsewhere if infection is rampant and staff shortages are commonplace.

Under circumstances like these, ethical concerns can arise that challenge service professionals. As you study these chapters, consider if sufficient resident autonomy is permitted in nursing facilities when administrators are hyper-focused on lawsuits and health department inspections. Is it just to remove home health care services from older adults who fail to comply with service plans, especially when doing so may lead to self-neglect? Can treatment be considered nonmaleficent or beneficent if it is likely to cure the disease but leave the hospitalized patient with radically diminished quality of life? And is it respectful of autonomy and self-determination to override the wishes of a patient at the request of the patient's family by providing treatment that may prolong life when the patient has stated a preference to be allowed to die under similar circumstances? Is hospice care truly beneficent if delivered too early or too late?

These and similar questions will challenge readers' thinking as the chapter authors describe ethical dilemmas that arise in the context of various care arrangements. There is much to consider as the reader navigates these complex aspects of an older person's life in the pursuit of a just world.

10

RESIDENTIAL LONG-TERM CARE

Diane Menio, MS
Center for Advocacy for the Rights and Interests of the Elderly

Michele Mathes, JD
Center for Advocacy for the Rights and Interests of the Elderly

KEYWORDS

autonomy

commitments

ethics of responsibility

residential care

care ethics

decision making

life story

long-term care

Overview

The lifelong task of forming a meaningful life story continues for those receiving care in residential settings, even as others must help in crafting the narrative. Whether or not they have chosen to enter residential care, persons living in such settings face many medical and everyday decisions (Caplan, 1990; Powers, 2001) that can affect how the continuity of the self is perceived. Decision making may be complex even when residents are able to express their wishes clearly. However, staff members often must grapple with the basic question of whether or not the care receivers have decision-making capacity. Integral to this concern is the question of how to "hear" the voices of residents when they may no longer be able to tell their own stories. This chapter describes an education program developed to guide caregivers in residential care settings through an ethical reasoning process based on the commitments made to vulnerable elders receiving long-term care within the relational and narrative contexts of residential settings.

Today, possibly more than at any time in our past, the purposes of long-term care are being deeply examined, debated, and discussed. Resulting changes in policy and practice, though generally welcome, pose new ethical challenges for practitioners in the field. Residential care settings offer unique challenges for professionals and paraprofessionals. This chapter proposes a new approach to understanding the ethical foundations of residential long-term care in terms of the commitments that care providers make to the recipients of their care. It has benefitted from input from long-term care providers at every stage of its development. The framework presented in this chapter reflects both the nature of residential care and the experience of those providing care.

Working in residential settings brings unique challenges arising from both the setting and the vulnerability of the individuals receiving care, a significant proportion of whom have some degree of cognitive impairment. Those who move to residential facilities on a long-term basis are most often very frail with extensive ongoing health needs, including physical disabilities and often some degree of dementia requiring round-the-clock care.

Over the past several decades care in residential settings has evolved from the medical model to appreciation of the significance of residential settings as the *home* of those who live there. Hearing staff, especially direct care staff who have the day-to-day responsibility for hands-on care of residents, say "we are their family" is quite common. Daily personal care, getting to know a resident's family, living through holidays and occasions, celebration, and loss all create the possibility for intimate connection with those for whom care is provided.

Ethical Decision Making in Residential Care Settings

There are three principal components to deciding on a course of action in health care generally, and residential care settings are no different: the clinical, the legal, and the ethical.

The *clinical* component concerns determining all the possible ways of addressing a given situation. It calls for using good professional knowledge, skills, and judgment as well as awareness of available resources.

The *legal* component of care decision making involves determining what must or must not be done in the circumstances. What do applicable statutes, regulations, and case decisions require or prohibit in a given situation? Law essentially establishes a floor for behavior. It describes what society holds to be the minimally acceptable standard of conduct. If behavior falls below that standard, society will impose penalties in the form of civil or criminal liability, fines, sanctions, or the like. Law is the minimum standard of conduct society will permit without penalty.

The third component is the *ethical* component which is concerned with what *should* be done in a given situation. That is, considering the ways it is possible to address the situation (the clinical component), and with awareness of the things that must or must not be done (the legal component), what is the *right* thing to do in response to the situation before us? Ethics explores the options for action that go beyond the minimum acceptable behavior established by law and that reflect the values and principles of the individual, their profession, and/or their community.

Frameworks for Ethical Decision Making

Ethical (or moral) frameworks provide tools that can be used in deciding what the "right" thing to do is. They provide reference points for assessing choices for action. Virtue ethics (developing good character), deontological ethics (fulfilling moral obligations), and consequentialist ethics (doing what achieves the greatest good for the greatest number of people) offer approaches to judging right and wrong that have been discussed and debated for centuries and continue to hold a prominent place in any discussion of ethical reasoning. In recent years societal changes, scientific and technological advances and evolving and emerging concerns have led to a renewed focus on ethics and new ways of considering moral obligations.

A. Ethics as Community Values and Responsibilities

We know from experience that a broad diversity of moral values and sources of moral decision making exists among individuals (Berlin, 1998; Hunt & Hansen, 2007). Likewise, experience makes clear that what is considered right conduct in one community may be different from what is considered right in another community. In residential care, too, different communities may hold different moral values or different understandings of how moral values are fulfilled. In some long-term care facilities, tube feeding those residents who cannot accept food orally is regarded as a moral imperative while in other facilities, it may not be. In some facilities, administrators and staff may believe it is "right" to accommodate consensual intimate relationships between residents. In others, sexual intimacy outside of a marital relationship may be regarded as morally impermissible.

Ethical consensus reflecting community values makes possible a pluralistic approach to long-term care, allowing those with similar ethical views to create an environment that supports their moral beliefs as they exercise their responsibilities to residents or clients. Likewise, it makes *choice* available to consumers of long-term care. By choosing among care providers who reflect a variety of ethical approaches, recipients of long-term care can feel more secure that care decisions or choices will be made that are consistent with their own held moral values.

B. Ethics of Care

A framework for understanding the nature of ethical obligations was introduced with the publication of *In a Different Voice: Psychological Theory and Women's Development* (Gilligan, 1982). Based on his earlier longitudinal study of a cohort of male subjects, moral psychologist Lawrence Kohlberg (1976) had identified three stages of moral development. Kohlberg's "mature" stage was characterized by moral decision making that is independent of external influences. In her research with female subjects, Gilligan found that her subjects' moral decision making more often corresponded to Kohlberg's "adolescent stage" reflecting care for and sensitivity to the interests of others.

The basic and path-breaking premise of the ethics of care (Held, 2007) that grew out of Gilligan's work is that rather than being an individualistic endeavor of independent decision makers, ethics begins in and is responsive to the nature of relationship. Ethical problems arise, and choices must be made within the context of particular relationships. Ethical conduct consists of responding with care to the other within the relationship. Care ethics recognizes that mutual duties of care exist between or among persons within specific relationships, the *particular* duties of care being determined by the nature of the relationship itself.

Thus, care ethics accepts and assigns value to the reality that membership in family and community involves the exchange of some degree of individual autonomy in favor of some level of cooperation. While more traditional approaches to ethics start with the presumption of a rational and free decision maker, care ethics proposes that moral decision making is embedded in, responsive to, and influenced by interpersonal commitments including friendship, love, and caregiving. It implicitly, if not explicitly, recognizes the difficulties presented by conflicts that arise among these commitments and between commitments to others and one's personal aims.

Ethical Obligations in Residential Care Versus Acute Care

Most thinking about health care ethics has taken place within the context of acute care (Collopy, Boyle, & Jennings, 1991; Van der Dam, Abma, Kardol, & Widdershoven, 2012). The nature and concerns of residential care are profoundly different from those of acute care, however. For example, while acute care focuses primarily on physical illness and injury, residential care is concerned with the overall well-being of the resident, including emotional, spiritual, psychological, social, and physical health. While in acute care great importance is given to the exclusivity of the patient–provider relationship, in residential care, a resident's place within a web of relationships with family and friends is recognized, valued, and supported. Strategies to strengthen these relationships rather than establish barriers to them are encouraged.

Another way in which the prevailing models of health care ethics, having been developed in response to ethical issues arising in acute care settings, fails to capture the challenges of residential care is in their understanding of the relationship between the health care provider and the health care recipient. Ethics in acute care began with the ideal of patient and physician as independent and autonomous agents. The rights and responsibilities for decision making rest squarely with the patient, although a collaborative relationship is encouraged. In residential settings, however, most care recipients are physically frail and/or suffer from various forms of dementia and other cognitive impairments. Frail elders in residential settings are dependent on others to ensure their well-being. The experience of dependency is magnified by the sheer variety of ways in which the quality of the resident's daily life is reliant upon staff. In this context, the exercise of both decisional and executive autonomy is problematic. A model of decision making predicated on autonomy does not reflect the reality of residential settings.

Residential Settings Present Unique Ethical Issues

While care ethics sets out a vivid conceptual foundation for an ethics of personal relationships, it does not seem quite adequate to addressing the ethical issues that arise in the residential care setting. Although personal caring relationships may develop between caregiver and care receiver in the course of providing residential care, one of the essential and distinctive features of long-term care is the (professional) obligation to care regardless of one's personal feelings. Moreover, the "caring for" that reasonably may be asked of and be expected from residential care staff has boundaries. It is defined by job descriptions, terms and conditions of employment, and responsibilities to others with equal moral claim on the caregiver's time and attention. If asked to bathe a resident, for example, a charge nurse might say, "That's not my job," and the nurse might very well be right, at least so far as the job description is concerned. At shift's end, a nurse aide is entitled to leave even though a resident in distress pleads for the aide to stay. An aide may need to leave a resident's room to complete tasks for the day even though the resident will likely feel lonely or alone.

Margaret Urban Walker, writing from the perspective of feminist moral philosophy, offers an ethics approach that seems to respond to ethical issues that present themselves in residential care more fully than does the principlism (see Chapter 1) so widely adopted and applied in the context of acute care medicine. Walker (1998) has proposed the concept of ethics of responsibility. As she notes, "Responsibilities trace 'our configuration of social roles and the boundaries of our community' as well as 'the distribution of power between those suffering and those being held responsible.'" (Walker, 1998, p. 78, quoting Smiley, 1992, p. 13).

Walker endorses the concept that

> we are responsible for protecting those vulnerable to our actions and choices. ... What binds us to keep promises to the extent that we are so bound is the vulnerability we have occasioned in others by inviting reasonable expectations; that familial and spousal obligations arise from vulnerabilities supported by a particular history of connection as well as the prevalence of certain social customs and legal arrangements; that friends grow progressively more obligated as (and if) deepened involvement and trust cause them reasonably to depend ever more strongly in certain ways on each other. (Walker, 1998, p. 81).

Citing the work of Goodin (1985), Walker notes that the kind of vulnerability that creates responsibility in others arises when someone is "*actually depending on* or *circumstantially dependent upon a*nother to secure or protect [a particular interest] *because of* the nature of their existing relationship, some prior agreement between or by them, [or] a particular causal history between them" (Walker, 1998, p. 84).

In other words, vulnerability can be created through a relationship in which one person is actually dependent on another or through explicit agreement that one person has made to another that encourages or allows the dependence of the other person. For example, one's commitment to a friend to help in a crisis, or promise of fidelity to a spouse or partner, or assurance of care to an aging parent encourages or allows the other person to act (or refrain from acting) in ways that make these others vulnerable if the representations or promises are not fulfilled. This vulnerability, according to Walker, creates a moral responsibility to do as one has said.

An ethics of responsibility provides a framework for understanding the ethical obligations of those providing residential care. The very nature of a caregiving relationship gives rise to the care recipient's reliance and trust. Within the care recipient–caregiver relationship, the person whose care is entrusted to another is vulnerable to the caregiver's fulfillment of responsibilities implied in that relationship. "I will take care of you" is both the implicit and explicit commitment of the staff of residential facilities, both individually and as a whole. This, then, creates a moral responsibility in the one whose role is to provide care.

> An "ethics of responsibility" as a normative moral view would try to put people and responsibilities in the right places with respect to each other. Moral philosophers with diverse concerns—medicine, technology, feminism, partiality—have thought this kind of normative view might have important conceptual resources distinct from those of more familiar deontological, utilitarian, contractarian or virtue approaches. (Walker, 1998, p. 79)

The moral responsibilities of residential care providers arise not only from the nature of caregiving but also through the express statements made by facility administrators and staff to the care recipient as well as her or his family members. Organizations and facilities providing residential care seek to attract residents through descriptions of the quality and kinds of care they provide. Older adults and their families make choices about whom they will entrust with their own or a loved one's care based upon these representations. Residential care providers have an ethical (if not legal) responsibility to fulfill the representations that have been made.

An Ethics Framework for Residential Settings

The Center for Advocacy for the Rights and Interests of the Elderly (CARIE) initially developed and presented ethics education programs grounded in the four bioethical principles or principlism (see Chapter 1), proposed by Beauchamp and Childress (1979). However, principlism has not been without its critics (see, e.g., Clouser & Gert, 1990) and does not seem to respond to the nature of residential care or offer adequate guidance for addressing complexities of ethical dilemmas encountered in the context of residential care. What was needed was a new paradigm that more fully captured the particular nature and challenges of residential care. Walker's ethics of responsibility seemed to offer a helpful way to frame the ethics of residential care because it takes account of *both* the particular vulnerability of the care recipient and the moral obligations of the provider. With this theoretical foundation for the model of residential care ethics, CARIE developed and tested a training program for residential staff created specifically to address the nature of ethical challenges that arise in residential care settings and the unique needs of residents.

CASE STUDY 10.1

Anna was admitted to Willow Haven nursing home after a hospitalization for a stroke. During the six days she was in the hospital, Anna was given regular sponge baths. After she was admitted to Willow Haven, however, she soon learned that she was to have a bath three times each week. She told the staff that her habit since childhood was to bathe once a week, and she only wanted to have a bath on Saturday evenings. She said she would be okay with a sponge bath in between. Her aide responded that she would lose her job if Anna didn't have the baths as scheduled.

In acute care settings, the clinician sees the patient only episodically to address particular health care concerns. The patient may choose to take the clinician's advice or not, and the clinician does not have legal or, some would argue, even ethical responsibility for the patient's choice not to follow the clinician's recommendations. Care providers in residential settings, however, are held to be responsible for the overall well-being of residents in their care over extended periods of time. Inadequate bathing is universally regarded as a key indicator of poor-quality care. Residential care staff therefore must work with residents to ensure that threats to their health and well-being are properly addressed.

Within the principlist framework, this care issue most likely would be perceived as a tension between the principles of autonomy and beneficence. Its resolution would depend upon which interest was determined to have greater weight under these circumstances. The ethics of responsibility/commitment framework calls for a more contextual understanding of Anna's refusal to bathe. Through fulfilling their commitment to continue Anna's life story in a way that she recognizes as hers, staff discovered that Anna Smith was raised in a home without running water. Most days the family members took a sponge bath, but Saturday evenings were special. They each took a warm bath by carrying water from an outside pump and heating it on the stove. After learning this, staff worked with Anna to create ways to continue making Saturday baths a special occasion marking the end of the week. Anna became more amenable to alternating sponge baths with more routine bathing during the week.

The first step in the development of the long-term care framework was listening to those who provided residential care to learn how *they* understood their responsibilities to those for whom they provide care. CARIE heard from residential care administrators and staff at all levels. Not surprisingly, the providers identified scores of responsibilities they had to the residents of their facilities. By integrating residential caregivers' accounts of their responsibilities, CARIE's focus and experience as an elder advocacy organization, and scholarly literature examining the moral nature of long-term care, CARIE developed an ethics framework that proposes commitment to the resident as the ethical basis of residential care.

The Five Commitments of Long-Term Care

An in-depth review of the broad array of responsibilities identified by long-term care providers led to the recognition that these responsibilities fell naturally within five overarching themes: health, safety, pain and suffering, respect for the individual, and life story. Each of these themes were then framed as a commitment that the provider makes to care recipients. These commitments, then, are: (a) to respect the individual, (b) to preserve and promote health, (c) to protect safety, (d) to ease pain and suffering, and (e) to provide opportunity and support for the continuation and completion of life story.[1]

Residential care is an inherently ethical undertaking because it involves fulfilling commitments made to vulnerable older persons. The five commitments provide the framework for ethical decision making in the residential care setting. An ethical care decision, then, is one that honors the commitments made, whether the subject matter is life-sustaining treatment or bathing. Fulfilling these commitments requires skill, judgment, high-quality professional training and attention to best practice models. Staff also must be provided with the resources—human and material—that are needed to be able to fulfill their commitments to the residents for whom they provide care.

CASE STUDY 10.2

Meet Bill Gorman

Bill Gorman is 76 years old and living at the Town & Country Nursing Home. He's had Parkinson's disease for about 10 years but continued to live on his own until 7 months ago when he had surgery for esophageal cancer followed by a course of radiation treatments. Following the surgery on his esophagus and the radiation treatments, Mr. Gorman's Parkinson's symptoms (tremors, rigidity, and shuffling gait) became more pronounced and his sister persuaded him to move into Town & Country. He is mentally alert.

Mr. Gorman never married, and his only close relative is his sister, who lives in a nearby city with her family. Even though Mr. Gorman's cancer and its treatment have impaired his ability to swallow, Mr. Gorman says he wants "real food" and has refused to eat purees or mechanical soft meals. Until now, the nurse aides who care for him have been cutting his food into very small pieces, which he has been feeding to himself. Sometimes he chokes on his food, which has even required staff to perform the Heimlich maneuver on occasion.

Mr. Gorman's health has declined to the point that he cannot feed himself and he insists that the aides continue to cut up solid food and feed it to him. There is disagreement among Mr. Gorman, his family, and the staff at Town & Country about what is the right thing to do. In addition, Mr. Gorman's sister has expressed her concerns about her brother's choking and is worried that he will not get adequate nutrition

---

[1] It is interesting to note that not one provider among the hundreds who were asked to identify what they believed to be their responsibilities to residents ever identified "preserving life" or its equivalent as a responsibility, although all identified responsibilities fell within the five themes of promoting health, protecting safety, respecting the person, easing suffering and pain, and supporting continuation of life story.

eating the small amounts of solid food he can swallow. The ethical dilemma will be discussed at the next care plan meeting which will include the director of nursing, the dietician, nurse aides, Mr. Gorman, and his sister.

Commitment to Respect the Individual

"If I am not for myself, who will be? But if I am only for myself, who am I?"

—Hillel the Elder

Respect and deference for autonomous decision making reflects deeply held American values of self-determination, liberty, and reason. When a resident has the capacity to make and express an autonomous decision, the societal importance accorded autonomy requires that their decision receive deference.[2]

The ability to reason and to understand and evaluate options is an essential element of the ability to exercise true decisional autonomy. However, many of the older adults who move to long-term residential settings have impaired cognitive capacity that limits their ability to be fully autonomous in this way. The requirements for autonomous decision making do not fit many of the frail elders who live in residential facilities, who rely on others to meet many of their most basic and intimate needs. Might, then, according greater weight to values of community, connection, and interdependence better serve the interests of elders in residential settings?

The understanding of autonomy imported from acute care into the residential setting must be adapted to the particular nature and reality of residential care. Because residents live in a community of residents and staff, staff have responsibility for meeting residents. Sustained medical, instrumental, and personal care needs, and because there often are nonmedical decisions that residents face, the principle of autonomy frequently needs modification. Interpreted as noninterference, adherence to autonomy may cause residents to be left on their own when they most need guidance. However, a belief that caring for frail elders requires valuing beneficence over autonomy may result in elders in long-term care settings being denied opportunities to make choices that reflect long-held values and preferences that are consistent with who they are (Tulloch, 1990).

The notion of autonomy is premised on the idea that one should be left alone and that boundaries between persons should be respected. Vulnerable elders in residential settings, having left their connections in the communities from which they came—including their relationships with neighbors, shopkeepers, church, and community organizations that might have been built over decades—also need the opportunity to

---

2   The contours of this chapter do not permit an examination of the relevance of Goffman's concept of the total institution (Goffman, 1961) to residential care facilities and the broader meaning—and possibility—of autonomy within such settings. Rather, this chapter focuses on the ethics of practice within the realities of residential settings as they are and the way(s) in which the classic concept of individual autonomy does or does not enhance fulfillment of an ethics of responsibility to vulnerable elders in these settings.

forge new connections. To the extent that respecting autonomy entails taking a hands-off stance, it discourages the very sort of engagement that might support a vulnerable elder psychologically, emotionally, and physically.

However, notwithstanding the disconnect between the actual meaning of autonomy as reasoned decision making and self-determination and the reality of vulnerable elders' lives, the language of autonomy nevertheless has importance for its connection to the equally important concept of liberty. In the context of residential care, the principle of respect for autonomy may better be replaced by a commitment to respect for the individuality of each person. Although respect for the individual as used here incorporates significant aspects of the principle of respect for autonomy, such as truth telling, keeping confidences, and respecting privacy, it is broader than the principle of respect for autonomy. It requires caregivers to be attentive to more than just the decisions made by residents, often the focus of the requirement to respect autonomy. A person's individuality is expressed in many ways. One way, of course, is through the decisions and choices he or she makes. But individuality is also reflected in expressed preferences; in values and personal goals; through emotions; and creativity and through social interactions, personal relationships, and community membership.

One reason that the commitment to show respect for individuality of the person is so challenging for professional caregivers in residential settings is that its fulfillment often seems to be in tension with other commitments to the resident, for example to promote health or safety. Staff members who make a genuine effort to respect the wishes of residents who cannot speak for themselves encounter challenges in discerning their held values. Residents may have outlived the people in their lives who cared for them or may have always been alone (Chamberlain, Baik, & Estabrooks, 2018; Karp & Wood, 2003) and may not have anyone other than staff who knows them at all. Enacting the wishes of residents with impaired decision-making capacity may face obstacles, including real or perceived regulatory constraints (Hilliard, 2006; Kapp, 1998), the mission and values of the particular institution, staff roles and attitudes (Fetherstonhaugh, Tarzia, Bauer, Nay, & Beattie, 2014)—including the degree to which staff members understand and accept differing cultural values (Mullins, Moody, Colquitt, Mattiason, & Andersson, 1998)—and the resident's adherence to those values (Braun, Pietsch, & Blanchette, 2000; Bullock, 2011; Hyun, 2002). Families of residents may have differing views of their respective roles and of their right to speak for residents. Family caregivers may be struggling with feelings, including guilt, following the resident's move from community-based to residential care (Bauer, Fitzgerald, Haesler, & Manfrin, 2009; Dellasega & Nolan, 1997; Kellett, 1999) that impact their ability to make decisions from the perspective of the resident. Facilities may have shifting views of the surrogate role and may defer all decisions, even those residents could make, to family members (Kapp, 1998).

When a resident has the capacity necessary for autonomous decision making, respecting autonomy means deferring to the decision whenever possible. Respecting autonomy requires providing and explaining the necessary and relevant information to enable the resident to make the best decision (Engelhardt, 2000). In individuals with some degree of cognitive impairment, decision making can often be supported by listening to help identify the problem, simplifying options, exploring choices, choosing the best time for discussion, and choosing language that can be easily understood.

Even with supports for decision making, many but by no means all people who live in residential care may lack the capacity to make autonomous decisions. However, decision making is not the sole way of expressing one's individuality. Respecting individuality when a resident lacks capacity to formulate and express even a preference, whether verbally or nonverbally, may require others to make choices on behalf of the individual that are consistent with prior written and spoken directives and the values reflected through the resident's life story.

Finally, this commitment requires adherence to such basic and universally applicable norms as respect for personal privacy and confidentiality. These norms can be, and too often are, overlooked or disregarded in residential care but are essential to any concept of personal dignity and respect.

CASE STUDY 10.3

Who Is Mr. Gorman?

Mr. Gorman has been described as mentally alert. There is no indication that he lacks the capacity to understand and consider the risks involved in eating solid food, even if cut into small pieces. There is a tendency to question the capacity of someone, especially someone who is elderly, when they make a decision that seems foolhardy. It is important to keep in mind that *anyone* can make what others consider a bad choice. Indeed, most people at one point or another during their lifetime do just that. This is not and must not be taken to be evidence of impaired cognitive capacity and a basis for overriding an elder's decision.

However, this case is made more ethically complex by the fact that Mr. Gorman seeks to solicit the assistance of the nurse aides in doing what *they* consider to be wrong. In order for a person to be held to be morally responsible for their actions, they must have agency—that is, the freedom to choose to act one way or another. Residential care staff have made commitments to residents which they are morally obligated to keep. In this case, these other commitments conflict with Mr. Gorman's choice to have staff feed him food that may result in significant harm to him.

Commitment to Promote and Preserve Health

Many, if not most, elders receiving care in residential settings suffer with chronic and/or progressive illnesses such as diabetes, arthritis, Parkinson's disease, cancer, congestive heart failure, chronic obstructive pulmonary disease, disability, and/or dementia. For these conditions, cure is not the goal. While acute illness, when it occurs, requires appropriate medical attention, the heart of the commitment to promote and preserve the health of older adults in residential care settings is maximizing a resident's functional ability. It involves focusing efforts on remediating ways in which chronic illness or treatment of illness can impair a resident's ability for meaningful participation in day-to-day life.

CASE STUDY 10.4

Will Mr. Gorman's Condition Improve?

There is general consensus among Mr. Gorman's care providers that maintaining his current health status requires his getting sufficient nutrition. His sister is pressuring Town & Country to insist that he eat purées and mechanical soft foods to ensure that he is getting the calories and nutrients that she believes will keep him strong in the face of his multiple health conditions. The dietician, too, is concerned that Mr. Gorman will not get adequate nutrition without supplemental easily swallowed foods as well as about the impact that frequent choking will have on his fragile health.

Commitment to Protect Safety

The previous commitment, to promote and preserve the resident's health, addresses providers' responsibilities to address the ways in which illness, disease, or infirmity limit a resident's ability to participate in the life around him or her. The commitment to protect the resident's safety, on the other hand, addresses interactions with the external environment of the residential setting. Providers must create or arrange the environment of the residence so that it provides a physically, emotionally, and psychologically safe place to live. Because residents often cannot accurately assess environmental risks, fulfilling this commitment involves such obvious steps as ensuring that living spaces and common areas are safely navigable and that potential hazards are anticipated, identified, and remediated. Fulfilling the commitment to residents' safety includes enacting and enforcing policies to address potential risks such as protocols for monitoring medications appropriately for accuracy to having a zero-tolerance facility-wide abuse policy. Facility maintenance and the myriad ways that staff assist residents throughout the day must be done a manner that does not pose hazards for frail residents.

CASE STUDY 10.5

Is Mr. Gorman Safe?

Nurse aides refuse to feed Mr. Gorman small pieces of steak and other foods he wants to eat due to the risk he will choke. In addition to concerns about an ethical commitment to the safety of the vulnerable older adults who reside at Town & Country, administrators and staff are also worried about potential legal liability should Mr. Gorman aspirate his food as the result of this known risk.

Commitment to Ease Pain and Suffering

The fourth commitment care providers in residential settings make to the persons they care for is to ease their pain and suffering. Although *pain* and *suffering* are often referred to as if they were a single experience, they are, in fact, distinct and separable. While pain is a physical symptom, suffering is an emotional and/or spiritual experience. A person may be in great pain and yet not be suffering, or one may have no pain at all and yet suffer deeply. The nearly universal response to pain is to seek its reduction or, if possible, elimination. Adequate pain management is an ethical responsibility of the medical team, including staff in residential settings.

Persons who are suffering may, through religious or other convictions, seek to find meaning within the experience of suffering (Engelhardt, 2000). Honoring a commitment to treat and reduce both a resident's pain *and* suffering requires being alert to the differences and to identifying the most appropriate person to provide care (e.g., physician, nurse, chaplain, social worker, psychiatrist, psychologist). It is well documented that pain is too often undertreated in older adults (Denny & Guido, 2012). Developing skills and interventions to identify and respond to another person's pain and suffering is as much a professional (as well as human) ethical responsibility as is the duty to adequately and appropriately treat observable and/or measurable somatic symptoms.

CASE STUDY 10.6

Is Mr. Gorman Suffering?

Mr. Gorman insists he is strong and will eventually get well enough to leave Town & Country, but staff suspect that beneath his bravado he fears increasing debility and is scared of dying. He has become angry with his sister and her family when they visit, accusing them of acting as if they are making a sympathy call when they are solicitous of him. He has insisted that even though, as the doctors told him, they were not able to get all the cancer when they operated on his throat, he did better than expected after the Parkinson's diagnosis, living on his own all that time, and he will outlive their predictions about the cancer. As Mr. Gorman has said, he refuses to slowly become a "pathetic, mewling, vegetable of a person." Staff recognize a need to address Mr. Gorman's emotional and psychological pain as he contemplates what potentially lies ahead for him.

Commitment to Support the Continuation and Completion of the Care Recipient's Life Story

"I was not the self I knew myself to be."

—Sekou Sundiata (2002)

We are all aware of the dread most people have about needing long-term care, particularly in a residential setting. Entering residential care represents a radical shift in the trajectory of an individual's life story. Paraphrasing one bioethicist, the need for long-term care may lead an older adult to feel that his or her biographical life has ended while biological life goes on (Rachels, 1986). But surely this need not be the case. To support the integrity of the resident's continuing life story, it is important to know about the life that proceeded the need for care. It is necessary to ask, "Who is this person?" and to listen for the answer.

Too often medical records, admission forms, and information from family members are the basis for the history—the account of who that person has been—and who that person is now is often lost. But each of these narrative sources speaks in a voice that is its own, reflecting its own viewpoint, its own concerns, even its own biases. To care well for the resident requires that the person is not only seen through the prism of others' eyes but, much more importantly, through the resident's own eyes.

The awareness, sharing, and acknowledgment of one's life story hold great value for any individual. As explored below, the value of having one's life story known is magnified for those who live within the context of a residential care setting.

IT HELPS MAINTAIN SELF-IDENTITY

Imagine, for example, what it would be like for a person to wake up one morning with total amnesia. She has apparently suffered no injury and has the physical ability to go about her life much as she wishes. Where would she go? How could she find the answers to such questions as "Where do I live?," "Do I have a family?," and "Where do I work?" In short, she would be desperate to get her story back in order to know who she is. The move to residential care is a profound shock to an individual's sense of themselves—literally one's place in the world changes. The resident's relationship to and experience of the people and things that gave life meaning and shape, including home, possessions, routines, and relationships disappear or are dramatically altered. Encouraging residents to tell their stories, the stories that preceded and include the need for care, provides an opportunity over time to create coherence from what may feel like a story and identity irreparably ruptured.

IT ILLUMINATES MEANINGS

Life events and choices derive their meaning from the way they fit together. For example, take the statement "John is walking in the park." Suppose John works for a major corporation. John's wife left him recently. Colleagues have noticed that he has lost weight, and his eyes are perpetually red-rimmed. Now John has failed to show for an important ten o'clock meeting. When his assistant is asked where John is, she answers, "John is walking in the park." Now instead suppose that 3 months ago John was severely injured in a car accident and went through a long and difficult period of rehabilitation. It's ten o'clock in the morning. A friend of John calls and asks to speak with him. His wife says, "John is walking in the park." To understand the meaning *of* the identical fact requires being aware of the story of which it is a part.

To know what something as seemingly simple as a walk in the park means for John requires knowing John's story. In the same way, it's essential to know a resident's story in order to know the meaning that a particular aspect of care holds for him or her. What does it mean to Mr. Logan, a former football player, to need a wheelchair? What does it mean to Mrs. O'Malley, who used to love to cook for her large family, to need to be fed? What does it mean to Mrs. Jefferson to be bathed by nurse aides? Discerning the meaning *that* an experience has for a resident requires being aware of how it fits in the context of that particular resident's life.

IT INDIVIDUALIZES THE RESIDENT

Charts, case files, and protocols are absolutely essential for identifying critical data, for organizing information in an efficient and useful way and for responding with efficiency and consistency to care issues. This permits standardization of practice. Charting calls for communicating information about a resident in a professional and objective voice. Protocols are a way of recognizing commonalities and responding in established effective ways. Both are an integral part of providing good and efficient care, especially when time is the resource most at a premium.

Learning the resident's story is a counterbalance to the tendency to expect to see the familiar, to make assumptions based on what has been seen before. Knowing each resident's unique story overcomes reliance on perceived similarities rather than appreciating the parts of *this* resident's history and experiences that contribute to his or her distinctiveness.

IT PROVIDES A GUIDE FOR DECISION MAKING

In situations where a resident lacks capacity to make care decisions, knowledge of his or her story can be of great help in making a decision that gives coherence to the story. Residents have developed a powerful storehouse of wisdom in their own life stories; each is the world expert on his or her own story. Knowledge of past choices about how to live can guide those who now must decide in the person's stead. It permits decision making that is consistent with the individual's previously lived values, with his or her way of doing things. It enhances our ability to take the other's perspective, to discern the choice the person would have made were he or she able.

IT HELPS CREATE SOCIAL CONNECTION

The value of learning a resident's life story lies not only in the information that is imparted but also in the relational act of communicating and receiving the story itself. Listening as someone tells his or her story, not just at one occasion but over time, creates connection. The experience of being listened to as one recounts one's own story—of being heard—can be one of deep sharing. This storytelling can call forth reactions and responses from the listener, who may then share parts of his or her own life. The formation of relationships in this way offers an antidote to the isolation that often accompanies the experience of needing and receiving residential care.

IT HELPS TO SUSTAIN MEMORY

Reminiscing can be an aid to memory. Prompts, observations, questions, and comments from the listener can reinforce the resident's memory of past experiences and evoke additional memories. Through this process the power of recollection may be strengthened, and the narrative coherence sustained.

IT ENCOURAGES FEELINGS OF EMPATHY, COMPASSION, AND UNDERSTANDING

Listening to another person recount episodes from their life that are touching, funny, sad, or joyful; the challenges they have overcome; ways in which they cared for others and were cared for themselves; ambitions that went unrealized; events that gave pleasure; and times that brought grief diminishes differences and distances. The sharing of life stories promotes understanding, empathy, and compassion.

CASE STUDY 10.7

What Is Mr. Gorman's Story?

Mr. Gorman's life reflects the great value he has attached to personal courage, strength, and independence. He was a member of the military and enjoys telling staff stories of the hardships he faced in basic training and talks with pride of being an army grunt in the Vietnam War. He never married but has lived on his own all his adult life. After his Parkinson's diagnosis, he fought hard to continue to live independently. Mr. Gorman only (very reluctantly) agreed to move to Town & Country when he felt he was becoming a burden to his sister. He vowed early in his life that he would not be a burden to anyone, including himself. Mr. Gorman's sister and her family, including his two nephews, are his closest family. In a conversation with staff, she shared how much her brother had enjoyed Sunday dinners with her family for many years before he became ill, when visiting became too difficult.

Ought Implies Can

It is likely that care providers in residential settings will encounter situations in which it is not possible to fulfill one or more of the five overarching commitments described here. It is an accepted principle of ethics that one is not obliged to do that which it is impossible to do.[3] It makes no sense, for example, to hold that curing Mrs. Green's widely metastasized cancer is an ethical duty. Likewise, care providers are not obligated to honor commitments it is impossible to fulfill. However, when faced with a situation in which it is impossible to honor one of the ethical commitments, care providers continue to be bound by the remaining commitments. While in some cases it may not be possible to know what a resident would choose were he or she able or to know the story of his or her life before entering residential care, staff are still committed to preserving and promoting the resident's health, protecting his or her safety, and palliating his or her pain and suffering. It is essential, however, that *impossible* not be confused with expensive, inconvenient, time consuming, or problematic.

CASE STUDY 10.8

Fulfilling Mr. Gorman's Wishes

Prior to the care plan meeting, staff had met to review their commitments to Mr. Gorman, the relevant facts, and the challenge the situation presented. At the meeting, the director of nursing spoke to Mr. Gorman and his sister, expressing understanding of their concerns and explaining the ethical commitments that staff must not only honor Mr. Gorman's preferences but also to promote his health and protect his safety. The director then invited everyone—staff, including nurse aides, the dietician, and the social worker, as well as Mr. Gorman and his sister—to brainstorm and think

---

3   The roots of this principle are alternatively ascribed to the 18th-century moral philosopher Immanuel Kant and to the legal maxim *ad impossibilia nemo tenetur* (no one is held to do the impossible).

as creatively as possible about ways that meals can be designed so that Mr. Gorman's health and safety are supported while his concerns and choices are addressed. Many suggestions were offered. It is important in this process that at this stage no idea be rejected out of hand. The options and suggested ideas can be assessed after all the possibilities are on the table.

A plan was cooperatively developed; it incorporated ideas that had been offered. The dietician agreed to create meals that included "real" foods that were nutritious and safe for Mr. Gorman to swallow, such as custards (e.g., crème brulées), thick soups, eggs, milkshakes, and other possibilities as she continues to think about Mr. Gorman's needs. She would also plan meals with foods that Mr. Gorman would be able to safely feed himself. Mr. Gorman's sister suggested that she could come with the boys and her husband to have regular family dinners with Mr. Gorman. The director suggested that the facility might be able to arrange a private space for such dinners. Mr. Gorman's sister said she would bring table linens and dishes for Sunday dinners. At the conclusion of the meeting, Mr. Gorman felt he had been heard and respected, his sister felt reassured that the staff would not let him choke or starve (which seemed to her to be the options prior to the meeting), and the nurse aides also felt their concerns were heard and they were relieved that they would not have to fear being responsible for causing potentially serious harm to Mr. Gorman. Perhaps most significantly, the problem was approached as an opportunity for collaboration among all stakeholders rather than as a conflict between competing interests.

CONCLUDING OBSERVATIONS

This chapter has described a commitment-based framework developed to respond to the distinctive nature of residential care and the responsibilities that those who choose to care for vulnerable older adults in such settings assume. While professionals who practice in residential settings have their respective areas of expertise and experience, all share a commitment to the well-being of the whole person.

Special attention has been given in this chapter to two of the five commitments that comprise the ethics framework described: The commitment to respect the individual and the commitment to support the continuation and completion of their life story. While the other commitments—to promote health, protect safety, and ease suffering and pain—are self-evidently at the heart of quality residential care, through conversations with administrators and staff from all aspects and levels of residential care during the development of the framework it became clear that these two ethical commitments presented the greatest challenges, both conceptually and practically. Consequently, more extended discussion has been provided to explain their rationale and critical significance for doing good for the most frail and vulnerable older adults.

The approach to providing care for frail older adults in residential settings described in this chapter hopefully provides a useful framework for staff striving to fulfill their responsibilities to vulnerable elders.

DISCUSSION QUESTIONS

1. How does the nature of residential care impact the ethical responsibilities of care staff and other professionals compared with those serving vulnerable older adults in acute care settings?

2. What impact does the nature of residential care have on the ethical responsibilities of care staff and professionals compared with those providing home- or community-based services for vulnerable older adults?

3. How is the commitment to respect the individual that is described in this chapter different from the more traditional concept of respect for autonomy? How might this difference impact ethical decision making in residential care settings?

4. What particular skills are required to fulfill the five commitments to vulnerable elders in residential settings?

5. Do you believe the ethics framework described in this chapter has applicability for serving older adults in settings other than residential care? Why or why not?

REFERENCES

Bauer, M., Fitzgerald, L., Haesler, E., & Manfrin, M. (2009). Hospital discharge planning for frail older people and their family. Are we delivering best practice? A review of the evidence. *Journal of Clinical Nursing, 18*(18), 2539–2546. doi:10.1111/j.1365-2702.2008.02685.x

Beauchamp, T., & Childress, J. (1979). *Principles of biomedical ethics.* New York, NY: Oxford University Press.

Berlin, I. (1998). Isaiah Berlin on pluralism. *New York Review of Books, 45*(8). Retrieved from https://www.cs.utexas.edu/~vl/notes/berlin.html

Braun, K. L., Pietsch, J. H. & Blanchette, P. L. (2000). Cultural issues in end-of-life decision-making. Thousand Oaks, CA: Sage.

Bullock, K. (2011). The influence of culture on end-of-life decision making. *Journal of social work in end-of-life & palliative care, 7*(1), 83–98.

Caplan, A. L. (1990). The morality of the mundane: Ethical issues arising in the daily lives of nursing home residents. In R. A. Kane & A. L. Caplan (eds.), Everyday ethics: Resolving dilemmas in nursing home life. New York: Springer, at p. 375.

Chamberlain, S., Baik, S., & Estabrooks, C. (2018). Going it alone: A scoping review of unbefriended older adults. *Canadian Journal on Aging / La Revue Canadienne du Vieillissement, 37*(1), 1–11. doi:10.1017/s0714980817000563

Clouser, K. D., & Gert, B. (1990). A critique of principlism. *Journal of Medical Philosophy, 15*(2), 219–236.

Collopy, B. J., Boyle, P., & Jennings, B. (1991). New directions in nursing home ethics. Hasting Center Report, 21(2), S1 – S16.

Commonwealth of Pennsylvania v. Golden Gate National Senior Care LLC, et al., No. 16 MAP 2017 (PA Sup. Ct., September 25, 2018).

Dellasega, C., & Nolan, M. (1997). Admission to care: Facilitating role transition amongst family carers. Journal of Clinical Nursing, 6(6), 443–51.

Denny, D. L., & Guido, G. W. (2012). Undertreatment of pain in older adults: An application of beneficence. *Nursing Ethics, 19*(6), 800–809.

Englehardt, H. T. (2000). *The foundations of Christian bioethics.* Lisse, Netherlands: Swets & Zeitlinger.

Fetherstonhaugh, D., Tarzia, L., Bauer, M., Nay, R., & Beattie, E. (2014). "The red dress or the blue?" How do staff perceive that they support decision making for people with dementia living in residential aged care facilities? *Journal of Applied Gerontology, 35*(2), 209–226. doi:10.1177/0733464814531089

Gilligan, C. (1982). *In a different voice: Psychological theory and women's development.* Cambridge, MA: Harvard University Press.

Goffman E. (1961). *Asylums: Essays on the social situation of mental patients and other inmates.* New York, NY: Anchor Books/Doubleday.

Goodin, R. (1985). *Protecting the vulnerable.* Chicago, IL: University of Chicago Press.

Held, V. (2007). *The ethics of care: Personal, political and global.* New York, NY: Oxford University Press.

Hillel. (1984). In M. Zlotowitz, *Ethics of the Fathers: Pirkei Avos.* New York, NY: Mesorah.

Hilliard, J. L. (2005). The nursing home quality initiative. *Journal of Legal Medicine, 26*(1), 41–60. doi:10.1080/01947640590917945

Hunt, S. D., & Hansen, J. M. (2007). Understanding ethics diversity in organizations. *Organizational Dynamics, 36*(2), 202–216.

Hyun, I. (2002). Waiver of informed consent, cultural sensitivity, and the problems of unjust families and traditions. Hastings Center Report, 32(5), 14–22.

Kapp, M.B. (1998). Our hands are tied: Legal tensions and medical ethics. Westport, CT: Auburn House.

Karp, N. & Wood, E. (2003). Incapacitated and alone: Health care decision-making for the unbefriended elderly. Washington, D.C.: American Bar Association.

Kellett, U. (1999). Transition in care: Family carers' experience of nursing home placement. Journal of Advanced Nursing 29(6), 1474–81.

Kohlberg, L. (1976). Moral states and moralization: The cognitive-developmental approach. In T. Lickona (Ed.) (1976). *Moral Development and Behavior: Theory, Research and Social Issues* (pp. 31–53). New York: Rinehart and Winston.

Mullins, L. C., Moody, L., Colquitt, R. L., Mattiason, A-C., and Andersson, L. (1998). An examination of nursing home personnel's perceptions of residents' autonomy. Journal of Applied Gerontology, 17, 442–61.

Powers, B.A. (2001). Ethnographic analysis of everyday ethics in the care of nursing home residents with dementia: A taxonomy. *Nursing Research. 50*(6), 332–9.

Rachels, J. (1986). *The end of life.* New York, NY: Oxford University Press.

Smiley, M. (1992). *Moral responsibility and the boundaries of community.* Chicago, IL: University of Chicago Press.

Sundiata, S. (2002, November 20). Performance poet Sekou Sundiata. *Fresh Air,* NPR. Retrieved from https://www.npr.org/templates/story/story.php?storyId=848912

Tullock, G. J. (1990). From inside a nursing home: A resident writes about autonomy. Generations, 14(Suppl.), 83–5.

Van der Dam, S., Abma, T. A., Kardol, M. M., & Widdershoven, G. A. (2012). "Here's my dilemma": Moral case deliberation as a platform for discussing everyday ethics in elderly care. *Health Care Analysis, 20*(3), 250–267. doi:10.1007/s10728-011-0185-9

Walker, M. U. (1998). *Moral understandings: A feminist study in ethics.* New York, NY: Routledge.

LONG-TERM SERVICES AND SUPPORTS

Kelly Niles-Yokum, PhD
University of La Verne

Suzanne Beaumaster, PhD
University of La Verne

> *"The test of real and vigorous thinking, the thinking which ascertains truths instead of dreaming dreams, is successful application to practice."*
>
> —John Stuart Mill

KEYWORDS

long-term services
ethics
independent living

homeless older adults
treatment of older prisoners
role of the state

Overview

This chapter focuses on ethical considerations in the context of long-term services and supports (LTSS) for vulnerable older adults. Concerns for LTSS for vulnerable older adults can no longer adhere to a one-size-fits-all solution. The setting should be a primary determinant for the planning and implementation of services. Considerations regarding setting also present provocative considerations for those individuals, institutions, and organizations responsible for the design and delivery of services and supports. The intersection of vulnerability, old age, and community-based long-term services and supports presents a myriad of ethical issues. The settings and cases we will be highlighting will be a vehicle for discussing the principles of autonomy, beneficence, justice, nonmaleficence, and other ethical concepts and approaches including therapeutic jurisprudence and restorative justice. The very nature of policy, funding, and implementation tends to adhere to service delivery models from a very singular focus—economies of scale, as it were. The quest for a just society goes well beyond considering the critical issue of the vulnerability of the elders in our society; this pursuit provides a pathway for all of us to live in a world that both protects us all while giving us the freedom to live our lives with opportunities for self-determination and dignity.

CASE STUDY 11.1

Long-Term Services and Supports

Joanna is a 25-year-old woman who recently finished a graduate degree and started her career at a company in the Midwest. Her grandmother, who lives on the East Coast, was recently hospitalized and is back home receiving home health care services. These services allow her to stay in her own home, and assist her with personal care, including bathing as well as light housework. Joanna has started flying back to the East Coast every weekend to see to the care of her grandmother. As a result of these weekend trips, Joanna has been unable to socialize with coworkers and neighbors in her new community and is unavailable for weekend work. Although weekend work is not mandatory, Joanna realizes that she is likely to be passed over for promotions as a result of the caregiving choices she has made. As her grandmother's only family caregiver, the long-distance nature of her situation has significant implications for both her and her grandmother (Niles-Yokum & Wagner, 2018).

Introduction

In the United States, *LTSS* refers to the supports and services provided to individuals who, because of disability or impaired physical or cognitive functioning, require assistance in their activities of daily living and/or instrumental activities of daily living. These include assistance with bathing, dressing, meal preparation, financial, and/or medication management. There are a variety of settings and ways in which LTSS are provided, which range from informal care provided in one's own home to the continuum of care available throughout one's life, provided through community-based programs to assisted living and skilled nursing. In theory, the LTSS along the continuum of care permits older adults to choose to remain in their current settings or at least to make some decisions that best suit their needs as well as their preferences. The opening case is a general introduction to LTSS and a reminder that we all may have instances in our lives that might require us to access programs and services intended to help us get through our day so we can live our lives. These services might be for us or they might be for someone else—a family member, friend, or client.

When we think about the network of programs and services intended to support and serve us in our later years, it is important to acknowledge that families are diverse, in both size and scope, and may be geographically distant as we see in the case of Joanne and her grandmother. Additionally, economics and many other issues can impact the how, why, what, and when LTSS come into play for older adults (Niles-Yokum, 2006).

This chapter will examine some of those issues through the lens of gerontology and public administration and grounded in the ethical principles of autonomy, beneficence, justice, and nonmaleficence.

In developing public policy, a key question should be "How can we, as a society, be just, caring, and fair as we take care of our vulnerable elders?" From the perspective of social justice, should not this be one of the key measures by which any advanced society should be judged? American public policy has struggled with this question throughout its history. The development of the post–Great Depression welfare state was certainly an outcome of these policy issues. Today, we find ourselves embroiled in the ongoing concerns of health care policy, and within that maelstrom come questions of how to deal with the needs of our rapidly aging population. The provision of care occurs both through private channels and directly via public institutions; in many cases care is a combination of both. To date, U.S. public policy has been unable to develop universal approaches for dealing with the expansive demands of elder care across the spectrum of situations in which they exist. The nature of representative democracy, individual liberty, and a market-driven economy all impact the ability to develop universal policy approaches.

In addition to the complex policy concerns there are underlying ethical concerns for high-quality care. The overarching ethical concerns cover both the fundamental need for "good care" of our most vulnerable populations, and the concerns for the provision of ethically delivered care (Blasszauer, 1994). The key component here is a need for ethical approaches to focused policy development with a goal of effective and "good" care of our vulnerable elderly population.

This chapter provides a framework for our exploration of long-term services and supports in this context. The intersection of ethics and justice—and the expectations that they come together when we make policy—doesn't always play out in ways that work for the consumer or in ways that we would consider ethical. For example, considering what makes a just set of outcomes for individuals who are incarcerated, for persons who are homeless, and for those older adults who are living independently or require assistance with their daily activities can be extremely complex. We have expectations that those who work with older adults will have the beneficence to do the right thing both ethically and functionally. Human dignity and personal autonomy may be minimized in the face of resource allocation, regulations, and time/capacity considerations (just to name a few). But what is "right"?

Ethical considerations this chapter will explore raise questions about whether the person who is tasked with providing care, planning services, and implementing policy not only is competent but also comprehends the very important underlying ethical considerations. Different settings produce a multitude of different issues surrounding individual rights and vulnerable elders. The aim of this chapter is to connect those outcomes with real-life ethical considerations—the lived experience of long-term services and supports. What is that story, and how and why will we tell it and from whose perspective—that is the foundation of ethics and social justice.

One need only look at the U.S Census Bureau fact sheet to get a quick picture of the complexity of the elder care situation (Profile America Facts for Features, 2017): 47.8 million people were 65 or older in the United States on July 1, 2015, representing 14.9% of the population. According to the Department of Housing and Urban Development, in 2014, there were 306,000 homeless people over 50 (Henry, Watt, Rosenthal, & Shivji, 2016; Nagourney, 2016). The elderly prison population (those age 55 or older) grew from 26,300 in 1993 to 131,500 in 2013—10% of the total prison population (Carson & Sabol, 2016).

Long-Term Services and Supports

LTSS, also referred to as home- and community-based services, are those services and programs that are aimed at supporting older adults and their families as needs arise. LTSS are typically day-to-day care services and fall into a number of categories. The first, daily living, includes tasks such as dressing, toileting, bathing, and eating. Second are those instrumental activities including meal preparation, housekeeping, bill paying and management of financial affairs, and preparing and administering medication. Third, coordinated care activities including nursing facility care, adult day health care, aide services in the home, transportation services, and in some instances, support for family caregivers.

As a result of the passage of the Older Americans Act in 1965, the development of what is now known as the Aging Networks was implemented. The Aging Networks are those programs and services that exist to support older adults in a variety of settings. They may be delivered by public entities, not-for-profit agencies, and/or faith-based organizations. The Older Americans Act allowed for senior centers to be built, staffed, and funded; home-delivered and congregate meal programs to be developed and implemented nationwide; and other LTSS to be put in place. LTSS were developed and are sustained through the Area Agencies on Aging (AAA) network. Area Agencies on Aging were officially established in 1973 in order to provide every community a local focus for their investment in programming for older adults (Niles-Yokum & Wagner, 2018). There are now 622 AAAs in the United States as well as 256 Title VI Native American aging programs (National Association of Area Agencies on Aging,, 2019) responsible for planning and coordinating the service networks in their geographic locations. Service networks vary, but most include the following services:

- Meal programs (congregate sites and home-delivered meals);

- Senior centers;

- Adult day programs for elders with care needs;

- Family caregiver programs;

- Information and referral services;

- Senior transportation;

- Health promotion centers.

LTSS are intended to provide a pathway to continued independence and well-being in later life for older adults who are experiencing age-related changes so that they can remain in the settings of their choosing. Whether it is an individual living in a single-family home or apartment, in a residential setting, or in any number of other possible living arrangements, the goal is to maintain individual autonomy for as long as possible. Oftentimes LTSS also supports the families of older adults by filling in gaps that remain when families are at a distance, are employed, or are faced with their own challenges.

According to Kaye, Harrington, and LaPlante (2010), approximately 6 million older adults access services and programs that support them in their later years. According to the 2013 Centers for Disease Control study (Harris-Kojetin, Sengupta, Park-Lee, & Valverde, 2013) this number had grown in just 3 years to over 8.4 million. This increase is directly associated with factors of population aging and increased longevity. With the increase in the need for services and supports, it is likely that existing gaps related to need, access, and availability will widen; and as communities grapple with addressing those gaps, ethical considerations will take center stage. As our nation ages, we are undergoing a wave of changes that bring with them increased diversity in a myriad of contexts including race and ethnicity, sexual orientation, living arrangements, and preferences in services and supports.

Historically, home- and community-based care primarily focused on attending to the physical needs of adults aging at home. Moving forward, delivery of LTSS will need to be focused on the individual and his or her changing needs over time. Services will need to be flexible to meet those changing needs. The future of high-quality ethical LTSS is now, and it is wrapped in considerations of what is just, and what is right for that person, at that moment, understanding that flexibility is key. If the existing networks that focus on aging are going to continue to be the hub of the wheel for LTSS, change must start at the level of initial coordination through these networks. It is imperative that the notion that LTSS is intended to be an intervention for problems be reexamined, focusing instead on empowering the individual person and supporting his or her autonomy. The key will be to put well-being and individual preference at the center of decision making and long-term care plans. From an ethical perspective that entails a refocusing along the lines of what Holstein and colleagues (2011, p. 7) describe as "gives a structure to moral institutions and captures prevailing ideas about what ought to count." While initially these principles were applied primarily to medical or clinical decisions, beginning in the 1980s through the work of the Retirement Research Foundation's initiative "Personal Autonomy in Long-Term Care," application of the ethical principles of autonomy, beneficence, nonmaleficence, and justice has been extended to long-term care. The field of gerontology has explored these issues from a variety of foci and perspectives including social gerontology, critical perspectives, and theoretical considerations such as life course and cumulative disadvantage.

Holstein (2011, p. 15) reminds us that "many older adults who need long-term care services, encounter problems of biographical discontinuity, threats to their older adult status, and compromised identity and selfhood" (Charmaz, 1993; Kaufman, 1987). A just society for older vulnerable adults who require LTSS should be balanced with the critical issues of care and preference, personal identity, and individual rights.

Public Policy and Elder Care

From a public policy perspective, long-term services and supports for older adults falls under the auspices of social care and the welfare state. The ever-rising cost of health care, increased longevity, increased reliance on Medicare, and chronic diseases among older adults are among the reasons that the issue of LTSS has become, in large part, one for governments and policy makers. The reality of the situation is that Americans are living longer and often in a state of declining health. Families and individual health coverage options are not enough to cover the broad spectrum of needs present in this population of vulnerable older adults. The implications here are the same as most social welfare concerns: How do we develop policies and programs that best meet the needs of vulnerable older adults? How do we pay for the increasing costs associated with these programs? Daly and Lewis (2000) argue that a perspective of care that places expanded focus on political economy aspects allows for greater understanding of the care-centered intersection of the state, market, nonprofit institutions, and the family. They termed this "social care" (p. 281). Certainly, narrowly focused policy initiatives will miss the complexity of the environment—all aspects of which are critical to good and ethically delivered care. In fact, it is of fundamental importance that policy development in the area of elder care focuses on these interstices. Elder care has always existed in somewhat contradictory environments: paid and unpaid caregivers, public and private programs, contracted and noncontracted (Leira, 1992). Each of these presents significant dichotomous relationships that raise important questions about dependence and independence in later life.

With the rapid expansion of the elder population in the United States, no one focus will be enough to effectively deal with the needs of older Americans, not to mention those vulnerable elders within an already vulnerable population. The development of policy in this area runs into a number of issues that rest essentially in the very nature of care. It begins with the social norming of care for our elders as an obligation and personal responsibility to one's family. This is a kind of ethical focus and adds complexity to the question. That is, a culture of care cannot be evaluated based on labor or economic factors alone but must also take into consideration societal and individual perspectives on family roles and responsibilities. Over the past several decades, the conceptualization of care has been firmly planted in the arena of care as a labor activity, thus bringing to the forefront the work aspects, as well as care as a more general activity. In this dimension, those who are caregivers are also workers in the more traditional sense. As Daly and Lewis (2000) argue, caregivers as workers emphasize both the economics of the activity as well as the conditions of labor. Possibly the most important characterization of care as labor has to do with refocusing around the concerns of the state. This brings to the discussion issues related to language: Is using the terms *carework* and *care partners* (as opposed to *caregiving* and *caregiver*) more appropriate? These are also ethical considerations in terms of how we perceive carework.

The issue of cost must be considered when formalizing elder care policy and determining the role of the state in setting boundaries under which these activities take place. Certainly, the social cost of caring for elderly people is very high and growing as the U.S. population ages. The burden on taxpayers and our public delivery systems is clear: Medicare and Medicaid alone ($672.1 billion and $565.5 billion respectively) represented 37% of U.S. national health expenditures in 2016. In 2016, 46.3 million seniors received Medicare and 4.6 million received coverage through Medicaid. These expenditures are expected to grow at the rate of 5.6% through 2025 (Centers for Medicare and Medicaid Services, 2017). These costs are really the tip of the iceberg; out-of-pocket costs to caregivers, private costs, and those associated with nonprofit organizations are equally high. However, those costs can be calculated and planned in a somewhat efficient manner—the hidden costs present a more unique problem for policy makers; that is, the social and emotional costs to individuals and society at large.

Individual Autonomy and State Paternalism

In our attempt to provide "good" (that which is ethical and effective) care for our vulnerable elderly population we find ourselves in a difficult position, that of determining the viability of universal social policy programs within a market-driven system and the limits of private solutions for such an expansive set of concerns. Pierson (1994) states that the reason the United States and other liberal welfare states have such difficulty in this area is that "universal public programs compete with viable private sector alternatives" (p. 170). In government policy discussions, universal (or broad-based programs, i.e., Social Security, Medicare) public programs are viewed by conservative policy makers as large expenditure entitlements and a significant challenge to market-based perspectives. This leads us to a crossroads of publicly supported care and market-driven options. Both are viable, and both produce positive and negative outcomes for the elders in their care.

At the eye of the storm are the questions of individual autonomy and state paternalism. The increase in life expectancy carries with it the challenges of physical and mental changes related to normative aging, not to mention the considerations of pathological changes that may occur with advanced age. This raises questions of the elderly individual's ability to maintain self-care and individual self-determination along with expansion of the costs associated with care and longevity. Policy in this area seeks to do the most good when it comes to deciding on the most effective services and supports for older adults; the difficulty lies in the questions of economics and equity. The idea of control over one's own person and the right to live life as he or she chooses is fundamental to American ideology and should be protected with great concern. This focus on autonomy is also central to almost all ethical perspectives and provides a cornerstone for ethical decision making. From Kantian moral philosophy to Mill's utilitarian perspective, the importance of maintaining individual autonomy cannot be overstated. The issue becomes extremely complex when we take into consideration the many facets of an ethic of care.

While it stands to reason that expenditures by government of scarce resources should be used in the most effective manner, the practical application of that premise runs headlong into the personal attachment we have to our own quality of life and that of our loved ones. That is to say, rational economic decisions regarding ethical care break down when it becomes personal.

Ethical considerations frame our discussion and may provide a pathway to a just and ethical society in the context of vulnerable older adults. As stated previously, one of the key concerns when it comes to policy and the implementation of care initiatives is the concern for individual autonomy.

To look at this issue contextually, we must look at two key components to autonomy: (a) independent thinking and choice regarding the maneuverings of others, and (b) capacity to choose (Dworkin, 1988). When it comes to the issue of care for older adults, the question of capacity and independence is always at the forefront. In fact, it is the nature of individual autonomy that creates significant problems for policy and implementation regarding elder care and the state. State paternalism is at the heart of so many ethical dilemmas in the management and delivery of elder care. Typically, paternalistic interventions fall into two categories; interpersonal and policy related (Conly, 2013). The interpersonal refers to those interventions that impact a person's ability to choose actions or knowledge for themselves and tend to be viewed through social or moral norms. Those that fall under the policy category are simply those that are attached to formal rules or legal statutes. Ethical approaches to elder care and decision making should uphold a healthy respect for individual autonomy while still adhering to good care practices.

Application Cases

Moody (1992, p. 30) writes that "the study of the small details of life—everyday ethics—or the, morality of the mundane—has already illuminated some of the neglected questions of long term" services and supports. These issues have been explored for decades, presenting us with more questions than answers. We turn to ethics to help us explore these issues further and use a case approach to delve deeper into these critical issues that will only become more present and more pressing as our world ages. Below we attempt to apply the ethical principles of autonomy, justice, beneficence, and nonmaleficence to a variety of settings in an effort to help us see the landscape before us, and light a path forward toward a just society. We follow the Beauchamp and Childress (2001) definitions of the ethical principles, as referenced in Chapter 1; they will help guide us as we explore the cases to follow.

CASE STUDY 11.2

The Role of Society and the Integration of Long-Term Services and Supports for Homeless Older Adults

Sylvia is a 75-year-old White female who has been living on the streets of Los Angeles for 2 years. She currently has access to services and programs through the local homeless shelter but has made the choice to remain on the street in a community of others in her situation. Her choice to sleep on the streets at night is her own. Or is it? While complex and multifaceted, hers is not an uncommon scenario. From an ethical and social justice perspective, the real questions for us to consider include themes related to the role of society in the context of not only homelessness but this particular population. Older adults may require health care to address acute and chronic conditions that tend to multiply with a life on the streets. What is the role of society? Issues of mental health, substance abuse, elder abuse, lifelong victimization, and economic challenges are often just a few of the many factors that lead to homelessness. Perhaps it is worthwhile to think about whether society's public policy and on-the-ground long-term services and supports should be designed to foster a better outcome over time by addressing homelessness and the long-term consequences of the factors that can lead to homelessness? Ethical considerations of autonomy: Is Sylvia making her own decision to live on the street? Beneficence: What is the role of the community, our society at large, with regard to not doing harm? Nonmaleficence: Is harm being done here? What is that harm and who is its recipient? Justice: What role does justice play? Do we live in a just society if there are older adults like Sylvia (and others, regardless of age) who are homeless?

Discussion Questions

1. What is the role of society in this case? Consider from all four ethical concepts—autonomy, beneficence, nonmaleficence, and justice.

2. Is Sylvia making her own decision to live on the street? If so, why do you think someone would choose that living situation?

3. What services and supports in the aging network would be applicable in this situation and how might they be enhanced to integrate an ethical perspective for this vulnerable population?

CASE STUDY 11.3

Ethical Issues and the Role of Long-Term Services and Supports in the Treatment of Older Prisoners

Stanley, age 92, has been incarcerated since he was 50 years old. He was convicted of murder during a break-in of a convenience store. His criminal record was, up to that time, primarily petty crimes that resulted in short-term incarceration. His sentence in the murder of an innocent bystander during a theft was incarceration for life. During his 42 years of living in prison, Stanley has lost touch with family members and any friends he had. His son visited him monthly during the first few years he was in prison but he has had few visits for the past 20 years. He does, however, stay in touch with his family members by mail and they have told him he could live with them if he was released from prison.

The cost of keeping Stanley in prison is high and increasing as his health deteriorates, and he requires help with the activities of daily living such as bathing and dressing. He has multiple health problems that also require therapy and medication.

Discussion Questions

1. Stanley's situation is a common ethical dilemma as people age in prison. Should an older prisoner with multiple health problems and who is, as a result, no longer a risk to society be kept in prison?

2. Is prison a punishment or a protection for society?

3. Do age and frailty merit special protections?

4. What is your opinion about Stanley? Why do you hold that opinion?

5. What ethical principles might help you consider this situation and possible solutions?

CASE STUDY 11.4

Maintaining Dignity in the Face of Dementia

Robert is an 89-year-old dementia resident, currently residing in dementia care at a continuing care retirement community. He has no living relatives and has been a resident on the dementia unit for 2 years. Robert is in the middle stages of dementia. His day revolves around task-based care including bathing, feeding, medication management, and activities. Lately the staff have noticed that he has taken an interest in a fellow resident, Barbara. Barbara is 78 years old and also in the middle stages of her disease. Her husband comes to visit her regularly. She has shown an interest in Robert as well by reciprocating his affectionate advances. Recently, during a visit Barbara's husband witnessed the advances himself and demanded that the two be separated. Both Barbara and Robert spend their days looking for each other and are agitated most of the day. The staff are faced with decisions related to managing this situation on many levels; between the two residents who want to spend time together, with Barbara's spouse who insists the two be separated, and with fellow residents who are impacted by the stress of the situation within the unit. At the center of this case are two individuals with dementia. How is autonomy balanced with cognitive decline and diminished capacity? How are issues related to living with dignity in an environment where it is in short supply evaluated and managed? The care for persons with dementia has been largely task based with little consideration for the human condition of residents including loneliness, isolation, and boredom.

Should we prevent two people from connecting in human ways? Individuals in these situations are also mitigating the three most devastating issues in the life of persons with dementia—loneliness, isolation, boredom. What responsibility do we have as a society in designing on-the-ground long-term services and supports to foster better outcomes over time, by addressing not just the disease but the person and how he or she might best live the end of his or her life? Ethical considerations of autonomy: Are Robert and Barbara making their own decisions to be together? Beneficence: What is the role of the community, our society at large, with regard to not doing harm? Nonmaleficence: Is harm being done here by either allowing them to have their friendship—or on the other side, preventing it? Justice: What role does justice play? Is it a just society that keeps people apart? Or if someone has dementia, what does any of this look like?

Discussion Questions

1. What is the role of the community in this situation? How do you define *community* in this particular case?

2. What role do the four main ethical principles play here and how can they help us make decisions about how to move forward?

3. Consider the issue of autonomy from the multiple perspectives in this case. What does the story look like from each of those perspectives?

CASE STUDY 11.5

Independent Living and the Role of the State

Jose is a 75-year-old Hispanic male, living alone in a small one-bedroom apartment in an urban area. Jose has been able to manage his activities of daily living on his own since the death of his wife 5 years ago but has grown increasingly frail. His adult children live at a distance and are not part of his daily life. Recently, Jose had a fall in his bathtub and was found by a neighbor several days later. The neighbor called the local AAA and reported that he was worried about his friend and neighbor. This resulted in a visit from the agency in the form of a welfare check. Jose was surprised and embarrassed by this visit—particularly since Jose speaks very little English and the case manager does not speak Spanish. Following this visit there were more visits by strangers, all of whom have the best intentions but still, none spoke Spanish. Jose wants to remain at home, and has been consistent about that to his visitors from the agency. If Jose's choice is to remain at home, how can LTSS be ethically and appropriately brought in to help Jose remain at home safely and in accordance with his desire for autonomy?

Each of the cases presented in this chapter raise questions about public policy development and LTSS. Each asks "How do we take care of the most vulnerable among us?" From the perspective of social justice concerns, should not this be one of the key measures by which any advanced society should be judged?

CONCLUDING OBSERVATIONS

This chapter explored the ethical considerations of long-term services and supports for vulnerable older adults. It's clear that LTSS can no longer be a one-size-fits-all solution. As was discussed, the intersection of vulnerability, old age, and community-based long-term services in this time presents a myriad of challenges that directly impact the lives of those vulnerable older adults and their families as well. As we move into a place and time where population aging and increased longevity are becoming more relevant, the issues of home and place and where we decide we want to age, including independent living, or where we end up aging despite our preferences, including residential long-term care, correctional institutions, or in a state of homelessness, the ethical component will be even more critical. As we consider what it means to be a just society, we need to go beyond the one-size-fits-all mentality. We also need to rethink pathways to a just society vis-á-vis the Older Americans Act, the Aging Networks, and our own ideas about what it means to be old.

DISCUSSION QUESTIONS

1. What does "good" care for vulnerable older adults look like? How would you define it?

2. Should those who are responsible for designing LTSS have a background in aging? Does it matter? Why or why not?

3. How do we take care of the most vulnerable among us? And what ethical principles can help us down that path of good and just long-term services and supports?

REFERENCES

Beauchamp, T. L., & Childress, J. F. (2001). *Principles of biomedical ethics.* New York, NY: Oxford University Press.

Blasszauer, B. (1994). Institutional care of the elderly. *Hastings Center Report, 24*(5), 14–17.

Carson, A. E., & Sabol, W. J. (2016). *Aging of the state prison population, Bureau of Justice Statistics, 1993–2013.* Retrieved from http://www.bjs.gov/index.cfm?ty=pbdetail&iid=5602

Centers for Medicare and Medicaid Services (CMS), United States Department of Health and Human Services, (2017) 2016 CMS Statistics, retrieved from https://www.cms.gov/Research-Statistics-Data-and-Systems/Statistics-Trends-and-Reports/CMS-Statistics-Reference-Booklet/Downloads/2016_CMS_Stats.pdf

Charmaz, K. (1993). *Good days, bad days: The self in chronic illness and time.* Rutgers University Press.

Conly, S. (2013). *Against autonomy: Justifying coercive paternalism.* Cambridge: Cambridge University Press.

Daly, M., & Lewis, J. (2000). The concept of social care and the analysis of contemporary welfare states. *British Journal of Sociology, 51*(2), 281–298.

Dworkin, G. (1988). *The theory and practice of autonomy.* New York, NY: Cambridge University Press.

Harris-Kojetin, L., Sengupta, M., Park-Lee, E., & Valverde, R. (2013). Long-term care services in the United States: 2013 overview. *Vital and Health Statistics, 3*(37). Retrieved from https://www.cdc.gov/nchs/data/nsltcp/long_term_care_services_2013.pdf

Henry, M., Watt, R., Rosenthal, L., & Shivji, A. (2016). *The 2016 Annual Homeless Assessment Report (AHAR) to Congress. Part 1: Point-in-time estimates of homelessness* (Report, Department of Housing and Urban Development, November). Retrieved from https://www.hudexchange.info/resources/documents/2016-AHAR-Part-1.pdf

Holstein, M. B., Waymack, M., & Parks, J. A. (2010). *Ethics, aging, and society: The critical turn.* Springer publishing company.

Kaufman, M. (1987). The construction of masculinity and the triad of mens violence, in (M. Kaufman, Ed) Beyond patriarchy: essays by men on pleasure, power, and change, edited by Michael Kaufman. Toronto, Canada, Oxford University Press, Toronto, 1–29.

Kaye, H. S., Harrington, C., & LaPlante, M. P. (2010). Long-term care: Who gets it, who provides it, who pays, and how much? *Health Affairs, 29*(1), 11–21.

Leira, A. (1992). *Welfare states and working mothers.* Cambridge: Cambridge University Press.

Moody, R. (1992). *Ethics in an aging society.* Baltimore, MD: Johns Hopkins University Press.

Nagourney, A. (2016, May 31). Old and on the street: The graying of America's homeless. *The New York Times.* Retrieved from https://www.nytimes.com/2016/05/31/us/americas-aging-homeless-old-and-on-the-street.html

National Association of Area Agencies on Aging (N4A) (2019) Definitions of Common HCBS, Retrieved from https://www.n4a.org/

Niles-Yokum, K. (2006). *Older adults and consumer direction: Factors that play a role in choice and control* (Dissertation, University of Maryland, Baltimore County).

Niles-Yokum, K., & Wagner, D. L. (2018). *The aging networks: A guide to program and services (8th ed.).* New York, NY: Springer, forthcoming.

Pierson, P. (1994). *Dismantling the welfare state? Reagan, Thatcher, and the politics of retrenchment.* New York, NY: Press Syndicate of the University of Cambridge.

Profile America Facts for Features. (2017). Older Americans Month: May 2017. US Census Bureau. Retrieved from https://www.census.gov/newsroom/facts-for-features/2017/cb17-ff08.html

12

HEALTH CARE DECISION MAKING

Carol Miller, MSN, RN-BC
Nurse Consultant

KEYWORDS

health care decision making
surrogate decision makers
comfort care
do not resuscitate orders
shared decision making

advance directives
durable power of attorney for health care
living wills
ethical decision making

Overview

Health care decision making is a process that is directly linked to vulnerability and ethics in many ways because health conditions, especially those that are progressive, put people at risk for vulnerability. When health care decisions involve questions about autonomy, beneficence, or nonmaleficence, ethical issues arise for the patient and the people or institutions who have personal or professional bonds with the patient. Ethical issues related to justice can arise when health care decisions are based on institutional or governmental policies that determine the use of resources. This chapter focuses on ways in which professionals of all disciplines can prevent and address ethical issues that are associated with health care decision making. Content is based on the following premises:

- Older adults with progressive health conditions are vulnerable because health care decisions influence their well-being and sometimes their length of life.

- Advance directives are a means of limiting or preventing vulnerability of patients with progressive conditions when health care decisions need to be made.

- The involvement of a legally appointed surrogate decision maker who is trustworthy in advocating for the patient's wishes can limit the patient's vulnerability.

- Shared decision making is a process that can prevent ethical issues by supporting autonomy, beneficence, and nonmaleficence.

- Numerous resources are available to address ethical issues related to health care decision making.

Emphasis of this chapter is on roles of professionals in both preventing and addressing ethical issues when health care decisions are made for vulnerable older adults. These issues range from everyday decisions about treatments, diagnostic tests, safety issues, or activities of daily living to more complex decisions about initiation or discontinuation of life-prolonging or life-supporting procedures. In this context, older adults are considered vulnerable when they have conditions that involve decisions related to any aspect of their health care. In this chapter, the term *professionals* refers not only to direct health care providers but also to the many other care providers who can be involved with health care decision making. Thus, the content is pertinent to diverse disciplines including medicine, nursing, legal, ethical, mental health, social service, rehabilitation therapists, and spiritual or religious based care providers.

Advance Directives and Surrogate Decision Makers

From an ethical perspective, advance directives provide a foundation for respecting the autonomy of the patient when the person is not capable of engaging in health care decisions. Advance directives are legally binding documents that allow competent people to document what medical care they would or would not want to receive if they were not capable of making decisions and communicating their wishes. Advance directives also enable a person to appoint a surrogate decision maker who is responsible for communicating and honoring the person's wishes if he or she becomes incompetent or unable to communicate them. Ethical issues are likely to arise under circumstances such as the following:

- in the absence of advance directives stating the person's wishes (e.g., no living will)

- when questions are raised about whether the surrogate decision maker is acting in the best interest of the patient (e.g., if the surrogate decision maker is making decisions that are contrary to the patient's stated wishes)

- when a surrogate decision maker is not available (e.g., never appointed or no longer involved)

- when the authority of the surrogate decision maker is questionable (e.g., accusations that the surrogate decision maker was appointed under undue pressure)

Advance directive documents must be drawn up when the person is capable of understanding their intent, and they become effective only when the person lacks the capacity to make a particular health-related decision. Thus, it is imperative to address advance directives before the onset of any condition that can affect functioning and cognitive abilities. When a diagnosis of a progressive disease such as dementia has already been made, decision-making capacity should be evaluated and documented as early in the process as possible and specifically in relation to the task of executing advance directive documents. This may necessitate a comprehensive assessment by an interdisciplinary team including a mental health professional such as a geropsychologist or geropsychiatrist. It also is imperative to recognize that a person's decision-making capacity can fluctuate significantly acutely, intermittently, or long term.

Although federal and state laws do not *require* that people have advance directive documents, these laws encourage discussions about health care decisions and *suggest* that people have advance directives. State laws vary regarding details (e.g., scope, type of document, conditions for application of advance directives, and requirements for updates) of advance directives, and not all states honor out-of-state advance directives. Box 12.1 provides information about specific types of advance directives.

BOX 12.1

Types of Advance Directives

Durable Power of Attorney for Health Care

- Is considered the most important advance directive

- Designates a surrogate health care decision maker who is authorized to represent the person during any time of incapacity, provide informed consent, and make health care treatment decisions

- Provides written guidelines stating the person's wishes on issues, such as termination of life support measures

- Should be supplemented by discussion of the person's wishes about medical treatments with their primary care provider, other health care workers, and the surrogate decision maker befor a crisis develops.

Do Not Resuscitate (DNR) Orders
- Is a very specific advance directive that compels health care providers to refrain from cardiopulmonary resuscitation if the person is no longer breathing and has no heartbeat

- Is not associated with directives to withhold other medical treatments readily accessible

Comfort Care DNR (also called DNR-Comfort Care, CC/DNR, or Comfort Care-Only DNR),

- Direct health care professionals to provide designated comfort care measures but not resuscitative therapies if the person is in full respiratory or cardiac arrest or if the person is near this condition

- Specify comfort care measures defined such oxygen therapy, airway suctioning, pain management, control of bleeding, and emotional support of patient and family

Living Wills

- Address preferences for a broad range of medical treatments that the person wishes to have or not have when he/she is considered terminally ill

- Affirms the right of a person to receive or refuse treatment

- Are limited in that the document cannot anticipate and address all circumstances that are likely to develop

Professional responsibilities related to advance directives include the following:

- being knowledgeable about pertinent state laws related to advance directives

- teaching patients about advance directives

- encouraging patients to execute such documents if they have not done so

- encouraging patients to review and update their advance directives whenever their situation or that of their surrogate decision maker changes

- assuring that advance directives are available in patient charts

- communicating with other professionals about a patient's advance directives

- documenting conversations about advance directives in patient charts

- facilitating referrals to appropriate professionals in the absence of advance directives or when questions arise about these documents

Many resources are available for helping people learn about and execute advance directives. For example, technological advances are helping people learn about and execute advance directives through interactive "e-planning" websites. Making Your Wishes Known is an example of a comprehensive website that provides educational materials and thought-provoking questions to help participants develop advance directives that communicate their preferences about care to health care providers. Box 12.2 lists some Internet resources that are pertinent to both patients and professionals for information and decision aids related to advance directives.

BOX 12.2

Internet Resources Related to Advance Directives

Information about Advance Directives and State Laws

- Caring Connection, http://www.caringinfo.org

- American Bar Association Commission on Law and Aging, http://www.americanbar.org

- Compassion and Support at the End of Life, http://www.compassionand-support.org/index.php

- Family Caregiver Alliance, http://www.caregiver.org

- Websites with interactive tools and educational videos

- Making Your Wishes Known, http://www.makingyourwishesknown.com

- Prepare for Your Care, http://www.prepareforyourcare.org

- Physician Order for Life-Sustaining Treatment, http://www.polst.org

- Aging With Dignity Five Wishes, https://agingwithdignity.org

Ethical Decision Making and Vulnerable Elders

Ethical decision making is based on a process of shared decision making, which is a collaborative process that enables patients and their providers to make health care decisions together, based on discussion of the best scientific evidence available and the patient's values and preferences. In health care settings, these decisions typically involve the following components: (a) provision of evidence-based information by a health care provider about predictions of likely outcomes based on many variables, including the probable risks and benefits of using or not using an intervention, and (b) discussion of personal goals of the patient, as expressed by the patient himself or herself or by a surrogate decision maker based on the wishes of the patient.

Shared decision making is particularly relevant to the ethical principle of autonomy because, when it is done appropriately, the process protects the right of the individual to be involved in decisions about his or her health care. The process emphasizes autonomy and challenges paternalistic approaches in which physicians make decisions for patients. In addition, it is pertinent to the ethical principles of beneficence and nonmaleficence because it requires the health care professional and the patient to choose tests and treatments based on a full discussion of potential benefits and harms within the context of the patient's unique situation. Despite widespread agreement that shared decision making is valuable, many barriers interfere with application of this process during patient care (See examples in Box 12.3).

BOX 12.3

Barriers to Shared Decision Making for Vulnerable Elderly

Barriers Arising From Society and Institutions

- Pervasive ageism (e.g., perception of older adults as unwilling or unable to participate in health care decisions that affect themselves)

- Lack of evidence-based information applicable to vulnerable older adults (e.g., those who are frail, those who have complex medical issues)

- Lack of societal emphasis on the importance of advance directives

- Paternalistic approach within health care systems

- Diagnostic labels that are associated with an individual's lack of ability to participate in decisions (e.g., dementia)

- Guidelines based solely on chronologic age of the patient (e.g., 85 and older)

- Lack of time

- Inadequate reimbursement from health insurance

- Lack of policies about shared decision making

Barriers Associated With Vulnerable Older Adults

- Common perceptions of physicians as infallible

- Long-standing practice of not being involved in health care decisions

- Lack of confidence in one's own ability to understand health care issues

- Personal desire to allow physicians to make decisions independently

- Fear of making poor decisions

- Lack of trustworthy surrogate decision maker

- Actions and decisions of surrogate decision makers who do not act in the best interest of the older adult

Currently many health care organizations and academic centers are publishing guidelines related to the process of ethical decision making. For example, faith-based health care settings, such as Catholic or Jewish institutions, publish guidelines that are mandated for patients who receive health care services in their facilities. Professionals can use the information in Box 12.4 as a guide to ethical decision making.

BOX 12.4

Process of Ethical Decision Making in Patient Care

Step 1: Identify the ethical questions: Focus on who *should* make this decision.

Step 2: What are the clinically relevant facts, including what is already known and the facts that will be gathered?

Step 3: What are the values at stake for all relevant parties and what are the conflicting values of various parties? (e.g., beneficence, nonmaleficence, autonomy, truth telling, confidentiality, fairness, respecting life).

Step 4: List options: Focus on what *could* you do?

Step 5: Chose the best option from the ethical point of view: Focus on what *should* be done.

Step 6: Justify your choice by explaining why this option is better than others and why the other options are less appropriate.

Source: Adapted from University of West Virginia Geriatric Education Center, n.d.

The following cases illustrate ethical dilemmas that involve decision making for older adults who are vulnerable. The first case involves everyday ethical issues and the next two cases illustrate ethical issues related to initiation or discontinuation of life-sustaining treatments. The cases take place across acute care, long-term care, and home care settings where health care is provided under Medicare, Medicaid, or other insurance policies. Information is provided about resources and technology that are commonly available to health care providers to address the ethical issues.

CASE STUDY 12.1

Everyday Ethical Issues About Decision Making for Those Who Are Vulnerable Due to Risks to Safety

Mr. H. is an 86-year-old man with long-term diagnoses of osteoporosis, osteoarthritis, and Parkinson's Disease and a recent diagnosis of acute myelocytic leukemia. He is admitted to the hospital and identified as high risk for falls due to history of three falls in the 2 months prior to hospitalization; he also is high risk for fractures due to his diagnosis of osteoporosis. Despite the falls, Mr. H. walked 2 miles every day and participated in water aerobics three times weekly until recently. According to hospital procedures for patients who are high risk for falls and fractures, he is not allowed to walk unattended, even to the bathroom. Mr. H. expresses concern about losing his muscle strength during his hospitalization because he has been admitted for several weeks while receiving chemotherapy. In addition, he considers the required assistance as a violation of his rights and he resents the long waits for staff to answer his call light. Mr. H. insists that he be allowed unrestricted ambulation, including walking in the halls for extended periods when he is not undergoing treatments. However, when Mr. H.'s daughter visits, she tells the staff that the restrictions are necessary and good because his falls at home were due to his poor judgment. Moreover, she states that as her father's health care proxy, she has the right to override his wishes about independent ambulation.

The hospital staff are considering using any of the following technological devices to alert them if Mr. H. gets out of bed without calling for assistance: motion-sensitive monitors worn on his clothing, pressure-sensitive bed or chair pads, or alarms clipped to his clothing or gowns. These devices are designed to sound an alarm at the nurses' station when the patient attempts to get out of bed. When Mr. H.'s daughter requests that the staff keep full bed rails up when he is in bed, the staff inform her that this would violate hospital policies because these are a type of restraint and studies indicated that restraints are associated with higher incidence of falls and more serious fall-related injuries. Box 12.5 summarizes ethical issues and interventions to resolve the issues.

BOX 12.5

Ethical Issues Associated With Mr. H.'s Desire to Walk Independently

Autonomy

- Mr. H. states that as long as he is competent to make his own decisions, he will walk without assistance while he is in the hospital.

- Mr. H. is entitled to walk freely as long as he does not interfere with anyone else or endanger any equipment.

- If Mr. H. falls, that's his choice because he has the right to choose between benefits and risks.

- Mr. H. has the right to refuse the use of any technological device to monitor his movements and he views these as a violation of his rights.

Beneficence

- Hospital staff have the duty to protect Mr. H. from fractures and other injuries due to falls.

- Hospital staff cite data about inpatient falls as the most commonly reported adverse event in hospitals.

- Hospital staff and Mr. H's daughter perceive that their judgement is better than his and therefore they are acting in his best interest by restricting his mobility.

Nonmaleficence

■ Studies show that restricting a patient's mobility during hospitalizations increases the risk of pneumonia, pressure ulcers, and deep vein thrombosis. Hospital staff should not impose this risk on Mr. H. by restricting his mobility.

Justice

■ Hospital staff cannot provide extra attention to help Mr. H. walk if it takes away from limited resources for addressing needs of other patients.

■ The hospital has the right to impose standards to protect themselves from liability, including lawsuits.

Resolution and Use of Resources: After a physical therapy evaluation was done, a care conference was held with Hr. H., his daughter, nursing staff, and the physical therapist. The following plan was initiated:

■ Mr. H. would be allowed to walk in his room as long as he used the walker provided by the physical therapist and left at his bedside

■ Mr. H. would participate in group exercise sessions on days when he was not actively receiving chemotherapy

■ Mr. H.'s daughter would walk with him in the hallways during her visits

QUESTIONS FOR DISCUSSION

■ What other health care decisions that affect a patient's ordinary activities might have ethical implications?

■ How do the ethical issues about Mr. H.'s safe mobility differ from those that arise when he is in his own home?

■ If Mr. H. also had a diagnosis of dementia, would his daughter automatically have the right to decide about his ambulation?

■ If Mr. H. also had a diagnosis of dementia, would the staff have the right to use an alarm device to alert them to his movements?

Decision Making About Initiating Life-Sustaining Treatments for Those Who Are Vulnerable Due to Inadequate Food and Fluid

Health care decisions about initiating artificial nutrition and hydration (ANH) are among the most common ethical dilemmas for patients with progressively declining conditions that affect their nutritional intake. ANH refers to methods of bypassing the upper gastrointestinal tract to deliver hydration and nutritional substances. A percutaneous endoscopic gastrostomy (PEG) tube (sometimes referred to as a *feeding tube*) is the most commonly used approach for long-term management of ANH. Nasogastric tubes, which are inserted through the nose to the stomach, are considered for short-term ANH, but they commonly are removed after a short period and replaced with a PEG tube for long-term nutrition and hydration.

Initially developed during the 1980s for short-term use in pediatric patients, the PEG tube gradually became a standard intervention for long-term use for patients of all ages and with many conditions. By 2010, PEG tubes were widely used in long-term care facilities for residents with advanced dementia, and questions about the risks versus benefits were raised by ethicists, policy makers, and medical professionals. Recent research supports the use of ANH for people with conditions that directly affect their ability to chew and swallow (e.g., head and neck cancer) but *not* for people with advanced dementia. Decisions about ANH are often initiated because the person is losing weight, has significant difficulty swallowing, or requires considerable and time-consuming assistance with feeding. Another reason the issue of ANH arises is because families and health care providers may have optimistic—but not evidence-based—expectations about the benefits of ANH, or they are concerned that the person will starve to death.

Although ANH is sometimes specifically addressed in advance directives; ethical issues are often associated with decisions about this life-sustaining intervention. The principle of autonomy may be challenged under circumstances such as the following:

- when the patient's wishes are not known
- when the patient's surrogate decision maker does not support the patient's wishes
- when the patient's prognosis is unpredictable
- when recommendations are based on outdated or otherwise inaccurate information

The ethical principles of beneficence and nonmaleficence may come into play when ANH is recommended without full consideration of the potential risks and benefits or when decision makers do not fully understand and accept the evidence. For example, PEG tubes may be recommended for someone who has advanced dementia and is losing weight with the intent of improving nutrition and overall physical health (i.e., beneficence). Current evidence indicates that the risks of PEG tubes in people with advanced dementia outweigh the benefits; however, decision makers may minimize the risks and focus disproportionately on the benefits (Abu et al., 2017; Gieniusz et al., 2018; Goldberg & Altman, 2014). In many situations, the principle of beneficence dominates the decision about a PEG tube and the principle of nonmaleficence is overlooked.

The following examples illustrate situations in which ethical dilemmas arise.

CASE STUDY 12.2

Case Studies

Mr. S. who is 86 years old and in moderate-stage dementia due to strokes. He lives with his daughter and has gradually lost 15 pounds during the past year. During a hospitalization for aspiration pneumonia, a swallowing evaluation determines that dysphagia significantly increases the risk for recurrent aspiration pneumonia. Subsequently, the physician asks Mr. S.'s daughter, who is his surrogate decision maker, to give permission for a PEG tube to be inserted. Mr. S. has not indicated his preferences about ANH in his advance directives, but his daughter states that her father has told her many times that he does not want any extraordinary interventions to prolong his life. She refuses to sign consent for the PEG tube; however, her two older brothers tell the doctor that their father should have the PEG tube so he doesn't starve to death. Moreover, they state that their sister simply wants him to die and they will bring charges against the doctor if he does not insert the PEG tube.

Mr. T. is 79 years old and is a resident of a nursing facility. During the care conference, the team raises concern that he has lost 10% of his weight in 6 months. It has become increasingly more time consuming to feed him, requiring more staff time. The nursing facility has been cited for the high number of their residents who have lost weight, and they recommend that Mr. T.'s family consider having him evaluated for a PEG tube. This would presumably improve his nutrition, and he would qualify for skilled care reimbursement, at least temporarily. The out-of-pocket expenses for the family would decrease temporarily, and the facility's rating would improve. Mr. T.'s family has made his health care decisions for the past 6 months, and his advance directives do not address any issues about ANH. Mr. T.'s family agrees to the PEG tube.

Because ANH has been widely used for decades, guidelines are available for health care professionals and many so-called decision aids are available to guide patients and surrogate decision makers. Professional responsibilities related to decisions about ANH involve communicating evidence-based information about ANH and encouraging the use of decision aids. Box 12.6 lists resources that professional can consider when decisions about ANH involve ethical concerns.

BOX 12.6

Resources for Ethical Decision Making About ANH

Resources for Professionals

- Care conference involving patient and surrogate decision makers and the following health care disciplines as appropriate: medicine, nursing, dietician, speech/swallowing therapist, social worker, mental health professionals, and religious/spiritual supports

- Palliative care team (described in next topic)

- Ethics committee if conflicts arise

- Cultural, religious, or spiritual support when religious or cultural beliefs of the individual, the surrogate decision maker, or the professional's influence the decision-making process

Decision-Making Tools for Patients and Surrogate Decision Makers

- Making Choices: Long Term Feeding Tube Placement in Elderly Patients (interactive Internet site and brochure), https://decisionaid.ohri.ca/docs/Tube_Feeding_DA/PDF/TubeFeeding.pdf

- Compassion and Support at the End of Life, http://www.compassionand-support.org/index.php/for_patients_families/life-sustaining_treatment/artificial_hydration_and_nutrition

- Health in Agin, http://www.healthinaging.org/resources/resource:feeding-tubes-for-those-with-advanced-dementia

- New York State, guide for patients and families for deciding about health care (available in English and Spanish), http://www.health.ny.gov/publications/1503

- University of North Carolina School of Medicine, video and other resources for improving decision making about feeding options in dementia, http://www.med.unc.edu/pcare/resources/feedingoptions

- Monroe County Medical Society and Community-wide Guidelines on Tube Feeding/PEG Placement for Adults, http://www.mcms.org/resources/Documents/QC/Tube%20FeedingPEG%20Placement/Tube%20Feeding_2017%20Complete%20Guideline.pdf

QUESTIONS FOR DISCUSSION

- How can professionals use shared decision making about the decision to initiate a PEG tube for Mr. S., particularly when current guidelines apply primarily to people with advanced dementia rather than moderate dementia? (Hint: Use resources in Box 12.6 to support your answers.)

- Does the decision about a PEG tube for Mr. T. involve ethical issues related to financial gain or benefits for the institution?

Decision Making About Discontinuing Life-Sustaining Treatments for Those Who Are Vulnerable Due to Progressive Conditions

The rapid development of medical devices for management of serious chronic conditions has created new ethical issues related to decisions about withdrawing treatments that are used to support essential life functions. Most medical, legal, and ethical experts state that decisions about withdrawing treatments are equivalent to decisions about never starting a treatment (Sprung et al., 2014). In clinical practice, however, decisions about withdrawing a treatment are more psychologically challenging for health care professionals and more emotionally laden for patients, families, and surrogate decision makers (Chung, Yoon, Rasinski, & Curlin, 2016; Somers, Grey, & Satkoske, 2016). Ethical issues often arise about withdrawing a treatment, as in the following examples:

CASE STUDY 12.3
Case Studies

Mr. A. is a resident of a nursing home and receives dialysis treatments three times a week for management of end-stage renal disease. After a stroke left him with significant physical and cognitive limitations, his family raised questions at a care conference about discontinuing the dialysis since his quality of life is poor. They also state that when their mother died 6 months ago, he told them that he did not want to keep living. His advance directives designate his son as his surrogate decision maker; however, they do not address his preferences about dialysis. Nursing home staff state they are obligated to continue the treatment since Mr. A. began it when he was capable of making that decision. Moreover, because the nursing home is a faith-based facility, staff need to adhere to policies of the institution.

While Mrs. B. is in relatively good health, she agrees to have a pacemaker device inserted to correct an ongoing cardiac arrhythmia. Several years later, Mrs. B. has metastatic cancer and advanced dementia. A decision needs to be made about turning off the pacemaker.

While Mr. C. was in the intensive care unit and not able to be involved with decisions about his care, his surrogate decision maker gave permission for dialysis to be initiated with the expectation that he would recover. When Mr. C. does not recover, a decision needs to be made about continuing or withdrawing the treatment.

In each of these situations, ethical issues might be avoided if patient preferences had been clearly defined in advance directives and if a reliable and trustworthy surrogate decision maker were involved in shared decision making. Ethical issues that arise are similar to the ones discussed in the section on ANH. In the absence of these advance directives, or whenever ethical issues arise related to withdrawing life-supporting treatments, professionals can seek guidance from palliative care teams.

Palliative care is both a philosophy of care and an organized system for achieving best possible quality of life for patients and their family caregivers who are facing problems associated with a broad range of persistent, life-threatening, or recurring conditions that adversely affect their daily functioning or will predictably reduce life expectancy. Problems include decisions about discontinuing life-sustaining treatments and ethical dilemmas about care or decision-making capacity (National Consensus Project for Quality Palliative Care, 2013). Palliative care models are based on an interprofessional team approach, with emphasis on respecting individual preferences and promoting self-directed care.

Palliative care services were initially developed within hospice services but in recent decades they have been developed within other health care settings. The proportion of hospitals with more than 50 beds that had palliative care models increased from 25% in 2000 to 75% in 2015 (Cassel, Bowman, Rogers, Spragens, & Meier, 2018). Increasingly, palliative care services are recognized as an essential resource for health care decision making for patients with conditions such as advanced dementia, end-stage renal disease, and heart failure (Lloyd-Williams, Mogan, & Dening, 2017; Maciver & Ross, 2018; Schmidt, 2017). Palliative care services are covered by Medicare, Medicaid, and other health insurance programs.

Professionals have an important responsibility to facilitate referrals for palliative care when issues related to withdrawing life supporting treatments arise. The National Consensus Project for Quality Palliative Care (2013) is an excellent resource for up-to-date guidelines and information about palliative care services. Hospital settings and hospice programs provide information about local resources for palliative care services. It is important to teach patients and families that although palliative care is provided through hospice programs, the services differ significantly in that palliative care can be provided throughout the course of a serious progressive illness; whereas hospice care is provided during the terminal phase of an illness.

QUESTIONS FOR DISCUSSION

- In each of these situations, how would you involve palliative care in addressing ethical issues?
- What resources do you have as a professional for using palliative care services?

CONCLUDING OBSERVATIONS

Professionals have essential roles in both preventing and addressing ethical issues related to health care decision making. Professionals can help prevent ethical issues by assuring that patients' preferences are known and honored through advance directives and shared decision making, as discussed in the first sections of this chapter. Interactive decision aids are rapidly being developed and available online through nonprofit organizations. Professionals can encourage patients and surrogate decision makers to actively engage in the decision-making process about the interventions they may or may not want during serious illness and end of life. When conflicts or issues arise, professionals are responsible for using available resources to resolve the situation, as described throughout this chapter.

REFERENCES

Abu, R. A., Khoury, T., Cohen, J., Chen, S., Yaari S., Daher S., ... & Mizrahi, M. (2017). PEG insertion in patients with dementia does not improve nutritional status and has worse outcomes as compared with PEG insertion for other indications. *Journal of Clinical Gastroenterology, 51*(5), 417–420.

Cassel, J. B., Bowman, B., Rogers, M., Spragens, L. H., & Meier, D. E. (2018). Palliative Care Leadership Centers are a key to diffusion of palliative care innovation. *Health Affairs, 37,* 231–239.

Chung, G. S., Yoon, J. D., Rasinski, K. A., & Curlin, F. A. (2016). US physicians' opinions about distinctions between withdrawing and withholding life-sustaining treatment. *Journal of Religion and Health, 55*(5), 1596–1606.

Gieniusz, M., Sinvani, L., Kozikowski, A., Patel, V., Nouryan, C., Williams, M. S., ... & Wolf-Klein, G. (2018). Percutaneous feeding tubes in individuals with advanced dementia: Are physicians "choosing wisely"? *Journal of the American Geriatrics Society, 66,* 64–69.

Goldberg, L., & Altman, K. (2014). The role of gastrostomy tube placement in advanced dementia with dysphagia: A critical review. *Clinical Interventions in Aging, 9,* 1733–1739.

Lloyd-Williams, M., Mogan, C., & Dening, K. (2017). Identifying palliative care needs in people with dementia. *Current Opinion in Supportive and Palliative Care, 11,* 328–333.

Maciver, J., & Ross, H. (2018). A palliative approach for heart failure end-of-life care. *Current Opinion in Cardiology, 33,* 202–207.

National Consensus Project for Quality Palliative Care. (2013). *Clinical practice guidelines for quality palliative care.* Retrieved from http://www.nationalconsensusproject.org

Schmidt, R. (2017). Incorporating supportive care into the hemodialysis unit. *Current Opinion in Nephrology and Hypertension, 26*(6), 530–536.

Somers, E., Grey, C., & Satkoske, V. (2016). Withholding versus withdrawing treatment: Artificial nutrition and hydration as a model. *Current Opinion in Supportive Palliative Care, 10*(3), 208–213.

Sprung, C. L., Paruk, F., Kissoon, N., Hartog, C. S., Lipman, J., Du, B., ... & Feldman, C. (2014). The Durban World Congress Ethics Round Table Conference Report I: Differences between withholding and withdrawing life-sustaining treatments. *Journal of Critical Care, 29*(6), 890–895.

University of West Virginia Geriatric Education Center. (n.d.). Process of ethical decision making. Retrieved from http://www.wvnec.org/media/1250/process-of-ethical-decision-making-new.pdf

13

END OF LIFE

Alina M. Perez, JD, MPH, LCSW
Nova Southeastern University

Kathy Cerminara, JD, JSD, LLM
Nova Southeastern University

Angana Mahapatra, DO
Nova Southeastern University

KEYWORDS

end of life
advance directives
medical futility
vulnerable elders

medical ethics
palliative care
end-of-life choices and the law

Overview

This chapter continues the previous chapter, about health care decision making, in a specific context: end-of-life care. Death is something every person will encounter, both in others and personally. Yet it is difficult to think about and discuss end-of-life issues for a variety of psychological and cultural reasons. This chapter is designed to encourage thought and discussion, first regarding the case it presents and analyzes, but then on a more personal level for every reader. If the governing principle of this chapter is to do what the patient wanted (and it is), then one of the goals of this chapter is to enable each reader to seriously consider and perhaps make some decisions about treatment near the end of life, and to consider the special circumstances that can render an elderly person vulnerable in this setting.

In pursuing this goal, this chapter will address the legal and ethical implications of a case involving an elderly Hispanic woman on ventilator support. The previous chapter has discussed basic principles of decision-making capacity, so it will rely upon that chapter for definitions and approaches to determining such capacity. Instead, it will address an unfolding scenario in which an elderly woman's capacity may be in question, and it will proceed from there through the end of her life.

CASE STUDY 13.1

Withdrawal of Ventilator Support

Ms. Gonzalez, a 78-year-old Hispanic woman, resident of a small rural community, was brought to the local community hospital's emergency department by her neighbor, Mr. Jones. At that time, he noted that she was "not herself" and appeared to be "short of breath." Mr. Jones had been frequently visiting Ms. Gonzalez and her long-time romantic partner, Ms. Johnson, for the past several months, since he noticed disrepair both inside and outside their home. Ms. Gonzalez had recently given power of attorney to Mr. Jones so that he could assist them "with their house issues." Neither Ms. Gonzalez nor Ms. Johnson had any local family support. Ms. Gonzalez had a son who lived outside the United States, but she had not seen or spoken with him in several years due to family arguments over Ms. Gonzalez's lesbian relationship.

At the emergency department, the physician determined that Ms. Gonzalez had suffered an embolic stroke due to an underlying heart condition. Upon transfer to the hospital, Ms. Gonzalez's condition deteriorated rapidly. She became unresponsive and unable to breathe on her own. Ms. Gonzalez was quickly intubated and transferred to the intensive care unit (ICU) under heavy sedation. Medically stabilizing Ms. Gonzalez required various invasive medical interventions including ventilator support, intravenous antibiotics, and the placement of several monitoring devices. Initial attempts to wean Ms. Gonzalez off sedation medication were followed by periods of severe agitation during which she became combative and tried to pull out the tubes and lines attached to her body for the monitoring of her medical condition.

Ms. Gonzalez's partner, Ms. Johnson, informed the medical team that, during their 20-year relationship, Ms. Gonzalez had told her several times that she would not want "tubes or other medical equipment attached to her body." Despite this, the team refused to discontinue treatment. The attending physician, Dr. Smith, explained to Ms. Johnson that Ms. Gonzalez did not suffer from a terminal illness, so all treatments were appropriate to alleviate or cure her multiple medical problems. Doing so would allow Ms. Gonzalez to live longer with a better quality of life, "something," he said, "all Hispanics want at the end of life." Dr. Smith also told Ms. Johnson that she could not make treatment decisions for Ms. Gonzalez without a signed legal form appointing her as a surrogate decision-maker. Despite Ms. Johnson's protests, and Mr. Jones's claims that he had the legal right to make medical decisions for Ms. Gonzalez because she had given him power of attorney, Dr. Smith located and contacted Ms. Gonzalez's son as her next of kin. The son authorized all forms of treatment for his mother, stating that he wanted everything done for her "because disconnecting the ventilator or not giving her treatment would be like murder."

After three more weeks in the ICU, Ms. Gonzalez's physical and mental condition began to improve, but she still could not breathe without the help of the ventilator. She communicated in writing and through an interpreter that she wanted to "die in peace." After a consulting psychiatrist deemed her as having capacity to make health care decisions, Ms. Gonzalez requested that the hospital and physicians discontinue all treatments, including the ventilator. With the aid of the hospital's palliative care and hospice teams, she died comfortably shortly thereafter, with Ms. Johnson by her side.

Contrasting and Comparing
End-of-Life Choices

Before delving into the ethical considerations relevant to end-of-life decision-making for vulnerable elders such as Ms. Gonzalez, it is crucial to remember that definitions matter. Confusion in terminology has plagued the field, sometimes interfering with well-meaning attempts to do what is "right" as patients near the end of their lives. Since the dawn of end-of-life decision-making law with the *Quinlan* case in 1976, legal and medical focus has shifted from ensuring that patients execute documents memorializing their treatment wishes (***advance directives***) to facilitating conversations about patients' values and treatment goals (***advance care planning***) (Institute of Medicine [IOM], 2014).

The IOM defines a *good death* as "one that is free from avoidable distress and suffering for patients, families and caregivers, in general accord with patients' and families' wishes; and reasonably consistent with clinical, cultural, and ethical standards"(IOM, 1997, p. 4). Understanding the terms involved and discerning the sometimes subtle differences between them is crucial to appropriately navigate the path to that goal.

As patients near the end of life, it has become commonplace for medical professionals to raise the issue of ***withholding or withdrawing life-sustaining treatment*** of various types. Withholding, for example, takes place if ventilator support is never initiated, while withdrawal occurs if a patient's ventilator is disconnected. If a patient has decision-making capacity, medical professionals will appropriately address the issue directly with him or her. If not, however, medical professionals must rely on a person making decisions on behalf of the patient or existing advance directives (See Table 13.1).

Withholding or withdrawal can take place with respect to any sort of medical treatment, including ***medically supplied nutrition and hydration*** such as that provided through a tube after a patient can no longer safely ingest nutrition and hydration by mouth. Even before that medical stage, a patient who has decision-making capacity may ***voluntarily stop eating and drinking***, and many medical professionals will assist with the clinical management of that process if the patient chooses it (Quill, Ganzini, Truog, & Pope, 2018).

Any patient with capacity may leave ***advance directives*** behind to guide a surrogate, proxy, holder of a medical power of attorney, or guardian—as well as clinicians and other professionals—in making end-of-life decisions after that patient's loss of capacity. Advance directives may be oral or written (Meisel et al., 2004), but the term is most often used to refer to written documents. Related to advance directives, and certainly a part of the advance care planning process, are ***Do Not Resuscitate (DNR)*** orders and ***Physician Orders for Life-Sustaining Treatment (POLSTs)*** (See Table 13.1).

All of these tools are intended to assist patients (and their decision-makers if the patients lack capacity) in refusing or authorizing withdrawal of life-sustaining treatment while still maintaining comfort and remaining pain free. In some instances, however, patients or their decision-makers wish to begin or continue treatment that physicians believe is futile. ***Medical futility*** may be ***quantitative***, if it produces no medical benefit,

TABLE 13.1   Definitions of Key Terms

Do Not Resuscitate (DNR) Order	A medical order instructing medical professionals to refrain from resuscitation efforts if a patient were to stop breathing or if a patient's heart were to stop beating.
Guardian	A person a judge has appointed to speak on behalf of a patient who lacks decision-making capacity.
Living Will	An advance directive in which a person gives instructions regarding end-of-life choices he or she would make.
Physician Order For Life-Sustaining Treatment (POLST)	A medical order operationalizing a variety of patient treatment choices near the end of life. Names vary; a POLST may be called a MOLST, a MOST, or another such acronym as one moves from state to state.
Surrogate, Proxy, or Holder Of A Durable Power Of Attorney For Medical Decision-Making	Various names, determined by state law, for a person whom a patient has designated to speak on his or her behalf in case of loss of decision-making capacity. State law also usually designates a person to speak on the patient's behalf if the patient has not designated anyone.

or it may be **qualitative**, meaning that it will result in very little medical benefit at great cost, such as pain or suffering (Schneiderman, 2011).

As patients enter the terminal phase of illness, or sometimes shortly before a terminal diagnosis, they may choose palliative rather than curative care. **Palliative care** is medical care intended to alleviate symptoms associated with illness, whatever the patient's prognosis (IOM, 2015). A patient meeting certain requirements may even choose a particular form of palliative care known as hospice. **Hospice care** is care provided at the end of life and includes palliation of physical symptoms along with psychological, spiritual, and family support through an integrated team of professionals (IOM, 2014).

Distinct from all of these concepts are two concepts that are often confused. In contrast to withholding or withdrawal of life-sustaining treatment, **euthanasia** occurs when someone (who need not be a medical professional) administers a drug to a person or takes an action with the purpose of ending that person's life. This is illegal even if the person taking the action is doing so at that patient's request, because that patient is near death anyway, or to end the patient's excruciating pain. This differs significantly from **aid in dying** (also known as **assisted suicide**) because there, the patient himself or herself takes the final step, most commonly by self-administering a drug. When the person who assists by prescribing or providing the drug in aid in dying is a physician or other medical professional, the process is termed **physician aid in dying** or **medical aid in dying**.

End-of-Life Choices and the Law

Intrinsically related to the ethics of choices made by individuals at the end of their lives is the legality of those choices. Laws governing end-of-life decision-making vary from state to state in the United States and from country to country in the rest of the world. The laws among the various states within the United States are reasonably uniform with respect to withholding or withdrawal of life-sustaining treatment and euthanasia, but states contrast sharply with respect to physician aid in dying. Other countries similarly vary; some, such as the Netherlands, authorize withholding and withdrawal of life-sustaining treatment, physician aid in dying, and euthanasia (Preston, 2018); while others, such as Italy, have only recently authorized withholding or withdrawal of life-sustaining treatment through advance directives (Sulmasy, 2018).

Withholding and withdrawal of life-sustaining treatment in accordance with a patient's wishes is legal in all 50 U.S. states. The U.S. Supreme Court has even suggested that citizens nationwide enjoy a fundamental constitutional right to refuse life-sustaining treatment, including medically supplied nutrition and hydration (*Cruzan v. Director, Mo. Dept. of Health*, 1990). The Supreme Court also has indicated that adequate pain relief must be afforded to citizens nationwide (*Glucksberg v. Washington*, 1997). In addition, many states have passed legislation intended to assure that medical professionals provide sufficient pain relief to patients who need it. This contrasts with the condemnation of euthanasia as being illegal in all 50 states.

A small but growing minority of states has legalized physician or medical aid in dying in the United States. To qualify, an adult patient must be terminally ill, have decision-making capacity, make a series of requests (some oral and some written), and endure waiting periods between each of the requests. Physicians or other medical professionals such as physician assistants must inform patients of all available palliative care options, including hospice care, and must refer any patient thought to lack decision-making capacity to a mental health professional for evaluation. At the conclusion of the process, the patient receives a prescription to fill and to use to end his or her life as he or she sees fit, if desired. Many patients do not fill their prescriptions, instead choosing to die naturally even after buying the prescribed medication (Oregon Health Authority, Public Health Division, 2017).

Internationally there is wide variety in legality, as described earlier. Notably, the Netherlands has long authorized physician aid in dying and euthanasia—over recent years expanding its authorization to children (allowing parents to make the decision for their children) and to cases involving mental disorders in addition to physical suffering (Preston, 2018). In Belgium, legislation includes chronically ill children as among those who may request euthanasia (Brouwer et al., 2018). Further, in Switzerland, aid in dying need not be provided by a physician or other medical professional. Anyone may aid a qualified person in dying, as long as he or she is doing so ethically (Bosshard, Broeckear, Clark, Matersvedt, Muller-Busch, 2008).

Principles of Biomedical Ethics and the Dying Vulnerable Elder

Ethics is the study and resolution of conflicting principles. A principle is a basic foundational belief that guides actions. A number of conflicting ethical principles may be relevant and applicable to any difficult medical situation. How patients, physicians, staff, and family rank and value these principles and how conflicting rankings are resolved constitutes the main work of clinical ethics.

Ethical principles involved in end-of-life care include ***autonomy, beneficence, nonmaleficence,*** and ***justice.*** While it is important to recognize that various principles may play more distinctive roles from situation to situation, the ethical principles of autonomy (the patient's right to control his or her own body); beneficence (the belief that a practitioner should act in the best interest of the patient); and nonmaleficence (not harming or inflicting the least harm possible to reach a beneficial outcome) are central to the process.

Autonomy

Autonomy, which stands for a patient's right to freely make informed choices about medical care based on his or her wishes and values, plays a central role at the end of life, often framed by issues of capacity or even cultural values, as we will see in the discussion of our case. When end-of-life treatment and choices are involved and the elder has capacity, autonomy can be exercised through the elder's direct expressions of his or her wishes regarding treatment options. When elders lack capacity, autonomy may be exercised through previously drafted advance directive documents or by others legally authorized to make decisions on behalf of the patient.

As in the case of Ms. Gonzalez, autonomy can be limited by various factors. Elders suffering from diminished or absent capacity due to stroke, dementia, memory loss, or mental illness, who had not previously communicated wishes to proxies—in writing or otherwise—would have to rely on others such as family members or professionals to approximate their wishes during the decision-making process. Resulting decisions may or may not be a truthful representation of what the patient would have wanted.

In direct opposition to the ethical principle of autonomy is ***paternalism.*** Sometimes health care professionals make decisions for their patients, believing they are acting in their best interest. Paternalism occurs in many instances due to the disparity of power and knowledge in medical settings but sometimes occurs as an expression of cultural or individual values where familial or group decision-making rather than autonomy is preferred (Searight & Gafford, 2005).

Beneficence

The principle of beneficence calls for the health care professional to act as advocate for patient decisions and wishes, to prevent harm, to remove the source of harm when it is being inflicted, and to bring about positive good. In the context of end-of-life care for elders, beneficence translates into the acceptance of the patient's choices regardless of the professional's own moral or religious values. When patients have not previously and cannot concurrently express their wishes, the professional's duty is to advocate for those approaches that would promote good care at the end of life (Cavalieri, 2001). For example, once Ms. Gonzalez recovered her decision-making capacity, she requested the ventilator support to be discontinued, knowing that death would ensue but preferring such an end to the medical treatment that would keep her alive but "depending on machines and medical treatment" as she always said she did not want to be. In this case, the positive good (beneficence) is represented by the fulfillment of the Ms. Gonzalez's long-expressed wishes and the alleviation of physical and emotional symptoms for a better quality dying process.

Many would argue that physicians have an obligation to practice beneficence by providing all means to alleviate pain, regardless of the source of the suffering (Quill et al., 2018). In some situations, this could be at odds with other ethical principles. For example, a patient who voluntarily refuses nutrition and hydration to hasten death may be trying to exercise his or her autonomy and control and to reduce the possibility of suffering during the later stages of dying (Quill et al., 2018). Such practice has been the center of ethical, legal, and professional debates. A physician faced with the need to manage the symptoms of such a patient may find himself or herself caught in an ethical dilemma: Given that some would equate that patient's actions with committing suicide, and suicide is morally wrong, is it wrong to provide the means to alleviate the pain and suffering the patient's actions may cause?

Nonmaleficence

Often discussed in tandem with beneficence, the principle of nonmaleficence is about avoiding infliction of intentional harm. One can find conflicts between beneficence and nonmaleficence in almost any clinical situation. The dichotomy between the two principles is the foundation for a risk/benefit analysis in many end-of-life situations. One response to the above example, for instance, would be that anything done to assist an immoral action is immoral itself. If the patient's actions in refusing nutrition and hydration constitute the immoral act of suicide, a physician helping alleviate symptoms because of the patient's actions would also be inflicting intentional harm (maleficence) by contributing to the act of suicide, even if his or her intentions were just to alleviate pain.

The effects of balancing the principle of nonmaleficence against that of beneficence can give rise to the doctrine (or principle) of ***double effect***, which is often invoked to explain the permissibility of an action that causes a serious harm—such as the death of a human being—as a side effect of promoting some good end (Meisel et al., 2004). Application of the principle of double effect to our case would lead to the conclusion that Dr. Smith's actions were legally and ethically acceptable when he stopped ventilator support and all other medical treatment as requested by Ms. Gonzalez, because they were done to achieve a "good" result (support the patient's autonomy) while alleviating her physical and emotional suffering coming from the unwanted treatment (also good), even if the actions resulted in a "bad ending" (death).

Justice

The ethical principle of justice emphasizes fairness and equity among individuals. It involves the duty to fairly allocate limited health care resources and defines the role of health care providers as arbiters on decisions about resource allocation. When end-of-life issues are involved, the justice principle may be used to assure both fair treatment for individual patients and, at the population level, access to education about and resources for care at the end of life.

Many contextual factors would determine the application of this principle in end-of-life situations, especially those involving vulnerable elders. Culture, socioeconomic status, and prevalent societal values will shape the outcomes of the considerations (Pew Research Center, 2013; Perez & Cerminara, 2010). How does society make sure that persons from various cultures understand their choices? How does society accommodate those choices when they do not match accepted medical treatment? How should professionals deal with the mistrust of some ethnic and racial groups when discussing end-of-life choices and utilization of available resources? Ms. Gonzalez's son is an example of how mistrust of the health care system and cultural and religious beliefs of some ethnic and racial groups can shape the response to end-of-life choices.

Ms. Gonzalez's Case: Legal and Ethical Issues

When older adults are near the end of their lives, there are myriad physical, mental, and social conditions that may compromise their ability to function or to protect themselves from harm arising from neglect, exploitation, or abuse—or even from exercising their legal rights. Let's take the example of Ms. Gonzalez presented at the beginning of the chapter.

What Makes Ms. Gonzalez a Vulnerable Elder?

First and foremost, being near the end of life due to chronic illness potentially could implicate many deficiencies in the physical and mental functioning of an elderly person that would make him or her vulnerable. Such deficiencies in functioning could result in a greater exposure to different types of harm. His or her inability to carry out daily activities may result in physical injury from a fall, for example, or in the development of dangerous environmental conditions such as poor sanitation or lack of safety due to disrepair of the home. In Ms. Gonzalez's case, her chronic heart condition, associated with weakness and shortness of breath, provides the context for a diminished ability to maintain the house, which in turn could contribute to unsanitary conditions fostering the development of infections. Impaired cognitive function caused by a history of strokes and other cardiovascular conditions could play a significant role in altering judgment or capacity, leading to an inability to make decisions involved in the activities of daily living and rendering the elder vulnerable to the influences of others, who are not always guided by beneficent motives. Giving power of attorney to another person is a very serious legal action with devastating consequences when the powers are misused. Was Ms. Gonzalez's judgment impaired by illness when she gave power of attorney to her neighbor Mr. Jones?

In addition to the living conditions and mental impairment associated with illness, geographic issues could contribute to the vulnerability of elders at the end of life. Living in a rural area, as Ms. Gonzalez does, adversely affects quick and efficient access to resources due to many factors such as the perhaps inadequate number of providers in the area, distance from hospitals, and availability of certain specialized end-of-life services such as hospice or palliative care units (Rainsford et al., 2017).

Other social and systemic factors may also play significant roles in creating or exacerbating vulnerability in older adults at the end of life. Existing literature shows that cultural barriers, stigma associated with homosexuality for certain groups and individuals, language issues, erroneous cultural assumptions on the part of health care professionals, and lack of knowledge about legal options for making wishes known could significantly increase vulnerability to poor outcomes and quality of care at the end of life (Czaja et al., 2016; Krakauer, Crenner, & Fox, 2002).

Legal Issues

As presented earlier in the chapter, the IOM defines a *good death* as one that supports the wishes of patients and families at the end of life while avoiding distress and suffering for patients, families, and caregivers. While recent reviews of preferences among patients, families, and health care providers show that themes converge and diverge across stakeholders, those most frequently identified seem to empirically support that definition (Meier et al., 2016). The possible divergence also, however, emphasizes the need for dialogue among those involved to ensure envisioning a good death from the most important viewpoint: that of each individual patient.

Ms. Gonzalez's case represents the divergence of opinions between family members and health care providers, resulting in the nonfulfillment of a patient's expressed oral wishes to avoid being connected to machines or tubes at the end of life. This situation, however, was also strongly shaped by existing ethical standards and legal requirements.

First, only patients with capacity to consent may determine contemporaneously what type of treatment they wish to receive. Did Ms. Gonzalez have capacity to consent to treatment at the time she was taken to the emergency room? There appears to have been no emergency situation justifying treatment in the absence of consent, and patients are deemed to have capacity unless they demonstrate otherwise; but here there is some room for ambiguity, given Ms. Gonzalez's state when Mr. Jones brought her in. If she had capacity, did she require an interpreter? If she did, was an interpreter used to explain the need for and options for treatment? If so, was her level of health literacy sufficient to comprehend what the treatment involved? Was her mastery of the English language strong enough to make her wishes known? These questions illustrate the complexity of factors that may work against elders from racial and ethnic minorities even when they have capacity to consent.

Second, incapacitated patients can express their wishes through previously written advance directives or through surrogates or proxies. Even if Ms. Gonzalez had capacity at admission, at some point thereafter she clearly became incapacitated through heavy sedation. She apparently had not completed any written advance directives or designated anyone to serve as medical decision-maker to carry out her wishes. She had orally communicated her wishes to her partner and long-term companion, Ms. Johnson, but Dr. Smith disregarded those wishes when Ms. Johnson discussed them with him.

The power of attorney Ms. Gonzalez granted to Mr. Jones does not suffice to confer medical decision-making power upon him. Such powers of attorney usually are meant to convey financial power over bank accounts and bill paying, a conclusion buttressed in this case by Ms. Gonzalez's reference to the power of attorney being intended to assist with upkeep of the home. Medical decision-making must be specifically mentioned for a power of attorney to convey medical decision-making power in most states, and the power of attorney must be identified as "durable" to last beyond a patient's loss of capacity.

Ms. Gonzalez may not have executed written advance directive documents due to cultural, ethnic, and racial factors. Statistics show much lower rates of completion of advance directives among Hispanics and other minorities (Perez & Cerminara, 2010). Moreover, ethnic minorities and gay or lesbian older adults experience greater health disparities and are at risk for poorer health outcomes, including disability and mental distress, than heterosexual adults (Czaja et al., 2016).

In the absence of a written advance directive or a patient-designated medical decision-maker, health care professionals seek consent for treatment decisions from a list of people designated by state statute. Most if not all such state statutes prioritize spouses over adult children, but, despite a United States Supreme Court ruling supporting the constitutional right of same-sex couples to be spouses (*Obergefell v. Hodges*, 2015), some state statutes still purport to treat same-sex couples as "close friends." Close friends may be on a state's list of legally authorized decision-makers, but they rank below adult children in priority. Here, for example, Dr. Smith called Ms. Gonzalez's son, who likely knew nothing about his mother's end-of-life wishes due to his long, complete estrangement from her.

Giving legal priority to an estranged family member over a long-time partner can increase the vulnerability of the dying elder and the possibility of poor outcomes. Allowing persons disengaged from the actual care of the patient to make decisions increases the probability of results that do not reflect the elder's true wishes, as was the case with Ms. Gonzalez. It could also create conflict with those involved in the elder's care (Carr & Luth, 2017; Kramer & Yonker, 2011).

Ms. Gonzalez's son, moreover, was considering inappropriate factors in deciding whether to continue or authorize withdrawal of her ventilator support. First, he indicated that treatment should be continued because withdrawal would constitute murder, which is incorrect as a matter of law. Second, he did not refer to his mother's wishes when making his decision. As noted earlier, as a matter of both law and ethics, the goal in end-of-life decision-making is to make the decision the patient would have made if the patient had capacity to decide.

A final legal issue raised by these facts relates to fraudulent influences at the end of life. The U.S. Department of Justice considers financial exploitation one of the most frequently reported forms of elder abuse. Financial exploitation costs older adults more than $2.9 billion dollars annually, and the problem is only expected to increase as the population ages (MetLife Mature Market Institute, 2011). It results from cognitive deficiencies and loss of functioning that increase dependence on others, and it increases elders' vulnerability to poor outcomes at the end of life by depriving them of resources and subjecting them to arbitrary decisions that may not accord with their wishes. For example, in the case of Ms. Gonzalez, if Mr. Jones had a durable power of attorney for health care, would he have continued treatment to continue benefiting from the access to her financial resources provided by his financial power of attorney? Other factors also indicate the potential for vulnerability: How did he obtain power of attorney over her finances in the first place? The answers to those questions have important legal and ethical implications for Ms. Gonzalez's mental and physical well-being, as well for the well-being of other vulnerable elders similarly situated at the end of life and facing the risk of financial exploitation.

Ethical Dimensions of Ms. Gonzalez's Case

Earlier, this chapter said that autonomy and beneficence were at the center of end-of-life care for vulnerable elders. In certain situations, however, those essential principles may be at odds with each other when involving treatment decisions at the end of life. Ms. Gonzalez's case exemplifies that conflict.

At the time of arrival at the hospital, Ms. Gonzalez's condition was dire, although seemingly not emergent. Without knowledge or documentation of her wishes, the medical team did what was necessary to stabilize the patient. The team acted in the patient's best interest given the circumstances.

On the other hand, due to the nature of her deteriorating physical and mental status and her inability to communicate, Ms. Gonzalez's wishes for a peaceful death were met with roadblocks. In direct contrast with her exercise of autonomy were the beneficent actions of the intensivists who implemented aggressive and invasive treatments and measures intended to keep her alive and to cure her nonterminal ailments.

The autonomy of Ms. Gonzalez was compromised further when her son was made her proxy decision-maker in spite of the incongruence of their positions regarding medical treatment at the end of life. Ms. Gonzalez was unable to make her wishes known through the person who knew her the best—her partner and companion of 20 years, Ms. Johnson. It may be, upon further factual inquiry, that Dr. Smith decided to contact the son not only to follow the state statutory list but also, beneficently, to provide Ms. Gonzalez and her estranged son with the opportunity to reunite at the end of her life, perhaps for closure and emotional healing. In this difficult situation, the hospital overall may have maintained an ethical approach. The end-of-life decision from the next of kin was respected until the patient was able to communicate her requests.

Also arising from the facts of this case is the possible argument that the team was causing harm to the patient, thus engaging in maleficence, by continuing to treat after learning of her wishes through Ms. Johnson. Treating Ms. Gonzalez to alleviate her symptoms simultaneously likely caused emotional distress over being treated against her wishes. While prolonging her life allowed time to say goodbye, it could have also caused both Ms. Gonzalez and, presumably, Ms. Johnson at least emotional discomfort and harm. However, without appropriate legal documentation, with the son's preference having been learned, the hospital's hands were tied until Ms. Gonzalez displayed decision-making capacity and could communicate her wishes.

The ethical principle of justice is also at issue in this case. As said earlier, the ethical principle of justice emphasizes fairness and equity among individuals. It involves the duty to fairly allocate limited health care resources and defines the role of health care providers as arbiters on decisions about resource allocation. Given the rural nature of the hospital in this case, the ethical principle of justice might counsel one to consider how scarce valuable resources such as ICU beds are, juxtaposed against the risk of causing hardship to a vulnerable elder and his or her loved ones near the end of life by premature withdrawal of ventilator support. This is the time to balance the benefits of the medical intervention to Ms. Gonzalez against the burdens caused by treating her. Was she better off than when she was brought to the hospital? What did she gain by being treated? Was she treated fairly? Did she achieve a peaceful death at the end? How were the resources of the hospitals utilized? Were there other cases in which the same resources could have been utilized, to greater benefit to other individuals or to the community?

CONCLUDING OBSERVATIONS

End of life is associated with a substantial burden of suffering (Rao, Anderson, & Smith, 2002). With the increase in cancer mortality and the aging of the population in the early 21st century, many elders are suffering from chronic, unrelieved pain in their final days. Research shows that their caregivers and loved ones also find the process emotional and life changing, with a profound impact on their own health and financial status (Wozniak & Izycki, 2014). End-of-life care also has a significant financial impact on society in the United States, where Medicare pays for much of the care provided near the end of life (IOM, 2014).

The case of Ms. Gonzalez presents a multitude of interrelated ethical and legal issues similar to ones that will arise for the vast majority of elders near the end of life. When examining cases involving vulnerable elders, it is essential to recall and analyze not only the general ethical and legal principles but also the particular circumstances of each case's facts and the state's laws where each case takes place. It is also wise to involve the expertise of ethics committees for an interprofessional discussion of any complex case.

With changing societal values and new moral norms increasing the public attention paid to issues such as aid in dying and euthanasia, physicians and the entire health care team need to be conscious of the legal, ethical, and professional impact of caring for patients at the end of life (Cavalieri, 2001). Understanding both the legal and biomedical ethical principles guiding decision-making at the end of life is essential to improving access and quality of life for dying vulnerable elders and their families while assuring a just allocation of resources.

DISCUSSION QUESTIONS

1. An elderly patient with a terminal illness arrives at the emergency department unresponsive and in need of resuscitation. Quick review of the patient's medical record reveals no DNR on file. The medical team responds immediately with resuscitation efforts. Shortly thereafter, the patient's spouse arrives with a copy of the patient's living will expressing the wish to not be resuscitated. Did the medical team act ethically?

2. Identify situations described in the case study where health care professionals engaged in **paternalism**. Can you think of other situations involving vulnerable elders where paternalism can interfere with the principles of autonomy and beneficence?

3. What is **medical futility**? How may controversies resulting from the application of this principle impact quality of care at the end of life?

4. In the case presented, what violations of the ethical principle of justice might be argued? What further information might inform those arguments?

REFERENCES

Bosshard, G., Broeckear, B., Clark, D., Materstvedt, L.J., & Muller-Busch, H.C.(2008). A role for doctors in assisted dying? Analysis of legal regulations and medical professional positions in six European countries. *Journal of Medical Ethics, 34*(1), 28–32.

Brouwer, M., Kaczor, C., Battin, M.P., Maeckelberghe, E., Lantos, J.D., & Verhagen, E. (2018). Should pediatric euthanasia be legalized? *Pediatrics, 141*(2), e20171343. doi:10.1542/peds.2017–1343

Carr, D., & Luth, E. A. (2017). Advance care planning: contemporary issues and future directions. *Innovation in Aging, 1*(1), igx012.

Cavalieri, T.A. (2001). Ethical issues at the end of life. *Journal of the American Osteopathic Association, 101*(10), 616–622.

Cruzan v. Director, Mo. Dept. of Health, 497 U.S. 261 (1990).

Czaja, S.J., Sabbag, S., Lee, C.C., Shulz, R., Lang, S., Vlahovic, T., ... & Thurston, C. (2016). Concerns about aging and caregiving among middle-aged and older lesbians and gay adults. *Aging and Mental Health, 20*(11), 1107–1118.

Glucksberg v. Washington, 521 U.S. 702 (1997).

In re Quinlan, 355 A.2d 647 (N.J. 1976).

Institute of Medicine. (1997). *Approaching death: Improving care at the end of life.* Washington, DC: National Academies Press. Retrieved from https://doi.org/10.17226/5801

Institute of Medicine. (2014). *Dying in America: Improving quality and honoring individual preferences near the end of life.* Washington, DC: The National Academies. Retriced from http://www.nationalacademies.org/hmd/~/media/Files/Report%20Files/2014/EOL/Report%20Brief.pdf

Institute of Medicine. (2015). *Dying in America: Improving quality and honoring individual preferences near the end of life.* Washington, DC: National Academies Press. Retrieved from https://doi.org/10.17226/18748

Krakauer, E.L., Crenner, C., & Fox, K. (2002). Barriers to end of life care for minority patients. *Journal of the American Geriatrics Society, 50*(1), 182–190. doi:10.1046/j.1532-5415.2002.50027.x

Kramer, B. J., & Yonker, J. A. (2011). Perceived success in addressing end-of-life care needs of low-income elders and their families: What has family conflict got to do with it?. *Journal of pain and symptom management, 41*(1), 35–48.

Meier, E.A., Gallegos, J.V., Montross-Thomas, L.P., Depp, C.A., Irwin, S.A., & Jeste, D.V. (2016). Defining a good death (successful dying): Literature review and a call for research and public dialogue. *American Journal of Geriatric Psychiatry, 24*(4), 261–271. doi:10.1016/j.jagp.2016.01.135

Meisel, A., Cerminara, K. L., & Pope, T. M. (2004). *The right to die: The law of end-of-life decision making.* Aspen Publishers Online.

MetLife Mature Market Institute. (2011). The MetLife Study of Elder Financial Abuse: Crimes of occasion, desperation, and predation against America's elders. Retrieved from http://ltcombudsman.org/uploads/files/issues/mmi-elder-financial-abuse.pdf

Obergefell v. Hodges, 135 S. Ct. 2584 (2015).

Oregon Health Authority, Public Health Division. (2017). *Oregon Death With Dignity Act: Data summary 2016.* Retrieved from http://www.oregon.gov/oha/PH/

PROVIDERPARTNERRESOURCES/EVALUATIONRESEARCH/DEATHWITH-
DIGNITYACT/Documents/year19.pdf

Pew Research Center. (2013). Views on end-of-life medical treatments. Retrieved from
http://assets.pewresearch.org/wp-content/uploads/sites/11/2013/11/end-of-life-sur-
vey-report-full-pdf.pdf

Perez, A., & Cerminara, K.L. (2010). *La caja de Pandora*: Improving access to hospice care
among Hispanic and African-American patients. *Houston Journal of Health Law&
Policy, 10*, 255–308.

Preston, R. (2018). Death on demand? An analysis of physician-administered euthanasia
in the Netherlands. *British Medical Bulletin,125*(1), 145–155. doi:10.1093/bmb/ldy003

Quill, T.K., Ganzini, L., Truog, R.D., & Pope, T.M. (2018). Voluntarily stopping eating and
drinking among patients with serious advanced illness—clinical, ethical, and legal
aspects. *JAMA Internal Medicine,178*(1), 123–127. doi:10.1001/jamainternmed.2017.6307

Rainsford, S., MacLeod, R.D., Glasgow, N.J., Phillips, C.B., Wiles, R.B., & Wilson, D.M.
(2017). Rural end-of-life care from the experiences and perspectives of patients and
family caregivers: A systematic literature review. *Journal of Palliative Medicine,31*(10),
895–912. doi.org/10.1177/0269216316685234

Rao, J.K., Anderson, L.A., & Smith, S.M. (2002). End of life is a public health issue.
American Journal of Preventive Medicine, 23(3), 215–220.

Schneiderman, L.J. (2011). Defining medical futility and improving medical care. *Journal
of Bioethical Inquiry, 8*, 123–131. doi:10.1007/s11673-011-9293-3

Searight, H.R., & Gafford, J. (2005). Cultural diversity at the end of life: Issues and
guidelines for family physicians. *American Family Physician, 71*(3), 515–522.

Sulmasy, D.P. (2018). Italy's new advance directive law: When in Rome. ... *JAMA Internal
Medicine, 178*(5), 607–608.

Wozniak, K., & Izycki, D. (2014). Cancer: A family at risk. *PrzMenopauzalny, 13*(4), 253–261.
doi:10.5114/pm.2014.45002

VULNERABILITY: ABUSE, NEGLECT, AND EXPLOITATION

Section IV examines vulnerability through the lens of abuse, neglect, and exploitation whether at the hands of another or through one's own actions or failures to act (self-neglect). The section includes timely and emerging new topics, such as the bullying of older vulnerable adults and incarcerated elderly inmates.

The chapters demonstrate that abuse, neglect, and exploitation can create vulnerabilities or be an outcome of vulnerabilities. For example, adult abuse may result in physical injury, emotional suffering, and financial loss leading to other further harm. Consider the older parent whose life savings have been stolen by a child and now cannot pay for needed medical care and is self-neglecting.

Alternatively, older adults may be targeted because of their vulnerabilities, such as dementia, compromised health, or mental health conditions. Often seen as "good victims" by perpetrators, older adults may be victimized because they are unable to escape, defend themselves, report their victimization, or testify in court.

Once an older adult has been victimized, professionals and families want to protect that person—sometimes even at the cost of overriding the older adult's preferences and autonomy. Professionals and family members may seek guardianship for the abused elder in an effort to protect from further harms. While seemingly acting with beneficence, the result may deny the older adult his or her rights to autonomy and justice and actually result in doing harm (maleficence).

In recent years the punishments for many crimes have been increased, resulting in historical levels of older prisoners serving time in prison. These prisoners often need expensive medical care and are at risk of attacks by younger and stronger inmates. What duty does the government owe older inmates to health care and safety? Is it just to release them on compassionate grounds?

These chapters should raise many more questions: How should professionals deal beneficently with a neglected older adult who has been victimized by a caretaker who refuses services? How can the justice systems assure access to justice for older victims of abuse, neglect, and exploitation? How do entities create environments that protect participants or residents from bullying and criminal victimization at the hands of staff, other participants and residents, and outsiders? The perspectives in this section's chapters should fuel thoughtful and lively discussions.

14

ABUSE, NEGLECT, AND EXPLOITATION OF OLDER VULNERABLE ADULTS

Candace J. Heisler, JD
National Trainer and Consultant

Pamela B. Teaster, PhD
Virginia Tech

Georgia J. Anetzberger, PhD, ACSW
Case Western Reserve University

KEYWORDS

elder abuse	elder mistreatment
abuse	financial exploitation
ageism	polyvictimization
mandatory reporting	perpetrators
capacity	justice systems

CASE STUDY 14.1

Sarah has a career in public service working with troubled families. For it, she receives a respectable income that somehow gets depleted all too quickly and often, with little tangible to show. Sarah also has been a member of Alcoholics Anonymous for decades, relapsing repeatedly, including now. She blames her drinking and other problems on her mother, Pearl, whom she finds upsetting at best and impossible usually. Pearl is nearly 80, with multiple chronic conditions but is still able to live independently in another city a short distance from Sarah. Widowed and with few friends, she regularly travels to see Sarah, her only child. These visits often are filled with anger, accusations, and lately, assault. According to Sarah, it begins with Pearl's criticisms that she spends recklessly and drinks too much. According to Pearl, Sarah's behavior is frequently out of control, particularly after an evening at the bar, and recently includes taking money from Pearl's purse without permission and slamming Pearl on social media. Sarah's reactions to Pearl's criticisms may have begun with expletives and name calling, but they have now evolved into physical attacks, including pushing, punching, and throwing kitchenware and trash at Pearl. Thus far Pearl's injuries have been limited to bruises and cuts. Still, both women fear things could get much worse. Pearl is increasingly afraid of Sarah and has become anxious and depressed.

Sarah and Pearl's example illustrates *elder mistreatment,* a matter of growing concern worldwide (Pillemer, Burnes, Riffin, & Lachs, 2016; Podnieks, Anetzberger, Wilson, Teaster, & Wangmo, 2010). First recognized in the mid-1970s by physicians in the United States and Great Britain (Burston, 1975; Butler, 1975), it is now described across multiple professional disciplines as a social problem and social justice issue by social workers; as a medical syndrome and public health issue by health care providers and researchers; and as a violation of human rights and criminal laws by courts, legislators, attorneys, and law enforcement. Elder mistreatment is part of the larger construct of *elder abuse,* which also includes self-neglect and abuse and maltreatment by strangers and casual acquaintances. (Anetzberger, 2012).

There is no single universally accepted definition of elder abuse or elder mistreatment. Researchers often use the definition developed by the National Research Council, which uses the term *elder mistreatment,* while the medical field may prefer the Centers for Disease Control and Prevention (CDC) term *elder abuse.* Justice system professionals more typically address the issue using the Elder Justice Roadmap definition and framework of *elder abuse.* Table 14.1 describes these definitions.

The definitions in Table 14.1 are not legal definitions. Individual jurisdictions have enacted laws with their own definitions for such purposes as defining crimes, elder and vulnerable adult reporting requirements, civil actions, and probate matters. For purposes of this chapter, the terms *elder abuse* and *elder mistreatment* are used interchangeably and have the same meaning.

TABLE 14.1   Selected Definitions

Source of Definition	Definition
National Research Council (2003)	*Elder mistreatment:* "intentional actions that cause harm or create serious risk of harm, whether or not intended, to a vulnerable adult by a caregiver or other person who stands in a position of trust to the elder, or failure by a caregiver to satisfy the elder's basic needs or to protect the elder from harm" (p. 39).
CDC (Hall, Karch, & Crosby, 2016)	"An intentional act or failure to act by a caregiver or another person in a relationship involving an expectation of trust that causes or creates a serious risk of harm to an older adult" (p. 28).
U.S. Department of Justice Roadmap Project (Connelly, Brandl, & Breckman, 2014)	*Elder abuse:* "Physical, sexual or psychological abuse, as well as neglect, abandonment and financial exploitation of an older person by another person or entity that occurs in any setting (e.g., home, community or facility), either in a relationship where there is an expectation of trust and/or when an older person is targeted based on age or disability" (p. 3).

These definitions share three key elements: (a) status as an elder/vulnerable adult; (b) intentional or neglectful acts that cause or are likely to cause harm to the elder/vulnerable adult; and (c) a relationship between the parties in which there is a societal expectation of trust such as that of caregiver, family member, or fiduciary.

These definitions acknowledge that elder abuse can assume different forms, including physical abuse, emotional abuse, sexual abuse, financial abuse, neglect, and self-neglect. Table 14.2 defines each of these forms. (National Center on Elder Abuse, 2019).

The case study depicts *polyvictimization;* that is, multiple forms of abuse committed against the same person (Ramsey-Klawsnik & Heisler, 2014; Teaster, 2017). All forms of abuse occur in domestic settings (located in the community) as well as institutional settings, the latter encompassing residential facilities such as nursing homes, licensed care facilities, and other types of assisted living arrangements, in which the perpetrator is usually obligated to provide care or protection as a result of law or contract.

Large-scale national prevalence studies suggest that 1 in 10 community-dwelling older Americans experience past-year elder mistreatment, with exploitation and neglect most common (Acierno et al., 2010). Country prevalence research outside of the United States reveals a 0.8% (Spain) to 79.7% (Peru) range, with significant variation across cultures and nations, fueled in part by varying study definitions and methods (Marmolejo, 2008; Silva-Fhon, del Río-Suarez, Motta-Herrera, Fabricio-Webhe, & Partezani-Rodrigues, 2015). A meta-analysis of such studies globally resulted in a pooled prevalence rate for elder mistreatment of 15.7% (Yon, Mikton, Gassoumis, & Wilbur, 2017).

Less is known about elder mistreatment in residential facilities, due in significant part to a lack of sound investigatory practices in these settings. Further, mistreatment in them can be more complicated, with many more potential perpetrators (e.g., staff and volunteers, visiting family members, and other residents). Abuse and neglect in a facility setting can also involve different conduct, such as the failure to provide a timely response to call lights and inappropriate use of physical or chemical restraints (Miller, 2017). Still, several studies suggest that elder mistreatment in residential facilities may be widespread, with neglect and emotional abuse most common (e.g., Natan & Lowenstein, 2010; Phillips, Guo, & Kim, 2013). In contrast, reports from state long-term care ombudsman programs and Medicaid fraud control units indicate the highest frequencies for physical abuse (Daly, 2017). Despite the frequency of its occurrence, elder mistreatment typically goes unreported to those charged with investigating it or providing

TABLE 14.2   Forms of Elder Abuse and Their Definitions

Form of abuse	Definition
Physical abuse	"Intentional use of physical force that results in illness, injury, pain or functional impairment." (para. 2)
Sexual abuse	"Non-consensual sexual contact of any kind" (para. 3)
Emotional abuse	"Inflicting mental pain, anguish, or distress on a person" (para. 6)
Neglect	"Caregivers or other responsible parties failing to provide food, shelter, health care, or protection" (para. 4)
Self-neglect	"A person who fails to perform self-care tasks such that it threatens his/her own health or safety" (para. 7)
Financial abuse	"Misappropriation of an older person's money or property" (para. 5)

assistance. A recent large-scale New York survey revealed that the state prevalence rate was nearly 24 times greater than the number of cases reported to social service agencies, law enforcement, and legal authorities (Lachs & Berman, 2011). That same study found an alarming reporting rate of 1 in 44 cases when the abuse was financial in nature.

Any older adult can become victimized, and any caregiver or other trusted person can be a perpetrator. In fact, as in the case study, most perpetrators are family and spouses of the victim (Acierno, Hernandez-Tejada, Muzzy, & Steve, 2009; Lachs & Pillemer, 2015; Peterson et al., 2014). The risk of being abused seems especially great for older adults with dementia (Dong, 2015; Wiglesworth et al., 2010).

Research suggests that elder abuse is often associated with particular characteristics on the part of the victim, perpetrator, or context in which they interact. These risk factors[1] seem to vary somewhat by form of elder mistreatment, but generally for the victim they include: functional limitation and problematic behavior; for the perpetrator: mental disorder, substance abuse, hostility, and financial or housing dependence; and for the relationship between victim and perpetrator: shared living arrangement and social isolation or lack of social support (Anetzberger, 2013; Dong, 2015). Many of these risk factors are evident in the Sarah and Pearl case study, including mental disorder, excessive drinking, and bursts of hostility and anger by Sarah as well as Pearl's chronic illnesses.

Finally, the consequences of elder mistreatment can be severe. For Pearl, victimization has meant distress and declining mental health, physical injury, and financial loss. For others, it may lead to such other harms as increased morbidity or mortality; and for society, it can result in costs associated with greater use of health and other resources, including emergency departments and hospitals (Baker et al., 2009; Dong & Simon, 2013; Schofield, Powers, & Loxton, 2013).

How Elder Mistreatment Has Been Handled by Professionals

Because elder mistreatment has been identified in a variety of ways, including as a social service, health care, and legal issue, this section will address how each of these disciplines addresses it. Key ethical principles for each of these disciplines also will be identified.

Social Service Professionals

Social workers comprise a "practice-based profession and an academic discipline that promotes social change and development, social cohesion, and the empowerment and liberation of people" (International Federation of Social Workers, 2019, para. 2). Social workers are dominant among social service professionals, who work in a variety of practice settings but adhere to shared goals, philosophies, and ethical precepts. Social

---

1   Risk factors are "attributes, characteristics, or exposure that may increase an individual's likelihood of experiencing elder abuse or increase a perpetrator's likelihood of directing abusive behavior" (Chen & Dong, 2017, p. 93).

service professionals also were the earliest professionals concerned about what is now termed *elder mistreatment.* Social workers in the United States led in the formation and implementation of adult protective services during the 1950s and early 1960s, as it became a federally supported state public welfare program aimed at assisting impaired persons who were unable to manage their own affairs or were neglected or exploited (O'Neill, 1965).

Fundamental to a social worker's ethics is a client's right to self-determination and autonomy (Hall, 1971). Honoring that right is often challenging to apply in Adult Protective Services (APS) program situations where workers sometimes have to make difficult choices balancing risk and danger with the client's right to make his or her own life decisions (autonomy/self-determination). Social workers are charged with doing good/doing no harm (practicing beneficence). How then does the worker balance doing no harm with respecting a client's rights to autonomy and self-determination, when the result is that the client remains in danger or at risk? What should an APS worker do when a client who has been abused and exploited either chooses to remain in a dangerous environment or refuses help altogether?

It is not surprising that ethical issues were recognized early as the primary concern of protective services, given the potential use of legal and professional authority and their impact on client autonomy (Collins, 1982; Hobbs, 1976). This concern was especially meaningful at the time, since protective services came of age during the civil rights era. However, the role of social work in addressing elder mistreatment has never been limited to adult or elder protective services. Social workers function across multiple systems, from health care and behavioral health to the aging services network and domestic violence programming, clinically encountering situations of elder mistreatment and having various potential responsibilities in problem recognition, prevention, and/or treatment (Anetzberger, 2005). They are also responsible for community action designed to improve society's overall response to elder mistreatment, such as raising awareness about the problem and advocating for systemic change to more effectively address it (Herman, 2014). In every context, social workers confront thorny ethical questions such as whether or not to report an elder abuse situation, how to allocate scarce resources to address reoccurring mistreatment, and the value and propriety of committing overextended staff to participate in community multidisciplinary assessment and intervention teams (Donovan & Regehr, 2010).

Justice System Professionals

The *justice system* (Stiegel, 2017) describes two separate and distinct court systems—criminal and civil. The role of the civil justice system is to resolve private disputes between parties through lawsuits and restraining order proceedings and to protect vulnerable or incapacitated persons who are unable to manage aspects of their lives through creation of guardianships/conservatorships. In contrast, the criminal justice system's role is to determine culpability for criminal acts, to hold offenders accountable for those crimes, to protect the victim and the greater community, to attempt to rehabilitate offenders, and to make victims whole for their losses.

Comprehensive rules, derived from laws, regulations, rules of court, and case law, define how the justice systems function. While many laws are based in ethical principles, there are times when multiple ethical standards may be in conflict with one another or when the law is at odds with the ethical principles, discussed in Chapter 1. Laws will prevail over ethical rules. For example, in criminal justice cases the elder's right to self-determination does not override law enforcement's duty to arrest or the court's authority to sentence someone to prison over the elder's objections.

While once considered a private matter or a social service problem, elder/vulnerable adult abuse has been criminalized with the enactment of new crime laws, increased penalties, and procedural changes to improve the elder victim's access to justice paralleling what happened with domestic violence. Research and human stories changed the perception of elder abuse as primarily caused by caregiver stress to recognition of the widespread—sometimes predatory—nature of the conduct, the use of power and control tactics to control victims, and motivations of greed and entitlement to justify the conduct (Acierno, Hernandez-Tejada, Muzzy, & Steve 2009; Brandl, Dyer, Heisler, Otto, Stiegel, & Thomas, 2007; National Research Council, 2003).

Criminalization of elder abuse means that once a matter is brought to the criminal justice system, authority to make decisions passes from the victim to the criminal justice system. Protection of the community, including the victim (beneficence), and holding the offender accountable (justice) will guide the criminal justice system's decisions. These principles may conflict with Pearl's ethical concerns. Suppose, in the case study at the beginning of this chapter, Sarah was arrested and charged with a crime. Pearl may feel parental responsibility to protect her child (fidelity) and may not wish to cause her daughter harm (nonmaleficence). She may not want her child arrested, incarcerated, or convicted (justice). Pearl may worry what will happen to Sarah, fear loss of her companionship, love, and future care, and the disapproval of other family members and friends. She is concerned that a criminal conviction will make it difficult for Sarah to maintain employment.

The civil justice system operates very differently from the criminal justice system. In the civil justice system, the authority to bring, pursue, and terminate actions rests with the party bringing the action (the plaintiff) in lawsuits for elder abuse—related causes of action and applications for restraining or protective orders. Pearl as the moving party (plaintiff) would decide whether the action is filed, the relief that is sought, and the terms of any pretrial settlement.

Probate actions for appointment of a guardian or conservator are different from other civil actions. Such cases are brought on behalf of a vulnerable adult in need of protection who is believed to lack capacity to make decisions about his or her own life. In recent years, guardianship practices and legal presumptions have changed to give vulnerable older adults some degree of self-determination and control over their lives (autonomy), to narrowly tailor terms to only those needed to protect, and to use supported decision-making as an alternative to guardianship whereby the elder is assisted in making personal decisions now and in the future (Wood, Teaster, & Cassidy, 2017).

Efforts to enhance the older adult's access to justice in all court settings have included expanded professional training and education, development of multidisciplinary case responses, creation of specialized court calendars, improvements in case coordination and management, and greater availability of accommodations (*State v. Dye*, 2012; Stiegel, 2017; Stiegel & Teaster, 2011).

Judges, professionally licensed court staff, and attorneys are all subject to ethical standards or canons of conduct. Attorney standards of conduct have been established by the American Bar Association and individual states. Attorneys fulfill three roles: "(A) representative of clients, an officer of the legal system and a public citizen having special responsibility for the quality of justice" (American Bar Association Model Rules of Professional Conduct: Preamble & Scope, 2016). Criminal prosecutors and defense attorneys are subject to additional rules.[2] Similarly, judges are subject to ethical rules formulated by states, the American Bar Association, or others: "A judge shall uphold and promote the independence, integrity, and impartiality of the judiciary, and shall avoid impropriety and the appearance of impropriety" (American Bar Association, Model Code of Judicial Conduct, Canon 1, 2010).

These varied roles and duties create ethical dilemmas. For example, how does the civil plaintiff's attorney separate her older adult client's desires from those of her family? How should the prosecutor balance and weigh the victim's desires not to proceed against the prosecutor's duties to protect the greater community? What is the ethical responsibility of the defense attorney if his or her client says he or she will hurt the victim? What role does decision-making capacity play in the legal process? What is the court's responsibility to ensure that elderly victims are not unfairly treated during the court process? In short, how do the legal systems balance the older adult's rights of autonomy, least restrictive alternatives, justice, and fidelity with society's goals of protection, doing no harm (nonmaleficence), and accountability (justice)?

Health Care Professionals

Health care professionals includes an array of providers, including physicians from many specialties, nurses, pharmacists, dentists, therapists, public health practitioners, and mental health providers who focus on the physical and mental health of vulnerable older adults. While each brings unique expertise and experience caring for vulnerable adults, they share unique access to the older patient/client. Indeed, these professionals may be the only outsider who sees an older person (Mills, 2015). Medical professionals enjoy a special relationship of trust and respect with their patients (National Committee for the Prevention of Elder Abuse, 2008) which may result in disclosures of abuse, sharing of confidential personal information, and willingness to accept medical care, services, and other interventions.

Health care professionals help prevent, identify, report, and provide assistance to victims and perpetrators of abuse, neglect, and exploitation by recognizing signs and indicators of abuse, distinguishing abuse from accidental or age-related causes (Dyer, McFeeley, & Connelly, 2003), treating injuries and underlying medical conditions, assessing cognitive status, and providing expert consultations, reports, and testimony. Health care providers recommend social supports and provide referrals to community services to assist the older adult and the perpetrator.

---

2   See for example, American Bar Association, Criminal Justice Standards for the Defense Function; American Bar Association, Standards for the Prosecution Function; *Berger v. United States* (1935).

Health care professionals operate within ethical guidelines and codes. For example, the American Psychological Association's *Ethical Principles of Psychologists and Code of Conduct* (n.d.) list five guiding aspirational principles for professional conduct including beneficence and nonbeneficence, fidelity and responsibility, integrity, justice, and respect for people's rights and dignity. Physicians are bound by the American Medical Association's (AMA) code of ethics which describes the patient–physician relationship as "fundamentally a moral activity that arises from the imperative to care for patients and to alleviate suffering" (AMA, n.d., Model Code of Ethics, 1.1.1). This relationship of trust "gives rise to physicians' ethical responsibility to place patients' welfare above the physician's own self-interest or obligations to others, to use sound medical judgment on patients' behalf, and to advocate for their patients' welfare" (AMA, n.d., 1.1.1).[3]

Many health professionals are mandated to report suspected vulnerable adult abuse to law enforcement, protective services, prosecutors, or designated other agencies. Many also have a duty to warn an identifiable target of danger posed by a patient or client. (*Tarasoff v. Regents of the University of California,* 1976).

Returning to Sarah and Pearl's case at the beginning of this chapter, medical professionals could have evaluated and treated Pearl's injuries. Had she been admitted to the hospital, her needs as part of a safe discharge plan would have been assessed. Pearl could have been referred to domestic violence and aging services programs to obtain counseling, legal advocacy, and participation in a support group to help her overcome loneliness, isolation, and emotional dependence on Sarah. If Pearl lived in a mandatory reporting state, the medical provider likely would have been required to document and report the suspected abuse. Were Sarah a member of a health care practice, her provider could have offered her medical care and counseling and treatment for alcohol and anger problems and could have examined her for underlying medical problems.

Provision of health care services to vulnerable older victims and perpetrators gives rise to ethical conflicts. How is the duty to do no harm (nonmaleficence) balanced against a patient's refusal of life-saving care (autonomy)? Will reporting suspected abuse as required by law make the situation worse (justice vs. nonmaleficence)? What role does the older adult's decisional capacity play? What should a nurse or physician do if there is a strong belief that abuse has occurred, but the patient adamantly denies it has occurred? How does the health care provider legally protect private patient information shared in confidence while meeting legal reporting requirements (Health Insurance Portability and Accountability Act, 1996; Heisler, 2015)?

---

3   Examples of other ethical codes for health care professionals include the American Nurses Association *Code of Ethics for Nurses* (2015); the American Dental Association's *Principles of Ethics and Code of Conduct* (2018); and the American Public Health Association's *Principles of the Ethical Practice of Public Health* (2002).

Ethical Considerations: Mandatory Reporting Laws

As previously noted, there is ethical tension between protection and autonomy when an elder does not wish to report abuse or participate in a protective services investigation and those desires conflict with mandatory elder/vulnerable adult reporting laws. Mandatory reporting laws exist in virtually every state, the District of Columbia, and U.S. territories. Laws often include criminal and/or civil sanctions for a mandatory reporter's failure to report. Little proof is required to trigger a duty to report. To encourage reporting, statutes usually include civil and criminal immunity protections for good-faith reporting, even if the report is not found to be supported by sufficient legal proof. Some statutes do not distinguish between older adults who have full capacities and those who have diminished decisional capacity. While enacted to increase safety and protect older and vulnerable persons, strong objections have been raised. Standards for what must be reported are described as vague, uncertain, and poorly understood. These concerns may explain the low rate of reporting by health care professionals (Ahmad & Lachs, 2002; Koenig & DeGuerre, 2005; Mosqueda & Dong, 2011; Teaster et al., 2007).

Returning to the case study of Pearl and Sarah, assume that Pearl spoke to her doctor and shared her history of abuse at the hands of Sarah. Assume also that they live in a state where health care professionals are required to report to protective services. While Pearl is adamant that she does not want the matter reported, the physician is aware of his legal responsibilities. As a helping professional committed to doing no harm, the doctor may legitimately fear that reporting will not be helpful and may actually make the situation worse, will interfere with his relationship with Pearl and her family, and could result in liability or professional discipline if the report is found to have been erroneous.

The concerns about making the situation worse may have some justification. A basic rationale for mandatory reporting is the "presumed availability of services" (Mixson, 2010). An effective APS response requires a "functioning, interdisciplinary, community-wide response system" (Mixson, 2010, p. 32) within a framework of core services including social, health, housing, mental health, and legal, that are available when needed. Sadly, in some communities there is a very limited response system, if any, and many APS programs are underfunded and have inadequate services and resources to offer to clients (Regan, 1985).

Assume that while Pearl does not want to involve protective services or law enforcement, she does wish to talk with a community-based advocate. Core ethical principles of community-based advocacy are that the client is in the best position to decide what to do in a situation and should be allowed to make his or her own decisions (a philosophy of empowerment and person-centered, trauma-informed care). This presupposes that there is a legally protected confidential relationship between client and advocate. If the client's information is not confidential, then the ability to openly share information and even to seek confidential services is compromised. Mandatory reporting may well discourage Pearl from confiding in her advocate and seeking help to deal with an abusive or exploitative situation.[4]

Pearl may see these reporting laws as paternalistic and an unwanted governmental intrusion into her life. She may also fear that her disclosure will lead to involuntary appointment of a guardian, loss of her home and independence, and interference with her familial, social, and other relationships. Additionally, for some older vulnerable adults the fear of governmental interference in their lives is made worse by a history of past trauma, genocide, oppression, and war.

Ethical Considerations Related to Capacity

As a society, most agree that adults who are capable of making informed decisions should be allowed to do so. But what happens when a person is no longer able to make informed decisions? Should the governmental interest in safety and welfare take precedence over the individual's right to control his or her life? What is the standard for when a person's autonomy must give way to outside intervention? Should the person lose all control over decisions about his or her life or just some? All of these questions turn on findings of capacity.

Capacity is the ability to do something. Capacity "broadly refers to an individual's ability to receive and evaluate information and make and express a decision" (American Bar Association Commission on Law and Aging & American Psychological Association, 2008, p. 113). It is not all or nothing. A person can have some capacities while lacking others. Persons can also have degrees of diminished capacity. There are many different kinds of capacity, such as capacity to give a gift, make a will, enter into a contract, agree to medical treatment, testify as a witness (sometimes called testimonial capacity or competency to testify), dress or feed oneself, or drive a car. Each requires a different set of skills and abilities. Capacity is a clinical determination rather than a judicial decision, though capacity evaluations are used in legal proceedings to assess a person's ability to handle various aspects of life (American Bar Association Commission on Law and Aging & American Psychological Association, 2005).

Capacity is not static; it may change according to time of day, effects of medications, illness, nutrition, and hydration (American Bar Association Commission on Law and Aging & American Psychological Association, 2008). It also varies by the complexity of the decision to be made. For example, consent to accept a flu shot requires less capacity than consent to undergo a complex medical operation with multiple steps and alternatives. Capacity to give a beloved child $10 for his or her birthday requires less capacity than entering into a multimillion-dollar contract to erect a shopping center.

Capacity assessments begin with identifying what capacity is in question and determining the effect of that ability on relevant functional ability. For example, if the issue is whether a person understood the legal ramifications of deeding his or her home to a caregiver, the fact that a person has the capacity to dress himself or herself is not relevant or helpful. Similarly, if the capacity at issue is the ability to manage financial

---

4 Exceptions typically exist for child abuse and situations in which there is a duty to warn targets of violence that a person has expressed intent to harm them.

affairs and understand a complex trust, then the capacity to consent to a basic medical procedure will not provide needed information.

Because of the far-reaching and life-changing consequences of an incapacity determination, findings should be based on validated evidence-based evaluations. In reality, determining present capacity (or capacity in the past when a critical event occurred) is challenging. Brain science research continues to change knowledge of when a person may begin to lose certain abilities, especially those related to reasoning and management of financial matters. Measuring those changes and identifying when changes affect function are as yet imprecise. In social settings the vulnerable adult may appear socially competent and able to give informed consent to a financial transaction, when in reality brain changes are diminishing memory, reducing the ability to understand business transactions, and impacting the capacity to weigh and make a reasoned choice. How is autonomy/self-determination evaluated and balanced against the need for protection and intervention in such situations? What is a just and ethical evidence-based evaluation of decisional capacity when knowledge is changing rapidly?

Incapacity or diminished capacity is a risk factor for abuse, neglect, and exploitation (Chen & Dong, 2017 and citations therein). Therefore, development of protections for the care needs and financial assets of the older adult are critical. Various legal tools and programs are available while the vulnerable adult has some degree of decision-making capacity which continue on in times of incapacity. These tools offer opportunities to balance the elder's need for protection with his or her right to make decisions about his or her own life (autonomy/self-determination).

Returning to the case study, assume that Pearl is having some memory problems and her ability to navigate to Sarah's home is becoming more difficult. She has gotten lost several times and reached Sarah's home thanks to the efforts of police. Mail has been piling up on her kitchen table, and Pearl has forgotten to pay several bills. She has already received several reminder notices. She does not know how much money is in her checking account and has bounced two checks even though she has plenty of money in her savings account.

Pearl's situation raises concerns about her capacity to manage her financial affairs and keep herself safe. If these changes are due to dementia, her situation will worsen as her disease advances. Pearl may have already set up arrangements to deal with a possible loss of decision-making capacity. These may be informal such as arranging for family or friends to pay bills, get groceries and cook meals, and drive her to appointments. She may have enrolled in direct payment and representative payee services programs and arranged for Meals on Wheels and senior transportation services to help her. She may even have moved into a senior residential setting where many of her daily needs are met.

Alternatively, she may have executed advanced directives for health care decisions, a trust, or power of attorney.[5] If none of these steps are in place, she still may be able to engage family and friends for informal support or create simple legal instruments so

---

5   A power of attorney is a legal document created by a person with decisional capacity appointing another person (the agent) to make decisions on behalf of the person who created the power of attorney (the principal) when the principal is unable or no longer wishes to make those decisions. Powers of attorney are not monitored by a court.

long as she retains sufficient capacity to act for herself. She may benefit from supported decision-making in creating those documents.[6]

If Pearl could not or did not create alternatives to guardianship or if arrangements proved ineffective, as a last resort the court could be asked to intervene and create a guardianship.[7] That guardianship could be tailored to leave as much control and decision-making in her hands as is safe. Though guardianship is the most restrictive placement, these steps would achieve the ethical goals of protecting Pearl's autonomy while doing no harm.

Confronting the Ethical Issue of Societal Ageism

Ethical issues confronting vulnerable older adults who have experienced abuse, neglect, and exploitation must be considered in the context of a society that prizes youth and has a long history of applying an ageist lens to resource allocation (Government Accountability Office, 2011; National Research Council, 2013). How does that society assure that older vulnerable adults are treated fairly and equitably (justice)? For decades, child abuse funding for services, research, and staffing has far outstripped funding allocated for vulnerable elders. These practices occur against a demographic backdrop of many more older persons, including those who are vulnerable, living today than at any time in history. This demographic shift will continue for at least the next 30 years and far outstrips the current birth rate. There is evidence of age bias in many situations.

Cases involving vulnerable older adults not only compete for attention and priority against cases involving children, they also compete for priority against other kinds of crimes including street crimes, drug offenses, and gang actions (justice). Given the limited resources available to criminal justice agencies, how are priorities identified? Is it based on which cases most affect the greater community, or which ones will take more time to solve or prove or be more difficult and costly to prosecute (beneficence, justice)? How should cases of vulnerable adult abuse be handled—should they be turned over to protective services to investigate and manage rather than criminally investigated by the criminal justice system (beneficence, justice)?

Protective services programs are expected to conduct investigations sufficient to allow appropriate cases to be handled in the criminal and civil justice systems, not to be a substitute for the roles of criminal and civil justice system professionals. Protective

---

6 Supported decision-making is "a process of supporting and accommodating an adult with a disability to enable the adult to make life decisions, including decisions related to where the adult wants to live, the services, supports, and medical care the adult wants to receive, whom the adult wants to live with, and where the adult wants to work, without impeding the self-determination of the adult," Texas Estates Code § 1357.002(3). See also the National Resource Center for Supported Decision-Making (http://www.supporteddecisionmaking.org).

7 Guardianships are viewed as the most restrictive intervention a court can impose. Not only do protected persons lose rights to manage aspects of their lives, but in some states they lose various civil rights such as the right to marry and the right to contract. Over time courts have moved from creating global guardianships, which stripped the elder of the right to make nearly all life decisions to more limited guardianships with regular review of the continuing need for a guardian.

services programs were created to fulfill an entirely different role—to reduce risk and offer assistance to vulnerable and elderly victims of various types of mistreatment, most of which are not criminal. Most programs have insufficient resources and staffing to handle the cases currently reported to them. Protective services workers are not trained to be or to replace law enforcement officials in criminal cases. In addition to blurring the lines between social services and criminal justice, expecting protective services workers to investigate and handle criminal cases raises questions of fairness and justice. What is the societal commitment to equal treatment of offenses committed against vulnerable adults? How does treating crimes against older adults differently from other crimes achieve nonmaleficence (do no harm)? Will disparate treatment of older victims actually increase danger to safety, well-being, and financial security by emboldening abusers to continue to victimize vulnerable older adults, knowing there will be no consequences for their actions?

The overarching question posed throughout this chapter is how does a just society assist and respond to vulnerable adults who are victims of abuse, neglect, and exploitation? This chapter has raised many questions that challenge ethical principles of autonomy, when the state may need to take action even at the cost of the individual's independence (beneficence), the extent of an ethical state intervention (nonmaleficence), and what is justice for vulnerable older victims of abuse, neglect, and exploitation.

DISCUSSION QUESTIONS

1. Assume that you are a professional who is mandated to report vulnerable adult abuse to APS or law enforcement. Your client, who has decision-making capacity, is adamant that she does not want you to tell anyone about her son's abusive acts. How would you ethically manage the situation? What if your client lacked decision-making ability? Would that change what you would do?

2. You are working with a client/patient and have concerns that he or she may have been financially exploited. The client insists that she wanted to loan her son the large sum of money that is involved, even if it means that she may not have enough money left to live out her days. You are not sure about the client's capacity to give the loan to her son. You also have concerns that the son has been less than truthful to his mother; has isolated her from family, advisors, and friends; is a substance abuser; and has manipulated her. The client wanted you to know but does not want you to do anything. What are your ethical dilemmas?

3. You are the defense attorney in a criminal matter in which your client is alleged to have physically attacked and threatened a 75-year-old man. During a discussion about his defense your client tells you he knows how to "make the case go away." He says he is sure the elderly victim can be "scared off" from coming to court. You are concerned that your client is planning to harm the alleged victim. Do you have any ethical duties to the victim, your client, or the court?

4. You are part of a community multidisciplinary team that reviews cases of abuse, neglect, and financial exploitation of vulnerable older adults. You are a community-based advocate who has been working with the subject of today's

discussion, whose son is charged with various theft crimes committed against her. The client has shared personal information with you that she has not shared with APS, her doctor, the prosecutor, or law enforcement. That information would cast considerable doubt about her prior statement to law enforcement and her credibility. What are your ethical duties to your client and the multidisciplinary team? Should you participate in the team at all? What about in this case?

REFERENCES

Acierno, R., Hernandez, M.A., Amstadter, A.B., Resnick, H.S., Steve, K., Muzzy, W., & Kilpatrick, D.G. (2010). Prevalence and correlates of emotional, physical, sexual, and financial abuse and potential neglect in the United States: The National Elder Mistreatment Study. *American Journal of Public Health, 100*(2), 292–297.

Acierno R., Hernandez-Tejada, M., Muzzy, W., & Steve, K. (2009). *National Elder Mistreatment Study* (Grant Final Report, National Institute of Justice). Retrieved from https://www.ncjrs.gov/pdffiles1/nij/grants/226456.pdf

Ahmad, M., & Lachs, M. S. (2002). Elder abuse and neglect: What physicians can and should do. *Cleveland Clinic Journal of Medicine, 69*(10), 801–808.

American Bar Association. (2016). Model rules of professional conduct: Preamble & scope. retrieved from https://www.americanbar.org/groups/professional_responsibility/publications/model_rules_of_professional_conduct/model_rules_of_professional_conduct_preamble_scope.html

American Bar Association. (2010). Model Code of Judicial Conduct, retrieved from https://www.americanbar.org/groups/professional_responsibility/publications/model_code_of_judicial_conduct/

American Bar Association Commission on Law and Aging & American Psychological Association. (2005). *Assessment of older adults with diminished capacity: A handbook for lawyers*. Washington, DC: Authors.

American Bar Association Commission on Law and Aging & American Psychological Association. (2008). *Assessment of older adults with diminished capacity: A handbook for psychologists*. Washington, DC: Authors.

American Dental Association. (2018). Principles of ethics and code of conduct. Retrieved from http://www.ada.org/en/about-the-ada/principles-of-ethics-code-of-professional-conduct

American Medical Association. (n.d.). Code of medical ethics. Retrieved from https://www.ama-assn.org/delivering-care/ama-code-medical-ethics

American Psychological Association. (n.d.). Ethical principles of psychologists and code of conduct. Retrieved from http://www.apa.org/ethics/code/index.aspx

American Public Health Association. (2002). Principles of the ethical practice of public health. Retrieved from https://www.apha.org/~/media/files/pdf/membergroups/ethics_brochure.ashx

Anetzberger, G.J. (2005). *Clinical management of elder abuse: General considerations.* In G.J. Anetzberger (Ed.), The clinical management of elder abuse (pp. 27–41). New York, NY: Haworth Press.

Anetzberger, G.J. (2012). An update on the nature and scope of elder abuse. *Generations, 36*(3), 12–20.

Anetzberger, G.J. (2013). Elder abuse: Risk. In A. Jamieson & A. Moenssens (Eds.), *Wiley encyclopedia of forensic science* (2nd ed.). West Sussex, UK: Wiley.

Baker, M.W., LaCroix, A.Z., Wu, C., Cochrane, B.B., Wallace, R., & Woods, N.F. (2009). Mortality risk associated with physical and verbal abuse in women aged 50–79. *Journal of the American Geriatrics Society, 57*(10), 1799–1809.

Berger v. United States, 295 US 78 (1935).

Brandl, B., Dyer, C. B., Heisler, C. J., Otto, J. M., Stiegel, L. A., & Thomas, R. W. (2007). *Elder abuse detection and intervention: A collaborative approach*. New York, NY: Springer.

Burston, G.R. (1975, September 6). Granny-battering. *British Medical Journal*, p. 592.

Butler, R.W. (1975). *Why survive? Being old in America*. New York, NY: Harper & Row.

Chen, R., & Dong, X. (2017). Risk factors of elder abuse. In R. Chen (Ed.), *Elder abuse: Research, practice and policy* (pp. 93–107). Cham, Switzerland: Springer International.

Collins, M. (1982). *Improving protective services for older Americans, a national guide series: Social worker role*. Portland: Human Services Development Institute, University of Southern Maine.

Connelly, M.T., Brandl, B., & Breckman, R. (2014). The elder justice roadmap: A stakeholder initiative to respond to an emerging health, justice, financial and social crisis. Retrieved from http://Ncea. Acl. Gov/Library/Gov_Report/Docs/EJRP_Roadmap. Pdf

Daly, J.M. (2017). Elder abuse in long term care and assisted living settings. In X. Dong (Ed.), *Elder abuse: Research, practice and policy* (pp. 67–91). Cham, Switzerland: Springer International.

Donovan, K., & Regehr, C. (2010). Elder abuse: Clinical, ethical, and legal considerations in social work practice. *Clinical Social Work Journal, 38*, 174–182.

Dong, X. (2015). Elder abuse: Systematic review and implications for practice. *Journal of the American Geriatrics Society, 63*(6), 1214–1238.

Dong, X., & Simon, M.A. (2013). Elder abuse as a risk factor for hospitalization in older persons. *Journal of the American Medical Association Internal Medicine, 173*, 911–917.

Dyer, C., McFeeley, P.,& Connelly, M. T. (2003). The clinical and medical forensics of elder abuse and neglect. In R. J. Bonnie & R. B. Wallace (Eds.), *Elder mistreatment: Abuse, neglect, and exploitation in an aging America (pp. 339–381)*. Washington, DC: National Academies Press.

Government Accountability Office. (2011). *Stronger federal leadership could enhance national response to elder abuse* (Report to the Chairman, Senate Special Committee on Aging). Retrieved from http://www.gao.gov/assets/320/316224.pdf

Hall, G. (1971). Protective services for adults. In R. Morris (Ed.), *Encyclopedia of social work, Vol. II* (16th ed., pp. 999–1007). Washington, DC: National Association of Social Workers.

Hall, J. E., Karch, D. L., Crosby, A. E. (2016). *Elder abuse surveillance: Uniform definitions and recommended core data elements for use in elder abuse surveillance, version 1.0*. Atlanta, GA: Centers for Disease Control and Prevention. Retrieved from http://www.cdc.gov/violenceprevention/pdf/ea_book_revised_2016.pdf

Health Insurance Portability and Accountability Act, Public Law 104–191 (1996). Retrieved from http://www.hhs.gov/ocr/privacy/hipaa/administrative/combined/index.html

Heisler, C. J. (2015). Health Insurance Portability and Accountability Act: Implications for Adult Protective Services. Retrieved from http://www.napsa-now.org/wp-content/uploads/2015/07/TA-Brief-HIPAA.pdf

Herman, C. (2014, Summer). Elder abuse, neglect, and exploitation. *NASW Practice Perspectives.*

Hobbs, L. (1976). Adult protective services: A new program approach. *Public Welfare, 34*(1), 28–37.

International Federation of Social Workers. (2019). Social work. Retrieved from http://www.ifsw.org/get-involved/global-definition-of-social-work

Koenig, R. & DeGuerre, C. (2005). The legal and governmental response to domestic elder abuse. Orlando, FL: Elsevier Saunders.

Lachs, M., & Berman, J. (2011). *Under the radar: New York state elder abuse prevalence study* (Final report). New York: Lifespan of Greater Rochester, Weill Cornell Medical Center of Cornell University, & New York City Department for the Aging.

Lachs, M., & Pillemer, K. (2015). Elder abuse. *New England Journal of Medicine, 373,* 1947–1956. doi:10.1056/NEJMra1404688

Marmolejo, I.I. (2008). *Elder abuse in the family in Spain.* Valencia, Spain: Centro Reina Sofia para el Estudio de la Violencia.

Miller, C.A. (2017). *Elder abuse and nursing: What nurses need to know and can do about it.* New York, NY: Springer.

Mills, T.J. (2015). Emergency care department. In Elder Abuse Treatment and Management. Medscape. Retrieved from https://emedicine.medscape.com/article/805727-treatment

Mixson, P.M. (2010). Public policy, elder abuse, and Adult Protective Services: The struggle for coherence. *Journal of Elder Abuse & Neglect, 22*(1/2), 16–36.

Mosqueda, L., & Dong, X. (2011). Elder abuse and neglect: "I don't care anything about going to the doctor, to be honest." *JAMA, 306,* 532–540.

Natan, M.B., & Lowenstein, A. (2010). Study of factors that affect abuse of older people in nursing homes. *Nursing Management, 17*(8), 20–24.

National Committee for the Prevention of Elder Abuse. (2008). Health and medical professionals. Retrieved from http://preventelderabuse.org/elder abuse/professionals/medical.html

National Center on Elder Abuse. (2019). Frequently asked questions: What is elder abuse? Retrieved from http://ncea.acl.gov/FAQ.aspx

National Research Council. (2003). *Elder mistreatment: Abuse, neglect, and exploitation in an aging America* (R. J. Bonnie & R. B. Wallace, Eds.). Panel to Review Risk and Prevalence of Elder Abuse and Neglect. Washington, DC: National Academies Press.

National Research Council. (2013). *Elder abuse and its prevention: Workshop summary.* Washington, DC: National Academies Press. Retrieved from http://nap.edu/download.php?record_id=18518

O'Neill, V. (1965). Protecting older people. *Public Welfare, 23*(2), 119–127.

Peterson, J., Burnes, D., Caccamise, P., Mason, A., Henderson, C., Wells, M., & Lachs, M. (2014). Financial exploitation of older adults: A population-based prevalence study. *Journal of General Internal Medicine, 29*(12), 1615–1623. doi:10.1007/s11606-014-2946-2

Phillips, L.R., Guo, G., & Kim, H. (2013). Elder mistreatment in U.S. residential care facilities: The scope of the problem. *Journal of Elder Abuse & Neglect, 25*, 19–39.

Pillemer, K., Burnes, D., Riffin, C., & Lachs, M.S. (2016). Elder abuse: Global situation, risk factors, and prevention strategies. *Gerontologist, 56*(S2), S194–S205.

Podnieks, E., Anetzberger, G.J., Wilson, S.J., Teaster, P.B., & Wangmo, T. (2010). Worldview environmental scan on elder abuse. *Journal of Elder Abuse & Neglect, 22*, 164–179.

Ramsey-Klawsnik, H., & Heisler, C. (2014). Polyvictimization in later life. *Victimization of the Elderly and Disabled, 3–14*, 15–16.

Regan, J.J. (1985). *Adult Protective Services policy issues for the '80s*. Conference on Working With Victims of Abuse and Neglect, San Antonio, TX, November.

Schofield, M.J., Powers, J.R., & Loxton, D. (2013). Mortality and disability outcomes of self-reported elder abuse: A 12-year prospective investigation. *Journal of the American Geriatrics Society, 61*(5), 679–685.

Silva-Fhon, J.R., del Río-Suarez, A.D., Motta-Herrera, S.N., Fabricio-Webhe, C.C., & Partezani-Rodrigues, R.A. (2015). Domestic violence in older people living in the district of Breña, Peru. *Revista de la Facultad de Medicina, 63*, 367–375.

State v. Dye 2170 Wn. App. 340, 283 P. 3d 1130 (Wash., 2012).

Stiegel, L.A. (2017). Elder abuse victims' access to justice: Roles of the civil, criminal, and judicial systems in preventing, detecting, and remedying elder abuse. In X. Dong (Ed.), *Elder abuse: Research, practice and policy* (pp. 343–362). Cham, Switzerland: Springer International.

Stiegel, L., & Teaster, P.B. (2011). *A multi-site assessment of court-focused elder abuse initiatives* (Report, National Institute of Justice, Washington, DC), available at https://www.ncjrs.gov/pdffiles1/nij/grants/238287.pdf

Tarasoff v. Regents of the University of California17 Cal.3d 425, 131 Cal. Rptr. 14, 551 P.2d 334; 45 CFR 164.512(c)(1)(i) (1976).

Teaster, P. B. (2017). A framework for polyvictimization in later life. *Journal of Elder Abuse & Neglect, 29*(5), 289–298.

Teaster, P. B., Dugar, T. A., Mendiondo, M. S., Abner, E. L., Cecil, K. A., & Otto, J. M. (2007). *The 2004 survey of state Adult Protective Services: Abuse of adults 60 years and older* (Report prepared by National Committee for the Prevention of Elder Abuse & National Adult Protective Services Association). Washington, DC: National Center on Elder Abuse.

Wiglesworth, A., Mosqueda, L., Mulnard, R., Liao, S., Gibbs, L., & Fitzgerald, W. (2010). Screening for abuse and neglect of people with dementia. *Journal of the American Geriatric Society, 58*(3), 493–500.

Wood, E., Teaster, P.B., & Cassidy, J. (2017). Restoration of rights in adult guardianship: Research and recommendations. ABA Commission on Law and Aging with the Virginia Tech Center for Gerontology. Retrieved from https://www.americanbar.org/content/dam/aba/administrative/law_aging/restoration%20report.authcheckdam.pdf

Yon, Y., Mikton, C.R., Gassoumis, Z.D., & Wilbur, K.H. (2017). Elder abuse prevalence in community settings: A systematic review and meta-analysis. *Lancet Global Health, 5*, e147.

15

SELF-NEGLECT

Carmel B. Dyer, MD, AGSF, FACP
McGovern Medical School at UTHealth

John M. Halphen, JD, MD
McGovern Medical School at UTHealth

Jessica Lee, MS, MS
Division of Geriatric and Palliative Medicine

KEYWORDS

self-neglect   autonomy
multidisplinary team   mental capacity
social support
frailty

Overview

Elders suffering from self-neglect are among the most vulnerable in our society. In fact, many of the vulnerable conditions addressed in the chapters of this textbook occur simultaneously in self-neglecting elders. Self-neglecters often have compromised health and/or tenuous care situations, becoming victims of abuse, neglect, and exploitation at the hands of others. Most self-neglecters are living in the community, and these once autonomous adults slowly and invisibly become more vulnerable. The ethical principles of autonomy, beneficence, nonmaleficence, and justice must be considered in any intervention in the highly complex cases of self-neglect.

This chapter will address the history and epidemiology of self-neglect, the applicable ethical principles, social and medical approaches, the use of technology, and the future direction of practice and research. Although self-neglect is characterized by excessive clutter and an unkempt environment, many self-neglecters live in squalor with serious threats to their health. Self-neglect is a risk factor for hospitalization, victimization, and death. In subsequent pages the authors demonstrate that intervention in these cases requires the skills of professionals from social services, medicine, nursing, law enforcement, ethics, and justice.

CASE STUDY 15.1

Medical and Environmental Self-Neglect

In this case of self-neglect, a 70-year-old woman named Rose was referred to Adult Protective Services (APS) due to her lack of medical follow-up for severe leg wounds and unsanitary living conditions. APS had been involved with her previously when both Rose and her husband were reported to APS for living in a hoarding environment. APS had helped her and her husband move to a senior-friendly apartment; however, he had passed away the year prior and she steadily declined in her ability to perform high-level activities of daily living such as cooking and cleaning, as well as basic activities of daily living such as bathing and grooming. She did not have any close relatives or friends and had a mistrust of anyone who offered assistance.

The most recent referral to APS had come from the senior apartment complex manager who noted that she had seen roaches coming from Rose's apartment despite multiple attempts to fumigate and offers to clean the apartment. Rose had been able to pay her rent on time and was seen walking with a rollator walker around the complex. Her car was filled with garbage bags and open containers of food, but it was unclear whether she was actually driving the car. Her primary care physician of 4 years had noted that her hygiene was an issue. Her podiatrist also corroborated that she was able to make it to clinic appointments but also noted that whenever he tried to put home health services into place, she would refuse due to mistrust of "government agencies." Per her APS caseworker, Rose had been hospitalized 3 months prior for leg wounds but upon discharge had again refused to allow anyone into her home to treat her legs.

Due to concerns about lack of treatment for her leg wounds, APS requested an evaluation from a university-based geriatric multidisciplinary team. At the time of the house call, Rose was noted to be extremely emaciated and weak. She was unable to stand or even keep her head up to speak and was unable to move out of the doorway after she unlocked the door. She was sitting on her rollator walker and said that she had not eaten in several days, though she did have food in the apartment. There were cockroaches in every room, along with a foul odor. There was no air conditioning, despite summer temperatures in the 90s. Her leg wounds were covered with decaying tissue from her toes to her shins, and there were maggots as well as roaches in her wounds. Rose was unaware that there were insects in her wounds, nor was she able to explain how she got the wounds. Her mental status test score was 21 out of 27 (she had vision issues and was unable to complete the entire exam); she was disorientated, unable to perform numerical calculations, and her memory was impaired.

Given her acute medical issues, emergency services were called and she was taken to the hospital for treatment. Due to concerns that she was unable to adequately provide for her own medical care and maintain an adequate home environment, she was declared incapacitated and a request for guardianship was filed on her behalf.

Relevant Information About Self-Neglect

Definitions

Self-neglect is defined by the National Committee for the Prevention of Elder Abuse and the National Adult Protective Services Association as

> an adult's inability, due to physical or mental impairment or diminished capacity, to perform essential self-care tasks including (a) obtaining essential food, clothing, shelter, and medical care; (b) obtaining goods and services necessary to maintain physical health, mental health, or general safety; and/or (c) managing one's own financial affairs. (Teaster et al., 2007, p. 10)

Another manifestation of self-neglect is hoarding. Hoarding, also known as Diogenes syndrome, has come under national attention due to recent reality television shows. Other names used in the literature for this phenomenon are: the aged recluse, senile breakdown syndrome, social breakdown, squalor syndrome, collectionism, or Noah's syndrome. This phenomenon results from excessive accumulation of items, even items with no or little apparent value. At times, these behaviors result from schizophrenia or other psychotic disorders in some and lifelong patterns of collecting in others. However, in elders who self-neglect there appears to be a lack of editing or removing the excess items that accumulate. Items that are delivered to the residence on a recurring basis are not discarded such as newspapers, mail, and used food containers. The accumulation of items prevents older persons from performing their activities of daily living due to lack of space as rooms become filled with items and become unusable. In some cases hoarding has led to morbidity or mortality when heavy objects fell onto the older person or first responders could not get to the older person in a timely fashion.

Epidemiology

The prevalence of self-neglect in the literature has a broad range, since it includes study populations such as cases reported to state agencies like APS and hospitalized patients. Based on a number of studies, the incidence of self-neglect tends to be low, between 0.5 to 7 per 1,000 elders per year. It is clear that far more cases exist than are ever reported to social services or medical providers. This number reflects papers from North America, Europe, Asia, and Australia.

The risk factors for self-neglect are similar to those for elder abuse as described in Chapter 14. Age is one of the most common risk factors for self-neglect, while gender is not. Psychological state may contribute and reports detail premorbid personality traits such as poor interpersonal relationships; being aloof, detached, suspicious, quarrelsome, or unfriendly; or displaying reclusive and/or hoarding behaviors (Halliday, Banerjee, Philpot, & Macdonald, 2000; Reyes-Ortiz, 2006; Wrigley & Cooney, 1992). Psychiatric disorders as noted above specifically include obsessive-compulsive, paranoid, schizoid, and delusional disorders.

Other disorders commonly seen in self-neglecting elders are schizophrenia, dementia, alcohol abuse, and psychosis; dementia is the most common (Clark, Mankikar, & Gray, 1975; Dyer, Pavlik, Murphy, & Hyman, 2000; Hurley, Scallen, Johnson, & De La Harpe,

2000; Macmillan & Shaw, 1966; Pavlou & Lachs, 2006; Snowdon, 2007). Functional impairment and physical disability were noted in 17% to 44% of subjects in two studies (Macmillan & Shaw, 1966; Wrigley & Cooney, 1992). In one study, 64.8% of older self-neglecters were deemed to be frail (Lee, Burnett, & Dyer, 2016). Decline in sensory function complicates the medical and psychiatric profiles of self-neglecters. Multimorbidity is common and includes a combination of cognitive impairment, depression, delirium, medical illness (stroke, hip fracture), functional and social dependence, stressful events (e.g., bereavement), history of social isolation, and alcohol and substance abuse in self-neglecting elders (Abrams, Lachs, McAcay, Keohane, & Bruce, 2002; Dyer, Goodwin, Pickens-Pace, Burnett, & Kelly, 2007; Lachs, 1998; Naik, Burnett, Pickens-Pace, & Dyer, 2008; Reyes-Ortiz, 2006). In fact, cognitive impairment and clinically significant depressive symptoms were independent predictors of self-neglect over time. In a longitudinal follow-up in the Chicago Health Aging Project (CHAP) study (1993–2005), decline in executive function was associated with increased risk of reported and confirmed elder self-neglect. Also, decline in global cognitive function was associated with increased risk of greater self-neglect severity (Dong et al., 2010).

TABLE 15.1 Common Risk Factors And Associated Disorders for Self-Neglect

Older age

Isolation

Lack of social support

Poverty

Personality disorders

Hoarding

Mental disorders: Dementia, depression, substance abuse, etc.

Functional impairment

Clinical Findings

An observational study revealed that there are three phenotypes of self-neglect (Burnett et al., 2014). The first is environmental neglect. In these cases there is the hoarding as described above, as well as a general lack of cleanliness. The furniture, utilities, and the home itself are often in complete disrepair. Old food is not discarded; animal and even human feces litter the floor in some cases. In many cases, there are excessive numbers of animals such as dogs and cats; these homes often reek of animal urine. In the case study of Rose, her car was filled with garbage and her apartment lacked utilities and was infested with insects. Medical neglect is the second phenotype. In these cases, the lack of medical care may be evidenced by out-of-control blood sugar and blood pressure and untreated tumors or wounds, such as the decaying leg wounds seen in Rose's case. Physical neglect is the third phenotype and is characterized by poor personal hygiene. Self-neglecters often have overgrown hair and nails and are dirty and unkempt; a lack of bathing is apparent. Their clothes are often old and stained with a foul odor. Generally, environmental and/or medical neglect occur first; physical neglect is seen in the more serious, advanced cases. In Rose's case, her serious physical neglect led to her need for emergency hospitalization.

These cases are difficult to detect in an office visit. Patients often clean up for their medical visits and without an in-home evaluation, the extent and severity of self-neglect would not be known. In Rose's case, she was seen fairly regularly by her primary care physician as well as a podiatrist, but neither detected that she was self-neglecting. APS performs in-home evaluations and can often provide critical firsthand information. The Self-Neglect Severity Score is an observational tool that was developed to characterize and quantify the extent and severity of the self-neglect. This tool does not rely on self-reporting (Dyer et al., 2006).

The most common medical conditions associated with self-neglect include depression, dementia, psychiatric disorders, substance abuse, and executive decontrol (Dyer et al., 2007; Hansen, 2015; Hildebrand, Taylor, & Bradway, 2014; Pavlou & Lachs, 2008). These disorders are often undiagnosed due to lack of medical attention. Like other geriatric syndromes, self-neglect is associated with medical comorbidities. These include hypertension, dementia, diabetes mellitus, arthritis, stroke, depression, urinary incontinence, or delirium (Dyer et al., 2007; Pavlou & Lachs, 2006).

Self-neglecters are characterized by their refusal to seek or accept either medical or social services. They often refuse or do not have family support. In Rose's case, once her husband passed she was increasingly unable to maintain her own activities of daily living (ADLs) or instrumental activities of daily living (IADLs) and she refused to accept any services in her home. A model of the interplay of medical and social factors is shown in Figure 15.1.

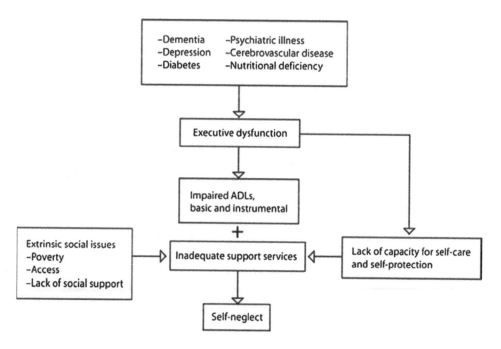

FIGURE 15.1 TEAM Institute Model of Self-Neglect (Dyer et al., 2007)

Mortality and Other Health Outcomes

Self-neglect is an independent risk factor for death. Indeed, in the New Haven EPESE, self-neglecting elders had an increased risk of 3-year all-cause mortality (OR 1.7; 95% CI 1.2–2.5), when compared with other members of the cohort (Lachs, 1998). Also, in the CHAP study, self-neglecting elders had an increased risk of 1-year mortality (hazard ratio=HR 5.82; 95% CI 5.20–6.51), which remained significant over the entire 9-year follow-up period, but was greatly reduced starting in year 2 (HR 1.88; 95% CI 1.67–2.14) (Dong, 2009).

Probably due to the severity of self-neglect and accompanying comorbidity or health complications, self-neglecters may have increased use of health services. These include increased likelihood for nursing home placement (HR 5.23; 95% CI 4.07–6.72) (Lachs, Williams, O'Brien, & Pillemer, 2002), hospice utilization (HR 2.34, 95% CI 2.10–2.81) (Dong & Simon, 2013), hospital utilization (rate ratio=RR 1.47, 95% CI 1.39–1.55) (Dong, 2012), and emergency department utilization (RR 1.42, 95% CI 1.29–1.58) (Dong, Simon, & Evans, 2012b). However, once self-neglecters are brought into the healthcare system, they are no more expensive than other similar patients (Franzini & Dyer, 2008). In a recent report of the CHAP study, elder self-neglect was associated with increased risk for 30-day hospital readmission (HR 2.50, 95% CI 2.02–3.10) (Dong & Simon, 2015).

Interestingly, interventions that include acute hospitalization of patients who self-neglect often resulted in worse outcomes compared with patients treated in the outpatient setting for the same conditions (Clark et al., 1975; Wrigley & Cooney, 1992). This was described by MacMillan and Shaw (1966), who found that hoarders that were admitted to the hospital had higher mortality rates than those left in their environments.

Studies have evaluated medication nonadherence in the elder self-neglect population. Turner, Hichshild, Burnett, Zulfiqar, and Dyer (2012) reported that 90% of 100 elder self-neglecters were nonadherent to at least one medication and the majority of self-neglecters were nonadherent on approximately four medications. Nonadherence was associated with the number of prescribed medications as well as lower objective physical function. A summary of main outcomes associated with elder self-neglect are listed in Table 15.2.

Current State of the Field

Although the most common case reported to APS, self-neglect does not fit nicely into the criminal justice paradigm of elder abuse, neglect, and exploitation. There are of course no

TABLE 15.2 Health Outcomes of Self-Neglect

Hospitalization

Hospital readmission

Disability due to loss of limb or stroke

Malnutrition

Increased use of all health services

Exacerbation of chronic diseases

Death

perpetrators. While self-neglect does pose a danger to the elder, how does governmental protection play a role? Are professionals who intervene in these cases protecting elders from themselves? Many experts in the field, including clinicians and researchers, strongly believe that self-neglect is not part of the abuse, neglect, and exploitation syndrome. Yet the very same disciplines that are involved with abuse, neglect, and exploitation are also integral to effective interventions in self-neglect. Furthermore, in all but 13 states self-neglect is reportable to the APS agency (Teaster et al., 2007).

Like cases of abuse, neglect, and exploitation, a multidisciplinary approach to self-neglect appears to be the most effective and efficient (Brandl et al., 2006). Multidisciplinary teams that address self-neglect require members from social services, medicine and nursing, law enforcement, ethics, and justice (civil more likely than criminal). Interventions by these teams include social remedies like increased social services, medical treatments for diagnosed disorders, assistance with finances, or placement in the safest yet least restrictive environment.

Nearly every case of self-neglect requires a capacity assessment since elders with capacity are free to make what others may consider to be unwise choices. Many times guardianship results from the more severe cases. Often, due to a lack of family support, the state becomes the guardian in cases of self-neglect. The use of state power greatly heightens the ethical concerns regarding the protection of self-neglecters due to the greater resources of the state.

Discussion of Applicable Ethical Principles and the Determination of Capacity

Often in an effort to make the right decision on behalf of the self-neglecting patient or a client, there are competing ethical principles to weigh. This discussion will address ethical considerations raised by the case presented in this chapter as well as the concept of capacity and how it is determined.

Most situations involving self-neglect involve a tension between autonomy and beneficence (Halphen & Dyer, 2017), but the principles of nonmaleficence and justice may also apply.

Those persons that are considered legal adults are presumed to have the capacity to make their own decisions and govern their own actions (American Bar Association Commission on Law and Aging, American Psychological Association, & National College of Probate Judges, 2006). They are also allowed to carry out their decisions within the constraints on liberty imposed by law. This is the case even when the decisions and actions of the adult with capacity are not considered advisable (Cooney, Kennedy, Hawkins, & Hurme, 2004; Smith, Lo, & Aronson, 2013). For religious or other reasons, people may reject conventional medical care or make other decisions that seem to be ill advised. The patient may have long-held values demonstrated by behaviors or words over a period of time that dictate these choices. It is not the advisability of the choices made but the way the choice is made that is important (American Bar Association Commission on Law and Aging et al., 2006; Cooney et al., 2004).

It is true that dementia is more frequent in the elderly. However, to assume that an older person does not have the capacity to live independently without supervision is an example of the prejudice called ageism. Respect for autonomy requires that we do not presume incapacity in the elderly and mentally ill (Cooney et al., 2004). It also would be offensive to the moral principles of justice and nonmaleficence for a clinician to make this presumption.

In the case presented, Rose was not keeping her apartment reasonably sanitary, arranging for adequate food or clothing, or managing her health needs. She had leg wounds that required ongoing care at home. However, she was refusing to allow home health care services to help her because she thought they represented government interference. Respect for autonomy would normally argue for not interfering with an older adult who refuses offered assistance, but not in this case.

Rose's case brings up the important topic of the determination of capacity. Adults have capacity if they are able to make and carry out decisions regarding their needs and safety (Cooney et al., 2004; Naik et al., 2008). In Texas, where Rose lived, incapacity is found when the individual is "substantially unable to: provide food, clothing, or shelter for himself or herself; care for the person's own physical health; or manage the person's own financial affairs" (Estates Code Chapter 1002, 2014). This is a definition based on the ability of the person to function, and many other jurisdictions have similar definitions for those who are incapacitated. In order to make the decisions about providing for these needs, adults must be able to understand and remember relevant information, appreciate their circumstances, reason about options, and make a choice (Appelbaum, 2007). Then to carry out their decisions, adults need to have sufficient executive function to plan their actions and adjust behavior based on circumstances (Cooney et al., 2004; Naik et al., 2008). There are a number of formulas and tools to assess capacity (Dunn, 2006; Kelton, Kunik, Regev, & Naik, 2010; Mills et al., 2014).

Rose was failing to meet her needs and had refused the help that may have prevented the deterioration of her condition. She did not appreciate her inability to take care of herself and she did not take reasonable steps to get help. Her lack of appreciation for her inabilities and circumstances caused her to be unable to make sound decisions to meet her needs and so caused her to lack the capacity to arrange for them. Because of this lack of capacity, she was unable to exercise autonomy in arranging for the care of her health, shelter, food, and other needs.

Her failure to provide for her self-care calls for the clinician to apply the moral principle of beneficence. The clinician should try to foster support for the provision of the needs of the neglected. This may even amount to helping the state through APS and the courts to impose emergency removal from the home or supervision without the agreement of the patient if that is the least restrictive way to proceed (American Bar Association Commission on Law and Aging et al., 2006). It is well established by federal law that the state may not deprive a person of liberty using means more restrictive than necessary to achieve the legitimate state interest in protecting vulnerable persons (Appelbaum, 1999). In an ideal situation, a family member or friend could help supply the assistance and supervision and an imposition of removal or supervision by the state would not be necessary.

Rose was found to be very weak, cachexic, and her wounds were in bad condition. It was believed that she would be in danger of serious harm from her condition and circumstances if she did not get immediate attention in a hospital setting. Fortunately, she did agree to go with the ambulance services to the hospital for evaluation and treatment.

Had she refused to allow urgent evaluation and treatment, it would have been possible to seek intervention by a court with appropriate jurisdiction to have her emergently removed. For a court to order her removal to the hospital without her consent, the court would have had to determine her to have been suffering from abuse, neglect, or exploitation presenting a threat to life or physical safety, and that she lacks the capacity to refuse the intervention (Texas Human Resources Code, 2002). The geriatrician that saw her at the home would have been able to produce evidence of her incapacity to refuse and her risk of harm. This would have been a case where the client's autonomy interest would have given way because she would not have had the capacity to make the refusal. Beneficence would have required an effort to protect her from the choices she could have voiced in protest, but which she did not have the ability to make because of her inability to appreciate her situation.

Later, Rose was deemed to be totally incapacitated by the court. In her case there was no one available that she trusted to help guide and protect her. A guardian was appointed to make decisions on her behalf. Justice and nonmaleficence require the clinician to carefully evaluate the client before supplying evidence to the court, which would help the state restrict a client's autonomy by a nonconsensual removal from the home or the appointment of a guardian.

The Application of the Topic to Older, Vulnerable Adults

Issues Concerning Frailty

Frailty is an age-related syndrome that can be considered a "condition in which the individual is in a vulnerable state at increased risk of adverse health outcomes and/or dying when exposed to a stressor" (Morley, 2013, p. 392). Frailty can be physical, cognitive, and/or psychological and is associated with poor outcomes such as disability and mortality (Fried et al., 2001). Frailty is usually classified into three states: frail, prefrail, and robust (not frail). Frail older adults have a twofold increase in risk of mortality, while prefrail older adults have a onefold increased risk of mortality when compared to robust older adults. A 2016 secondary analysis of frailty in older self-neglecters found that 35% were frail and 62% were prefrail, when compared to 7% frail and 47% prefrail in community-dwelling older adults (Lee et al., 2016). The majority of self-neglecters in the analysis were African American women with lower self-reported education and income levels. Interestingly, they had normal grip strength; tended to be overweight or obese; and did not show evidence of significant memory impairment, depression, or exhaustion. The main frailty characteristic the self-neglecters exhibited was slow walking speed, along with decreased physical activity, which may be why self-neglecters are unable to perform many of their own daily activities. Another important point is that the majority of the self-neglecters were prefrail, which indicates that there may be interventions which can help prevent them from becoming frail, leading to more positive outcomes.

Maintaining Persons In Their Own Environment

As the population ages, there has been an increase in the prevalence of homebound and semi-homebound older adults. In a 2011 study, 20.6% of community dwellers age 65 years and up were unable to leave their home at all or could occasionally go out but needed the assistance of others (Ornstein et al., 2015). Homebound status has been conceptualized as the cumulative effect of multimorbidity, functional impairment, poor social support, and low environmental resources that make it difficult to leave home to access appropriate care, contributing to poor health outcomes such as a 2-year mortality rate of 40.3% (Soones, 2017). Despite the increased risk of mortality, in a 2014 U.S. Census Bureau survey, nearly 90% of older adults stated that they wanted to remain in their communities, preferably in their homes, for as long as possible (Mermelstein & Reynolds, 2016). This desire to stay at home is reflected in many self-neglecters who would rather stay in their homes at all costs, even if they are unable to meet their own basic needs. Unfortunately, only 11.9% of the completely homebound population receive any primary medical care services at home (Ornstein et al., 2015). Interventions for self-neglecters to assist them with being able to stay in their own homes could include home-based primary care programs, if they are available.

Lack of Societal Support Systems

Self-neglecters are often isolated and lack the social support systems to be able to maintain themselves in their homes. There are clear differences when a person has good social support versus when they lack social support. For example, in Rose's case, she experienced significant deterioration after her husband died. Prior to that, she and her husband were able to rely on each other to perform their ADLs and IADLs such that they did not need to be institutionalized. However, after her husband passed, she was unable to keep up with her basic needs. In the United States, societal support systems are fragmented and often rely on informal caregiver support. These caregivers are not given any compensation or relief for providing care, which is often very demanding and all-consuming. The medical system rarely pays for providers who can assist with ADLs and IADLs and the majority of older adults cannot afford such care on their own. Thus it is not surprising that self-neglect is the most prevalent form of elder mistreatment.

Interventions in Self-Neglect

Multidisciplinary Team Interventions

Multidisciplinary teams to address elder abuse and self-neglect are becoming more common in jurisdictions around the United States. These teams include but are not limited to members from multiple disciplines including social work, law enforcement, civil and criminal justice, medicine, and ethics. The purpose of these teams is to address the multiple dimensions of these complex cases, develop a comprehensive intervention plan, reduce waste and duplication of services, and develop a personalized strategy for assisting self-neglecting older adults. Most believe these teams to be highly effective

(Snowdon & Halliday, 2009; Twomey et al., 2010). They do, however, require strong team dynamics and dedicated members. Currently most multidisciplinary teams can serve only a fraction of self-negelcters reported to APS.

The Importance of Home Evaluations

One of the key components to identifying and assisting self-neglecters is the home evaluation. Rose's doctors did not have adequate information about her home circumstances. The home evaluation is essential to assessing the ability of elders to adequately maintain themselves in their homes such as arranging for food, clothing, shelter, care of their physical health, and management of their finances. In the home, the clinician can assess home safety, gather detailed medical and social history, and conduct a basic physical exam. This home visit often includes the components of a comprehensive geriatric assessment such as an evaluation of fall risks, nutrition, functional ability, ADLs, IADLs, mental status, cognitive function, depression screening, social support, social history, advanced directives, basic finances, and the environment (Gazewood, 2009). Seeing the patient in his or her home environment is key to determining whether the patient is truly able to meet his or her own basic needs, rather than relying on what he or she might tell someone in another setting. Another benefit of home evaluations in self-neglecters is that on some occasions, the physicians have helped to facilitate emergency medical care for patients who have critical medical issues. In Rose's medical self-neglect case, she was so emaciated and weak that she might have had a much more serious outcome, including death, if she had not had a home evaluation. The home visit provides a much broader view of the patient which also informs the capacity assessment. In some instances, if clients are unable to safely care for themselves, the home evaluation can provide the evidence needed to determine and request guardianship for appropriate patients.

Technology in the Evaluation of Self-Neglect

As mentioned in the above paragraphs, the best way to evaluate self-neglect includes a visit to the home of the alleged self-neglecter as well as determination of an intervention plan by a multidisciplinary team. Through home visits, members of intervention teams can gain a better understanding of the challenges faced by vulnerable persons and their abilities to meet those challenges (Dyer et al., 2006; Iris, Conrad, & Ridings, 2014). An evaluation done during a home visit is ideal but difficult to accomplish due to time, distance, and scarcity of trained and willing evaluators beyond APS workers. Multidisciplinary team meetings require time and getting all parties to the table at one time. Technological advances in telecommunication can make both home visits and mutlidisicplinary team meetings more feasible and available to more older adults.

Telecommunication developments, which include a web-based portal and the use of videophone technology through cell phones, have been used in mental health assessments and more and more for dermatological assessment and other medical evaluations. The UTHealth team in Houston, Texas, is using a telecommunication portal to perform evaluations of the home environment and the mental health of APS clients. These services are now assisting APS throughout Texas providing access to a multidisciplinary evaluation for all forms of abuse. Although based in Houston, Texans reported to APS in both rural and urban areas are being served.

The principles of justice and beneficence are served by being able to properly assess more vulnerable adults, and the principle of nonmaleficence is served by using the best information available to help carefully evaluate self-neglecters and their environments. The videophone technology plus the facilitation of the APS specialist on-site with the client allows a mental health assessment for capacity. There has been a history of the use of effective and efficient mental health assessment via telecommunication technology (Brossart et al., 2013; Dautovich, Shoji, Stripling, & Dzierzewski, 2013).

CONCLUDING OBSERVATIONS

This chapter underscores the fact that self-neglect cases are incredibly complex. The description of Rose demonstrates to the reader a combination of intertwined medical, social, psychological, legal, and ethical issues commonly seen in these cases. The many facets are difficult to sort out, and each professional, most naturally, sees the case through his or her own professional lens. Many experts in the field believe that self-neglect and other forms of elder mistreatment are best managed by multidisciplinary teams. Together the team members prioritize the key elements and determine the appropriate remedies and intervention and the sequence in which these should be enacted or delivered. The ultimate goal is a holistic approach that helps prevent unintended consequences and maleficence, respects the rights of the person, and balances safety versus autonomy.

The key step in the evaluation of older adults who self-neglect is the assessment of capacity. In most states, physicians are charged with performing the assessments, the results of which are forwarded to a judge to make the final determination. Capacity assessment is a joint medical–legal action. One of the challenges is that outside of psychiatry, geriatrics, and primary care, many physicians are not trained to perform this task. (In some jurisdictions, social workers and nurses can make these determinations when there is risk for imminent harm.) The physician's experience with decision-making capacity generally revolves around the acceptance of a medical procedure or intervention. However, the issues in cases of self-neglect are much broader and include decisions about one's living situation, control of one's finances, and—through guardianship—the removal of all rights.

Perhaps the most salient ethical issue in cases of self-neglect is the clash between safety and autonomy. The heart of the ethical issues in cases of self-neglect lay in assessment of capacity. The result of these assessments could result in partial or full guardianships. The assessments are often not clear-cut. No one wants to err and inappropriately remove all rights from an autonomous adult. Neither does anyone want to leave an older adult without capacity in a precarious situation that leads to death or disability. Here the principle of beneficence would require that capacity assessments are done by trained individuals and according to standards. It would also require that if an adult lacks capacity then the least restrictive alternative for his or her safety and well-being is employed, such as staying with relatives (if possible), as opposed to moving to a nursing facility. Nonmaleficence would require that persons who lack capacity are not abandoned and appropriate safeguards to their health and well-being are put in place.

These cases often evoke emotional responses to abrogating a person's rights, removing them from their homes, and just the witnessing of human suffering. There are further clashes when individual rights such as owning multiple pets, or not wanting to exterminate roaches infringes on the rights and well-being of one's neighbors or community. The cases challenge our own feelings about the reach of government versus the rights of the individual. In every case of self-neglect, autonomy, beneficience, non-maleficence, and justice should be thoughtfully and carefully addressed.

DISCUSSION QUESTIONS

1. Liz is an 82-year-old woman who lives alone; she is starting to fail mentally and physically. Her husband is deceased and she has no children. Her closest relative is a nephew who helps manage her money but provides no personal care. A friend brings her to a geriatrician for an evaluation. She is found to have high blood pressure, insomnia, and memory impairment. She is not always taking her medications properly. The geriatrician diagnoses her with Alzheimer's disease, and recommends that she not live alone. The geriatrician believes that she lacks decision-making capacity. She is still driving. Her physician does not believe she can safely drive.

   Liz is very articulate, and does not think that she has anything wrong with her. Her nephew—although he notices that she is starting to have some difficulties caring for herself—believes that her changes are just due to old age. The physician advises the nephew that he must report the case to APS as they live in a state with mandatory reporting. The nephew requests that the physician not report and promises that he will oversee her care more closely.

   - Which ethical principles are inherent in this case?
   - Should this case be reported, since there is a potential caregiver?
   - What concerns does her driving raise?
   - What other disciplines could be helpful to her case?

2. A 76-year-old man, Mel, lives alone in a small house in the suburbs. The house is in disrepair. He is thin and appears malnourished. He has over 30 cats living with him; this is upsetting to neighbors and he is reported to APS. They learn that animal control services have been called several times over the past 5 years. The cats are thin, and some are in ill health. The home reeks of cat urine. Mel pays his bills on time and his hygiene is good. A medical evaluation is requested by APS.

   A physician makes a house call since Mel does not have a primary care physician. He is evasive on exam. He does not make eye contact. Although very thin, his physical health is good. He undergoes mental status testing. He is not depressed nor demented. Mel is found to have normal mental capacity.

   The local multidisciplinary team reviews his case and all the reports.

- Which ethical principles are being demonstrated in this case?
- What actions can the team recommend for Mel?
- Can Mel be removed from the home?
- What can be done to protect the animals?

REFERENCES

Abrams, R., Lachs, M., McAvay, G., Keohane, D., & Bruce, M. (2002). Predictors of self-neglect in community-dwelling elders. *American Journal of Psychiatry, 159*(10), 1724–1730.

American Bar Association Commission on Law and Aging, American Psychological Association, & National College of Probate Judges. (2006). Judicial determination of capacity of older adults in guardianship proceedings. Retrieved from https://www.apa.org/pi/aging/resources/guides/judges-diminished.pdf

Appelbaum, P. (1999). Law & psychiatry: Least restrictive alternative revisited: Olmstead's uncertain mandate for community-based care. *Psychiatric Services, 50*(10), 1271–1280.

Appelbaum, P. (2007). Assessment of patients' competence to consent to treatment. *New England Journal of Medicine, 357*(18), 1834–1840.

Gazewood, J. D. (2009). Assessment of the older patient. In C. Arenson, J. Busby-Whitehead, J. O'Brien, M. Palmer, & W. Reichel (Eds.), *Reichel's care of the elderly: Clinical aspects of aging* (6th ed., pp. 14–30). New York, NY: Cambridge University Press.

Brandl, B., Dyer, C. B., Heisler, C. J., Otto, J., Stiegel, L., & Thomas, R. (2006). *Elder abuse detection and intervention: A collaborative approach.* New York, NY: Springer.

Brossart, D., Wendel, M., Elliott, T., Cook, H., Castillo, L., & Burdine, J. (2013). Assessing depression in rural communities. *Journal of Clinical Psychology, 69*(3), 252–263.

Burnett, J., Dyer, C., Halphen, J., Achenbaum, W., Green, C., Booker, J., & Diamond, P. (2014). Four subtypes of self-neglect in older adults: Results of a latent class analysis. *Journal of the American Geriatrics Society, 62*(6), 1127–1132.

Clark, A., Mankikar, G., & Gray, I. (1975). Diogenes syndrome. *Lancet, 305*(7903), 366–368.

Cooney, L., Kennedy, G., Hawkins, K., & Hurme, S. (2004). Who can stay at home? *Archives of Internal Medicine, 164*(4), 357.

Dautovich, N., Shoji, K., Stripling, A., & Dzierzewski, J. (2013). Clinical geropsychology: Treatment and research approaches with rural older adults. *Clinical Gerontology, 37*(1), 64–75.

Dong, X. (2009). Elder self-neglect and abuse and mortality risk in a community-dwelling population. *JAMA, 302*(5), 517.

Dong, X., & Simon, M. (2013). Association between elder self-neglect and hospice utilization in a community population. *Archives of Gerontology and Geriatrics, 56*(1), 192–198.

Dong, X., & Simon, M. (2015). Elder self-neglect is associated with an increased rate of 30-day hospital readmission: Findings from the Chicago Health and Aging Project. *Gerontology, 61*(1), 41–50.

Dong, X., Simon, M., & Evans, D. (2012). Prospective study of the elder self-neglect and ED use in a community population. *American Journal of Emergency Medicine, 30*(4), 553–561.

Dong, X., Simon, M., Wilson, R., Mendes de Leon, C., Rajan, K., & Evans, D. (2010). Decline in cognitive function and risk of elder self-neglect: Findings from the Chicago Health Aging Project. *Journal of the American Geriatrics Society, 58*(12), 2292–2299.

Dunn, L. (2006). Assessing decisional capacity for clinical research or treatment: A review of instruments. *American Journal of Psychiatry, 163*(8), 1323.

Dyer, C., Goodwin, J., Pickens-Pace, S., Burnett, J., & Kelly, P. (2007). Self-neglect among the elderly: A model based on more than 500 patients seen by a geriatric medicine team. *American Journal of Public Health, 97*(9), 1671–1676.

Dyer, C. B., Kelly, P. A., Pavlik, V. N., Lee, J., Doody, R. S., Regev, T., ... & Smith, S. M. (2006). The making of a Self-Neglect Severity Scale. *Journal of Elder Abuse & Neglect, 18*(4), 13–23.

Dyer, C., Pavlik, V., Murphy, K., & Hyman, D. (2000). The high prevalence of depression and dementia in elder abuse or neglect. *Journal of the American Geriatrics Society, 48*(2), 205–208.

Estates Code Chapter 1002, 82nd Leg., R.S., Ch. 823 (H.B. 2759), Sec. 1.02 (2014). Definitions. Retrieved from http://www.statutes.legis.state.tx.us/Docs/ES/htm/ES.1002.htm

Franzini, L., & Dyer, C. (2008). Healthcare costs and utilization of vulnerable elderly people reported to Adult Protective Services for self-neglect. *Journal of the American Geriatrics Society, 56*(4), 667–676.

Fried, L., Tangen, C., Walston, J., Newman, A., Hirsch, C., Gottdiener, J. ... & McBurnie, M. A. (2001). Frailty in older adults: Evidence for a phenotype. *Journals of Gerontology Series A: Biological Sciences and Medical Sciences, 56*(3), M146–M157.

Halliday, G., Banerjee, S., Philpot, M., & Macdonald, A. (2000). Community study of people who live in squalor. *Lancet, 355*(9207), 882–886.

Halphen, J., & Dyer, C. (2017). Elder abuse and neglect. In A. G. Catic (Ed.), *Ethical considerations and challenges in geriatrics* (pp. 123–136). Cham, Switzerland: Springer International.

Hansen, M., Flores, D., Coverdale, J., & Burnett, J. (2015). Correlates of depression in self-neglecting older adults: A cross-sectional study examining the role of alcohol abuse and pain in increasing vulnerability. *Journal of Elder Abuse & Neglect, 28*(1), 41–56.

Hildebrand, C., Taylor, M., & Bradway, C. (2014). Elder self-neglect: The failure of coping because of cognitive and functional impairments. *Journal of the American Association of Nurse Practitioners, 26*(8), 452–462.

Hurley, M., Scallen, E., Johnson, H., & De La Harpe, D. (2000). Adult service refusers in the greater Dublin. *Irish Medical Journal, 93*, 208–211.

Iris, M., Conrad, K., & Ridings, J. (2014). Observational measure of elder self-neglect. *Journal of Elder Abuse & Neglect, 26*(4), 365–397.

Kelton, F., Kunik, M. E., Regev, T., & Naik, A. D. (2010). Determining if an older adult can make and execute decisions to live safely at home: A capacity assessment and intervention model. *Archives of Gerontology and Geriatrics, 50*(3), 300–305.

Lachs, M. (1998). The mortality of elder mistreatment. *JAMA, 280*(5), 428.

Lachs, M., Williams, C., O'Brien, S., & Pillemer, K. (2002). Adult Protective Service use and nursing home placement. *Gerontologist, 42*(6), 734–739.

Lee, J., Burnett, J., & Dyer, C. (2016). Frailty in self-neglecting older adults: A secondary analysis. *Journal of Elder Abuse & Neglect, 28*(3), 152–162.

Macmillan, D., & Shaw, P. (1966). Senile breakown in standards of personal and environmental cleanliness. *British Medical Journal, I,* 1032–1037.

Mermelstein, T., & Reynolds, J. (2016). *A spotlight on aging: Houston, Harris County and beyond.* Retrieved from https://www.unitedwayhouston.org/news/publications

Mills, W., Regev, T., Kunik, M., Wilson, N., Moye, J., McCullough, L., & Naik, A. (2014). Making and Executing Decisions for Safe and Independent Living (MED-SAIL): Development and validation of a brief screening tool. *American Journal of Geriatric Psychiatry, 22*(3), 285–293.

Morley, J., Vellas, B., van Kan, G. A., Anker, S., Bauer, J., & Bernabei, R. ... & Fried, L. P. (2013). Frailty consensus: A call to action. *Journal of the American Medical Directors Association, 14*(6), 392–397.

Naik, A., Burnett, J., Pickens-Pace, S., & Dyer, C. (2008). Impairment in instrumental activities of daily living and the geriatric syndrome of self-neglect. *Gerontologist, 48*(3), 388–393.

Ornstein, K., Leff, B., Covinsky, K., Ritchie, C., Federman, A., Roberts, L., ... & Szanton, S. L. (2015). Epidemiology of the homebound population in the United States. *JAMA Internal Medicine, 175*(7), 1180.

Pavlou, M. P., & Lachs, M. S. (2006). Could self-neglect in older adults be a geriatric syndrome? *Journal of the American Geriatrics Society, 54,* 831–842.

Pavlou, M., & Lachs, M. (2008). Self-neglect in older adults: A primer for clinicians. *Journal of General Internal Medicine, 23*(11), 1841.

Reyes-Ortiz, C. (2006). Self-neglect as a geriatric syndrome. *Journal of the American Geriatrics Society, 54*(12), 1945–1946.

Smith, A., Lo, B., & Aronson, L. (2013). Elder self-neglect—how can a physician help? *New England Journal of Medicine, 369*(26), 2476–2479.

Snowdon, J., & Halliday, G. (2009). How and when to intervene in cases of severe domestic squalor. *International Psychogeriatrics, 21*(06), 996.

Snowdon, J., Shah, A., & Halliday, G. (2007). Severe domestic squalor: A review. *International Psychogeriatrics, 19*(01), 37–51.

Soones, T., Federman, A., Leff, B., Siu, A., & Ornstein, K. (2017). Two-year mortality in homebound older adults: An analysis of the National Health and Aging Trends Study. *Journal of the American Geriatrics Society, 65*(1), 123–129.

Teaster, P. B., Dugar, T. A., Mendiondo, M. S., Abner, E. L., Cecil, K. A., & Otto, J. M. (2007). The 2004 survey of state adult protective services: Abuse of adults 60 years of age and older. National Center on Elder Abuse. Retrieved from http://www.ncea.aoa.gov/resources/Publication/docs/APS_2004NCEASurvey.pdf

Texas Human Resource Code § 48.208 (b). (2002).

Turner, A., Hichshild, A., Burnett, J., Zulfiqar, A., & Dyer, C. B. (2012). High prevalence of medication non-adherence in a sample of community-dwelling older adults with adult protective services-validated self-neglect. *Drugs and Aging, 29*(9), 741–749.

Twomey, M., Jackson, G., Li, H., Marino, T., Melchior, L., & Randolph, J. (2010). The successes and challenges of seven multidisciplinary teams. *Journal of Elder Abuse & Neglect, 22*(3–4), 291–305.

Wrigley, M., & Cooney, C. (1992). Diogenes syndrome—an Irish series. *Irish Journal of Psychological Medicine, 9*(01), 37–41.

16

OLDER ADULTS IN CORRECTIONAL SETTINGS

Anita N. Blowers, PhD

Associate Professor Emeritus, Department of Criminal Justice and Criminology, UNC Charlotte

KEYWORDS

prison	recidivism
older offenders	prisoners
prisoner rights	criminal justice
sentencing	prison programming

Overview

This chapter examines the complex issues associated with older adults in correctional facilities. While all prisoners are vulnerable to a greater or lesser extent and the vast majority come from difficult and deprived backgrounds (Enggist, Møller, Galea, & Udesen, 2014), older inmates have different needs from the rest of the correctional population. Correctional facilities currently work under the assumption that incoming prisoners will be young and still will be young when released. The rapid increase in the older prison population brings significant managerial and human rights challenges for correctional officials as they grapple with how to provide programs and services that meet the specific needs of elderly inmates (Blowers, Jolley, & Kerbs, 2014; Hurley, 2014; Kerbs & Jolley, 2014).

Defining Elderly Inmates

Although there is no clear-cut consensus, most researchers recommend that correctional agencies adopt age 50 as the chronological starting point for defining older inmates. Because of the unhealthy lifestyles of many individuals before incarceration, the lack of medical care associated with that lifestyle, and the stress of incarceration, the physiological age of an inmate usually surpasses chronological age. The functional age of a typical male inmate is approximately 12 years older than his nonconfined counterpart (Anno, Graham, Lawrence, & Shansky, 2004; Blowers, et al., 2014). Thus, an incarcerated 50-year-old is likely to be physiologically similar to a 62-year-old person outside of prison.

The Rise in the Aging Prison Population

The United States has the highest incarceration rate in the world. While elderly inmates represent a relatively small proportion of the total prison population, they also are the fastest growing prison population. The number of prisoners aged 50 and above today is twice that in 2001 and five times as large as it was in 1990 (Haugebrook, Zgoba, Maschi, Morgen, & Brown, 2010). At the end of 2016, prisoners aged 50 and older accounted for 19.8% of the total prison population of 1,505,400 (Carson, 2018). It is estimated that this population will make up about one-third of the prison population by 2020 (Blevins & Blowers, 2014; Blowers et al., 2014; Enders, Paterniti, & Meyers, 2005).

The increase in the number and percentage of older inmates reflects several realities. One factor is the global trend that people are living longer and the proportion of older adults comprises a larger part of the general population in the United States. In general, people are staying healthy longer, are living longer, and are capable of committing crimes longer. At the same time that we are experiencing trends in the aging of our population at large, recent trends in criminal justice policies have contributed to an increase in older inmates. One of the most obvious reasons for the aging of the inmate population, apart from the aging of the general population, is what Rikard and Rosenburg (2007) refer to as the *convergence of trends* in the U.S. correctional system. One such trend has been movement away from a prevailing concern for rehabilitation to more of a so-called get-tough approach. This change in punishment philosophy has had a dramatic impact on sentencing practices across the nation. For example, the late 1980s and 1990s saw a rise in the creation of tougher sentencing law. This time period is characterized by the war on drugs, a time when great attention was paid to escalating crime rates in almost all states. Mandatory sentencing policies, such as three-strikes laws, along with truth-in-sentencing laws,[1] became popular during this period in an effort to dissuade criminal behavior, and these policies have resulted in increases to the rate and length of prison sentences (Rikard & Rosenburg, 2007; Smyer & Burbank, 2009; Williams, 2006). Sentencing practices like these mean that more young persons are receiving sentences of life without parole, which will continue to contribute to the

---

1   Truth-in-sentencing laws require "offenders to serve a substantial portion of the prison sentence imposed by the court before being eligible for release. Previous policies which reduced the amount of time an offender served on a sentence, such as goodtime, earned-time and parole board release, are restricted or eliminated under truth-in-sentencing laws. The definition of truth-in sentencing laws and amount of time required to be served are primarily governed by state laws, which vary by state" (USLegal, n.d., para. 1).

already escalating prison population as a whole, and to the number of inmates who will grow old in prison.

Increasing numbers of people in prison, combined with longer sentences, creates a stacking effect (Blowers, et al., 2014; Rikard & Rosenburg, 2007). Those with long sentences remain in prison, and each year more people are added to the total, straining capacity in facilities throughout the United States. As Rikard and Rosenburg (2007, p. 152) suggest, "more sentences, longer sentences, and mandatory sentences coupled with medical advances that keep older prisoners alive longer, have led to the current growth of the older prisoner population." It is also important to note that one of the unintended consequences of mandatory sentencing practices is that these policies often result in long-term incarceration for nonviolent offenders. In fact, a large proportion of offenders serving time in state and federal prisons are there for nonviolent offenses (Carson, 2018). Thus, many aging inmates are serving time for offenses like drug crimes, property crimes, and other nonviolent crimes. Given the projected trends fostering the explosion of the older inmate population, it is crucial that greater attention be placed on understanding the legal, ethical, and pragmatic considerations related to older inmates.

CASE STUDY 16.1

Why Should We Care About the Treatment of Older Inmates?

Consider the following scenario:

At the age of 35 Delray Jones was convicted of possession of crack cocaine. Because this was his third felony, Delray was sentenced to serve a minimum of 25 years in prison. He is now 50 years old, but due to accelerated aging he looks as though he is in his mid-60 s. In the past few years Delray has been diagnosed with depression, cirrhosis of the liver, kidney failure, and also appears to be showing early signs of dementia. He is frail and must use a wheelchair to move about the prison. He must be transported to the hospital 30 miles away for biweekly dialysis treatment.

This scenario raises a variety of legal, ethical, and pragmatic concerns over how our society should handle older offenders. The following sections in this chapter highlight the complexities involved in dealing with older inmates like Delray Jones.

Legal Considerations

It is reasonable to expect that when an individual is convicted of a crime and sentenced to a term of incarceration, the offender loses his or her right to freedom and has his or her rights curtailed. However, that does not mean that inmates are without basic legal and human rights. The U.S. Supreme Court has consistently held that prison systems are required to protect the physical and mental health and well-being of prisoners (Ruggiano, Lukic, Blowers, & Doerner, 2016).

Case law on prisoner rights has established that even the most hardened criminal retains basic rights protected by the U.S. Constitution and requires that prisoners be treated as humanely and decently as possible given the practical realities of administering safe and secure correctional facilities. For example, prison officials have a duty under the Eighth Amendment to provide humane conditions of confinement. They must ensure that inmates receive adequate food, clothing, shelter, and medical care, and must protect prisoners from violence at the hands of other prisoners (*Estelle v. Gamble*, 1976; *Farmer v. Brennan*, 1984). In *Estelle*, the Court ruled that prisoners were entitled to: (a) access to care for diagnosis and treatment, (b) receipt of a professional medical judgment, and (c) administration of the treatment prescribed by the physician. In 1998, the U.S. Supreme Court also ruled that the Americans With Disabilities Act (ADA) applies in the prison context and that prisoners are entitled to reasonable accommodations for their disabilities under Title II of the ADA (*United States. v. Georgia*, 2006). The ADA requires that inmates with disabilities have equal access to facilities, equal participation in programs and proceedings, and accommodations within a facility. While older prisoners are not necessarily disabled, they are at high risk to be disabled, to become disabled, or to develop conditions that require special accommodations. Thus, disability legislation plays an important role when determining whether older prisoner rights are being violated.

Ethical Considerations

Aside from legal obligations, there are also ethical considerations. While age does not change the rights of people who are incarcerated, it may change what prison officials must do to ensure those rights are respected. Because of the aging process, elderly inmates develop unique mental, physical, and behavioral problems that necessitate a different approach than that afforded to the younger inmate population. Simply put, an aging inmate who is frail and fraught with a myriad of physical and mental issues should not be treated the same as a healthy 25-year-old (Human Rights Watch, 2012).

The incarceration of aging inmates raises two important ethical concerns: (a) Are current prison conditions sufficient to address the unique needs of aging inmates? In other words, do the conditions in prison meet the minimum threshold needed to protect basic legal and human rights? (b) Does the continued incarceration of aging offenders constitute disproportionately severe punishment and violate human rights, even assuming acceptable conditions of confinement?

One could argue that an inmate's advanced age and related health problems may dictate that continued incarceration is no longer warranted.

> While a prison term may have been proportionate when the inmate was first sentenced as a young offender, at what point can it be argued that the challenges faced by being old in prison may change the calculus against continued incarceration and in favor of some form of conditional release? (Human Rights Watch, 2012, p. 88)

The argument of the need to be cautious about incarcerating a large number of aging inmates is grounded on the premise that continued incarceration does not serve the four traditional goals of punishment (American Civil Liberties Union [ACLU], 2012;

Human Rights Watch, 2012). Retribution (ensuring that the punishment fits the crime) is not served by continued incarceration as many aging prisoners have already served far more time behind bars than their crimes warrant, especially when so many of the inmates are serving very long sentences for nonviolent offenses. In fact, it can be argued that recent get-tough sentencing practices have eroded a proper sense of proportionality, which is essential to a retribution philosophy of punishment. The goals of incapacitation (preventing a prisoner from committing a crime by locking him or her up) and deterrence (punishing someone to dissuade them and others from committing future offenses) also have little value when dealing with aging prisoners. The literature on correlates of crime has consistently found that people tend to commit fewer crimes as they get older, regardless of control variables, such as type of offense, race, and gender (Smyer & Burbank, 2009). Furthermore, elderly offenders have the lowest recidivism rates of all offenders. In fact, only about 1% of elderly offenders ever face a second conviction (Miller, 2011). Lastly, the goal of rehabilitation becomes less relevant to those nearer the end of their lives, and most prison programming is targeted to the needs of young offenders, so little effort is focused on rehabilitating the older inmate. Thus, it is challenging to see how the continued incarceration of aging inmates serves any of the purposes for which the sentences were originally imposed (Human Rights Watch, 2012).

Practical Considerations: The Unique Needs of Older Inmates

Prisons currently work under the assumption that incoming prisoners will be young and still will be young when released, and thus most jurisdictions have not done an adequate job in meeting the needs of older prisoners. It is generally estimated that the current cost of housing, programming, and providing medical care to older offenders is three to four times that of younger offenders (Blowers, et al., 2014). It also means that more of a prison's budget and attention will be used for a small percentage of the prison population. Therefore, states will be forced to make policy decisions on what to do with elderly inmates within their penal systems as they struggle to provide medical treatment and special accommodations to meet the needs of aging inmates.

Healthcare

By far the biggest challenge for correctional administrators in dealing with older inmates is the issue of healthcare. Inmates of all ages tend to experience more physical and mental health problems because they often come from poor backgrounds, have less education, have a greater likelihood of drug and alcohol abuse, and have had restricted access to healthcare, particularly when they were young (Anno et al., 2004; Hill, Williams, Cobe, & Lindquist, 2006; Sterns, Lax, Sed, Keohane, & Sterns, 2008; Williams & Abradles, 2007). The pervasiveness of health issues is much more pronounced as inmates age in prison.

Elderly inmates require a disproportionate amount of medical attention. This is due to a combination of two factors. First, prisoners typically come into the prison having led a very unhealthy lifestyle and often having had limited access to proper healthcare. Second, because of the physical environment and the emotional stresses of imprisonment, inmates age faster than people who are not incarcerated. This accelerated aging may lead to the need for more medical care. The increased need for healthcare among older inmates places burdens on already strained prison health facilities as it is not easy to provide healthcare in prisons, which by their nature are designed for safe custody and operate so as to enhance security (Enggist et al., 2014).

Chronic diseases are prevalent among older prisoners and often lead to functional impairments that interfere with daily life. Further complicating the issue is the fact that comorbidities (the presence of one or more disorders co-occurring with a primary disease) are more commonly found among older inmates. It is generally estimated that elderly inmates experience on average three chronic conditions at the same time (Anno et al., 2004; Mitka, 2004). Many of these chronic medical conditions are similar to those found in the general older U.S. population (for example, chronic obstructive pulmonary disease, arthritis, diabetes, heart disease, and other conditions common to the aging process). Elderly inmates also have diseases with unusually high prevalence rates in prison, such as HIV/AIDS and other sexually transmitted diseases, viral hepatitis, and advanced liver damage due to alcohol abuse. According to the *Journal of the American Medical Association*, as many as 20% of inmates older than 55 have a mental illness (Mitka, 2004).

One particular mental health disorder that is likely to be associated with older inmates is dementia. As the inmate population ages, dementia will become increasingly common in our jails and prisons. In the free world, the rate of new cases of dementia is expected to double in the next four decades. There is reason to think that the prevalence of dementia among inmates is likely to be two to three times higher than in the community but potentially more difficult to diagnose (Wilson & Barboza, 2010). Because of the regimented life prison requires, diagnoses such as mild cognitive impairment and early-stage dementia are less likely to be discovered or reported until the problem reaches more advanced stages (Sterns et al., 2008).

Prisons are run on hierarchical, militaristic models of strict obedience to rules governing every aspect of behavior. This environment is not conducive to inmates with mental health issues. While the prison staff must enforce strict adherence to prison rules, they are often ill equipped to differentiate when an inmate is deliberately breaking a rule or when an inmate, due to their mental illness, is unable to control their behavior. This sets up an environment where inmates experiencing mental illness are subject to punishments for infractions that often may be beyond their control, thus violating their basic human rights (Fellner, 2008). The challenge for correctional administrators is to address

> the delicate balancing act required by administrators to maintain order while trying not to punish inmates for behavior that is beyond their control because of mental illness, especially when some inmates are not able to clearly understand the rules or even comprehend that the rules have been broken. (Adams & Ferrandino, 2008, p. 917)

Given the fact that aging and chronic illness are progressive, it is inevitable that a number of inmates with these conditions will reach a terminal stage. Elderly inmates have mortality rates that are five times greater for cancer and heart disease than any other age group (Williams & Albraldes, 2014). Treating a terminally ill individual in prison is difficult at best. Inmates are usually isolated from their friends and family on the outside precisely when they need them most. Terminally ill inmates tend to cycle in and out of infirmaries and hospitals. As their conditions worsen, they often require round-the-clock nursing services from a prison healthcare system not originally designed to provide sophisticated and intensive care to large numbers of chronically ill and/or elderly inmates. These inmates require a level of medical care and treatment well beyond that provided to the general inmate population.

Although a significant proportion of older inmates require and are legally entitled to medical treatment, they are not necessarily receiving adequate medical care (Aday, 2003; Anno et al., 2004). According to Gibbons and Katzenbach (2006), there are several policy barriers that prevent inmates from receiving quality healthcare. These impediments include inadequate funding of prison healthcare systems, lack of collaboration and partnerships between correctional facilities and primary and public health care providers in the community, lack of consistent screening for infectious diseases, required copayment by inmates for medical and oral health care, and the inability of inmates to receive Medicare and Medicaid while incarcerated. Thus, there is no doubt that that the aging prison population will need a disproportionate number of resources. Additionally, prisoners are the only people in the United States who have a constitutional right to health care (Gibbons & Katzenbach, 2006; Mitka, 2004). In spite of increasing need and legal rights to medical care, provision and receipt of those services often does not occur.

Functional Ability and Facility Design

Acclimating to the prison setting is a challenge to all inmates as they adjust to the loss of their familiar ways of life and become isolated from their support groups. However, these problems are exacerbated for older inmates who, because of their physical and mental health issues, often require additional assistance in managing their institutional lives. Chronic diseases and the natural aging process associated with older prisoners often lead to functional impairments that interfere with daily activities. Functional ability reflects the extent to which an older person is independent and is measured by assessing a person's need for help with their Activities of Daily Living (ADLs): bathing, dressing, eating, transferring, and toileting. The prevalence of ADL dependence increases with advancing age and chronic illnesses. Prison life requires inmates to be able to climb on bunk beds, hear orders from staff, drop to floor alarms, and walk to dining halls for meals, all of which may be especially difficult for elderly inmates (Williams et al., 2006).

Many older inmates need a combination of healthcare services, assistive devices (such as walkers, wheelchairs, hearing aids, and breathing aids), and even special housing. Many older inmates require physical accommodations that are not easily provided in the typical prison environment. Environmental issues such as limited temperature control, lack of adequate lighting, loud noises, and crowded facilities present problems for older or disabled inmates. Inmates with respiratory problems need to be housed in areas where they will not be exposed to cigarette smoking, prisoners with spinal cord injuries must be assigned to air-conditioned units, and those with arthritis should not be housed in cold, damp environments. The following quote from the Human Rights Watch report on older inmates (2012, p. 1) sums this up well:

> Life in prison can challenge anyone, but it can be particularly hard for people whose bodies and minds are being whittled away by age. Prisons in the United States contain an ever growing number of aging men and women who cannot readily climb stairs, haul themselves to the top bunk, or walk long distances to meals or the pill line; whose old bones suffer from thin mattresses and winter's cold; who need wheelchairs, walkers, canes, portable oxygen, and hearing aids; who cannot get dressed, go to the bathroom, or bathe without help; and who are incontinent, forgetful, suffering chronic illnesses, extremely ill, and dying.

Although functional impairment and the environment's functional requirements may be mismatched in the community, mismatches are intensified in prison (Williams et al., 2006). Prisons, which are generally designed for young and healthy inmates without functional limitations, often lack basic assistive devices (e.g., bathroom handrails) commonly found in living environments for elderly adults living in the community (Williams et al., 2006). Frail inmates and those with seizure disorders will require a bottom bunk. Those suffering from heart disease, certain respiratory conditions, or difficulty in ambulating should be housed on lower tier cells to avoid the need to climb stairs. Even older inmates without mobility impairments might require additional supervision or assistance in certain circumstances, such as walking while handcuffed, since this is more difficult for older adults and can make them unsteady, putting them at increased risk for falls (Hill et al., 2006). Certain chronic care patients, particularly those with respiratory ailments, require placement in nonsmoking cells or dorms, and inmates with certain spinal cord injuries must be housed in air-conditioned areas. Even if corrections staff are aware of limitations that aging offenders may have in their ability to function in their living environment, assessing functional skills and capabilities of offenders is not one of their formal responsibilities; it is not something they are trained to do, and overcrowding may make it impossible to do sufficiently.

Appropriate Prison Programming for Older Inmates

In addition to considerations regarding the physical layout of a prison, an aging prison population also will require correctional administrators to adjust the way in which they manage and interact with older inmates. Older inmates differ from younger inmates in terms of their psychosocial needs (Aday, 2003). Generally speaking, older inmates have difficulty coping with the typical routines of the prison day and feel more agitated when they cannot escape from the continuous noise and distracting activities of other inmates. They tend to be uncomfortable in large groups and need more privacy and time alone. Older inmates also need more orderly conditions, emotional feedback, and familial support than younger prisoners (Aday, 2003; Sterns et al., 2008). Older inmates find it progressively harder to maintain ties with their families as the years go by, and given the fact that many will die in prison, terminally ill inmates often experience increased anger and depression and are at increased risk of suicide (Anno et al., 2004).

While the numbers of elderly inmates continues to rise, programming for elderly inmates has not kept pace. Few older inmates participate in programs and activities offered by the institution which involve interaction with other prisoners, including social and recreational activities and/or formal programs such as counseling, education, and vocational training. As a result, the elderly in prison tend to become idle (Aday, 2003; Hill et al., 2006; Smyer & Brubank, 2009). As one expert noted, "the present modality of 'warehousing' these inmates with minimal programming or activities intensifies day-to-day management concerns and significantly contributes to the general decline in the individual which escalates daily cost of institutional and health care" (Florida House of Representatives, 1999, p. 23). The growing aging population in prison necessitates that correctional administrators provide more individualized programming that responds to the older adults' biological, psychological, and social levels of functioning. Keeping older inmates active is important. They should be offered activities that are practical for their ages and physical conditions and should be allowed to keep reasonable assignments in the institutional work force as a way of maintaining dignity and positive self-image (Aday, 2003; Blowers, et al., 2014; Crawley, 2005; Crawley & Sparks, 2006; Florida House of Representatives, 1999; Hill et al., 2006; Smyner & Brubank, 2009). New approaches to existing policies and procedures which encourage older inmates to improve their lifestyle and maximize their level of functioning will reduce institutional management concerns and the cost of care.

Risk of Victimization

Most of the research examining inmate-on-inmate victimization suggests that older inmates may be more at risk of victimization when they are mainstreamed into age-integrated facilities. Many elderly prisoners feel especially vulnerable to the intimidating and predatory behavior of younger inmates (Aday, 2003; Blowers, et al., 2014; Florida House of Representatives, 1999; Kerbs & Jollie, 2010; Ornduff, 1996; Rikard & Rosenburg, 2007). In comparison to younger inmates, older inmates tend to report higher levels of anxiety and nervousness, and an inmate's perception of the risk of abuse may intensify as the inmate ages and becomes more physically and emotionally frail (Aday, 2003). The following examples from a video illustrate the tensions these older inmates often feel. Elmore Elliot, a 64-year-old prisoner in a New Hampshire facility, pled guilty to manslaughter in the early 1990s. After four hospital visits, two bypass surgeries, and the installation of a pacemaker, he spoke to an interviewer about his day-to-day experience, "It's like living in a minefield, when you're my age, in a place like this." Elliot said, "you don't know what you're going to step on next, whether it's going to blow up in your face" (WBUR, 2000, at 00:52). Similarly, another prisoner stated: "We all know grandparents who complain they're afraid of walking at night because of crime. Imagine being geriatric in a neighborhood where everyone is certifiably violent" (Gubler & Petersilia, 2006, p. 6).

In their review of the literature, Kerbs and Jollie (2010) suggest that the socio-cultural environment in prison provides some explanation as to why older inmates perceive higher risks of victimization. Similar to the elderly in society, older inmates may find that they no longer get the respect that they once received when they were younger. As inmates age, older inmates may lose their status in the prison's hierarchy, which therefore puts them at greater risk of being victimized by the younger, more aggressive inmates.

Costs of Housing Older Inmates in Correctional Facilities

As our correctional facilities continue to deal with a growing older prisoner population, the greatest challenge by far is the cost associated with housing inmates. The cost for incarcerating a geriatric prisoner is approximately three to five times that of a younger prisoner (Blowers, et al., 2014). It is not uncommon for states to pay $70,000 per year for each aging inmate compared to $27,000 per year for a younger inmate. The substantially higher cost of housing an elderly inmate is due in large part to higher healthcare expenses among geriatric prisoners, including hospitalization, medications, diagnostic tests, and skilled nursing care. In addition, there are substantial custodial costs associated with off-site health care, related to providing security (Blowers, et al., 2014). If left unchecked, the rising cost of providing healthcare to inmates in general and specifically to elderly inmates will overtake annual correctional budgets.

Balancing the Need for Public Safety With Pragmatic and Ethical Concerns

Given the astronomical costs associated with housing older inmates, it is time for criminal justice officials and legislators to seriously consider the wisdom in continuing to implement get-tough sentencing policies that have proliferated a situation where inmates are literally growing old in prison and question the utility in keeping old and often infirm offenders in prison. Imprisoning more of the most expensive cohort of prisoners might make sense if these prisoners were more dangerous than any other group and proportionality warranted such lengthy incarceration. However, as previously discussed, that is not the case. Aging prisoners are, in fact, the least dangerous of any cohort of prisoners. If prisoners no longer pose a public safety risk because of age and infirmity, and they already have served some portion of their prison sentence, one could argue that continued incarceration may constitute a violation of their right to a just and proportionate punishment (Human Rights Watch, 2012). Within a human rights framework, imprisonment is only an acceptable sanction for crime if it is not disproportionately severe relative to the crime and the legitimate purposes to be furthered by punishment. Therefore, the continued long-term incarceration of an older inmate plagued with physical and/or mental health issues may in fact constitute a human rights violation.

Another factor to consider when addressing the efficacy of keeping offenders in prison when they have reached advanced age is the argument that incarceration may be seen as too punitive for some older offenders. Since older offenders often come into the prison system with a host of physical and psychological ailments, older inmates may be perceived as more vulnerable to the stressors of the prison environment than younger inmates. Further, when one considers the prison sentence as a proportion of an offender's remaining life, a year of imprisonment given to an older offender is much more severe than a year of imprisonment for someone in their early 20s (Porcella, 2007). Further, there remains ample evidence that older prisoners continue to be at risk of medical and social care neglect, lack of access to human rights, loss of relationships, and lack of age-appropriate discharge planning (ACLU, 2012; Enggist, et al., 2014; Human Rights Watch, 2012; Hurley, 2014; Maschi, Viola, Morgen, & Koskinen, 2015).

We also need to recognize that most inmates will eventually be released. The aging prison population has resulted in more geriatric inmates being released from prison. While successful reentry into the community is challenging for inmates of all ages, it is particularly problematic for older offenders. Many elderly inmates are released from prison with significantly more health problems than similarly aged individuals in the community, and have more challenges reconnecting with family and friends, finding housing and employment, and readjusting to a life where they are required to make individual decisions for themselves after many years of institutional dependency (Blevins & Blowers, 2014).

The current status of warehousing older offenders begs the question of whether basic principles of justice espousing fairness and equality among individuals is being compromised when older and infirm offenders are being kept in prison for long periods of time. The ACLU's (2012, p. 52) in-depth examination of the United States' population of aging prisoners reveals that

> limited resources, resistance to changing longstanding rules and policies, lack of support from elected officials, as well as insufficient internal attention to the unique needs and vulnerabilities of older prisoners, all lead to inadequate protection for the rights of the elderly.

Thus, keeping elderly offenders in prison for long periods of time when they are not likely to pose a public threat violates society's legal and ethical obligations.

To minimize the mass incarceration of older prisoners without jeopardizing public safety, correctional systems are beginning to implement strategies, such as building separate geriatric prisons, utilization of telemedicine, and greater use of early-release mechanisms like compassionate release (Blevins & Blowers, 2014; Chiu, 2010; Williams et al., 2012). Early release for older inmates has attracted attention because it promises cost savings at relatively low risk to public safety, and many states have implemented policies to release elderly individuals as a potential cost-cutting measure. In 2008 and 2009, for example, several states—including Alabama, North Carolina, and Washington—enacted policy reforms that would allow some older inmates to serve the remainder of their sentences in the community. While progress is being made in rethinking polices for older offenders, the challenge lies in getting legislators and correctional administrators to actually follow through with these reforms. For example, at the end of 2009, 15 states and the District of Columbia had provisions for geriatric release. However, a report on the use of these programs indicates that jurisdictions rarely use these provisions (Chui, 2010). The challenge is to make existing policies more effective and to identify and assess new approaches to managing an aging population that is expected to grow.

CONCLUDING OBSERVATIONS

The burgeoning "graying"of America's inmate population mandates that we rethink our current sentencing policies more carefully and consider the moral and ethical care for the most vulnerable inmates, those who are aging behind bars (Hurley, 2014). Society has a legal and ethical obligation to ensure that every individual's basic rights to life, health, fairness and justice, humane treatment, dignity, and protection from ill treatment remain intact regardless of circumstance. As Mahatma Gandhi once stated, "The true measure of any society can be found in how it treats its most vulnerable members." This obligation should not end when one enters a correctional facility. Clearly, there are ways to honor the legal and ethical obligations we have to those who are spending their end-of-life years in prison without jeopardizing public safety. Too often, the treatment of older prisoners is compromised by strained resources, isolation, and pressures to conform to the punitive aspects associated with correctional environments. While we cannot—and should not—dismiss those concerns, we also must ensure that the conditions of confinement of older prisoners do not infringe on society's obligation to ensure their human rights are respected (Human Rights Watch, 2012).

DISCUSSION QUESTIONS

1. What is meant by the "graying" of the prison population?

2. What factors have influenced the mass incarceration of older offenders?

3. Discuss the unique challenges faced by older prisoners. What strategies should correctional administrators implement to address the needs of older offenders living behind bars?

4. Discuss the legal and ethical considerations that need to be addressed when considering the rise in the older prison population.

5. What modifications could reduce the population of elderly prisoners without appreciable risk to public safety?

6. Given that convictions and punishments should be based on sound legal factors, is there ever justification to considering increasing age and infirmity to determine if continued incarceration is warranted? Refer back to the scenario of Delray Jones presented earlier in the chapter. Assuming that his prison sentence was an appropriate punishment at the time of his conviction, is it appropriate to

now consider his advanced age and infirmity to determine if continued incarceration is warranted? What arguments can be made to justify the use of early release mechanisms for inmates like Delray?

REFERENCES

Adams, K., & Ferrandino, J. (2008). Managing mentally ill inmates in prisons. *Criminal Justice and Behavior, 35*(8), 913–927.

Aday, R.H. (2003). Housing and programming for aging inmates. In *Aging prisoners: Crisis in American corrections* (pp. 143–170). Westport, CT: Praeger.

American Civil Liberties Union. (2012). *At America's expense: The mass incarceration of the elderly.* New York, NY: Author.

Anno, B.J., Graham, C., Lawrence, J.E., & Shansky, R. (2004). Correctional health care: Addressing the needs of elderly, chronically ill and terminally ill inmates. *National Institute of Corrections Accession, 018735.* Middletown, CT: Criminal Justice Institute.

Blevins, K.R., & Blowers, A.N. (2014). Community reentry and aging inmates. In J.J. Kerbs & J.M. Jolley (Eds.), *Senior citizens behind bars: Challenges for the criminal justice system* (pp. 201–222). Boulder, CO: Rienner.

Blowers, A.N., Jolley, J.M., & Kerbs, J.J. (2014). The age segregation debate. In J.J. Kerbs & J.M. Jolley (Eds.), *Senior citizens behind bars: Challenges for the criminal justice system* (pp. 133–156). Boulder, CO: Rienner.

Carson, E.A. (2018). *Prisoners in 2016.* Washington, DC: Department of Justice, Bureau of Justice Statistics.

Chiu, T. (2010). *It's about time: Aging prisoners, increasing costs, and geriatric release.* New York, NY: Vera Institute of Justice.

Crawley, E. (2005). Institutional thoughtfulness in prisons and its impacts on the day-to-day prison lives of elderly men. *Criminology and Criminal Justice, 2*(4), 350–363.

Crawley, E., & Sparks, R. (2006). Is there life after imprisonment? How elderly men talk about imprisonment and release. *Criminology and Criminal Justice, 6,* 63–82.

Enders, S.R., Paterniti, D.A., & Meyers, F.J. (2005). An approach to develop effective health care decision making for women in prison. *Journal of Palliative Medicine, 8,* 432–439.

Enggist, S., Møller, L., Galea, G., & Udesen, C. (2014). *Prisons and health.* Copenhagen: World Health Organization.

Estelle v. Gamble, 429 U.S. 97 (1976).

Farmer v. Brennan, 511 U.S. 825 (1994).

Fellner, J. (2008). The failure of U.S. prisons to address adequately the special needs of prisoners with serious mental illness, including in their disciplinary systems. *Harvard Civil Rights–Civil Liberties Law Review, 41,* 391–412.

Florida House of Representatives, Criminal Justice and Corrections Council, Committee on Corrections. (1999). *An examination of elder inmates services: An aging crisis.* Tallahassee, FL.

Gibbons, J. J., & Katzenbach, N. D. B. (2006). *Confronting confinement* (Report, Vera Institute of Justice Commission on Safety and Abuse in America's Prisons, Washington, DC). Retrieved from https://www.vera.org/publications/confronting-confinement

Gubler, T., & Petersilia, J. (2006) *Elderly prisoners are literally dying for reform* (Working paper, California Sentencing and Corrections Policy Series).

Haugebrook, S., Zgoba, K. M., Maschi, T., Morgen, K., & Brown, D. (2010). Trauma, stress, health, and mental health issues among ethnically diverse older adult prisoners. *Journal of Correctional Health Care, 16*(3), 220–229.

Hill, T., Williams, B., Cobe, G., & Lindquist, K. (2006). *Aging inmates: Challenges for healthcare and custody* (Report for the California Department of Corrections and Rehabilitation, Lumetra, San Francisco).

Human Rights Watch. (2012). *Old behind bars: The aging prison population in the United States* (Report, Human Rights Watch, Washington, DC).

Hurley, M.A. (2014). *Aging in prison: The integration of research and practice.* Durham, NC: Carolina Academic Press.

Kerbs, J.J., & Jolley, J. M. (Eds.). (2014). *Senior citizens behind bars: Challenges for the criminal justice system.* Boulder, CO: Rienner.

Maschi, T., Viola, D., Morgen, K., & Koskinen, L. (2015). Trauma, stress, grief, loss, and separation among older adults in prison: The protective role of coping resources on physical and mental well-being. *Journal of Crime and Justice, 38,* 113–136.

Miller, D. (2011). Sentencing elderly criminal offenders. *National Academy of Elder Law Attorneys Journal, 7*(2), 221–247.

Mitka, M. (2004). Aging prisoners stressing health care system. *Journal of American Medical Association, 292,* 423.

Ornduff, J. (1996). Releasing the elderly inmate: A solution to prison overcrowding. *Elder Law Journal, 4,* 173–200.

Porcella, K. (2007). The past coming back to haunt them: The prosecution and sentencing of once deadly but now elderly criminals. *St. John's Law Review, 81,* 369–397.

Rikard, R.V., & Rosenburg, E. (2007). Aging inmates: A convergence of trends in the American criminal justice system. *Journal of Correctional Health Care, 13,* 150–162.

Ruggiano, N., Lukic, A., Blowers, A., & Doerner, J. (2016). Health self-management among older prisoners: Current understandings and directions for policy, practice, and research. *Journal of Gerontological Social Work, 59*(7–8), 627–641.

Smyer, T., & Burbank, P.M. (2009). The U.S. correctional system and the older prisoner. *Journal of Gerontological Nursing, 35,* 32–37.

Sterns, A., Lax, G., Sed, C., Keohane, P., & Sterns, R.S. (2008). Growing wave of older prisoners: A national survey of older prisoners' health, mental health and programming. *Corrections Today, 70*(4), 70–72, 74–76.

United States v. Georgia, 546 U.S. 151(2006).

US Legal. (n.d.). Truth in sentencing law and legal definition. Retrieved from https://definitions.uslegal.com/t/truth-in-sentencing

WBUR. (2000). The price of punishment: Growing old in jail—follow-up conversation with sixty-four year old inmate [Radio broadcast]. NPR. Retrieved from http://www.wbur.org/special/prison/elderly.shtml

Williams, B., Lindquist, K., Sudore, R., Strupp, H., Willmott, D., & Walter, L. (2006). Being old and doing time: Functional impairment and adverse experiences of geriatric female prisoners. *Journal of the American Geriatric Society, 54,* 702–707.

Williams, B., & Abraldes, R. (2007). Growing older: Challenges of prison and reentry for the aging population. In R. Greifinger (Ed.), *Public health behind bars: From prisons to communities* (pp. 56–72). New York, NY: Springer.

Williams, B., Stern, M. F., Mellow, J., Safer, M., & Greifinger, R. B. (2012). Aging in correctional custody: Setting a policy agenda for older prisoner health care. *American Journal of Public Health, 102,* 1475–1481.

Wilson, J., & Barboza, S. (2010). The looming challenge of dementia in corrections. *CorrectCare, 24*(2), 12–14.

17

CRIMINAL VICTIMIZATION OF OLDER ADULTS

Christina Policastro, PhD
University of Tennessee at Chattanooga

Katelyn Hancock
University of Tennessee at Chattanooga

KEYWORDS

victimization
crime
victims
criminal justice
restorative justice

National Crime Victimization Survey (NCVS)
Uniform Crime Report (UCR)
police
Alternative Dispute Resolution (ADR)

Overview

The study of criminal victimization among elderly adults is a relatively new area of interest in the traditional fields of criminal justice and criminology, as well as their related subfield of victimology. Criminologists have often justified their focus on younger offenders and victims by citing findings based on large population-based sources of criminal victimization data like the National Crime Victimization Survey (NCVS) and the Uniform Crime Report (UCR). These data sources generally indicate that older adults have significantly lower rates of victimization compared to their younger counterparts (Klaus, 2005; Morgan & Mason, 2014; Payne, 2011; Payne & Gainey, 2006). Recent studies and emerging changes in the U.S. population, however, have led criminologists to begin to reconsider their inattention to older adults and a growing body of literature has emerged that focuses on the unique characteristics of victimization incidents involving older victims, as well as the experiences of these victims if and when they become involved with the criminal justice system. Despite this increasing attention, criminal victimization of older adults still comprises a minority portion of the extant criminal justice and criminological literature. This disparate attention is especially noticeable when considered in the context of the substantially larger body of literature examining elder abuse and neglect in other disciplines such as public health, social work, and gerontology.

For elderly victims of crime, this inattention can translate into ineffective responses by criminal justice entities and additional trauma caused by criminal justice system involvement in their cases, which some may consider a form of revictimization, so to speak, by the system. To consider the ethical implications of the criminal justice response to victimization of older adults, this chapter will provide the reader with a broad overview of elder victimization and then will present a more nuanced discussion of some of the potential ethical problems that may arise once a case enters the criminal justice system. Throughout this chapter, we will use the case of Anne, a 75-year-old female, to illustrate some of the common characteristics of elder victimization cases. Her victimization experience also raises important questions about the criminal justice system's response to older victims and how this response may not be effective.

CASE STUDY 17.1

Anne and Simon

Anne had lived alone in her home since her husband of 50 years passed away 5 years ago. She had a regular schedule where she would go to the store on Monday mornings, attend ladies' Bible study meetings on Wednesday evenings, and go to church every Sunday. For the remainder of the week, she was content staying at home and working in her garden. She had no children and her closest living relative was a niece who lived over 300 miles away. Anne had managed to live fairly well on her own, even though she had experienced some health problems in the past year that led her to rely on a walker. She knew some of her neighbors, and they would check in with her occasionally. One of her neighbors, Simon, was a 17-year-old male who lived at home with his parents and had never really interacted with Anne. Despite their lack of interaction, Simon had noticed Anne's predictable weekly routine and thought that he could get some quick cash by sneaking into her house while she was at Bible study one Wednesday evening. Unfortunately, that Wednesday her class had been cancelled and Anne was home when Simon squeezed in through her living room window. Startled by Simon, Anne began screaming and tried to run to the front door when she fell and severely injured her hip. The neighbors, hearing Anne's cries for help, called the police and Simon was arrested for burglary, as well as assault due to the injuries Anne sustained. Anne's hip injury resulted in severe mobility limitations and led to her being unable to live independently in the community. Unable to afford the care facility near her home, she was placed in a nursing home about 50 miles from her community, which was something she had wanted to avoid.

Overview of Elder Victimization

As will be discussed below, the case of Anne and Simon is not an unusual case of elder victimization. It is important to consider the prevalence of and trends in criminal victimization among older adults to have the proper contextual grounding necessary to reflect on the potential ethical concerns involved in the criminal justice response to elderly victims. This also provides a background for understanding why the problems with the current system response may exist. The majority of what we know about crimes against older individuals is gleaned from the elder abuse and neglect literature, which is a more focused field of study that is generally restricted to an examination of offenses committed by trusted caregivers and family members (see Bonnie & Wallace, 2003). Although abuse and neglect are considered criminal offenses in many situations, for the purposes of this chapter, elder victimization is conceptualized as encompassing all types of victim–offender relationships, including incidents involving strangers.

Prevalence of Elder Victimization

Data derived from large, population-based studies of victimization allow for direct comparison of elder victimization patterns to those identified among younger adults. Data from victim-based sources such as the NCVS or official data such as the UCR, Supplementary Homicide Reports (SHRs), and/or the National Incident Based Reporting System (NIBRS) generally identify much lower victimization rates among older adults compared to younger adults. The NCVS is based on self-reports from a nationally representative sample of over 40,000 American households and includes data on both reported and unreported victimizations drawn from over 70,000 individuals ages 12 and older. In comparison, the UCR, NIBRS, and SHRs are all derived from official data submitted by law enforcement agencies, thus only include statistics based on crimes that have been reported to the police.

Using NCVS data from 2003 to 2013, Morgan and Mason (2014) report that older victims consistently accounted for only 2% of all violent victimizations and 2% of all serious violent victimization incidents reported to the NCVS. Although studies have shown older adults are less likely to be victims of traditional property crimes compared to younger people (Klaus, 2005; Morgan & Mason, 2014), it appears that like younger adults, nonviolent property offenses comprise most victimization events reported by older persons (Morgan & Mason, 2014). Moreover, recent NCVS data indicate that theft is the most common property crime reported by older persons (Morgan & Mason, 2014). Examining characteristics of violent victimization incidents, NCVS data suggest that the majority of violent victimizations involving elders occur near the victim's home and nearly 49% of offenders were known to the elderly victim (Morgan & Mason, 2014). Importantly, Morgan and Mason (2014) note that although 43% of offenders were strangers to the elderly victim, older adults only comprise 2% of victims of stranger crime. These characteristics are reflected in the case of Anne and Simon. Simon had attempted a burglary (nonviolent property offense), but Anne ended up being at home and consequently was injured when she was frightened by his entry into her residence. Further, despite their limited interactions, Simon was not a stranger to Anne.

Issues With Prevalence Estimates of Elder Victimization

Even though NCVS findings and other sources of victimization data match the general characteristics of Anne and Simon's case, there are several problems associated with the use of NCVS and official crime data to determine the scope of elder victimization. Payne (2002) identifies three specific issues related to NCVS and UCR data, including nonreporting, exclusion of fraud cases, and exclusion of offenses occurring in institutional settings, specifically nursing homes. The first and possibly most significant issue is related to underreporting. Overall, the NCVS data for 2016 suggest that less than half of violent crimes and roughly 36% of property crimes were reported to the police (Morgan & Kena, 2017). While some data suggest that older adults are more likely to report victimization compared to younger adults (Morgan & Kena, 2017; Morgan & Mason, 2014), elder abuse studies find that a considerable proportion of older victims do not report their victimization to law enforcement and/or social services (Acierno et al., 2010; Pillemer & Finkelhor, 1988; Tatara, 1998). Thus, it is likely that a number of older victims may not disclose their victimization in NCVS interviews and/or to police to be recorded in UCR statistics. Returning to the case of Anne, it is useful to consider what would have happened had Anne not been home when Simon broke in. Would Anne have noticed he had taken some of her cash or possessions? Would she have reported it to police?

The second issue with NCVS and FBI data is related to the ability of these data sources to capture the prevalence of fraud victimization. Again, if Simon had defrauded Anne in some way rather than burglarized her home, then this would not be a victimization incident adequately captured by these resources. Fraud cases are always excluded in the UCR, whereas the NCVS has only recently begun to incorporate measures of fraud in the identity theft supplement to the main victimization survey. The incorporation of the identity theft supplement is an improvement to the NCVS, but it does not tap into the broad range of fraud offenses that victims, especially elderly victims, may experience. This is especially problematic considering that research suggests that older individuals are at substantial risk of falling victim to fraud (Burnes et al., 2017; Mears, Reisig, Scaggs, & Holtfreter, 2016; Pak & Shadel, 2011). In a study of 2,000 adults ages 60 and older living in two states, Holtfreter, Reisig, Mears, and Wolfe (2014) identified that nearly 60% of their sample reported that they were targets of fraud in the past year and almost 14% reported that they had been victimized by fraud in the past year. Moreover, data from the Consumer Sentinel Network (2017) indicate that individuals ages 60 and over made up the majority of complaints (37%) for consumer fraud in 2016.

Finally, the NCVS does not survey individuals who reside in nursing homes, nor are many crimes that take place within this setting typically reported to police. Research has indicated that abuse, particularly financially motivated crime in the form of theft, is relatively common in nursing homes (Friedman, Santos, Liebel, Russ, & Conwell, 2014; Harris & Benson, 1998; Tilse & Wilson, 2013). What if Anne was not living in the community at the time this incident occurred, but instead resided in a nursing home and a nursing home aide had stolen some of her possessions? Would this have come to the attention of authorities?

Impact of Prevalence Estimates on Elderly Victims

Overall, our picture of crimes committed against elderly individuals is quite limited when we base our estimates solely on traditional sources of crime and victimization data. Elder abuse scholars often refer to the *iceberg theory* of elder abuse when discussing prevalence and incidence estimates. The iceberg theory simply suggests that only the most visible and severe cases of elder abuse, and as an extension other forms of elder victimization, come to the attention of authorities like adult protective services and the police (Tatara, 1998). Researchers have also argued that many older victims may not report their victimization in community-based surveys due to feelings of embarrassment and fear (Payne & Gainey, 2009). One must question whether Anne would have reported her victimization had she not been injured or had not been home the day Simon burglarized her home. It is likely that our understanding of the scope of elder victimization is not a complete picture and that even the best estimates are still only the tip of the proverbial iceberg.

Ultimately, this may translate into inefficient criminal justice system responses and an inability to achieve justice in elder victimization cases, as criminal justice budgets for programming and training are frequently designed to address what is perceived as the greatest social problem. This highlights a broader ethical issue related to how problems are defined as worthy for attention by the criminal justice system. Scholars have argued that policymaking, including criminal justice policy, is often driven by a cost–benefit analysis where policymakers identify policy goals, explore multiple methods of achieving stated goals, establish the costs and benefits associated with different methods, and compare the costs and benefits of the various methods (Banks, 2017; Tong, 1986). Public opinion also factors into policy decisions (Banks, 2017). If scholars, policymakers, and the public do not define elder victimization as a problem worthy of attention, then this corresponds with a lack of funding afforded to strategies that would combat this specific problem. If the goals of the system are defined by what traditional crime data sources like the NCVS and UCR identify as significant crime problems, then elder victimization may not be viewed as a priority; and how can law enforcement justify creation of specialized units like Elder Abuse Response Teams (EARTs) when victimization statistics do not support such an expenditure? This is especially troubling considering that research has highlighted a host of consequences associated with victimization broadly, and victimization of elders more specifically.

Generally, victimization research has indicated that victims experience physical, mental/psychological, and financial consequences as a result of victimization (Daigle, 2016). Further, financial abuse may deplete older adults' life savings and may possibly affect their access to healthcare, as well as even their ability to live independently (Choi, Kulick, & Mayer, 1999). Anne experienced a severely injured hip as a result of her victimization, which led to her placement in a nursing home facility. This ultimately affected her autonomy as she was no longer able to move freely and engage in the activities she enjoyed prior to her injury. This was especially true of the church activities she was now unable to attend, which led her to feel socially isolated from her small but influential social support network.

Anne's case highlights a major issue that older victims may face when they sustain a life-changing injury and have no informal care providers (i.e., family members) to help them remain in the community. Placement in a nursing home facility may be a major form of revictimization that adds insult to injury for older adults who had successfully lived independently prior to the victimization incident. It is safe to suggest that some older victims, especially those victimized by caregivers, may be reluctant to report their victimization or cooperate with legal authorities in an effort to avoid involuntary placements in facilities. An awareness of these unique consequences is necessary for law enforcement and other criminal justice professionals, like prosecutors and judges, who may be working with these victims as their cases process through the system. It also raises questions about our society's responsibility to provide some sort of social safety net for older victims that allows them to remain in their homes and maintain their autonomy despite the need for additional care that some may be unable to afford.

A Crime Problem: Effects of Disciplinary Boundaries and Fragmentation

The victimization experiences of older adults garnered additional attention in the 1990s as researchers and policymakers began to frame elder abuse as a crime problem rather than a social problem (Payne & Berg, 2003). As demonstrated by law enforcement's involvement in Anne and Simon's case, elder abuse and other forms of victimization experienced by older adults have evolved from a social problem into a distinct crime issue. The study of this phenomenon crosses multiple disciplinary boundaries and is mirrored by the diverse array of professionals who are involved in the response to criminal cases involving older victims.

Although this cross-disciplinary interest has produced considerable insight into this complex issue, it has also led the literature as well as the response to crimes against older adults to be somewhat fragmented. Although scholars generally agree that elder abuse and victimization involve a broad range of behaviors and occur in diverse settings, there is considerable variation across disciplines regarding what types of behaviors fall within each category of abuse, who is considered a perpetrator of elder abuse versus elder victimization, and at what age an individual is classified as an *elder*. These differences in perspectives and inconsistencies across studies can lead to conflicting policy recommendations and subsequent confusion across disciplines when attempting to collaborate in response to elder victimization.

For instance, although elder abuse has been effectively criminalized, many scholars consider elder abuse to be distinct from more traditional criminal acts committed against elders like theft and burglary. This is the approach taken in the current chapter and shifts the focus to a more circumscribed set of circumstances and crimes. The case of Anne is considered elder victimization, as Simon is a socially distant offender rather than a trusted family member or caregiver. This lends to a differential response to victims of situations that are defined as traditional criminal victimizations versus abuse incidents. The police may have still been involved had Simon been older and served as a full-time, informal caregiver who helped Anne remain in her home. Consider an alternative version of Anne and Simon's case where he is Anne's caregiver and the details of the case are more in line with what many would define as an abusive situation. In this altered version of their story, Simon is Anne's 45-year-old nephew who provides 24-hour care for her. He has stolen from Anne in order to pay bills he was unable to afford because he had to leave his job to attend to her daily needs. He may have even occasionally handled Anne roughly out of frustration about his care commitment and lack of training on proper care.

Although both the original victimization incident and now the new abuse incident may be dealt with via the criminal justice system, a response to the abuse incident may be accompanied by additional social service responses for Anne as well as for Simon. In the case of abuse, Adult Protective Services and other social services agencies may work with Simon to help ensure he receives additional support to provide appropriate care to Anne. This may include access to respite care for Anne that allows him to take a break from his responsibilities as caregiver. Due to the nature of the incident and the context surrounding the abuse, Simon may not be subject to criminal justice penalties and if he is, he may receive diversion where he is involved in an alternative sanction that keeps him from becoming involved in the correctional system. In comparison, in the original incident outlined at the beginning of the chapter that aligns more with a traditional criminal offense, Simon would not be offered such a diverse array of services. Instead, he would be more likely to be brought into the criminal justice system and potentially subject to stiffer penalties such as time in a correctional facility.

Fragmentation and Its Implications for Police Response

These two definitions may also have implications for how professionals approach these types of cases and whether victims are treated in an appropriate manner within the system. As police officers are often considered the gatekeepers of the criminal justice system, it is of significance to consider their roles in case processing and responding to elderly victims. For example, the criminal justice literature has highlighted how police officers may perceive their role in society by differentiating between the view of law enforcement as either crime fighters or public servants. Officers' predisposition for one role over the other informs the use of discretion, as well as influences the definition of duty and ethical obligation to respond to a given case (Pollock, 2019). As originally outlined by Packer (1968), the crime fighter orientation suggests that officers are in a war against real criminals and they should pursue repression of "real" crime (i.e., violent street crime), while resolving cases in the most efficient manner possible. This minimizes officers' perceptions of the duty to maintain order and provide services beyond strict crime control to the public.

Packer's (1968) public service model of policing stands in stark contrast to the crime fighter by emphasizing the officers' duty to serve all members of the public—even offenders. This orientation recognizes that the police have a limited ability to control crime due to the complex nature of criminal offending; thus the police have to deal with a range of problems beyond just crime and must approach cases with a willingness to provide a service, not just enforce the law. Depending on an officer's view of his or her role as public servant or crime fighter, and how he or she defines elder victimization, he or she may approach similar cases differently, which does not yield a fair, just response to older victims. More specifically, if police officers view elder victimization as a social problem rather than a crime problem, then they may use their discretion to overlook an offense or pass the responsibility for responding to a case to another agency, especially if the officer responding to an incident views his or her role as that of a crime fighter. This may occur even despite mandatory reporting requirements in place for suspected elder abuse that have emerged across many jurisdictions in the United States.

For instance, consider again the case posed at the beginning of the chapter and the alternative version where Simon was Anne's abusive caregiver. In the original crime scenario involving Anne and Simon, a police officer may view Simon as a potential threat and although a young, likely first-time offender, view his criminal potential as high and therefore in need of a stern criminal justice response. Would this best serve Anne in the long run? Would it best serve Simon and encourage him to make amends to Anne? In comparison, would the crime fighter deem the altered abuse scenario, in which Simon was Anne's caregiver, as worthy of criminal justice intervention? What about the public servant—how might he or she approach these two different cases and what may be the implications for both the victim and offender? Would justice be served? Would the response be fair to both parties? Which role, crime fighter or public servant, would lead to a greater consideration of beneficence as it relates to all parties in the two situations?

A Different Approach to Elder Victimization: The Promise of Restorative Justice

Research on victims' experiences in the criminal justice system indicate that some victims, namely domestic violence victims, report they feel disempowered by their involvement with law enforcement and the courts (Belknap & Sullivan, 2003; Hotaling & Buzawa, 2003). As previously noted, Anne's placement in the nursing home is a prime example of how disempowering a victimization incident can be. As a result, there has been a call in the literature to consider more victim-centered approaches to criminal justice (Caplow, 1998; Cattaneo & Goodman, 2010; Hartley, 2003). These approaches generally take into consideration the victim's needs and safety as priorities rather than focus solely on the punishment of the offender. One such approach is found in the restorative justice model, which involves the victim, offender, and the community in the criminal justice process and allows input from all parties when considering the outcomes or justice in a particular case (Zehr, 2002). Restorative justice can be viewed within the context of alternative dispute resolution (ADR), which in general refers to methods of settling private disputes without the use of civil litigation and may include techniques such as mediation and arbitration (Blake, Browne, & Sime, 2016). The ideas behind ADR and restorative justice are similar in that these two methods encourage innovative solutions to private and public wrongs.

At restorative justice's core is a focus on repairing the harm done by a criminal offense and the restoration of relationships between all parties affected by crime, even those not traditionally considered direct victims like the community at large. One of the ultimate goals of restorative justice programs is to reintegrate both offenders and victims back into the community rather than attach stigma to parties involved in a victimization incident (Zehr, 2002). Restorative justice may take the form of a victim–offender mediation, family/community group conference, and/or a peacemaking/sentencing circle (Daigle, 2016). Despite being rooted in indigenous practices, restorative justice has emerged as a new approach to responding to crime in the United States. It stands in stark comparison to the retributive justice model, which is offender and punishment focused. Scholars have begun to consider the utility of such an approach for elderly victims, particularly those who have been victimized by family members (see Groh & Linden, 2011). By applying this to elder victimization cases, the needs and wishes of the older person would be integral when considering the services and interventions necessary for a specific case. This type of approach requires multiagency collaboration and leads to unique, innovative case resolutions that are often beyond what traditional criminal justice remedies have generally provided. Elements of the restorative justice model have been employed in the Waterloo region in Manitoba, Canada, where there is an established EART trained to provide individualized responses to elder abuse cases. Groh and Linden (2011) report that early results indicate that the program is a promising model for collaboration in elder abuse cases. This model has been primarily utilized to address abusive situations involving perpetrators who are caregivers and family members; thus the literature has not fully examined the utility of this approach for a broader range of criminal victimization incidents involving older victims.

Anne's case may be appropriate for a restorative justice resolution involving both Anne and Simon, as well as other members of the community affected by the incident, the social services agencies that could assist the victim and offender, and the criminal justice professionals responsible for holding Simon accountable. Restorative justice has often been used with first-time juvenile offenders like Simon to provide him with an outlet for discussing why he may have committed the offense and as a resource for him to receive help for any issues that contributed to his offending behavior. Further, restorative justice could serve to restore some sense of power to Anne by giving her a voice in the process by allowing her to tell Simon how his offending has had an impact on her life. She would also have a role in determining appropriate sanctions for Simon.

There are some important considerations, however, that affect the promise of restorative justice approaches in cases involving elderly victims. Importantly, victim empowerment is a key piece of restorative justice practices and scholars have argued that it is important to level the playing field, so to speak, when engaging in this type of case resolution. Like domestic violence cases, there may be an inherent power differential between victim and offender that must be properly addressed for the restorative justice process to be effective. This means that victims must be afforded a proper voice and afforded the full right to participate in the process. To be in line with the ideals of the restorative justice framework, victims should not be forced or coerced into participating, nor should their concerns be dismissed by others who participate in the process. Focusing on mediation, Barry (2015) further notes that mediators and others involved in the resolution may be tempted to approach older adults from a paternalistic viewpoint, which may lead others to infringe upon the older victim's right to autonomy and could contribute to solutions that may not be in his or her best interests. Placing the victim's needs as well as safety at the center of this process and ensuring that facilitators are properly trained can help ensure that power imbalances are not reinforced by the restorative justice process (Zehr,

2002). Considering the two versions of Anne and Simon's case, which scenario would be more likely to exhibit some of the issues identified above? How could these issues be addressed in order for restorative justice to be a viable solution to this case?

CONCLUDING OBSERVATIONS

The U.S. Census Bureau projects that over 88 million U.S. residents will be 65 years old or older by 2050 (Vincent & Velkoff, 2010). This means that 1 in 5 Americans will be 65 or older by 2050, which is unlike any other time in U.S. history. Although NCVS data indicate that crime rates against older adults are declining (Morgan & Mason, 2014), it is likely that the U.S. criminal justice system will encounter more victims like Anne in the next several decades, simply because of the sheer increase in number of individuals in this age group. Considering the flaws associated with using traditional crime data sources and evidence of underreporting among this segment of the population, it is vital that policymakers and the public do not dismiss elder victimization as a policy priority due to some evidence that older adults are less likely to be victims compared to younger adults. This leads to the promotion of policies that fail to serve a growing segment of the population and may result in injustice for this group of victims. Moreover, there are concerns with how our current criminal justice system may respond to and handle cases involving elderly victims. Differing views on how to define and respond to elder victimization may lead criminal justice professionals to be unprepared to respond to elder victimization cases, and this lack of preparation may hinder efforts to respond to older victims. Current responses may affect the autonomy and safety of older victims, as well as fail to hold perpetrators accountable for their behavior. Finally, restorative justice appears to be a promising way to respond to cases involving elderly victims, and this approach may address the drawbacks of the traditional criminal justice response to crime.

DISCUSSION QUESTIONS

1. Considering the weaknesses of traditional sources of crime data and the implications of these sources for policy development, what is a better way to measure and capture elder victimization? What are some of the barriers that exist when attempting to measure victimization among this population?

2. There is evidence of underreporting among older victims of crime. Why do you think older individuals may be reluctant to report that they have been victimized?

3. What are the implications of the varying perspectives on how to define *elder abuse* and *elder victimization* for the response to elderly victims of crime?

4. Given that older adults comprise a smaller proportion of crime victims, how would you convince policymakers and the public that it is necessary to allot resources to programs and policies directed at addressing crimes against this population?

5. Do you think that restorative justice is an effective response to elder victimization? What are its potential strengths and drawbacks?

6. Do you think a traditional criminal justice response to crimes against the older adults would result in justice for older crime victims? Moreover, do you think the system is prepared to appropriately address crimes against older adults?

7. What are the biggest challenges that the criminal justice system will face in the next several decades as the American population "grays" and older victims, witnesses, and offenders ultimately become more involved in the system?

REFERENCES

Acierno, R., Hernandez, M. A., Amstadter, A. B., Resnick, H. S., Steve, K., Muzzy, W., & Kilpatrick, D. G. (2010). Prevalence and correlates of emotional, physical, sexual, and financial abuse and potential neglect in the United States: The national elder mistreatment study. *American Journal of Public Health, 100(2),*292–297.

Banks, C. (2017). *Criminal justice ethics.* Thousand Oaks, CA: Sage.

Barry, L. (2015). Elder mediation: What's in a name? *Conflict Resolution Quarterly, 32(4),* 435–444.

Belknap J., & Sullivan, C. M. (2003). *Longitudinal study of battered women in the system: The victims' and decision-makers' perceptions: Final report.* Washington, DC: National Institute of Justice.

Blake, S., Browne, J., & Sime, S. (2016). *Alternative dispute resolution.* Oxford: Oxford University Press.

Bonnie, R. J., & Wallace, R. B. (2003). *Elder mistreatment: Abuse, neglect, and exploitation in an aging America.* Washington, DC: National Research Council.

Burnes, D., Henderson, C., Sheppard, C., Zhao, R., Pillemer, K., & Lachs, M. (2017). Prevalence of financial fraud and scams among older adults in the United States: A systematic review and meta-analysis. *American Journal of Public Health, 107(8),* e13–e21.

Caplow, S. (1998). What if there is no client? Prosecutors as "counselors" of crime. *Clinical Law Review, 5,* 1–45.

Cattaneo, L. B., & Goodman, L. A. (2010). Through the lens of therapeutic jurisprudence: The relationship between empowerment in the court system and well-being for intimate partner violence victims. *Journal of Interpersonal Violence, 25(3),* 481–502.

Choi, N. G., Kulick, D. B., & Mayer, J. (1999). Financial exploitation of elders: Analysis of risk factors based on county adult protective services data. *Journal of Elder Abuse & Neglect, 10(3/4),* 39–62.

Consumer Sentinel Network. (2017). *Consumer Sentinel Network data book for January-December 2016.* Washington, DC: Federal Trade Commission.

Daigle, L. E. (2016). *Victimology.* Thousand Oaks, CA: Sage.

Friedman, B., Santos, E., Liebel, D., Russ, A., & Conwell, Y. (2014). Longitudinal prevalence and correlates of elder mistreatment among older adults receiving home visiting nursing. *Journal of Elder Abuse & Neglect, 27(1),* 1–31.

Groh, A., & Linden, R. (2011). Addressing elder abuse: The Waterloo restorative justice approach to elder abuse project. *Journal of Elder Abuse & Neglect, 23(2),* 127–146.

Harris, D. K., & Benson, M. L. (1998). Nursing home theft: The hidden problem. *Journal of Aging Studies, 12*(1), 57–67.

Hartley, C. C. (2003). A therapeutic jurisprudence approach to the trial process in domestic violence felony trials. *Violence Against Women, 9*, 410–437.

Holtfreter, K., Reisig, M. D., Mears, D. P., & Wolfe, S. E. (2014). *Financial exploitation of the elderly in a consumer context* (Final report, National Institute of Justice, Washington, DC). Retrieved from https://www.ncjrs.gov/pdffiles1/nij/grants/245388.pdf

Hotaling, G., & Buzawa, E. S. (2003). *Forgoing criminal justice assistance: The non-reporting of new incidents of abuse in a sample of domestic violence victims* (Document No. 195667). Washington, DC: National Institute of Justice.

Klaus, P. (2005). *Crimes against persons age 65 or older, 1993–2002*. Washington, DC: Bureau of Justice Statistics.

Mears, D., Reisig, M., Scaggs, S., & Holtfreter, K. (2016). Efforts to reduce consumer fraud victimization among the elderly. *Crime & Delinquency, 62*(9), 1235–1259.

Morgan, R. E., & Kena, G. (2017). *Criminal victimization, 2016*. Washington, DC: Bureau of Justice Statistics.

Morgan, R. E., & Mason, B. J. (2014). *Crimes against the elderly, 2003–2013*. Washington, DC: Bureau of Justice Statistics.

Packer, H. (1968). *The limits of the criminal sanction.* Stanford, CA: Stanford University Press.

Pak, K., & Shadel, D. (2011). *AARP Foundation National Fraud Victim Study.* Washington, D.C.: American Association of Retired Persons.

Payne, B. K. (2002). An integrated understanding of elder abuse and neglect. *Journal of Criminal Justice, 30,* 535–547.

Payne, B. K. (2011). *Crime & elder abuse: An integrated perspective* (3rd ed.). Springfield, IL: Thomas.

Payne, B. K., & Berg, B. L. (2003). Perceptions about the criminalization of elder abuse among police chiefs and ombudsmen. *Crime & Delinquency, 49*(3), 439–459.

Payne, B. K., & Gainey, R. R. (2006). The criminal justice response to elder abuse in nursing homes: A routine activities perspective. *Western Criminology Review, 7*(3), 67–81.

Payne, B. K., & Gainey, R. R. (2009). *Family violence & criminal justice: A life-course approach* (3rd ed.). New Providence, NJ: Lexis Nexis.

Pillemer, K., & Finkelhor, D. (1988). The prevalence of elder abuse: A random sample survey. *Gerontologist, 28*(1), 51–57.

Pollock, J. M. (2019). *Ethical dilemmas and decisions in criminal justice* (10th ed.). Boston, MA: Cengage.

Tatara, T. (1998, September). *The National Elder Abuse Incidence Study: Final report.* New York, NY: National Center on Elder Abuse.

Tilse, C., & Wilson, J. (2013). Recognising and responding to financial abuse in residential aged care. *Journal of Adult Protection, 15*(3), 141–152.

Tong, R. (1986). *Ethics in policy analysis.* Englewood Cliffs, NJ: Prentice Hall.

Vincent, G. K., & Velkoff, V. A. (2010). *The next four decades the older population in the United States: 2010 to 2050.* Washington, DC: US Census Bureau.

Zehr, H. (2002). *The little book of restorative justice.* Intercourse, PA: Good Books.

18

THE INTERSECTION OF ETHICS AND BULLYING IN THE PROVISION OF SERVICES FOR ELDERS

Katherine P. Cardinal, MS, LIC
Cardinal Gerontology

Pamela B. Teaster
Virginia Tech

> *"Ethics and the good society: It is in everybody's interest to seek those (actions) that lead to happiness and avoid those which lead to suffering. And because our interests are inextricably linked, we are compelled to accept ethics as the indispensable interface between my desire to be happy and yours."*

> —Dalai Lama (as cited in Craig, 2017)

KEYWORDS

older adults
retirement community
bullying
cyberbulling

ethics
nursing home
bystander effect
legislative interventions

CASE STUDY 18.1

The director of a retirement community received funds earmarked for anything serving the needs of residents. The funds were given in honor of a donor whose mother, Sue, currently lives in the assisted living facility. For two years, the donor has made comments, noting the need for new dining room furnishings and carpeting. He has also suggested replacing and updating the worn-looking building. The executive director of the entire retirement complex went to high school with the donor. Especially in the past two years, the social climate has been tremendously negative in the assisted living facility. The staff has pinpointed the problem to Sue, the mother of the donor, and a group of her "friends." To the best knowledge of staff, Sue has no cognitive challenges. She is the leader of a group of women who, on a regular basis, speak negatively about memory care unit residents. At mealtime, assisted living and memory care residents share the dining room. Although there are no assigned seats, Sue always reserves seats for her "friends," rudely telling memory care residents that they cannot sit down. While sitting at a table of eight, Sue and friends loudly mock other residents. One woman receiving memory care has stopped going to dinner entirely, and staff thinks that she is avoiding Sue and her group of friends. Another female resident moved out because Sue told her that her Muslim religion is sinful. It has gotten so bad that dining room staff avoid lingering near Sue's table because they don't want to confront her or overhear negative comments. Sue never says anything negative in earshot of you, the director. In fact, Sue acts welcoming and helpful in front of those in charge. The director of the retirement community would like some of the funds from Sue's son's donation to go toward antibullying staff training and improvements to the social climate. Sue has great influence not only over her current friend group, but also over future residents who may join the community. Sue is well connected in the community because her husband, who died two years ago, was very popular as the town's former chief of police. Sue and most of her friends pay full price for housing and services while the targets of her ridicule seem to have very few family visitors and are on Medicaid. It has become clear that Sue befriends certain individuals, treating them well while acting cruelly toward more vulnerable residents and staff.

Overview

The case study illustrates bullying behaviors and its consequences in the lives of older vulnerable adults. It highlights the need for a new sense of urgency within our culture and in aging services, which is to fully understand and effectively prevent bullying among older adults. To determine how to best protect vulnerable elders from harm by peers and others, it is important to determine appropriate ethical responses and ignite research efforts to establish evidence-based best practices designed to keep vulnerable older adults safe. Aging services professionals well understand that bullying occurs throughout the lifespan and therefore must seek to create and bolster programs and enact policies to protect older adults who fall prey to this kind of abuse. The scope of bullying among elders has yet to be determined due to lack of research. However, scholars and clinicians are exploring if resident-to-resident aggression, which studies indicate is a pervasive problem (Lachs, Teresi, & Ramirez, 2014; Rosen, Pillemer, & Lachs, 2018), can be viewed as one symptom of an underlying problem of bullying (Lake, 2014). Bullying can occur in a variety of venues, including but not limited to senior centers, congregate meal sites, senior high-rise apartments, assisted living facilities, and nursing homes. Professionals cannot wait for years of research in order to draw conclusions on how to proceed. Enough is known about bullying in other populations to extrapolate to older adults in order to implement approaches that encourage civility and do not cause harm (i.e., the ethical principle of nonmaleficence). Care must be taken, however, not to implement piecemeal programming that may backfire or inadvertently cause harm to targets of bullying. There must be a comprehensive cultural shift that recognizes elder-to-elder bullying as an important health concern. Current evidence-based research about elders and other populations makes clear the need to challenge notions that minimize bullying behaviors as part of life or as something with which elders must cope alone. Older adults have the right to be free from ridicule and entrapment in emotionally unsafe environments. Still in its infancy, the study of bullying among elders raises troubling questions. Awareness and education are important beginning efforts towards recognizing bullying and devising responses that keep older adults emotionally safe.

This chapter will provide readers with an understanding of bullying as a problem with the hope that solid interest and a commitment to further research takes hold. Specifically, answers to these questions are explored: Does society place adequate value on vulnerable elders and others in order to fully fund research that promotes social wellness and significantly counteracts bullying? Is bullying recognized as wrong and regarded as a problem to be addressed?

Bullying and Vulnerability

Bullying is, by its very nature, an ethical and social justice issue for older adults who find themselves devalued in a social hierarchy, vulnerable to those who may not always have their best interests at heart. In addition, since the social status of older individuals is fluid rather than static, even those not currently vulnerable may later join the category due to changes in health or ability. In addition to finding bullying difficult to identify and rectify, professionals may confront ethical dilemmas related to social bullying, as little evidence-based policy and practice exists. It is critical to learn the hallmarks of bullying and address it within the context of the social hierarchy in which it is fueled. It is equally important to view bullying as systemic within a community, rather than as single episodes of ridicule or harm directed toward a target.

Definitions and Understanding Bullying as Elder Abuse

Bullying is intentional, repetitive, aggressive behavior that involves an imbalance of power or strength (Hazelden Foundation, 2011). While this chapter focuses on bullying in residential settings, bullying occurs in other settings, including congregate meal sites and senior centers. Some researchers have noted that even one episode of harmful bullying can produce a detrimental impact on targets who fear that more will follow. Targets of bullies may suffer considerable emotional anguish as well as physical and psychological manifestations including but not limited to anxiety, depression, decreased self-worth, hopelessness, helplessness, and social withdrawal, among others (Bonifas, 2016). Table 18.1 shows that bullying falls along a continuum of actions, ranging from those that are subtle to those that are criminal. In contrast, Table 18.2 illustrates the impact of bullying on the target.

TABLE 18.1   Understanding Bullying—From Subtle Actions to Criminal Behavior

Subtle actions	Intensified actions	Criminal behavior
Ignoring another individual on purpose (repeatedly)	Bossing around, controlling resources to which a person is entitled	Verbal threats that make the target fearful with or without kicking, shoving, biting, hitting
Spreading rumors, gossip that is often untrue or exaggerated	Derogatory comments that may be racial or discriminatory in nature or regarding sexual orientation	Hurting an individual with a mobility device, cane, scooter, wheelchair
Motivating others to disassociate with an individual or group (refusing to sit with individual or excluding a person from activities meant for everyone)	Repeated gestures behind a person's back or to his or her face; eye rolls, grimaces, sticking out tongue, hand gestures	Cruelty to pets, damage to property, stealing

Source: Adapted from Bonifas, 2016, p. 63

TABLE 18.2   Target/Victim Perspectives of Bullying—from Emotional Discomfort to Character Assassination

Emotional discomfort	Increased emotional discomfort	Character assassination
An overall feeling of rejection	Decreased ability to manage activities of daily living (e.g., eating, bathing)	Talk of moving out or leaving the community
Depressive symptoms, including changes in sleep	Experiencing harassment in the form of derogatory, racial, homophobic, anti-Semitic or discriminatory comments	Injury from being hit by an individual with a mobility device, cane, scooter, wheelchair
Increased physical complaints	Damage to reputation	Suicidal ideation

Source: Adapted from Bonifas, 2016; Bonifas & Frankel, 2012.

Alternate Causes for Bully-Like Behavior or the Presence of Coexisting Conditions

Bullying behaviors sometimes overlap with behaviors exhibited in mental illnesses. Consequently, it is critical for psychotherapists, psychiatrists, and clinical social workers to assess individual situations. Some conditions associated with mental illness result in hallucinations or inappropriate, aggressive behaviors. Active addiction, either to substances or other behaviors, may also interconnect and/or overlap with individuals experiencing bullying. Substances may be used by bullies or by targets of bullies and bystanders when feeling trapped in a bully drama. When victims feel powerless and endure pain from bullying, addictive substances provide immediate relief by numbing the pain for those who feel powerless. In the bigger picture, such maladaptive strategies often make matters worse.

One of the greatest challenges to addressing bullying is the perspective of those who consider certain bullying behaviors nonharmful. Despite its definition, which is consistent with abusive behaviors that often lead to serious health consequences for targets, some still regard bullying as "part of life." In populations where bullying has been researched, largely among school-aged students, evidence of real harm suggests otherwise (Olweus, 1993, 2003; Olweus & Graham, 2001). Understanding its associated individual and collective social/emotional harm must precede efforts to affect individuals in systems that support or deter it. Finding ethical responses to bullying for the long-term well-being of individual targets and for the greatest community good can be elusive. A significant challenge is overcoming the denial and discounting of bullying by leaders who are poised to exert influence over the culture of a community.

Lack of Recognition of the Problem of Bullying

The chief research on bullying among older adults is a study of 121 residents in six assisted living facilities in the Netherlands (Trompetter, Scholte, & Westerhof, 2011). Researchers found a link between residents who were victimized by relational aggression and high levels of depression, anxiety, social loneliness, and lower life satisfaction. Nothing causal was found. However, important to note was that "nurse reports of relational aggression were not related to any of the measures of resident's subjective well-being" (Trompetter et al., 2011, p. 65). The study went on to say, "apparently nurses have difficulty discerning incidences of aggression that are perceived as hurtful by residents" (Trompetter et al., 2011, p. 65). The difference between what nurses perceived and what residents experienced differed greatly by facility. When researchers attempted to explain why nurses' perception of residents' experiences were so different from those of the residents, they posed two possible scenarios. The first was the use of indirect tactics by older adults; essentially, stealth on the part of the bully, and/or "possible non-transparency of groups of residents making systematic relational aggression hard to detect for nurses." The study highlights that that residents emphatically rejected the term bullying—saying that only children were bullies, even though behaviors were consistent with the definition (Trompetter et al., 2010). In the Trompetter study, it may be that nurses were not adequately focused on empathy for their patients but rather focused exclusively on medical aspects of their care, so that they were not aware of patients' social and emotional needs. Also and relatedly, according to Briles (2009), senior or more socially powerful nurses have been found to bully younger, more vulnerable nurses. This points to systemic, multilevel bullying problems that could become pervasive within communities.

Hidden and Misleading Actions of Individual Bullies

As shown in the case study at the beginning of the chapter, bullies act differently depending on who is in the vicinity. They will sometimes act civilly in front of individuals at their level or above in the social hierarchy, often reserving bullying tactics for targets when they are alone or accompanied by others who are equally powerless and vulnerable. The hidden nature of bullying presents a significant challenge for facility staff members who will only know more by involving themselves further in the social realms of residents or community members.

Anecdotally, when staffing and resources are low and the number of people attempting to access them is high, infighting and jockeying for positions to obtain scarce resources tends to occur. Bullies and more assertive individuals seek to have their needs met while more passive individuals wait and often receive fewer services and less attention. In an environment where the staff is conscious of this dynamic, the onus is on staff to insist that bullies wait their turn. Triaging based on need instead of tactical social aggression reinforces that a bully does not gain what he or she wants from negative behavior. Meeting underlying needs of bullies who have lost social status in their own families or who feel displaced because of having lost a lifelong job that offered a sense of identity can be helpful if staff is able to help the person replace the feeling of loss with a new role (Barbera, 2015). In other words, the bullying individual may feel out of control and may try to regain it by manipulating and controlling others. Meeting the underlying need and helping individuals create a new sense of belonging may ameliorate the problem (Barbera, 2015).

Lessons From School Bullying

Lessons from studies on school bullying (Berger, 2007; Espalage, 2014; Farrington, 1993; Gladden et al., 2014) can inform bullying among older individuals (Kreimer, 2012), social and emotional support for bullies and the bullied, as well as civility training, and can greatly improve the social climate within a community or environment. A question often asked is this: Have older adult bullies (Kreimer, 2012) been bullying their entire lives, or is the problem new in older adulthood as aging takes place? Though the answer is yet unknown, anecdotally, the biological sciences provide some direction. Traits that are hallmarks of bullying are identified in certain alpha animals and, strikingly, can be traced to animal behavior displayed in youth. In 2018, while studying adult bonobos (animals related to the ape family), Brian Hare, associate professor of evolutionary anthropology, and Christopher Krupenye, from Lola ya Bonobo Sanctuary in the Democratic Republic of Congo, described an emergent pattern of bullying and noted that individual animals who attempted to challenge the rising alpha bully's dominance had scarring, missing hair on their backs, and other evidence of physical attack from the leader who was solidifying his dominance over the group. Also remarkable were the reactions of onlookers who preferred to establish a closer relationship to animals seen as bullies and jerks among them, rather than an association with the bullied animals (Hare & Krupenye, 2018).

The Bystander Effect

To counteract this inclination to follow and take the side of the bully, also evident in humans, is bystander effect training (Scully & Rowe, 2009), an approach to counter diffusion of responsibility that people feel while in the presence of others. The bystander effect, also called the theory of diffusion of responsibility (Schneider, Gruman, & Coutts, 2005), occurs when multiple people are present and a person or group of individuals appears to need help. Each bystander tends to feel that because there are others, someone else will take action and do what is necessary. Eliciting a reduced burden of action on witnesses, onlookers seem less inclined to help bullied targets. Onlookers expect that someone else will intervene, with some even experiencing paralysis.

Ethical dilemmas for bystanders present themselves daily and demand values-based responses. Questions to consider include the following: What influences and motivates individuals to intervene when witnessing unkindness, or worse, bullying? Does remaining quiet or silently standing by a bully insure one's own safety? Individuals, consciously or unconsciously, evaluate, on some level, what they may lose, and then act (or not), facing the consequences from having either stepped up or done nothing in the face of bullying. Inadequate social support within a community's hierarchy can mean actions taken against bullying can backfire and bystanders who act with good intentions may themselves become targets.

Taking Responsibility at the Organizational Level

In addition to protecting individual older adults, organizations providing care for older adults and others with fiduciary responsibilities must be ethically driven to provide older adults with emotionally safe environments. The social climate, beyond medical and physical care, becomes increasingly important. Without regulations and legislation enabling communities to manage their social climate, responsibility is placed on individual leaders to model appropriate conduct, influence their communities, and provide proper staff training. The problem is then, when leadership changes, norms of civility also may change, and accountability for social wellness may be rejected outright or abandoned over time.

For example, bullying problems reported by older adult residents to nursing staff and social workers are often met by nurses' and aides' *ad hoc* interventions for dealing with emotionally aggressive residents (Lake, 2014; Span, 2014; Wood, 2007). Without protocols or evidence-based research or training, staff will address problems from their own sense of right and wrong and obligation to maintain residents' safety. In organizations where social aggression is more common, direct care workers may ignore what they see and hear from either their own helpless, hopeless feeling, or from not knowing that certain behaviors are unacceptable. Expecting unacceptable behavior as the norm can then escalate and become toxic.

Physical aggression may be documented by staff as an incident or accident report, which falls under state regulations and is addressed with policies and mandated reporting protocols. Alternately, little protects an older adult from social bullying, unless the offense involves discrimination, harassment, or violations associated with people in protected classes. Even then, bullies who figure out how to skirt harassment law will simply find ways to do damage without triggering legal and or criminal violations.

Critical to bullying intervention and prevention is the understanding of likely times and places that bullying is apt to occur (Voyer, 2005). Dining, activity, and exercise areas in older adult communities are considered "hot spots" and are noted by staff as typical locations where problems occur. If staff makes their presence known when a group prone to hurtful gossiping and other bullying behaviors is convening, it may significantly deter that conduct.

Resolutions for the Problem of Bullying
Resident-Level Interventions

Some evidence shows that when older adults feel valued and worthy of customized care, there is less social aggression because underlying needs are met. The personalized approach in Green House Project communities (i.e., innovative, home-like communities for residents needing nursing home–level care) with more home-like settings founded by Robert Wood Johnson, specializing in progressive, patient-centered care for older adults and those with disabilities, is one such example (Cardinal, 2015). Anecdotally, in settings with exceptionally high standards of customized care, community members may naturally uphold kinder social behaviors that tend to be inconsistent with bullying behaviors. Breaking certain social norms in settings where high behavioral expectations are solidly upheld may help ensure that bullying and other inappropriate behaviors are seen as outlier behaviors that are unwelcome. Positive behavior is therefore more apt to be displayed by community members, making civility self-reinforcing.

Dealing with physical bullying is difficult to manage in nursing homes. Residents, including those who engage in bullying, have the right not to be discharged or even moved to a different room in a facility without notice and appeal rights. Attempting to deal with aggressive behavior by using medication may run afoul of a resident's right to be free from chemical and physical restraints, as well as the right to consent to treatment under both state and federal law. Thus, the use of psychotropic drugs, even for a mentally ill and/or physically aggressive resident, can require a lengthy process and ultimately, court-ordered mandatory treatment to overcome a residents' right to be free from chemical restraints, reflecting the ethical principle of autonomy. Care providers need creative strategies, other than use of medication, to calm a resident's mental state and help with emotional regulation.

Bystander interventions can be effective for situations involving older adults. School bullying research indicates that "when bystanders intervene on behalf of the victim, they successfully abate victimization more than 50% of the time" (Polanin, Espelage, & Pigott, 2012, p. 48). To elicit the effect that bystander interventions have on school bullying in nursing homes, memory care, and assisted living facilities, nursing staff, nurse's aides, activities staff and other workers must learn effective bystander intervention strategies. Staff members are able to model to residents how to assert themselves without harming another resident. Staff also need to advocate for vulnerable residents, giving voice to what they may need and feel if they are unable to stand up for themselves.

Unfortunately, most front-line workers likely to witness incidents of bullying are neither trained in bullying prevention, nor do they inherently have specialized social work skills for managing social hierarchies and bullying situations. "Training would need to include methods of coaching residents to avoid aggression with peers in a way that is neither punitive nor infringes on a resident's right for self-expression" (Aaron, personal communication as seen in Cardinal, 2015, p. 23). Also, ethical dilemmas, often related to justice, arise when workers are not able to intercede with the goal of protecting targeted residents. Staff cannot expect to change a bully's particular views but can instead help the bully understand how a resident's individual views manifest in behavior that infringes on the right of another to live in an emotionally and physically safe environment. This concept reflects the ethical principle of autonomy. Prevention strategies could include a full calendar of engaging activities led by trained staff:

- Noise reduction (volume control especially in shared rooms and common areas)

- Music, art, Reiki, pet therapy, and other complementary and alternative medicines

- Increased staff-to-resident ratios (especially in busy hot spots)

- Lighting, aroma, and other ambiance factors which enhance mood

- Smaller group table configurations instead of large group dining tables (seating for 2–4 instead of 6–10)

- Not allowing seat saving (allows for less ability to form destructive groups or cliques)

- Private rooms and respectful practices for entering an individual's private space

- Size limits on the number of individuals who may participate in certain programs along with appropriate staff to resident ratios

Bullying is also a problem in independent living environments, which are typically regulated by hotel and restaurant management agencies. Virginia attorney Martin Donlan, who has provided legal counsel for nursing homes and assisted living organizations for more than 35 years, emphasizes that laws do not specifically address social, relational forms of bullying among residents. "Unless there are physical injuries or risk of injury, verbal abuse is generally seen as a management issue for caregivers to address" (Donlan, personal communication, May 1, 2015). Regulating these issues is difficult because in most states, the rights of residents are conflicting. Like many states, Virginia assures residents in nursing homes certain rights while residing in state-licensed facilities. A bullied resident may claim to be mentally abused or not treated with respect by rejection from a resident group, while the rejecting group may claim the right to associate with only certain residents by choice. The facility "has a duty to foster an environment in which abusive resident-to-resident behaviors are minimized without limiting the rights of residents to choose the residents with whom they associate" (Donlan, personal communication, May 1, 2015).

Organizational-Level Interventions

Care-providing organizations must consider whom they wish to attract when marketing their services and communities. Some organizations implicitly invite members of the same religious or socioeconomic group to join a community through covert marketing, which can subtly fuel an undercurrent of discrimination. Other communities promote inclusion and advertise the appeal of culturally rich and diverse membership as a community asset. Some experts believe that people tend to be happier in an environment congruent with their values and beliefs. However, proximity to family or economic necessity may entice an older individual to join a community with dissimilar people. Without kind and welcoming individuals in the community, a person can feel ostracized and develop a feeling of loneliness or a fear of being outcast. Recognizing that an individual's sense of belonging is critical to overall health as seen in Maslow's hierarchy of needs, a welcoming social climate is an ethically relevant criterion.

When strong cultural norms around civility and tolerance of others' differences are enforced by both staff and community members, the expectation for new members to conform is created. Group tendencies to act with caring toward others may be self-reinforcing, which reflects an ethic of care, as discussed in Chapter 1. From a human resources department that incorporates social wellness into hiring practices to resident/member manuals and environmental cues that reinforce kind behavior, civility norm building is continually evolving. Practices include staff training that revolve specifically around modeling civility, leadership fostering norms of civility (e.g., human resource hiring practices, training staff on civility, programming emphasizing inclusion and camaraderie among staff and residents, and organizational emphasis on resident emotional safety as a health issue).

An Attempted Legislative Intervention

In 2016, the state of Massachusetts enacted a landmark law establishing the nation's first legislative study commission to examine the impact of bullying on older people or those living with a disability in multifamily public and subsidized housing. The Beacon Hill Community in Boston highlighted problematic bullying issues and brought community stakeholders together to address what they considered a widespread problem. However, 15 months later, when an update on the progress of the commission was reported, funding and resources to combat the problem proved inadequate. Housing officials for Massachusetts asserted that bullying is a social relationship, one outside the scope of the Department of Housing and Community Development. In addition, the agency was stretched financially in taking physical care of the buildings themselves (Stop Bullying Coalition, 2019). It was noted that harassment law covered certain violations. However, bullying did not fall into the category of harassment law, and it remains an area for which individual housing managers do not take responsibility. In 2017, a survey of people from 1,400 housing developments consisting of approximately 92,000 housing units was still underway in order to explore the scope of the problem (Stop Bullying Coalition, 2019).

CONCLUDING OBSERVATIONS

Any form of bullying, no matter how subtle, should be considered both an ethical issue and a business problem. While it is obvious that physical bullying falls into the category of mandated incident/accident reporting and receives the immediate attention of nursing staff and management, the more subtle forms of social bullying that are ignored but become negative to the individuals served by the business must be addressed. Often, such problems result in ethical compromise and financial loss. The phenomenon of health care professionals who bully their colleagues is a parallel problem that exists in organizations and one that may impede leaders from addressing the issue or including it as a focal point in strategic planning where dollars are designated for making progress in various areas of the company. Large turnover in a certain department or throughout a company could be due to bullying issues or social issues where individuals are in conflict with one another (Briles, 2009). Workplace bullying must be addressed alongside resident-to-resident bullying if it is to influence community norms (Workplace Bullying Institute, 2014). If employees are to successfully manage resident-to-resident aggression, they must first learn how to manage it for themselves and understand that bullying is indeed problematic.

Trends in how other populations deal with social, relational aggression reveal the need for a new narrative with respect to bullying of older, vulnerable adults. The message from service providers to older adults is that their spirits, feelings, and lives matter. Denying that the problem exists is unacceptable from a moral and ethical standpoint. Realizing that bullying exists on a continuum and is never completely absent among human beings is critical to understanding and remedying the problem. Instead of being fearful from a public relations perspective, organizations should emphasize their investment in programming towards prevention and early detection and intervention. If industry leaders embrace and support research and test promising pilot programs in older adult populations, benefits would accrue to the entire industry.

Many older adults came of age in an era where bullying was considered a "part of life." There is a notable need for mass education on its real harm. It appears there are limits to legislation on social aggression and lack of civility, especially when many bullying behaviors are covert. However, programming can do much to help and may even contribute to lessening physical aggression, which is an associated serious issue. Leaders and managers must reflect on where, in the past, each has stood in their own experiences as a victim, bystander, or perpetrator. While the topic may create discomfort, self-reflection is part of the process of change and a necessary first step in addressing bullying as a serious health and social justice problem.

Cyberbullying Is a New Problem for Older Adults

With Baby Boomers already fully immersed in technology, cyberbullying has become a new problem, similar to that for youth and young adults (Dilmac, 2009). Occurring on smartphones and other digital devices, older adults are already contending with harassment and bullying via social media, forums, and in gaming where people engage with those they know and with others considered strangers. Teaching elders about "stranger danger," a phrase used by elementary school–aged students, is already necessary for older adults. Learning how to avoid becoming a target of online bullying is critical, and older adults must also learn how to maintain privacy and not become victims of online hoaxes which may damage one's reputation. It is considered cyberbullying to share harmful, false, or abusive content about someone else via text, e-mail, Tweet, post or other media. Private information that could be embarrassing when shared also contributes to the problem. Some cyberbullying crosses the line into unlawful or criminal behavior, and reporting this to authorities is critical.

Currently, cyberbullying occurs most commonly on social media, such as Facebook, Instagram, Snapchat, and Twitter (Tokunaga, 2010). Some forms of social media create a permanent public record of what a person views along with activities that they post as well as other information. Because the Internet is available to people around the clock, the amount of content is impossible to police. In addition, technology companies have done little to help people control their privacy. A person's reputation may be seriously affected by cyberbullying. Individual states have laws against cyberbullying with significant focus on protection of children. However, online bullying may harm adults and elders seriously as well and is a problem expected to continue to grow over time (Stopbullying.gov, n.d.).

Future Directions

There is a collective harm in the ethos that may not yet be scientifically measured but that can be intangibly felt when an individual or group engages in bullying. For those in authority in any community, understanding how to influence the social climate is vital to ensuring basic norms of civility and preventing harm to individual community members. It is incumbent on current and future generations to codify into law ways to address the effects of bullying and promote programming that enhances civility. Furthermore, defining leadership characteristics that align with upholding civility norms must be identified, understood, and articulated in job descriptions.

Environmental factors influence how people feel and can contribute to emotional and physical suffering. Conditions such as overcrowding, scarce resources, or how individuals feel about themselves when living in neglected properties may complicate matters of civility. Communicating a message of "you matter" to each and every community member, regardless of social status, race, religion, sexual orientation, or mental or physical ability, contributes to the overall social climate.

Bullying as an Issue of Justice

To conclude, it is short sighted for individuals as well as foundations, philanthropists, governments, and other funding sources to deny funding for examining social bullying in elders while supporting funding to study physical aggression. While the cost of health care is overwhelming, preventive measures may prove far less costly. Putting effort into solutions that address the root causes of violence in community and facility settings where elders dwell is critical to long-term management of the problem. Verbal and social aggression can become precursors to physical aggression and should be regarded as interconnected. Intervention at the source instead of where symptoms manifest themselves can save time, money, and unnecessary emotional and physical pain for victims of bullying and bystanders—which in many instances are health care workers who suffer alongside victims. While this chapter attempted to cover the topic of bullying as it relates to ethics and vulnerable elders balancing an individual's rights with justice, the field is open for further research and practice efforts, as both are in early stages of development. Importantly, elder-to-elder social aggression has finally made its way into the national dialogue.

DISCUSSION QUESTIONS

1. You are the new director of a brand-new senior center in town and want to establish the space as a place where group members can make meaningful connections, have fun, learn, and enjoy time together. You have a totally clean slate and can make this community whatever you want it to be. You want civility and

kindness to be of utmost importance in this new gathering space because your last job was working in a senior center where people were disrespectful and discriminatory. It was an effort to go to work and hear people being mean to each other. How do you create an inclusive and inviting space for everyone from the beginning?

2. From the perspective of a new director of an assisted living (an outside hire) how would you handle the following situation: After two months on the job, you find out that an elderly couple living in the building has been eating alone in their room for 2 years. Upon inquiry, you learn from staff that they have been socially rejected primarily because of the way they dress and their overall disheveled appearance. According to a long-time well-respected staff member, when they went for their first meal their first day, they walked into the dining room to eat breakfast. They went from table to table to join in with others where there appeared to be open seating. After multiple rejections, they took their breakfast trays, returned to their room, and never went back to eat in the dining room again. The staff didn't intervene because they "had each other" and so they felt loneliness would not be an issue. How would you approach this problem on the staff level, on the resident level, and within the community as a whole? What steps would you take immediately? What would you implement over time?

3. You are the new director of a continuing care retirement community. The old director who built and developed the organization over many years left suddenly but was previously directed by the board of directors after numerous complaints to attend anger management workshops. The story that slowly unfolds within the first two months of your tenure is that his style of social bullying included publicly reprimanding staff at team lunches, mocking individuals behind their backs to the residents (which undermined staff credibility), and quietly going up behind staff in the halls and startling them from behind then laughing at their vocal reactions. Although most staff were on edge from this behavior and were relieved at his departure, long-term staff that had only known his management style copy some of his behaviors, perpetuating this emotionally unsafe working environment. What would you do to turn things around and create a more emotionally secure environment, and how would you retrain staff and undo the damage done as it relates to the residents?

4. Doris, a new resident, starts complaining to other residents about her primary care aide, around whom she is uncomfortable because of her ethnicity. She is constantly making negative comments that indicate she is racist. Finally, she announces that she is not going to let anyone enter her room if they have dark skin. She has upset a number of people on the staff who care about the aide whom she is criticizing. Betty, another resident who has no racial bias, has been at the residence for years and is a favorite of all the aides. To get back at Doris for her prejudice, she begins calling Doris names in the hallway and tries to trip her with her cane. You are the social worker on the unit. What do you do?

5. A woman who entered a nursing home and was fully accepted by peers eventually made the decision to identify herself to her friends as a lesbian. For years, the

friends had thought of her as straight. The staff began noticing changes in her demeanor and she began to isolate and show signs of depression. Staff initially thought that the changes were due to a new diagnosis of Parkinson's disease and symptoms associated with that. However, nursing staff eventually learned that the woman's friend group began to reject her based on her newly disclosed sexual orientation. They refused to let her play bingo with them anymore. They would no longer let her join them for meals. How would you proceed to change this harmful dynamic?

REFERENCES

Barbera, E. F. (2015, March 4). Senior bullying: How to recognize it how to handle it [Web log post]. Retrieved from https://www.mcknights.com/blogs/the-world-according-to-dr-el/senior-bullying-how-to-recognize-it-how-to-handle-it

Berger, K. S. (2007). Update on bullying at school: Science forgotten? *Developmental Review, 27*, 90–126.

Bonifas, R. (2014, April 22). Recognizing and curtailing bullying among older adults. PowerPoint presented at the 17th Anniversary Arizona ALFA Spring Conference and Trade Show.

Bonifas, R. P. (2016). Bullying *among older adults: How to recognize and address an unseen epidemic.* Towson, MD: Health Professions Press.

Bonifas, R., & Frankel, M. (2012, Feb. 8). Senior bullying: Guest post by Robin Bonifas, PhD, MSW, and Marsha Frankel, LICSW [Web log post]. Retrieved from www.mybetternursinghome.com/senior-bullying-guest-post-by-robin-bonifas-phd-msw-and-marsha-frankel-licsw

Briles, J. (2009). *Stabotage! How to deal with the pit bulls, skunks, snakes, scorpions & slugs in the health care workplace.* Aurora, CO: Mile High Press.

Cardinal, K. (2015). *From social bullying in schools to bullying in senior housing: A new narrative and holistic approach to maintaining residents' dignity* (Capstone Project, University of Massachusetts, Boston). Retrieved from www.umb.edu/editor_uploads/images/mgs/mgs_gerontology/Cardinal. Katherine_Capstone_Gerontology_May_2015.pdf

Craig, M. (2017). *The pocket Dalai Lama.* Berkley, CA: Shambhala.

Dilmac, B. (2009). Psychological needs as a predictor of cyber bullying: A preliminary report on college students. *Educational Sciences: Theory & Practice, 9*(3), 1308–1320.

Espelage, D. (2014). Psychologist offers insight on bullying and how to prevent it. American Psychological Association. Retrieved from http://www.apa.org/news/press/releases/2014/09/prevent-bullying.aspx

Farrington, D. P. (1993). Understanding and preventing bullying. *Crime and Justice, 17*, 381–458.

Gladden, R. M., Vivolo-Kantor, A. M., Hamburger, M. E., & Lumpkin, C. D. (2014). *Bullying surveillance among youths: Uniform definitions for public health and recommended data elements, version 1.0.* Atlanta, GA; National Center for Injury Prevention and Control, Centers for Disease Control and Prevention, & US Department of Education.

Hamburger, M. E., Basile, K. C., & Vivolo, A. M. (2011). *Measuring bullying victimization, perpetration, and bystander experiences: A compendium of assessment tools*. Atlanta, GA: National Center for Injury Prevention and Control. Retrieved from http://www.cdc.gov/violenceprevention/pdf/BullyCompendiumBk-a.pdf

Hare, B., & Krupenye, C. (2018). Bonobos prefer individuals that hinder others over those that help. *Current Biology, 28*(2), 280–286. Retrieved from https://doi.org/10.1016/j.cub.2017.11.061

Hazelden Foundation. (2015). Olweus Bullying Prevention Program. Retrieved from http://hazelden.org/olweus

Kreimer, S. (2012, March). Older adults can be bullies, too. *AARP Bulletin*. Retrieved from www.aarp.org/relationships/friends-family/info-03-2012/older-adults-can-be-bullies-too

Lachs, M., Teresi, J. A., & Ramirez, M. (2014). *Documentation of resident-to-resident elder mistreatment in residential care facilities* (Final report, National Institute of Justice, Washington, DC).

Lake, N. (2014, November 14). Bullying is ageless: Conflict and violence widespread in nursing homes, study finds. WBUR.

Olweus, D. (1993). *Bullying at school: What we know and what we can do.* Cambridge, MA: Blackwell.

Olweus, D. J. (2003). A profile of bullying at school. *Educational Leadership, 60*(6), 12–17.

Olweus, D. J., & Graham, S. (2001). *Peer harassment: A critical analysis and some important issues.* New York, NY: Guilford Press.

Rosen, T., Pillemer, K., & Lachs, M. (2008). Resident-to-resident aggression in long-term care facilities: An understudied problem. *Aggression and Violent Behavior, 13*(2), 77–78.

Schneider, F. W., Gruman, J. A., & Coutts, L. M. (Eds.). (2005). *Applied social psychology: Understanding and addressing social and practical problems.* Newbury Park, CA: Sage.

Scully, M., & Rowe, M. (2009). Bystander training within organizations. *Journal of the International Ombudsman Association, 2*(1), 1–9.

Span, P. (2014, November 25). Aggressive neighbors in the nursing home. *The New York Times*. Retrieved from https://newoldage.blogs.nytimes.com/2014/11/25/violence-in-the-nursing-home

Stop Bullying Coalition. (2019). Website. Retrieved from https://stopbullyingcoalition.org/index.php/

Stopbullying.gov (n.d.). What is cyberbullying. Retrieved from https://www.stopbullying.gov/cyberbullying/what-is-it/index.html

Tokunaga, R. S. (2010). Following you home from school: A critical review and synthesis of research on cyberbullying victimization. *Computers in Human Behavior, 26*(3), 277–287.

Trompetter, H., Scholte, R., & Westerhof, G. (2011). Resident-to-resident relational aggression and subjective well-being in assisted living facilities. *Aging & Mental Health, 15*(1), 59–67.

Voyer, P. (2005). Prevalence of physical and verbal aggression behaviors and associated factors among older adults in long-term care facilities. *BMC Geriatrics, 5,* 13.

Weiner, J. (2015, January 17). Mean girls in the retirement home. *The New York Times,* Sunday Review. Retrieved from https://www.nytimes.com/2015/01/18/opinion/sunday/mean-girls-in-the-retirement-home.html

Workplace Bullying Institute. (2014). Who we are. Retrieved from http://www.workplacebullying.org/the-drs-namie

19

CONCLUSION: CHALLENGES IN ETHICAL DECISION-MAKING AND ISSUES FOR THE FUTURE

Georgia J. Anetzberger, PhD, ACSW
Case Western Reserve University

Candace J. Heisler, JD
National Trainer and Consultant

Pamela B. Teaster, PhD
Virginia Tech

KEYWORDS

older adults	ethics
compromised health	effective status
care arrangement	mistreatment
decision-making frameworks	multidisciplinary

Overview

In our quest for individual rights and a just society, we began this text with a journey into ethics, how it is defined, and how it serves as a guide for behavior and action. Attention was given to select ethical principles and predominant ethical theories before the role of law was considered. Throughout, of course, our focus has been on vulnerable elders, examining conditions and circumstances that render older adults particularly susceptible to harm, suffering, or loss. Chapter authors discussed these under four broad categories:

- Compromised health: Cognitive impairment, mental illness, physical disability

- Effective status: Gender, ethnicity, sexual orientation, religion, immigrant status

- Care arrangement: Residential long-term care, home and community-based services, health care decision-making, end of life

- Mistreatment: Abuse, neglect, and exploitation; self-neglect; correctional settings; criminal victimization; bullying

The creation of this book required making hard choices. It was impossible to include all conditions and circumstances that can result in vulnerability for older adults. Sometimes this happened because of the unavailability of authors who could write about technical subjects and then, using the lens of vulnerable elders, effectively address ethical challenges in real-life situations. More often, topics were not included simply because of page and space limitations. For example, there are no chapters on substance abuse or Native Americans. In addition, the chapter on ethnicity does not consider all ethnic groups and the chapter on religion fails to include all religions in the United States.

Reoccurring Themes

Although each chapter author examined ethical concerns as they relate to a distinct condition or circumstance for vulnerability, some reoccurring themes emerged that deserve mention. First, even when the origins of vulnerability are evident early in life—as may be the case for physical disabilities, for instance—their adverse effects can become more pronounced with advancing age, resulting in greater challenges for ethical decision-making. This especially can be seen in the lack of tolerance by others for what might be seen as risky acts (which, for example, might result in self-neglect or criminal victimization) or behavior (such as bullying) in older adults versus their younger counterparts. Also evident are the often different experiences of older adults versus younger adults in settings like hospitals or correctional facilities.

Second, the ability to manage vulnerability can diminish with age, leaving older adults dependent on others for assistance, association, or even the preservation of fundamental rights. These others, whether informal caregivers or formal service providers, may be ill prepared or ill inclined to ensure that the older adult's goals and preferences; strengths and capacities; and rights and relationships are central to intervention planning and implementation. In addition, decision-making by the older adult may be limited due to cognitive impairment, affecting the desired partnership between client or patient and service provider. This can be illustrated in inadequate or inappropriate care provided in home, residential, or community service settings, and is particularly evident in situations of abuse, neglect, or exploitation.

Third, as noted by several chapter authors, including those writing on gender and sexual orientation, intersectionality further complicates the situation of vulnerable elders. If the ethical issues and dilemmas faced by ethnic or religious minority elders are difficult to resolve, they are more so when that person is also transgender with poor mental health and is a recent immigrant to this country. Finally, perhaps the most dominant theme to emerge from the various chapters is that "doing ethics" (Johnson, 1999) is almost always hard, sometimes simply because the issues and dilemmas that emerge from situations involving vulnerable elders can have profound consequences. As evident toward the end of life, decisions made can result in life with meaning in the final stage or a "good death"—or not, as when systemic supports are inadequate.

Doing Ethics

Various techniques have been developed to promote ethical decision-making, although few are specific to issues and dilemmas surrounding vulnerable elders. Collectively they recognize ethical decision-making as a process. In this context ethical principles like autonomy and justice, and ethical theories like utilitarianism and communicative ethics, are foundational. They may not solve ethical issues and dilemmas, but they can offer perspective on how to approach these matters in order to better examine problems and determine courses of action for resolution.

Some principles, such as autonomy, may—and often do—take primacy over the others, and in doing so may either enhance the quality of life of a vulnerable elder or significantly detract from it. For example, autonomy, like capacity, can be detrimental to an elder if it is regarded as all or nothing (i.e., there is either complete autonomy or there is none). Such an approach to this important ethical principal may not be the best, and authors like Collopy (1988) have written elegantly on this distinction. The exercise of autonomy if not tempered by application of the other principles may prove to be an overt or covert excuse to do nothing should an elder initially refuse services or other interventions. In this regard it is important to remember that an initial refusal may not mean a permanent one. Thus, accepting and leaving the elder's first decision as the last decision may prove harmful or even fatal. Alternately, respect for an elder's autonomy turns out to be even more important to an elder than where he or she lives or his or her health (Rowe & Kahn, 1987; Sherwin & Winsby, 2011).

Most decision-making techniques can be classified as either guidelines or collaborations. Guidelines include decision-making frameworks and professional or organizational codes of ethics. Collaborations include consultations with supervisors or colleagues and ethics committees. Each of these will be described and illustrated below.

There is nothing inherently separate about these techniques. Although either classification or any technique can be used alone, their effectiveness is enhanced if combined. This means that professional or organizational codes of ethics can inform thinking when applying decision-making frameworks to situations involving vulnerable elders. Moreover, collaborations—whether with another person or an established committee—will provide added perspective, knowledge, and resources to case deliberation and ethical decision-making, whether or not a particular guideline is employed. As Johnson (1999, p. 339) states in her classic book on ethical issues in aging, "In the final analysis, we are all 'in it together'—we participate in the community either directly or indirectly when we make decisions. Together, we have a better chance of creating an ethical plan than if we act alone."

Decision-Making Frameworks

Decision-making frameworks provide steps or checkpoints to break down the ethical decision-making process into manageable components for analysis. These steps give order and logic to decision-making, making it an intellectual and rigorous activity. They also help promote more objective, reliable, and moral judgments (Glover, 2017). Kidder (1995), for example, suggests nine checkpoints for ethical analysis:

- Recognize that there is a problem.
- Determine the actor.
- Gather the relevant facts.
- Test for right-versus-wrong issues.
- Test for right-versus-wrong values.
- Apply ethical standards and perspectives.
- Look for a third way.
- Make a decision.
- Revisit and reflect on the decision.

In contrast, Day (2006) identifies three distinct phases of ethical analysis, each with specific elements of critical thinking:

- Situation definition: Definition of facts; identification of principles and values; and statement of ethical issue or question
- Analysis: Weighing of competing principles and values; consideration of external factors; examination of duties to various parties; and discussion of applicable ethical theories
- Decision: Rendering of moral agent's decision and defense of that decision based on moral theory

Both of the above frameworks emphasize complete and orderly inquiry. Kidder's model may evoke more creative solutions, but Day's incorporates moral theories; both are worthwhile. However, each framework fails to ensure action or implementation, which is at the crux of professional work with vulnerable elders. Further, each portrays ethical decision-making as linear, which may not apply to the real-life situations that professionals face involving vulnerable elders. For example, self-neglect may reoccur again and again, deepening and varying in its consequences; and chronic conditions may multiply, resulting in long-term care needs that appear more like a bouncing Ping-Pong ball than a declining plank.

Codes of Ethics

Codes of ethics are common for professions and organizations that target vulnerable elders as clients or patients (Teaster & Sokan, 2016). Their function is to serve as guides for conduct and practice. For instance, the National Association of Social Workers (NASW) Code of Ethics has four sections: preamble, which delineates the profession's mission and core values; purpose, which provides an overview of the Code's main functions and how to deal with ethical issues and dilemmas in practice; principles, as they reflect core values; and standards, essential for informing professional conduct (NASW, 2018). More specifically, NASW core values and related ethical principles follow:

- Service: Social workers' primary goal is to help people in need and to address social problems.

- Social justice: Social workers challenge social injustice.

- Dignity and worth of the person: Social workers respect the inherent dignity and worth of the person.

- Importance of human relationships: Social workers recognize the central importance of human relationships.

- Integrity: Social workers behave in a trustworthy manner.

- Competence: Social workers practice within their areas of competence and develop and enhance their professional expertise.

NASW ethical standards relate to six broad areas of professional activity, namely, social workers' ethical responsibilities to clients, to colleagues, in practice settings, as professionals, to the social work profession, and to the broader society.

Somewhat in contrast to that of NASW, the Code of Ethics for the National Adult Protective Services Association (NAPSA) focuses on the rights of mistreated elders or vulnerable younger adults rather than the professional conduct of persons providing adult protective services (NAPSA, 2018). The guiding value is that every action taken by adult protective services must balance the duty to protect the safety of the vulnerable adult with the adult's right of self-determination. The secondary value is that older persons and persons with disabilities who are victims of mistreatment should be treated with honesty, caring, and respect. Four principles follow these values:

- Adults have the right to be safe.

- Adults retain all their civil and constitutional rights, i.e., the right to live their lives as they wish, manage their own finances, enter into contracts, marry, etc. unless a court adjudicates otherwise.

- Adults have the right to make decisions that do not conform with societal norms as long as these decisions do not harm others.

- Adults have the right to accept or refuse services.

The above two codes of ethics can inform the practice of adult protective services program staff, more of whom are social workers than any other profession. However, because the principles lack hierarchal arrangement, their guidance is insufficient in responding to many situations of self-neglect or elder mistreatment. For example, following the NAPSA code we do not know if insuring the adult's safety is more or less important than preserving the adult's civil and constitutional rights. Yet the answer can be critical, especially in all-too-common situations involving incapacitated elders. Furthermore, the NASW code tends to be more of an aspiration than a practical set of guidelines, seeming to ignore the reality of service availability and provision. For instance, it is fine to have as our primary goal "to help people in need," but help is likely to be severely hampered in some locales by inadequate resources due to insufficient funding, lack of specialized providers, and inaccessible facilities, leaving both worker and client frustrated and discouraged.

Collaborations With Supervisors or Colleagues

Perhaps no technique for ethical decision-making is more widely used than consultation with supervisors or colleagues. It seems only natural to initiate such conversations with those in close contact and with whom we have shared experiences and backgrounds, particularly when theirs may be longer or more extensive. Some interactions may be informal, as in chance meetings "around the water cooler." Others may be formal, like scheduled supervisory sessions or case conferences. Whatever the format, consultations are notable for their emphasis on active listening, careful articulation of concerns, and exploration of options (Jurchak, 2000). They also can be limiting for effectively resolving ethic issues or dilemmas involving vulnerable elders. Barriers can include insufficient dedicated time, preexisting biases, differential authority, varying philosophies, incompetence, and disagreement about case goals and their achievement (Robinson & Reeser, 2008).

Ethics Committees

Ethics committees originated in the United States during the 1960s but were still uncommon until the late 1980s (Aulisio, 2016). They developed for several reasons, including advances in medical technology, prolongation of the dying process, criticism of physicians as paternalistic, emergence of the consumer rights movement, and various legal decisions, such as the Quinlan and Cruzan cases (Kelly, 2002). Ethics committees now are found in almost all hospitals and frequently in such other settings as social service agencies and nursing homes. In addition, they can exist as community resources, as illustrated in the roles of some interdisciplinary teams, where they tend to address ethical concerns that cross agency and institutional boundaries and "dramatically affect the community and those residing in that community" (Robbins, 1997, p. 51).

Most ethics committees have several functions that may include consultative case review, staff and community education, policy development and advocacy, and consideration of general ethical questions, perhaps resulting in the establishment of protocols for decision-making when professionals confront them (Pozgar, 2010). Wherever they are found and whatever their functions, ethics committees tend to meet regularly and operate using formal procedures. They also tend to be multidisciplinary in composition. Members may include representatives from the organization's board, administration, and key professions along with laypersons, academicians, clergy, and others. Although they do not make decisions, ethics committees can offer useful advice for those having to make decisions, mainly by identifying varied choices and the pros and cons of each choice.

Challenges can exist for ethics committees in addressing the ethical issues and dilemmas of vulnerable elders. These may include the time and costs required to establish and sustain committees, less than timely response to requests for case consultations, communication problems across disciplines and departments due to different goals and philosophies, status inequities among members, diverting attention to extraneous matters like organizational risk management, and failure to effectively use mediation or other measures to deal with conflict resolution.

Future Ethical Issues

In 2018 the Gerontological Society of America (GSA) asked the chairs of the four sections under which its membership falls to identify trends in aging. As the premier professional association in the United States for those invested in geriatrics and gerontology, the perspectives offered seemed an appropriate source for uncovering future ethical concerns for vulnerable elders. Therefore, we selected the identified trend from each section that appeared potentially most consequential for the targeted population of this book and most challenging in its ethical implications.

Longer Lives

Janko Nikolich-Zugich, MD, PhD, Bowman Professor of Medical Research at the University of Arizona and GSA Biological Sciences Section Chair, stated that:

> based on the animal models, it should be possible to extend the human lifespan into the early 100s, with commensurate extension of the health span. ... Health is not the absence of disease, but the ability to live in a satisfying manner (Posey, 2018a, p. 3).

For many of the vulnerable elders discussed by our chapter authors, a longer life may not be a satisfying one. For example, adding decades to the financial and social struggles of gender and ethnic minorities may be seen as neither just nor beneficent to a vulnerable elder, especially at a time of diminishing personal resources in a society with growing disparities. Moreover, it may be contrary to nonmaleficence for vulnerable elders in institutional settings, such those offering long-term care or corrections, to extend further in time their potential exposure to mistreatment and curtailment of autonomy.

Not Enough Professionals

Tomas L. Griebling, MD, MPH, Senior Associate Dean for Medical Education at the University of Kansas and GSA Health Sciences Section Chair, said, "Looking at a future with dramatic increases in the numbers of older adults, the biggest challenge our health care system faces are shortages in medicine, nursing, pharmacy, really all of the disciplines" (Posey, 2018b, p. 1).

The shortage of health care providers—especially those specializing in geriatrics—makes maleficence more likely in the treatment of older adult patients, whose reliance on health care is greater than other age cohorts, often as a result of complex chronic conditions. The failure of professional associations, educational institutions, and governments to adequately address the shortage also can be seen as a social injustice, perhaps in part reflective of the ageism that is so pervasive in this country and globally.

Caregiver Vacancies

Karl Pillemer, MA, PhD, Hazel E. Reed Professor of Human Development at Cornell University and GSA Behavioral and Social Sciences Section Chair, noted:

> We can't operate as if the family structure that cared for the parents of the baby boomers is going to continue. ... Indeed, we must rapidly begin to understand how care is going to be provided if we cannot rely on adult children and spouses (Posey, 2018c, p. 2).

The caregiving needs of vulnerable elders with compromised health can be profound, perhaps especially for those with cognitive impairment or chronic mental illness. Reliance on informal care sources can exploit caregivers or expose older adults to improper or insufficient assistance or even mistreatment and bullying. Unjust, too, is the failure of society to provide adequate supports to caregivers in order to enable them to fulfill effectively their important but often difficult roles.

Age-Unfriendly Communities

Marla Berg-Weger, PhD, LCSW, Professor of Social Work at Saint Louis University and GSA Social Research, Policy, and Practice Section Chair, explains,

> It's more cost effective to keep people supported and living in their home than it is for them to be in a skilled care facility. ... We're having to seriously think about whether our communities are prepared and able to support aging-in-place options (Posey, 2018d, p. 3).

Respecting autonomy means empowering and supporting vulnerable elders to live in the setting of their choice, with the structures and services in place to enable that choice. Compromised health and effective status may suggest additional considerations for the planning of age-friendly communities, but to ignore their importance would mean limiting the meaning of community and diminishing the importance of each resident within it. We are all less fortunate when that happens.

CONCLUDING OBSERVATIONS

Our concluding chapter began with the identification of reoccurring themes from the sections on conditions and circumstances of elder vulnerability. Then techniques for ethical decision-making were described and illustrated. Finally, we offered a brief look at future ethical issues of vulnerable elders by examining some trends in aging.

As is true of the book itself, the concluding chapter is meant to challenge the thinking and expand the perspectives of its readers. Like the book, too, this chapter is incomplete. However, the objective of any course, text, or chapter is not to tell the whole story or to cover everything, which is impossible anyway. Rather, it is to be interesting enough for you to continue the journey of learning more regarding the subject on your own. If that happens with respect to ethics and vulnerable elders, nothing would make us happier as editors and authors. More importantly, it may benefit the vulnerable elders with whom you have contact as clients or patients, making more possible a just society, where respect for individual rights becomes the default position in any intervention.

REFERENCES

Aulisio, M.P. (2016). Why did hospital ethics committees emerge in the US? *AMA Journal of Ethics, 18*(5), 546–553.

Collopy, B.J. (1988). Autonomy in long term care: Some crucial distinctions. *The Gerontologist, 28*(Supplement), 10–17.

Day, L.A. (2006). *Ethics in media communications: Cases and controversies, 5th ed.* Belmont, CA: Wadsworth/Thomson Learning.

Glover, J.J. (2017). Ethical decision-making guidelines and tools. In L.B. Harman & F. Cornelius (Eds.), *Ethical health informatics: Challenges and opportunities, 3rd ed.* (pp. 51–73). Burlington, MA: Jones & Bartlett Learning.

Johnson, T.F. (1999). Ethical issues in decision-making: A balanced perspective. In T.F. Johnson (Ed.), *Handbook on ethical issues in aging* (pp. 326–339). Westport, CT: Greenwood Press.

Jurchak, M. (2000). Report of a study to examine the process of ethics case consultation. *The Journal of Clinical Ethics, 11*(1), 49–55.

Kelly, D.F. (2002). *Critical care ethics: Treatment decisions in American hospitals.* Eugene, OR: Wipf and Stock Publishers.

Kidder, R.M. (1995). *How good people make tough choices: Resolving the dilemmas of ethical living.* New York, NY: Fireside.

National Adult Protective Services Association. (2018). NAPSA (or APS) code of ethics. Retrieved on July 1, 2018 from https://www.napsa-now.org/about-napsa/code-of-ethics

National Association of Social Workers. (2018). Read the code of ethics: Approved by the 1996 NASW. Delegate Assembly and revised by the 2017 NASW Delegate Assembly. Retrieved on July 1, 2018 from http://www.socialworkers.org/About/Ethics/Code-of-Ethics-English

Posey, L.M. (2018a). *Trends in the biological sciences: Longer lives, better lives: The search for an extended "health span".* Washington, DC: Gerontological Society of America.

Posey, L.M. (2018b). *Trends in the health sciences: Looking through a glass darkly: Challenges ahead in health care for older adults.* Washington, DC: Gerontological Society of America.

Posey, L.M. (2018c). *Trends in the behavioral and social sciences: We're all human: Aging trends through an international lens.* Washington, DC: Gerontological Society of America.

Posey, L.M. (2018d). *Trends in social research, policy and practice: After changing everything else, baby boomers turn to aging.* Washington, DC: Gerontological Society of America.

Pozgar, G.D. (2010). *Legal and ethical issues for health professionals, 2nd ed.* Sudbury, MA: Jones and Bartlett Publishers.

Robbins, D.A. (1997). Developing tools for addressing ethical issues. *Home Health Care Management Practice, 10*(1), 41–53.

Robison, W., & Reeser, L.C. (2008). *Ethical decision making in social work.* Torrance, CA: Homestead Schools, Inc.

Rowe, J.W., & Kahn, R.L. (1987). Human aging: Usual and successful. *Science, 237*(4811), 143–149.

Sherwin, S., & Winsby, M. (2011). A relationship perspective on autonomy for older adults residing in nursing homes. *Health Expectation, 14*(2), 182–190.

Teaster, P.B., & Sokan, A.E. (2016). Ethical standards and practices in human services and health care for LGBT elders. In D.A. Harley & P.B. Teaster (Eds.), *Handbook of LGBTQ elders: An interdisciplinary approach to principles, practices, and policies* (pp. 657–669). Cham, Switzerland: Springer International Publishing.

Index

CPSIA information can be obtained
at www.ICGtesting.com
Printed in the USA
LVHW061919300922
729626LV00001B/27